Four-Handed Monsters

Four-Handed Monsters

*Four-Hand Piano Playing and
Nineteenth-Century Culture*

ADRIAN DAUB

OXFORD
UNIVERSITY PRESS

Oxford University Press is a department of the University of
Oxford. It furthers the University's objective of excellence in research,
scholarship, and education by publishing worldwide.

Oxford   New York
Auckland   Cape Town   Dar es Salaam   Hong Kong   Karachi
Kuala Lumpur   Madrid   Melbourne   Mexico City   Nairobi
New Delhi   Shanghai   Taipei   Toronto

With offices in
Argentina   Austria   Brazil   Chile   Czech Republic   France   Greece
Guatemala   Hungary   Italy   Japan   Poland   Portugal   Singapore
South Korea   Switzerland   Thailand   Turkey   Ukraine   Vietnam

Oxford is a registered trademark of Oxford University Press
in the UK and certain other countries.

Published in the United States of America by
Oxford University Press
198 Madison Avenue, New York, NY 10016

© Oxford University Press 2014

First published as "Zwillinghafte Gebärden": Zur kulturellen Wahrnehmung des vierhändigen
Klavierspiels im neunzehnten Jahrhundert by Königshausen & Neumann GmbH, Würzburg, 2009

All rights reserved. No part of this publication may be reproduced, stored in
a retrieval system, or transmitted, in any form or by any means, without the prior
permission in writing of Oxford University Press, or as expressly permitted by law,
by license, or under terms agreed with the appropriate reproduction rights organization.
Inquiries concerning reproduction outside the scope of the above should be sent to the
Rights Department, Oxford University Press, at the address above.

You must not circulate this work in any other form
and you must impose this same condition on any acquirer.

Library of Congress Cataloging-in-Publication Data
Daub, Adrian.
Four-handed monsters : four-hand piano playing and nineteenth-century culture / Adrian Daub.
pages cm
Includes index.
ISBN 978-0-19-998177-9 (alk. paper)
1. Piano music (4 hands)—19th century—History and criticism.   I. Title.
ML706.D3813 2014
785'.6219209034—dc23
2013037919

This volume is published with the generous support of the AMS 75 PAYS Endowment of the
American Musicological Society, funded in part by the National Endowment for the Humanities and
the Andrew W. Mellon Foundation.

1 3 5 7 9 8 6 4 2
Printed in the United States of America
on acid-free paper

CONTENTS

Acknowledgments vii

Introduction 1

1. The Sonic Hearth and the "Piano Plague" 24

2. Four-Hand Piano Playing between Parlor Music and the Culture Industry 55

3. "At Best an Intruder, at Worst a Voyeur": Four-Hand Piano Playing and the Family Unit 82

4. Four-Handed Monsters 105

5. The Semantics of the Hand 135

6. Fordist Chords 163

7. Musical Platonism: Four-Hand Playing Among the Philosophers 186

8. Kakanian Variations: Four Hands and the Passing of the Nineteenth Century 212

Index 241

ACKNOWLEDGMENTS

This book isn't the product of years of impassioned four-hand playing. Instead, it constitutes an attempt to harness an outsider's glance at the phenomenon. It was at any rate that glance which occasioned it. Years ago I was fortunate enough to have exquisite seats to a concert given by Martha Argerich and Nelson Freire, and it was not just the intimacy with which the pair's seasoned pair of hand cavorted across the keys that struck me, but also the feeling that witnessing such intimacy put any observer in a strange position. I couldn't look away, but no more could I be certain that it was okay to keep looking. My gaze sought to read all manner of stories into these two pairs of hands—comedies, tragedies, romances—but at the same time each of my readings came to seem to me questionable, perhaps even inappropriate.

As the evening wore on, I started to clutch my ticket like a talisman. For I no longer felt as if it entitled me to witness what I witnessed. I realized that the performance was not intended for me, that I was out of place, and that my presence disturbed rather than ratified the performers. "I have heard the mermaids singing, each to each," we read in T. S. Eliot's "The Love Song of J. Alfred Prufrock," "I do not think that they will sing to me." The feeling that four-hand players were such sirens, who for all the allure of their song do not sing to me, never left me during my research or during the writing of this book.

What gave this book its shape was the realization that during the heyday of four-hand playing, literature, the press, and the visual arts approached the phenomenon with much the same eyes and ears as Prufrock did his mermaids. Whether this was due to a sense of shame as words and gazes threw themselves at a phenomenon that no longer required either language or looking, or whether it derived simply from some general human impulse to tell stories about things that may not have stories to tell, that will be one of the questions this book sets out to answer.

But above all, it will emerge that the eagerness with which I read into Argerich's and Freire's playing would have made me typical rather than special in the nineteenth century, that the mysterious configuration at the piano keyboard functioned as the screen on which bourgeois culture could project its obsessions (from the nature of the individual, of community, to the status of the body, or the possibility of becoming one with another). It is a history of ideas only in the sense of the Greek root: a story of something emerging as visible and the challenges it poses.

Since it was the project of a non-musicologist, this project required in both its German and its English versions constant guidance and critique by those who are professionally occupied with the topic. I was fortunate enough to speak to many piano duettists in writing the German book, and many pianists have written me since it was published. Their ideas were central in guiding me through the visions and revisions of the past seven years.

Many hands have guided the project during that time. The original version benefited immensely from support, criticism, and suggestions from Jeffrey Kallberg, Tim Ribchester, David Copenhafer, and Claudia Schmölders. My colleagues at Stanford, especially Paul Robinson, Tom Grey, Charlie Kronengold, and Sepp Gumbrecht, were instrumental in helping me rethink, clarify, and in many cases sharpen the ideas contained in the German edition. The Arthur Schnitzler Archive in Freiburg and the Adorno Archive in Frankfurt were kind enough to give me access to unpublished text by two of the most interesting writers on four-hand piano playing. Without the help of the Staatsbibliothek Berlin, the Österreichische Nationalbibliothek Vienna, the New York Public Library, and the Bibliothèque Nationale in Paris I would not have been able to assemble many of the texts and illustrations gathered in this book.

In its English edition, this work about four-hand piano playing is, appropriately enough, the result of a four-handed effort. My gratitude goes to Erik Butler who not only displayed great care and delicacy in translating my prose, but who was also generous enough to allow me to alter his after he was done. If translation is by its nature a generous and selfless enterprise, there is something particularly noble about it when you are aware that the text you write will be altered, at times beyond recognition, by the author. With roles reversed, I don't think I could have done it, and I owe Erik an immense debt.

From the beginning this English edition had a good deal of institutional support. Debra Satz and the H&S Dean's Office at Stanford supported the project financially. Without a fellowship at the Stanford Humanities Center I would not have been able to complete this manuscript. Without the generosity of the book's German publisher, Königshausen & Neumann, the transition across the Atlantic could not have gone as smoothly as it did. Norm Hirschy, Kate Nunn, and the staff at OUP were instrumental in getting the manuscript through the review and editing process smoothly, and they were patient with any and all crises that arose during that time.

I explicitly don't wish to thank the individual(s) who walked off with my MacBook in San Francisco's Mission District halfway through the editing process. You set this project back by almost a half-year; I hope you at least got some really good drugs out of the bargain. Kara Levy was instrumental not only in proofreading and critiquing the manuscript but also in nursing the book back to health after disaster struck. I dedicate this English edition to my mermaids.

Four-Handed Monsters

Introduction

A few years ago, the musicologist Thomas Christensen began an article on four-hand piano playing by setting the scene around a very specific piano: the grand in the parlor at his villa, Wahnfried, Richard Wagner's house in Bayreuth. Christensen luxuriates in descriptions of communal playing after dinner and the composer's impromptu discourses on the music being played, and he tells us who is playing and who is merely listening:

> After the dinner plates have been cleared, our couple retires to the parlor for their regular evening reading—this week, Walter Scott's *Waverly*. But Richard is in a mood for some four-hand music. Seidl and the other copyists are invited to join them. Richard takes out his worn copy of the Haydn symphonies and sits down at his new Steinway with Cosima. Together they read through Symphony No. 82 (the "Bear"). Everyone is enchanted.[1]

Christensen admits right away that this scene is pure montage—pieced together from a patchwork of diary entries of both Richard and Cosima Wagner. At first, the reader may feel a little taken aback; but if one lingers with the scenes of four-hand piano playing that populate the memoirs, diaries, dramas, and novels of the nineteenth and the early twentieth century in Central and Western Europe, one gets the sense that Christensen is not simply right to montage episodes in this way, it is almost imperative that he do so. The short, often quite banal episodes are transformed into fleeting glimpses of a larger phenomenon, which in itself was too quotidian and ubiquitous to merit discussion in its own day—and which has therefore disappeared from retrospective view in ours. When we are simply told that this or that piece was played four-hand, we'd like to know more. "Four-hand playing" begs for further explanation, much more so than if we were told that Richard Wagner lit a pipe or went for a walk after dinner. We tend to assume that something more hides behind these seemingly unimportant scenes, and sometimes we are even right.

---

[1] Thomas Christensen, "Four-Hand Piano Transcription and Geographies of Nineteenth Century Musical Reception," *Journal of the American Musicological Society* 52, no. 2 (1999): 255–96, here p. 255.

One gets a sense for just how much can hide behind them when one considers the exactitude with which literary works of the era record the minutiae of four-hand encounters. In Robert Musil's *Man Without Qualities*, the narrator relates how one player's "feelings were splashing like big raindrops on the keys."[2] In novels and plays the piano keyboard becomes a site for flirting, for confrontation, for negotiation. There is much to discover between the two players who "storm along side by side with twinned gestures of desperation and rapture."[3] Two people, two bodies on one piano that they are forced to share—it's a scene that often presents itself as anything but innocent, half *pas de deux*, half poker game. In chronicling their playing, Musil's narrator dips deep into all manner of metaphoric registers; we hear about feelings like raindrops, rushing trains, inflating bubbles, galloping horses, rutting bucks. Would such a thicket of connotations have attached itself to another form of music, such as a quartet or a *Lied*?

The scene that Christensen and Musil describe, a hundred years apart, is one that is largely native to the nineteenth century. It's become a rarity in our day; unless they play four-hand arrangements of Christmas songs, few families today would gather around a piano as did the Wagners at Wahnfried. Music enthusiasts and music professionals still play four-hands as a hobby or to practice. But in the nineteenth century, four-hand piano playing was at home in every bourgeois family. The piano was one of the most important pieces of furniture a family could own, and four-hand playing was one of the most defining forms of interaction, both within the family and between the family and the outside world. From the student bedsit to royal and imperial courts, from the fancy parlor to the dusty classroom, four-hand playing was everywhere, pursued with an enthusiasm, a dedication, and a sense of significance that the form never again attained.

If "four-hand" means two people playing on one keyboard, the phenomenon indeed is entirely limited to that century. Of course, there had been predecessors in the eighteenth century (for instance, four-hand organ playing), but before the "long" nineteenth century, piano duets were almost exclusively played on *two* keyboards—for instance, in Johann Sebastian Bach's Contrapuntus XIII in *The Art of the Fugue*. François Couperain's *Pièces de clavecin* (1730) are conceived for two cembalists, but *sujet, basse*, and *contre partie* cross in such a way that made playing the pieces on one keyboard all but impossible. Armand-Louis Couperin wrote three *Quatuors à deux clavecins*. Bach's sons wrote several enduring duets, but all of them were intended for two separate instruments.

Only at the very end of the eighteenth century did the British composer and historian Charles Burney (1726–1814), a friend of Christoph Willibald Gluck, Carl Philipp Emanuel Bach, and Johann Adam Hiller (as well as of Rousseau and

---

[2] Robert Musil, *The Man Without Qualities* (New York: Knopf, 1996), 155.
[3] Musil, *The Man Without Qualities*, 152.

Introduction

Diderot), write four-hand music to be played on the same keyboard.⁴ In 1776 he published *Two Sets of Sonatas or Duetts for Two Performers upon One Piano Forte* and referred to them in his introduction as "the first of this kind that have appeared in print."⁵ From the first, the novelty of this form of music was thus connected to its being in print. This connection if anything intensified in the course of the nineteenth century. Four-hand piano playing was a kind of music that was articulated through print culture and was directed at a reading public. Franz Joseph Haydn was an early practitioner of the form, as was Muzio Clementi (1752–1832), who, like Burney, will reappear in our story at a later point. Wolfgang Amadeus Mozart, who wrote several four-hand pieces, played four-hand piano with Clementi, as well as with Johann Christian Bach.⁶ It was after Mozart that four-hand piano playing truly began its rise to dominance.⁷ Only the early twentieth century saw a decline in both the number of publications and the number of amateurs and virtuosos who bought and played them. New works and new arrangements were now preferably written for four-hand on two pianos: the four-hand parlor music of the nineteenth century gave way to concert music written for two pianos.

Composers like Schubert, Schumann, and Brahms wrote extensively for four hands, and many of their compositions for the form are still part of the repertoire today. But there are hardly any nineteenth-century composers who did not write (and inevitably publish) at least some works for four hands. And even those with no four-hand pieces in their official list of works often made extra money by arranging the works of others for four hands—Wagner, Mahler, and Bizet, for instance, made arrangements either for money or as a token of friendship.⁸ This was because in the second half of the nineteenth century, the dominance of four-hand music was driven less by original compositions than by arrangements and transcriptions. Many such arrangements were intended for a single player. Since they were able to capture the symphonic repertoire better than two-hand transcriptions, and since they were also generally much easier to play, the number of transcriptions and

---

⁴ See Roger Lonsdale, *Dr. Charles Burney: A Literary Biography* (Oxford: Clarendon, 1965), 199.

⁵ Cited in *A Catalogue of a Miscellaneous Collection of Music, Ancient and Modern, Together with Treatises on Music and the History of Music* (London: Calkin and Budd, 1844), 22.

⁶ Susanne Beicken, *Studies in the Technique and Structure of Eighteenth Century Four-Hand One Keyboard Duets, as Examplified in the Three Sonatas by Johann Christian Bach* (M.A. Thesis, Stanford University 1969).

⁷ Howard Ferguson, *Keyboard Duets* (Oxford: Oxford University Press, 1995), 6.

⁸ Howard Shanet, "Bizet's Suppressed Symphony," *Musical Quarterly* 44, no. 4 (October 1958): 471. Marc-André Roberge's list of important composers who arranged the work of others either for profit or as a service to a friend includes many more names: Franz Liszt, César Franck, Johannes Brahms, Camille Saint-Saëns, Modest Mussorgsky, Nikolai Rimsky-Korsakov, Gabriel Fauré, Claude Debussy, Richard Strauss, Paul Dukas, Max Reger, Hans Pfitzner, Maurice Ravel, Alban Berg, Alexander Zemlinsky, and Anton Webern; see Marc-André Roberge, "From Orchestra to Piano: Major Composers as Authors of Piano Reductions of Other Composer's Works," *Notes* 49, no. 3 (1993): 927.

variations on established themes soon eclipsed in number the original compositions for four hands.

Howard Ferguson has argued that there are three reasons for the dramatic expansion of the market for four-hand transcriptions: (1) In the course of the nineteenth century, the pianoforte became mass-produced and was widely available, and wider and wider strata of society felt they needed one. Piano builders helped things along with marketing strategies intended to proliferate the instrument. (2) The shape of the piano was standardized along the dimensions familiar to us today. This norm particularly affected the width of the piano, and thus created a standard keyboard range. Thanks to this standardized range, two pairs of hands could comfortably find room on the keyboard. (3) The popularity of four-hand transcription rested on the ascent of the bourgeoisie, who were both the instrument's and the music's main customer base. This class sought the piano as a status symbol and then wanted music to play on it. As we shall see in chapter 1, four-hand playing is at home in the bourgeois living room, not in the courtly salon, and it reflects the desires, values, and interests of the ascendant bourgeoisie.[9]

But the mercantile spirit of the new class of customers came to infect the distribution forms of this new hobby: piano transcriptions were almost factory-like in their production, and were marketed in mass quantities. Between 1852 and 1859 alone, for instance, Mozart's symphonies appeared in more than a half dozen different four-hand transcriptions. This was not counting pirated and unlicensed transcriptions; composers wrote letters to major music journals warning their reading public against bad or unauthorized arrangements, slapdash affairs written mostly as cash-ins on the latest fads. The music journals, in turn, frequently advertised several competing arrangements, transcriptions, potpourris, and variations of the same piece in the same issue. In his advertisement of the *Two Sets of Sonatas*, the connection Burney made between print culture and four-hand versions was thus, if anything, intensified in the nineteenth century.

While the publishing houses and their underpaid scribblers feverishly pushed more product onto the market, it was lapped up just as feverishly by a nearly insatiable public. Original compositions, simplified versions of two-hand works, and above all transcriptions of popular orchestral works sold in comparatively large print runs. The customers played four-hands in their living rooms, practiced using four-hand music at the flourishing music schools, and performed it for one another in semipublic events. The keyboard was the meeting place for mothers and sons, teachers and pupils, siblings, lovers, and colleagues. Newspapers and journals remarked (often quite critically) on these consumers' compulsive need for new scores. The scene was ubiquitous: the keyboard gathered a veritable who's who of the nineteenth century, Frédéric Chopin and Georges Sand, Richard Wagner and

[9] Ferguson, *Keyboard Duets*, 5.

Friedrich Nietzsche, among them.[10] The crowned heads of Europe granted their subjects audiences on the keyboard; Carl Czerny, for instance, played four-hand piano with the young Queen Victoria, while the great nineteenth-century scholar of India, Max Müller, played with Victoria's son, Prince Leopold.[11] At the other end of the social spectrum, four-hand playing was used to bring music to the lower classes or, in the Americas, to "civilize" natives.[12]

But even those who dealt with music professionally found four-hand playing useful: in important music journals, famous reviewers would remark on works they could know and judge "only" by means of their four-hand transcriptions. When Robert Schumann reviewed Berlioz's *Symphonie fantastique*, he admitted that the verdict was based on Liszt's (two-hand) transcription, and G. W. Fink based his review of Mendelssohn's Overture to *A Midsummer Night's Dream* on the four-hand arrangement.[13] Given how difficult and expensive it was to travel, it is safe to assume that a majority of nineteenth-century composers knew the symphonic works of their friends and competitors only through four-hand transcription—to say nothing of how the average music consumer experienced these works. Engelbert Humperdinck discovered Bruckner's symphonies for himself by playing four-hand transcriptions of them—his partner was none other than Hugo Wolf.[14] This was even more common among nonprofessionals: it is likely that the vast majority of those who venerated Wagner's operas as the expression of an authentic German essence knew those operas only in transcribed form, and thus encountered the aura of Bayreuth only in the form of a copy. Prince Philip von Eulenburg, who would precipitate the defining scandal of the Second German Empire, developed his fervent Wagner idolatry while listening to his mother play the *Meister*'s works with Cosima—he, at least, received his copy straight from an original.[15]

Literature was quick to take notice of the new phenomenon. The first mention of four-hand piano playing in literature seems to have occurred in France, where Charles Pigault-Lebrun (1753–1835) mentions the practice in his *L'Enfant du carnival* (1792). Jean Paul (Johann Paul Friedrich Richter) mentions it in passing in his novel *Titan*, appropriately published in 1800, at the dawn of the century of four-hand piano playing.[16] Both Pigault-Lebrun and Jean Paul do little more than

---

[10] Curt von Westernhagen, *Richard Wagner: Sein Werk, Sein Wesen, Seine Welt* (Zürich: Atlantis, 1956), 500.

[11] Friedrich Max Müller, *Auld Lang Syne* (New York: Scribner, 1898), 278.

[12] See, for instance, an article on the Nez Percé tribe in *Revue des Deux Mondes* 65 (1895): 826.

[13] Christensen, "Four-Hand Piano Transcription and Geographies," 266. The reviews can be found in *Neue Zeitschrift für Musik* 3, nos. 10–13 (August 4–14, 1835) and *Allgemeine musikalische Zeitung* 13 (March 27, 1833): 201–204.

[14] Otto Besch, *Engelbert Humperdinck* (Leipzig: Breitkopf und Härtel, 1914), 50.

[15] Reinhold Conrad Muschler, *Philipp zu Eulenburg: Sein Leben und seine Zeit* (Leipzig: Grunow, 1930), 29–30.

[16] Jean Paul, *Jean Paul's sämmtliche Werke* (Berlin: Reimer, 1826), 2: 525.

mention it; but the literature of the mid-nineteenth century stages elaborate scenes of four-hand playing and makes them focal points of its action—especially in the realist novel and popular theater. The serialized novels of bourgeois realism in particular, which appeared in journals from the 1840s on (in Germany, this development, exemplified by periodicals like *Gartenlaube* and *Deutsche Rundschau*, was delayed by a few decades), turn to four-hand playing both for quiet scene setting and for dramatic reversals and revelations.

In Germany, for instance, four-hand playing features in the works of Theodor Fontane, Eduard Mörike, and Theodor Storm; in England, Charlotte Brontë, Charles Dickens, George Eliot, and William Makepeace Thackeray; in France, in Charles de Bernard; in Russia, in the work of Ivan Goncharov, Leo Tolstoy, Ivan Turgenev, and Anton Chekov; in the United States, Kate Chopin. Naturalism, too, turns four-hand playing into a popular motif—Gerhart Hauptmann's plays in Germany, the brothers Goncourt in France, and August Strindberg all turn to it for dramatic effect. The literature of early modernism (Frank Wedekind, Thomas Mann, Arthur Schnitzler, and Oscar Wilde) abounds in scenes of four-hand piano playing, often far more detailed and ambiguous than in the realist fiction from earlier in the century. Poetry is more reluctant to deal with the topic, though there are sporadic references to it, particularly in French poetry.

It appears that, Pigault-Lebrun's novel notwithstanding, French literature was much more hesitant in adopting four-hand piano playing as a topic than, say, British or German literature. In an exhaustive study, Danièle Pistone accumulated almost two thousand scenes involving pianos in French literature, most of them from the "long" nineteenth century; of those, only about a half dozen deal with piano *à quatre mains*.[17] In Germany, and to a lesser extent in England, the use of four-hand playing as a *topos* seems to have reached its high-watermark around 1900, only to recede in the following decades. The phenomenon instead increasingly appears as motif in memoirs or historical novels set in the cosmos of the nineteenth century; two such novels— Robert Musil's *Man Without Qualities* and Joseph August Lux's *Grillparzer's Love Story*—will be analyzed in chapter 8. This is another reason that, while this study aims to address four-hand piano playing in Europe in general, it will return again and again to the German-speaking world: four-hand playing may have been a common practice throughout Europe, but it became the stuff of literature above all in Germany.

Of course, just because four-hand piano playing was a mainstay in novel plots at the time doesn't mean that it was also the object of extensive reflection; even in German literature, four-hand piano playing is actually surprisingly invisible, or only fleetingly visible. It is mentioned quite often, but most texts don't really go

---

[17] Danièle Pistone, *Le Piano dans la littérature française* (Lille: Atélier Reproduction des Thèses, 1975).

beyond mentioning it. It seems to have played an integral part in the musical, educational, and social life of the era, but few seem to have given it serious thought. This is most likely due to the fact that it was so well integrated into the bourgeois lifeworld. Four-hand playing was background music in literature, diaries, and articles. It was not worth describing in the same way that soloist, orchestra, and singer were. It is the basic premise of this study that it was nevertheless understood as hugely significant, that a wide range of cultural meanings attached to the practice, and that there was a broader cultural awareness of them.

If the following chapters again and again turn to literary texts as their source, it is precisely for this reason: I proceed from the assumption that literature (but also the visual arts), especially in the nineteenth century, picked up on things that everyday praxis allowed to slide out of view, to speak about that which goes without saying. The basic method of this study consists in centering the seemingly marginal and scattered episodes, then putting them into dialogue with the historically verifiable fashion of four-hand playing. Four-hand piano playing was anything but epiphenomenal, anything but marginal in nineteenth-century culture. Rather, it constituted the staging ground for the subject, for community, and even for the nation. Perhaps more important, four-hand piano playing, both the performance itself and its observation, allowed for negotiations of the very nature of subjectivity, community, and nation.

The hermeneutic decision to center the seemingly marginal still only allows limited insight into the phenomenon. For a musical sociology of the phenomenon, the novels, diaries, and journals that will constitute a good part of our evidence would not be sufficient. After all, their presentations of scenes of four-hand playing are (a) selective in what they relate, which means they give us more of a sense of how people *wanted* four-hand playing to be practiced and to be perceived, not how it was actually practiced or perceived; and they are (b) shot through with the categories of nineteenth-century ideologies of the aesthetic, which means that the experience as presented in these texts comes to us "filtered" in ways that may falsify interpretation.

Earlier approaches to the topic (in particular those of Philip Brett and Richard Leppert[18]) have turned to two tricks in order to animate the scant and partial evidence that exists, neither of which is without risk. That having been said, it is worth admitting at the outset that this study will follow them down this less than scholarly path. The first such legerdemain is to rely on the phenomenology of four-hand playing: what it actually feels like to play four hands, what it looks like to those who observe it, how four-hand playing actually functions. Late-born observers can witness and experience these feelings and functions in the present, but adopting them as our guide to the nineteenth century runs the risk of a kind of "presentism"—that

---

[18] Philipp Brett, "Piano Four-Hands: Schubert and the Performance of Gay Male Desire," *19th Century Music* 21 (1997): 149–76; Richard Leppert, "Four-Hands, Three Hearts—A Commentary," *Cultural Critique* 60 (Spring 2005): 5–22.

is, the tendency to project unproblematically our own present onto the past and to assume that some experience (mis-)understood as immediate can be assumed as a constant between the past and our own time.

Unfortunately, this is a danger that is almost impossible to avoid. In talking about a certain four-hand piece today, our primary guides are notes on a page, as is playing them. The more scholarly studies of four-hand music and related phenomena, especially in Europe, stop there, and they restrict themselves to the notes, the composers who wrote them, where they were printed, and how they were sold.[19] That sort of data tells us nothing about the praxis, unless we take the score as a jumping-off point and use our playing experience as a means of analysis. We know how hands that played these notes move; we can assume that our improvisations, simplifications, and fingerings are those that would have made play easier or more fun for a layperson in the nineteenth century as well. We know how one moves on a piano stool today, and we know how to improvise on the piano. We thus assume that these "immediate" interactions with the instrument and the score would have proceeded along much the same lines in the nineteenth century, and that they were simply interpreted differently back then. Admittedly, this assumption is itself questionable. The work of Michel Foucault and Judith Butler, to name just two, crucially asserts just the opposite: that the body and its supposedly immediate relations to the lifeworld are always already shaped by "discourse," and that a "pre-discursive" (and thus safely transhistorical) immediacy is always necessarily fictitious.

But this questionable bridge to the past is all we really have in the case of four-hand playing. All we can do is admit that we are well aware of this potential problem—but that doesn't mean we can avoid it. We have to assume that the basic experience of four-hand piano playing (techniques, sensations, lines of sight) is shared between the nineteenth century and our own, and that the two diverge primarily in the interpretive techniques and the ideologies they bring to bear on this basic experience.

In a second legerdemain, we have to push our investigations into something approaching essayism. We have to try to fill gaps, to let stand hypotheses without finding evidence for them right away, and to risk fiction judiciously. What it *might* have been like, how certain scenes *must* have been seen—that will be our topic, again and again. Philipp Brett takes recourse to his own experiences playing Schubert's Rondo *à quatre mains* in order to substantiate his theses about Schubert's sexuality, or at least the sexuality of Schubert's duets. Thomas Christensen creates a montage of diary entries to imagine a coherent and sustained "scene" of four-hand piano playing. All of that cannot be finally verified, but analyses such as Brett's and Christensen's can claim to lay hold of the phenomenon only because they willingly take this risk.

---

[19] See, for instance, Helmut Loos, *Zur Klavierübertragung von Werken für und mit Orchester des 19. und 20. Jahrhunderts* (Munich: Katzbichler, 1983); and Johannes Lorenz, *Max Reger als Bearbeiter Bachs* (Wiesbaden: Breitkopf und Härtel, 1982).

The following chapters will proceed the way good four-hand piano players do: building bridges where the notes desert us, improvising and constructing shortcuts where our skill or our luck runs out, and in the end hoping to create something like a reasonably accurate piano transcription of a polyphonic and much richer reality.

Four-Hand Playing as a Constellation

The following chapters are intended to illuminate four-hand piano playing as a constellation. Our first step will be to sketch the outlines of that constellation. It will be my goal to draw on four characteristics of four-hand piano music and playing, which are all interrelated but which, taken together, describe what was unique about the practice in the nineteenth century. That does not mean that each of these characteristics was exclusively associated with four-hand playing, but that each of them attains a unique valence in the case of four-hand playing. The elements of this four-handed constellation are as follows:

(1) Music for four hands and its use in the home has a particular relationship to consumption: four-hand players are consumers in a different way from single pianists.
(2) Four-hand playing is "semi-private"; that is to say, it always mediates between the domestic sphere and a public of some kind.
(3) Four-hand playing is a visual spectacle—four hands, two people on one instrument; this configuration requires and rewards close scrutiny and careful interpretation, whoever the onlookers may be.
(4) Four-hand playing solicits this kind of attention precisely because hands and bodies interlock and interweave constantly in the process of playing four-hand. While in the nineteenth century piano playing in general was a central cipher for individual subjectivity, such subjectivity is radically undone in four-hand playing.

The first of these points concerns four-hand playing and consumer culture. To a much higher degree than for other kinds of music, four-hand music (especially when it came to piano transcriptions) was a consumer good and thus subject to market forces. Four-hand transcriptions were in many respects the CDs of the nineteenth century. The average music aficionado, who could not go to the opera or to concerts more than a few times a year, could acquire knowledge of pieces he needed to know in order to count as educated only by playing them himself, or by listening to others playing them. Just as the twenty-first century turns to the Internet to compress a wide world of musical references into the home, so too the nineteenth century imported symphonic music into the private sphere by means of four-hand transcriptions. Arrangements could be collected like CDs or records, and they looked none the worse on a bookshelf. But of course the transcription is a strange kind of CD—one that can be played only through the body of its collector.

Music for piano four hands is the most commodified, the most reified music of the nineteenth century, and yet it elicits and sustains utopian hopes for pure, unalienated creation. Owning four-hand scores allowed the layman to make music with a fullness of sound usually reserved for orchestras, court operas, and chamber ensembles. And through transcription he had access not just to an aristocratic sound but also to an aristocratic repertoire; he could domesticate public (or ecclesiastical) music. But the four-hand score as status symbol did not primarily derive from the amount of skill the owner, or his family, brought to playing it—here, too, education was more of "an adornment of the home," as the satirist Karl Kraus remarked scathingly, a musical equivalent of bibliophile obsessions with the surface rather than the content of things.[20] It is precisely its reification and its thorough integration into the accouterments of the bourgeois *intérieur* that make four-hand scores one of the defining musical objects of the long nineteenth century.

In some way, this industrialization penetrates deep into the form itself. In four-hand piano playing, the two parts are not determined by intrinsic musical logic (development or harmony) but, rather, by questions of efficiency. The keyboard is subdivided into parcels, and each pair of hands busies itself in its own domain. (This is precisely where four-hand piano playing differs from other chamber arrangements.) In this sense one can read four-hand piano playing as the division of the keyboard according to the logic of the score, as the terminal moraine of the decline of seventeenth- and eighteenth-century music's *harmonia*, which undertook to harmonize contrapuntal lines. When in doubt, the logic of four-hand piano playing is particularized and unmelodic—each hand attends to what is in reach.

Regarding the second point of the constellation, four-hand music's relationship to consumer culture shows the semi-public nature of this private pursuit. Four-hand music is *Hausmusik*, private and parlor music, but it also relies on publication, publicity, and publicness more than any other type of music. Its sound, but more importantly the traditions that developed around it, pointed beyond the family, beyond the private sphere. Just as four-hand transcription translated public music (music that could normally be played or experienced only at church, in the concert hall, or in the *Musikverein*) into the private sphere, so the instrument, once played four-handed, turned the family into a miniaturized orchestra, a domestic court, or a nuclear congregation. The exact essence of this translation is anything but clear—and the nineteenth century puzzled over it continuously. The puzzlement was heightened by four-hand playing's relationship to labor; after all, four-hand piano playing is located somewhere between (aesthetic) co-laboration and purely

---

[20] Karl Kraus, *Schriften X* (Frankfurt: Suhrkamp, 1986), 200.

nugatory community, and four-hand transcriptions are especially hard to place on the continuum between autonomous work of art and heteronomous use object.

The third point of the constellation has to do with the way this ambiguous scene was viewed, and the way viewing it was viewed. Four-hand playing relies on very peculiar forms of visibility and invisibility. Since two players share one instrument, the practice solicits a different gaze, but immediately frustrates that gaze as well. What two people do on one instrument is never fully private (the way a lone figure gazing out a window or dawdling on the keys might be), and their activity tended to be viewed accordingly. But if four-hand players encouraged spectatorship, they also shut out spectators far more radically than other forms of *Hausmusik*. After all, the two players at the keyboard do not look at each other; in fact, none of their communication is visual. The spectator, who has only visuality to go by, is thus *a priori* excluded from the musical goings-on. Compare this to the transparency of the quartet, the other preferred proto-CD of nineteenth-century domestic culture: scores, body language, tapping feet, eye contact—all are visual cues shared by the players and the onlookers.

The French poet François Coppée (1842–1908) wrote a poem with the title "Morceau à quatre mains," which describes this strange dialectic of eagerly solicited and always already frustrated visual desire. The poem appeared in 1872, at the height of the four-hand boom, in a collection entitled *Promenades et Intérieurs*, and not surprisingly, the titular "morceau à quatre mains"[21] is being played in an interior. The lyric "I" witnesses how the landscape outside is mirrored in the windows of the salon, and connects this observation to his young sisters' four-hand piano playing:

> The salon opens to the park
> Where the grand trees, a somber green,
> Unite their branches in an arch
> Above the lawns they bathe in shadow.
> If I turn suddenly back
> In the fauteuil in which I sit,
> I see again the garden
> Reflecting in the glass panes;
> And I savor the enjoyment
> Of having, to the left and to the right,
> Two parks, absolutely identical,
> Through the door and in the narrow mirror.
> Through a charming play of chance,
> The two young sisters, prettily
> Are seated at the piano

---

[21] François Coppée, *Poésies 1869–1874* (Paris: Lemerre, 1875), 139–40.

> To play a little bit of Mozart.
> Like the two parks in the ornament,
> They are entirely alike;
> Four identical golden jewels
> Sparkle in their ears.
> I examine them as much as I want,
> For their eyes are cast down onto the keys,
> The same flower in their hair,
> The same blossom on their two mouths;
> And from time to time, to see them better,
> Rather than hearing them better,
> I rise and lean against
> The piano made of rosewood.

Given our discussion so far, it should not surprise that both the four-hand playing and its observation unfold in a domestic context. But even in this emphatically domestic scene, four-hand playing refers to the extra-familiar cosmos; after all, the parallelism that structures the poem is between the sisters in their salon and the park outside. Both are understood optically.

Coppée's poem tells of and lives on mirrorings and doublings. It deals with four-hand playing, but it begins with the observation of nature, a park that is reflected in one of the glass panes of an open window. "If I turn suddenly back / In the fauteuil in which I sit, / I see again the garden / Reflecting in the glass." The mirroring of the two parks corresponds to the mirroring of the two girls at the piano. "Like the two parks in the ornament, / They are entirely alike." What connects these two diptychs, these two doublings, is in each case the word *jeu*: the sisters play ("jouent") "a little Mozart," but chance indulges its own "charming game" ("jeu charmant"), by coupling the two sisters to the two parks. Only this accident ("hazard") makes possible the analogy between the two interlacing pairs of hands "on the keys" and the way in which the trees outside "unite their branches in an arch."

The full extent of these interlocking "games" is only accessible to the spectator—that is to say, the lyric "I." For the sisters are no more conscious of their optic doubling than the park can enjoy its reflection in the glass; the "jeu charmant du hazard" depends on the fact that both mirrored park and mirrored sisters are object of one and the same consciousness, and give aesthetic pleasure to one and the same consciousness. "And I savor the enjoyment / Of having, to the left and to the right, / Two parks, absolutely identical, / Through the door and in the narrow mirror." But this "amusement" over the play of mirrorings is limited to the poetic subject; the sisters accomplish more than just play "a little Mozart" *only* when they are treated as objects. And even their simple observation becomes possible only when the two girls are unconscious of the fact that they're being observed. For only because "their eyes are cast down onto the keys" can the lyric "I" "examine them as much as I want."

Herein lies what is symptomatic about Coppée's poem: it says nothing of the movement of the hands, of the sound of the piano; and no "chance" inspires comparison between, say, the Mozart piece and the rustle of the "grandes arbres," to say nothing of an outright reflection. The reader never learns which piece is the "morceau à quatre mains" of the title, any more than he knows how the piece affects the lyric "I" or what it even sounds like. Four-hand playing enters the poem as a purely visual phenomenon. Not only does the lyric "I" refuse to speak of the sound of either trees or of the instrument, but the "jeu charmant du hazard" depends on the suppression of the sonic dimension, as though the poet had set his TV on mute. He says himself that he approaches the scene "to see them better, / Rather than hearing them better," for there is nothing to "entendre" here, nothing to hear or to understand: the play, the privilege of the poetic subject, is purely visual and is not really interpretable. Instead it is pleasing, accessible, and decorative, like a symmetrical wallpaper pattern.

In the poem, the wallpaper character of four-hand playing is owed to the disembodiment of the sisters. The more the girls become the focus of the poem, the more they seem to dissolve. The poem subdivides the sisters into tracts and puts those in harmony, sometimes in order to have the two bodies reflect each other—for instance, "the same flower in their hair, / The same blossom on their two mouths"—at other times to dissolve the two bodies into four organs without bodies ("Four identical golden jewels / Sparkle in their ears"). The poem treats as geometric not so much the sisters' bodies (which are "totally alike" in any case) but, rather, their isolated, dissected body parts.

The "decorative" mode of spectatorship is one a reader encounters again and again in nineteenth-century descriptions of four-hand piano playing. In memoirs, letters, and novels that feature four-hand playing, it is treated cursorily—even Coppée's own memoirs never go beyond a mere mention that he sometimes liked to play four-hand.[22] And even if the musical "content" of such playing is touched upon, that content is frequently reduced to just the score that's sitting on the instrument—for example, in Strindberg's *Taklagsöl* (The Topping Out Party), the monologizing narrator talks about four-hand playing mostly in order to then offer his opinions on Brahms's Hungarian Dances.[23]

Even Cosima Wagner's diaries mention four-hand playing only as a vehicle to then luxuriate in opinions (usually Richard's) about the piece itself.[24] In such moments, the four-hand piano playing becomes a pure medium, perfectly transparent and not worth talking about in itself—letter writers and diarists speak of the acts of playing no more than one would speak about the laser when talking about listening to a piece on CD. The gaze, the narration fleets effortlessly past the halting,

---

[22] François Coppée, *Oeuvres complètes* (Paris: Hébert, 1897), 6: 12.
[23] August Strindberg, "Taklagsöl," *Samlade Skrifter*, Vol. 44 (Stockhold: Bonnier, 1917), **23**.
[24] See, for example, Cosima Wagner, *Die Tagebücher* (Munich: Piper, 1976/77), 1:804, 2:243, 3:567.

moving bodies on their piano stool, and onto the eidetic pastures of the printed score. That is all the more remarkable, given that what Strindberg's narrator and what Coppée's lyric "I" observe at the piano is an extremely physical phenomenon. Instead of a disembodied laser there is an absolute surfeit of bodies twisting and wiggling on their far-too-small bench. The heaving of bodies, the constant conflict of the hands, the over and under of arms—this is the experience of both watching and playing four-hand piano.

But it is only onlookers spectating the scene who mention those bodies, onlookers like Coppée's lyric "I." Coppée's description dissects the bodies and then reassembles them—describes eyes, ears, hair. He partitions the objects of observation into smaller partial objects (eyes, ears, hair), renders the organ autonomous, and dissolves the bodily schema. That may well correspond to the experience of the players, but at least in the universe of Coppée's poem, it seems, they can't express that experience themselves. In this regard, too, Coppée's poem is symptomatic. There are exceptions, but even in descriptions that devote much time and ink to the interior life of the players (for instance in Musil's *Man Without Qualities*), the "stereoscopic" gaze of Coppée's poem prevails: the tendency to see the two players connected in a "jeu charmant du hazard"—that is to say, to see them as connected *from the outside*. And just like that, the two figures at the piano no longer are subjects in their own right but, rather, are objects, the eyes of which "are cast down onto the keys" and which can be observed, enjoyed, and interpreted only by the narrating, lyric, remembering "I."

But another important point of departure for this study can be gleaned from Coppée's poem. Speaking generally, the two objects with their eyes lowered on the keys do not have to be feminine—if Coppée's poem did not make clear the sex of the two players, nothing would necessarily make us think they had to be women—but it should be noted that in the visual vocabulary of the West, devoutly lowered eyes aren't exactly signifiers of hypervirility. Much more important is that the person watching the two players is a man. Unlike the sex of the *soeurs*, the observer's sex is never explicitly established, hiding him behind the seemingly ambiguous *je*. But it is clear that this is a male gaze, a gaze for which woman is a source of "amusement." After all, the poem plays with the double meaning of *reflection*: the two phenomena (doubled park, doubled sisters) are united by the fact that they *se reflètent*—they do not reflect *on* themselves; rather, they passively reflect either themselves or each other. The *reflexion* is something for an observer who can reflect on himself by means of objects. As so often in visual art, optical reflection of phenomena depends on the absence of self-reflection of the phenomena.

As symptomatic as Coppée's poem is for the way the nineteenth century stages four-hand piano playing, any actual four-hand player is liable to feel some resistance to Coppée's description. After all, anyone who has actually looked more closely at four-hand playing will be struck by how *unlike* mirror images the two players are.

Putting aside for a moment that four-hand playing, even with a well-practiced duo, is a far more chaotic affair than the placid image of the mirror would suggest, Coppée's park as reflected in the window pane differs from the park outside by being *its reflection*. Original and *eidolon* are absolutely separated, and it seems that the two players (who mirror the mirroring park) are supposed to relate in much the same way. But this is empirically hard to maintain, and it is not the common view of four-hand playing in the nineteenth century. Rather, the nineteenth century is ensorcelled, even bedeviled, by the fact of how *little* separates the two women at the piano and how *hard* they are to separate in observation. In the imaginary of the nineteenth century they are not mirror images or doppelgangers; they are (as Edward T. Cone called them) "four-handed monsters."[25]

The dividing line within this bestiary is clear: doppelgangers are threatening because they radically put into question the individuality of the subject; but in purely physical terms, the doppelganger is distinct from the subject. Monsters, by contrast, are marked by bodily indistinction: they have additional heads, have unclear boundaries, or ooze beyond those boundaries. The shock of observing four-hand piano playing is not that of witnessing two mutually indistinguishable Stepford-subjects but, rather, the creation of a music-making something, with four busy hands, two bopping heads, and "quatre oreilles." After all, every four-hand piece has passages in which the hands venture beyond their proper place on the keyboard, where they touch or where they cross. Moments with an erotic charge in an otherwise anomic arrangement. And these are, of course, the moments that hold the greatest interest for literature: Thackeray's strongly autobiographical *The Adventures of Philip on his Way Through the World* tells of a "pretty little duet *à quatre mains*, where the hands cross over, and hop up and down the keys, and the heads get so close, so close. Oh, duets, oh, regrets."[26]

This erotic charge is the fourth and final point of our constellation. Unlike in duets, trios, or quartets with different instruments, the two pairs of hands in four-hand pieces always enter the keyboard as *one* being, *one* identity. Even the spectator (implied or actual gaze) cannot pick up on nods, eye contact, or torso motion—the communication is somehow more private, more internal, more intimate. Calling this moment "erotic" may seem premature, though the nineteenth century generally had a hard time thinking of a private, internal, and intimate moment as anything but erotic. But for now I am simply describing something that appears thoroughly determined by a stark division of labor, yet at certain moments miraculously turns into togetherness, into oneness.

---

[25] Edward Cone, *The Composer's Voice* (Berkeley and Los Angeles: University of California Press, 1974), 135.

[26] William Makepeace Thackeray, *The Works of William Makepeace Thackeray in Ten Volumes* (Boston: Osgood, 1872), 6:321.

"A four-hand piece allows us reveries together with our beloved, provided she plays the piano," Robert Schumann notes.[27] This association between four-hand piano playing and eroticism is almost axiomatic in the nineteenth century. It has some basis in lived reality (in letters and memoirs, we find many couples that found one another, or at least tried to find one another, on the keyboard[28]), but literature was particularly fond of it. In Thomas Mann's early novella *Luischen* (*Little Lizzie*, written in 1897 and published in 1900), sadistic Amra convinces her husband to embarrass himself by dancing in a tutu and singing the titular song (about a prostitute named Little Lizzie). She accompanies the tune four-hand—with her lover: "Make sure you arrange it for four hands, you hear," she tells her paramour, "we'll accompany him together while he sings and dances."[29] Amra's husband's humiliation depends on the juxtaposition of the intimacy of the four-handed monster and the profound loneliness of the accompanied singer/dancer. It also juxtaposes the kind of spectatorship being solicited by each arrangement: the two four-hand players are sheltered from outside glances in their twinned idyll, while the lone soloist is brutally exposed and vulnerable before an uncaring audience.

In Arthur Schnitzler's *Märchen* (*Fairy Tale*, 1891), old Mr. Wandel flirts with beautiful young Klara Theren by bringing her scores—"if you'd permit me, we could play the four-hand pieces together."[30] Fritz Anders's "Skizzen aus unserm heutigen Volksleben" (*Sketches from Popular Life*) present Mr. Wandel's designs in fast-forward mode: "Playing together their hands had found each other. Eva, who had at first been reluctant to play together, but then had gotten a taste for it, had giggled and blushed, and the rest followed quite quickly. By the end of the lesson they presented themselves to her horrified mother as fiancées."[31]

In the world of theater, too, four-hand piano playing appears almost exclusively in the context of erotic transactions. Roderich Benedix (1811–1873), a popular writer of comedies in Leipzig, presents the following scene in his play *The Expelled Students* (*Die Relegierten Studenten*, 1869). The paterfamilias walks in on his daughter Emma trying to get her music teacher, Lindeneck, to kiss her. "You've been allowed into my house so you can play four-hands with my daughter from time to time. Was it four-hand playing I just saw?" Emma's girlfriend replies smart-alecky: "But of course! They were touching hands, thus it was certainly four-hand playing!"[32] Coppée's poem treated the

---

[27] Robert Schumann, *Gesammelte Schriften über Musik und Musiker* (Leipzig: Breitkopf und Härtel, 1891), 2:204.

[28] A famous example from the world of music is Edvard Grieg, who first confessed his love to his cousin Nina Hagerup while playing a transcription of Schumann's first symphony with her, marrying her soon after; Ernest Lubin, *The Piano Duet* (New York: Grossman, 1970), 3.

[29] Thomas Mann, *Frühe Erzählungen (Frankfurter Ausgabe, Band 2.1)* (Frankfurt: Fischer, 2004), 173.

[30] Arthur Schnitzler, *Das Dramatische Werk (Werke, Band 1)* (Frankfurt: Fischer, 1977), 144.

[31] Fritz Anders, "Skizzen aus unserm heutigen Volksleben," *Die Grenzboten* 62, no. 2 (1903): 421.

[32] Roderich Benedix, "Die Religierten Studenten," in *Ausgewählte größere Lustspiele* (Leipzig: Weber, 1882), 18:13.

"jeu charmant" as an "amusement," but there existed in the nineteenth century a pervasive suspicion that the "playing" in four-hand playing produced more than just music, and that this "more" might involve matters scandalous rather than amusing. Four hands "playing" was a dangerous proposition, and putting those hands on a keyboard often little more than a fig leaf.

The French novelist Charles de Bernard (1804–1850) creates a much more detailed scene of four-hand eroticism in his novel *Gerfaut* (1838). De Bernard traces a veritable *pas de deux* on the keyboard. The author eclipses the controlling gaze by putting it to sleep. The novel's hero, Octave Gerfaut, meets the object of his desire, the Baroness de Bergenheim, while playing the piano together, and immediately seizes his chance. Unfortunately, the Baroness is far from alone: her aunt, Madame de Corandeuil, is taking her afternoon nap on the fauteuil. What follows is a classic scene of four-hand erotics.

Madame de Bergenheim explains that Gerfaut does not need to worry about the old lady: "I have a special talent in making my aunt fall asleep.... If I wished it, she'd sleep till the evening time; but the moment I stop playing, the silence will wake her up."[33] This musical Sheherazade thus decides to play "the *Valse du duc de Reischstadt* [sic]," by "striking only the first chords of the accompaniment, to indicate to her lover where he was to place his fingers."[34] The scene thus relies on an old *topos*, the idea that four-hand playing is like dancing, but it quickly shifts from the barely sublimated eroticism of the dance (the waltz, no less, which even off the keyboard had the reputation of being too contact-intensive to be quite decent[35]) to the completely unsublimated kind: Madame de Bergenheim shows Gerfaut where to put his fingers; the mediating piano keyboard has disappeared from the sentence, and the turn of phrase barely qualifies as double entendre anymore.

In the image of Madame de Bergenheim telling her lover where to put his hands, the spectral presence of the piano keyboard still keeps guard between the flirting pair of hands. However nominally, the hands being guided, and moving furtively, at least get to cling to the alibi of the piano keys. And thanks to Madame de Bergenheim's way of "guiding" Gerfaut by playing the accompaniment, the fingers never come to rest on the same key at the same time. That restraint does not last long, and the echolike *pas de deux* turns into actual contact. This contact comes about because both players, as de Bernardt's narrator puts it, play their "roles" particularly well—Gerfaut plays a masculine "basse," and Madame de Bergenheim plays the sex-appropriate "chant," which consigns her hands to the upper registers of the keyboard. But since both of them thus busy themselves only on the extremes of the keyboard, "two of their hands remained underemployed, precisely those that

---

[33] Charles de Bernard, *A Fatal Passion, Or: Gerfaut*, trans. O. Vibeur (New York: G.W. Carleton, 1874) 192. [translations modified]

[34] de Bernard, *A Fatal Passion*, 193.

[35] Arthur Loesser, *Men, Women and Pianos: A Social History* (New York: Dover, 1990), 159.

were direct neighbors" in the middle of the keyboard. The narrator presents what happens next as an inevitable consequence: "Well, what could two such underemployed hands directly next to each other do?"[36]

Having lured him onto the keyboard, she suddenly hesitates, forcing Gerfaut to become active: "Before the end of the first reprise, the young white fingers of the 'clef of sol' imprisoned within those of 'the *clef* of fa,' without it lessening the piece in any way, for the old aunt was still fast asleep."[37] Besides the comedy of having the old lady fast asleep next to a burgeoning scandal, the Damocles sword of her awakening points to a secret connection between pianism and sex. The aunt sleeps as long as the four-hand playing continues. Playing four-hand piano and being intimate are secret allies: the former can hide the latter from the aunts of this world. Hands emerge as erogenous zones only when the watchful eyes are led astray by the narcotic power of music. Gerfaut makes his move on Madame de Bergenheim with his hands, and after a while "the hand was returning the kiss."

> A moment after, Octave pressed his mouth upon that somewhat trembling hand, as if he wished to impregnate with his soul its warm and perfumed skin. Twice the baroness attempted to extricate herself, for she felt the thrill of the caress circulating through her veins; twice her strength failed, and her attempts became changed into a pressure against the tenacious lips, which seemed as if fastened upon her heart; the hand was returning the kiss.
>
> It was becoming urgent that the old aunt should wake, but she was sleeping sounder than ever, for the waltz was still going on; and if a slight indecision was apparent in the treble, the left hand, on the contrary, struck its deep notes with an energy capable of metamorphosing Mademoiselle de Corandeuil into a second Sleeping Beauty.[38]

But observers so completely lulled into complacency by the tonic of four-hand music are rare in nineteenth-century literature—and if diaries, letters, and memoirs are to be believed, they were rare in the nineteenth century off the printed page as well. Normally people occupied the spot at which Madame de Corandeuil dozes, or imagined themselves occupying that spot, with a much greater degree of alacrity. The way the eroticism of four-hand playing relates to the spectating gaze can be made clear by a musical example. Johannes Brahms transcribed the third movement of his Third Symphony for four-hand piano himself. The movement is deeply lyrical and melancholy, a songlike *allegretto* in minor (the only one of its type in Brahms's symphonies[39]).

---

[36] de Bernard, *A Fatal Passion*, 193.
[37] de Bernard, *A Fatal Passion*, 193.
[38] Charles de Bernard, *A Fatal Passion*, 193.
[39] Walter Frisch, *Brahms: The Four Symphonies* (New Haven, CT: Yale University Press, 2003), 105.

In spite of its elegiac tone, Brahms's transcription of the movement is not easy to play. This is because in transcribing it, Brahms kept the melodic and contrapuntal lines consistent, and left them entirely to either the primo-player (the player sitting to the right, who usually covers the higher registers) or the secondo-player (the player sitting to the left, usually responsible for the lower registers), rather than splitting up melody and counterpoint to accommodate the relative positions of the two players. This leads to an astonishing hand constellation as the movement opens: the primo-player's left hand lies between the hands of the secondo; the two players have to sit extremely close, their wrists on top of each other, their hands interlaced. They are like lips resting on each other, contiguous, touching, but they speak only by parting.

Within a few bars the constellation changes completely. The two hands disengage, withdrawing into their own spheres. Their separation is not entirely complete: for several measures the score directs both primo and secondo onto one and the same key! At times the two little fingers miss each other by less than an eighth note, sometimes by a half measure. At least that's what the score decrees—in practice, the fingers of course arrive too early or leave too late. Again and again, they touch or come close to touching, and when the hands flutter back into their proper spheres, those players unfamiliar with the piece may feel a genuine sense of panic— a panic that one has played the other's key by accident, fear that one may have been in the other's way. Even players who know the piece well may experience a flash of fright at the sudden, and seemingly mistaken, touch. Only the observer, provided he hovers right behind the players, will know that there is no mistake here, but that the two fingers have to brush each other almost by design.

The beginning of Brahms's "Poco Allegretto" in its four-hand version contains a story of four-hand playing and its perception *en miniature*. It opens with a conspiratorial entwinement of hands, wrists, and even arms that quickly unravels and whose elements, although they retreat into their own separate spaces, still seem drawn to one another as if by magic. Instead of the constant contact of the opening, all they manage are almost accidental-seeming moments of contact, from which both hands almost seem to flee in fright. These brief, fragmentary moments of contact contain a distant echo of the original entwinement with which it all began. The hand constellations in the course of the piece, in other words, sign a tragic narrative: an idyllic unity doomed to dissolution, decomposing into atomized actors whose moments of contact are only accidental and momentary—oh duets, oh regrets!

And it is a tragedy that is visible only to the observer. A neophyte player, especially if sight-reading, does not recognize the moments of contact as short, frightful, and shocklike reminiscences, but as by-products of his unfamiliarity with the piece. But the spectator, in particular the one who reads along and turns pages, realizes there is a narrative here—the story of a fall from unity to isolation. This is the perspective that will be the focus of the following chapters: the perspective of the observer who either projects narratives onto the keyboard, or who is alone in being able to recognize them there. How objective this perspective is, whether it is a matter of apperception or projection, will remain secondary. It is our premise that, even as projection, as fiction, a *méconnaissance*, this way of looking had something almost like objectivity about it. At least for a time what it saw was there, if for no other reason than that there was a gaze that wanted to see it. What is beyond question is that this way of looking was omnipresent in the nineteenth century: diagnosing, interpreting, and narrativizing the seemingly innocent pairs of hands was a favorite pastime. Following the nineteenth century's gaze onto the four hands on their keyboard means exposing yourself to the curious situation in which two different observers could espy entirely different things in the same movements.

Overview of the Argument

In 1933, Theodor W. Adorno wrote a brief essay entitled "Four Hands, Once Again" ("Vierhändig, Noch Einmal"). As Richard Leppert has observed, there is a good reason the "once again" is in the title.[40] Something unique is being repeated here, a bourgeois fantasy that in being brought back for reflection (particularly in the era into which it is brought) necessarily seems cryptic, almost hieroglyphic, like a dream that you try to relate to others upon waking. Adorno writes:

> That music we are accustomed to call classical I came to know as a child through four-hand playing. There was little symphonic and chamber music literature that was not moved into home life with the help of those oblong volumes, bound uniformly green in landscape format by the bookbinder. They appeared as if made to have their pages turned, and I was allowed to do so, long before I knew the notes, following only memory and my ear.[41]

The "once again" has become, if anything, more cryptic since Adorno wrote these lines. Modern audiences no longer access "the music that we are used to calling classical" by playing it four-handed. Four-hand playing is now an object of nostalgia, and even those critics who lament its disappearance do so though they subconsciously know that it disappeared because its reasons for existing are no longer with us. Communal music making became a pastime for Christmas parties or the family life of the petite bourgeoisie. But four-hand piano playing could not survive there: for one, because the required free time was lacking among those who had to work for their leisure; for another, because the desires and promises of four-hand piano playing were those of another, higher social class. Nevertheless, remnants of

---

[40] Leppert, "Four Hands, Three Hearts," 5.
[41] Theodor W. Adorno, "Four Hands, Once Again," *Cultural Critique* 60 (Spring 2005): 1.

the libidinal economy of four-hand piano playing survive even in the guises into which the once-ubiquitous social practice has degenerated—the dying pastime of ever-smaller groups of musical amateurs, on the one hand, and highly virtuosic concert music, on the other.

This study wants to illuminate "once again" these promises, as well the fears ignited by four-hand playing. And just as the secret of a dream cannot be unlocked by simply narrating it, or by taking inventory of it, its chapters are not intended to tell one straightforward narrative; rather, they will approach the phenomenon from a multitude of—at times contradictory—directions. The first chapter takes up Adorno's claim that four-hand piano playing uniquely "befitted the home," and investigates the status of the piano as a piece of furniture, the setting for the four-hand boom. Within the bourgeois household, the piano functions primarily as a mediator, which (a) gives structure and contours to the domestic sphere, and (b) provides a means of communication and interaction between the household and its outside. Four-hand playing in particular offered a royal road between interior and outside, between the sphere of intimacy and the public sphere.

The second chapter deals with another fact mentioned by Adorno's essay: four-hand playing made symphonic music part of domestic life. It treats four-hand music as an object of consumption, and thus privileges the four-hand transcription. Admittedly, those transcriptions were only a subset of the available scores for piano four-hands; and admittedly transcriptions for one pianist were just as popular as those for two. There were plenty of arrangements for string quartet or piano quartet, or for piano four-hands with additional voices, either voices or instrumental. And all of these were at times represented in literature or in the visual arts. But the four-hand versions usually sold better than those for solo pianists: Beethoven's fourth symphony sold twice as many copies in the four-hand version by Lux than the solo transcription by Hummel with the same publisher; and Pauer's arrangement of the same symphony by the Schott publishing house also sold much better than the solo version.[42] Much more important, the vast majority of four-hand scores in bourgeois parlors were transcriptions. The second chapter focuses on the score as fetish: on the one hand, music becomes collectible, commodified, and fungible through transcription, turning into a fetish in the Marxist sense of the word; on the other hand, the transcription always has an inherent sense of its own ersatz character, the fact that it stands in for something else that the player, by playing the transcription, cannot lay hold of "in itself," which moves the four-hand score into the orbit of the Freudian conception of the fetish.

As the third chapter shows, both objectively and in the judgment of nineteenth-century observers, four-hand transcriptions are fetish objects, and it is this status that seems to require and legitimate constant control and judgment

---

[42] Loos, *Zur Klavierübertragung von Werken für und mit Orchester*, 10.

by the outside world. But even within the household, which so greedily consumed new four-hand scores and transcriptions, four-hand playing was subject to a highly ambivalent sort of scrutiny. It was accepted as a necessary cultural pursuit, but such acceptance is always tinged with a sense of threat. Four-hand playing structures the domestic community and threatens to destroy it. Drawing on literary examples from across Europe, this chapter sketches a more complete picture of this strange dynamic, and uses scores and journalistic texts to show on what basis four-hand piano playing was judged to be threatening.

The fourth chapter stays with four-hand transcriptions, but focuses on how transcriptions were created in the nineteenth century. Specifically, it shows the consequences that arose for the everyday consumer from the prevalent transcription practices in the publishing houses. The question is no longer what the consumer did with the glut of four-hand transcriptions; the question is now what those transcriptions did with the consumer. Here, the unlikely category of the "voice" comes into focus. For insofar as the piano can be said to possess such a thing, the four-hand "voice" does not speak for a single subject but is, rather, determined by two collaborating, and at times competing, subjects. Since the pedals are usually controlled by the secondo-player, while the primo normally carries the melody, one player "sings" while the other determines the primo's sound. Nineteenth-century writers were well attuned to the uncanniness of this arrangement. E. T. A. Hoffmann, for instance, himself a composer and music critic, comments on this problem in his stories of musical doppelgangers, strange monsters with extra limbs, of singing automata.

The fifth chapter deals with a much less frequently remarked aspect of four-hand piano playing: the hand. Most visual and literary representations of the phenomenon do not depict the hand itself. But the late nineteenth century also witnessed a veritable hand cult. In the last decades of the nineteenth century, a hand was not just a hand: its size, its form, its general appearance supposedly bespoke heredity, tendencies, and propensity for crime. The physiognomic albums compiled by Cesare Lombroso (or the photo volumes of hands that became popular in the early twentieth century) proceeded by way of montage and comparison. Two different hands (or more frequently "hand types") were juxtaposed in order to induce comparisons and suggest the terms by which they might proceed. Around the same period, prevalent piano technique kept the hands far more still than they are in our day—arm movement and a mobile upper torso were reserved for iconoclasts and virtuosos. The way hands were positioned on the keyboard around the time thus was ideal for looking closely at them; and since four-hand playing caged each pair of hands in a much smaller area, four-hand piano playing allowed for juxtapositions à la Lombroso.

While the fifth chapter deals with four-hand playing as a display of hereditary material, the sixth deals with practicing and teaching—that is to say, with the display of labor. In piano playing the entire body is submitted to a sort of dressage and is displayed like a dressage horse. Four-hand playing had an important role in both of these aspects, whether in the form of four-hand etudes or in teaching methods developed by Logier and others, in which two pupils had their hands affixed to a keyboard. Logier's method, which was rather controversial on the Continent, becomes a springboard for discussing how work and eroticism interact in four-hand playing, and conversely how work relationships can be presented, allegorized, and commented upon in four-hand playing.

This, then, is the topic of the seventh chapter: four-hand playing is like work in many respects, and in the eyes of many nineteenth-century observers, that served to condemn the phenomenon—what looked like intimate togetherness was in truth just an extension of industry by musical means. But other contemporaries pointed to the opposite possibility: that four-hand piano playing might provide a model for a better form of labor, unalienated and productless communal creation.

The study closes with a much more limited case study: by the turn of the twentieth century, music was pretty much the only thing still working in the tottering Hapsburg Empire, and contemporaries often characterized its final decades by means of musical scenes, among them scenes of four-hand piano playing. The eighth chapter deals with two texts that turn to four-hand playing with very different intentions and very different aesthetic programs. Joseph Lux's biographical novels on Franz Grillparzer and Franz Schubert fictionalize Vienna's "classical era," and attempt to resurrect through scenes of four-hand playing the apogee of the Austro-Hungarian double monarchy. Lux's novel was written in the run-up to World War I, and thus revisits the classical heyday of Austrian musical and political might just as the empire was nearing its dissolution. Four-hand piano playing allows Lux to stabilize after the fact a world that, in reality, was rather messy and unstable.

The second novel is set in 1913, though it was published in 1930, and thus after the double monarchy's demise. Robert Musil's *Man Without Qualities* offers probably the most detailed and most multivalent scenes of four-hand piano playing in all of literature. Musil turns to four-hand playing as an aesthetic analog to the royal-imperial double monarchy, on the one hand, and the "parallel action" with Germany thematized in the novel, on the other. However different these two novels are, Musil thus turns to four-hand playing with much the same questions as Lux, even though his diagnosis is of course a good deal more pessimistic. What Lux portrays as the good old days of Austrian cultural capital and political power, with all the kitschy nimbus of nostalgia, Musil caricatures and ironizes as "Kakanien," a country that runs on appearances and self-deceptions. Musil's judgments of four-hand playing thus constitute a verdict on Austro-Hungary in general: what to the uncritical eye looks like effortless unity, far removed from all that is mercantile, industrial, and public, under careful scrutiny turns out to be nothing but aesthetic Fordism.

1

The Sonic Hearth and the "Piano Plague"

It takes a peculiar kind of object to dominate a room even though it is pushed off to the side. Sir William Quiller Orchardson's painting *Her Mother's Voice* (1888) depicts a splendid parlor at nighttime (fig. 1.1), and although the piano occupies only a sliver of canvas on the extreme right, the painting's mystery is about that instrument at the margin. A young woman in white is playing the piano, next to her is an attractive young man, and across the room and across the visual field from her sits an older man with a look of distress. The piano has been moved, that much is clear. There is no reason for it to be stashed away in the corner, but its position opens up a colossal lack at the center of the painting. An emptiness has snuck into the opulence of the salon, eloquent yet difficult to decipher. There is too much space in this room for the few figures arranged in it, and one armchair has been pushed to the side, not to make room but, rather, to retire it from use.

Between the older man on the left and the two young people at the piano stretches a vast gulf, and although the older man is listening to the piano playing, he is gazing into that gulf. But what divides them, the duettists in their lively exchange and the isolated, introverted-looking figure on his armchair? Is he listening to them with envy, with suspicion, with sadness? Who are the two young people at the piano to each other, and who is the man who is supervising them in some way? Only the title gives some answers, as do the two lines from a Tennyson poem that accompany the picture. The man in the picture is a widower, we learn, and his daughter's voice startles him because, as she starts to sing, she sounds for a moment like her mother.

It is a little disappointing to have one's imagination so brusquely boxed in, for a painting to be so strident in reining in its ambiguity in the favor of treacly sentimentality. But between the moment of mystery and the moment when the mystery is solved is where we find the piano in the nineteenth century. Whenever the nineteenth century listened to it or watched it being played, the instrument managed to suggest a bedeviling range of possibilities—especially when, as in Orchardson's painting, two people are bent over the notes on the stand. But like Orchardson, the nineteenth century obsessively tried to foreclose on that range of possibilities: the scene's ambiguity had to give way as quickly as possible to a clear, preferably sentimental interpretation. Whether or not it was correct mattered less than the containment of the widening gyre of possibilities.

Figure 1.1 Her Mother's Voice (1888), by Sir William Quiller Orchardson. (Tate Gallery, London)

In the nineteenth century, four-hand piano playing was not the same activity that it is today. People played in much the same way, on instruments resembling ours, and largely drew on the same canon of works. Yet in performing the same gestures they managed to do very different things. Part of this study will involve seeing what was once a mass phenomenon as though it were still one—an obvious, largely unquestioned practice of everyday life, even though this is no longer that and we often tend to forget it ever was. People still play four-hand piano; passionate pianists still have stacks of scores draped around the piano. However, as a shibboleth allowing passage between nations and classes, it is now no less a foreign country to us than *cartes-de-visite*, panoramas, or Chicago's White City. To cast light on this universal phenomenon of yesteryear, which lies hidden today, the first part of this chapter will address three matters. First, it will investigate the piano as a piece of *furniture* and as an *institution* in the nineteenth-century interior, with a view to, second, assessing the *function* it performed in this bourgeois space; third, it will explore the *forms of sociability* that revolved around the piano at the end of the nineteenth and beginning of the twentieth centuries.

In a manner analogous to what Michael Baxandall has called the "period eye,"[1] the rest of the chapter concerns the mode(s) of perception associated with the

---

[1] Michael Baxandall, *Painting and Experience in Fifteenth Century Italy* (Oxford: Oxford University Press, 1988), 29.

"historical topography"[2] of playing piano with four hands: the forms of attention that it demands and the contents it was taken to be able to transport. This orientation requires changing focus from things that held true for piano playing in general to things specific to duet playing. What gaze does the nineteenth century customarily cast on the piano as such? How does it view those who play it? And what does this form of attention mean for the cultural perception of performances with four hands?

As Siegfried Kracauer described it, the piano is "a private creature"[3]—a part of the domestic sphere where people are not supposed to do labor but, instead, assemble freely and without economic pressure. In the chapters that follow, we will encounter time and again a tension between the fact that, on the one hand, four-hand performance belongs to a realm that banishes labor, while, on the other hand, it looks very much like work. It was possible to toil at the piano only when there was no need to toil for one's livelihood elsewhere. At the same time, the nineteenth century as a whole was obsessed with manual dexterity, with laboriously rehearsed etudes, and with hours upon hours of daily practice. In a bizarre way, then, the children of the bourgeoisie in the family parlor came to resemble at least in this one regard their less fortunate counterparts who slaved away in textile factories.

In the 1860s, the music critic Eduard Hanslick observed that "musical amateurs in Vienna" largely congregated within "the circle of the family." Of course, there was plenty of music to be enjoyed in public in a city like Vienna, at the "opera, [in] church, [or at a] *Tonkünstler-Societät*";[4] even the less-moneyed classes could attend dances or hear music played by military bands and at religious services. The piano, however, made it possible to transfer this public music to the private sphere, and in quantities that dwarfed whatever could be experienced in public venues. This was its primary function in the nineteenth century: to be, as Adolf Bernhard Marx put it, "the universal instrument"[5] that could encompass all that other ensembles large and small could produce, and fit it into the confines of the parlor.

The piano became a mediator between public and private, and it therefore became the instrument of the class that defined itself through that distinction. "By its innermost musical nature," Max Weber wrote in *The Rational and Sociological Foundations of Music* (*Die rationalen und soziologischen Grundlagen der Musik*, 1921), "the piano is a bourgeois instrument." Weber arrived at this conclusion by observing the intermediary space in which the piano is usually played or, perhaps better, the space that develops when a piano is played. He describes it as a sphere big enough

---

[2] Dolf Sternberger, *Panorama oder Ansichten vom 19 Jahrhundert* (Frankfurt: Suhrkamp, 1974), 7.

[3] Siegfried Kracauer, "Das Klavier," in *Schriften*, ed. Inka Mülder-Bach (Frankfurt: Suhrkamp, 1971), 5.1:345.

[4] Eduard Hanslick, *Geschichte des Concertwesens in Wien* (Vienna: Braumüller, 1869), 1:67.

[5] Adolf Bernhard Marx, *Die Musik des neunzehnten Jahrhunderts und ihre Pflege* (Leipzig: Breitkopf & Härtel, 1855), 273.

to afford lines of sight, to accommodate a range of viewing experiences, but not built in such a way as to focus attention on a single point (as occurs, for example, in a church)—a space that is too small to be public and political, but too large to be altogether private.

> Just as the organ demands a huge space, [the piano] demands a moderately large space to present its most appealing aspects.... It is no accident, then, that the carriers of piano culture are the northern peoples whose life, already in terms of climate, is tied to the house and centered on the "home," in contrast to the south. Because, in the south, care for bourgeois, domestic comfort was less advanced—for reasons of climate and history—the piano, although it was invented there, did not institute itself as quickly as has occurred here; nor has it, even today, achieved the status of bourgeois "furniture"—a matter that, among us, has long counted as self-evident.[6]

The dimensions of the space occupied by the piano varied enormously and, on occasion, exceeded the private sphere altogether, becoming a "home concert." When, for example, the world-famous virtuoso Sigismund Thalberg performed at the house of Prince Metternich, the event could hardly qualify as what the Germans called *Hausmusik*, music for the home.[7] Even beyond the world of the aristocracy, in the salons of wealthy bourgeois families during the first decades of the nineteenth century having more than a hundred guests for an evening of chamber music was not unheard of. However, over the course of the century, the triumph of the piano made it possible for the spaces—at salons or similar gatherings—to become smaller and smaller, and more modest, too. The groups that assembled around the piano became more intimate. And the performances changed as well. At the Schubert evenings in the home of the Spaun family and in the large salons of Viennese entrepreneurs, guests not only listened and sang but also danced, gambled, and enjoyed refined meals; in contrast, musical evenings during the second half of the century seemed to center on the music and, above all, the piano itself (consider Wagner's gatherings at his villa Wahnfried).

As the piano migrated into smaller domestic spaces, the piano became an item of furniture, with a fixed position at the center of the household. Characteristic though it proved for the emerging culture of bourgeois domesticity, the instrument did not fit amicably within the bourgeois interior. As Eric Hobsbawm has written, the instrument's position in the parlor was symptomatic for the rules of that space: "The first impression of the bourgeois interior, after the mid-nineteenth century, is clutter

---

[6] Max Weber, *Die rationalen und soziologischen Grundlagen der Musik* (Tübingen: J.C.B. Mohr/Siebeck, 1972), 77.

[7] Alice M. Hanson, *Musical Life in Biedermeier Vienna* (Cambridge: Cambridge University Press, 1985), 112.

and concealment: an oppressive array of objects."[8] This overloading found its "characteristic form" in the "grand piano, an altogether expansive, extremely artfully worked, and terribly expensive instrument.... No bourgeois interior could be called complete without it, and no daughter of a bourgeois household existed who did not have to practice interminable scales upon it."[9] But even if it is indeed typical, the piano is not one domestic trapping among others. It may have started out as that, but it mutated, transforming from a piece of furniture among others into an all-dominating usurper of domestic space. Thomas Christensen ironically called it a "sonic hearth."[10]

The story of this transformation can be gleaned from the guises that the instrument assumed before the dominance of the grand piano. The clavicytherium (a kind of vertical grand piano), for example, could be closed entirely and looked, from the outside, like a commode. Its design captures an interesting ambivalence that is still apparent in the grand piano itself. On the one hand, the instrument seems to be more furniture-like and practical: it can be stowed away, integrated into the republic of household objects. One could close it, push it against a wall, and put trinkets on it, and it would blend perfectly into the domestic ensemble. On the other hand, as Richard Leppert observes, "when played...the instrument appears eminently *impractical*, the preposterousness of its shape mirroring aristocratic privilege, where impracticality is a mark of class distinction."[11] The grand piano can be similarly described: a piece of furniture that, in its excess, displays the burgher's freedom from need.

For the same reason, it is also a piece of furniture that does not really allow itself to be integrated into any room at all: its shape brooks no contiguity with other pieces of furniture; its lid prohibits placing any objects on it whatsoever; and wherever it is located, the room is called the "piano room." In 1905, the art critic Joseph August Lux lamented the fact that the modern piano blocks "the best place in a relatively small living-room," that it is "broad and cumbersome" and makes impossible "any harmonious and purposeful division of the room that one might undertake."[12] The grand piano is just as much an item of furniture as the rest of the array of objects Hobsbawn describes—secretary desks, bookshelves, sewing tables, and so on. On the other hand, the grand piano structures the bourgeois lifeworld (as a hearth forms the

---

[8] Eric Hobsbawm, "Zum Zusammenhang von Erwerbsleben und bürgerlicher Familienkultur," in Heidi Rosenbaum (ed.), *Seminar: Familie und Gesellschaftsstruktur* (Frankfurt: Suhrkamp, 1978), 405.

[9] Hobsbawm, "Zum Zusammenhang," 406.

[10] Thomas Christensen, "Four-Hand Piano Transcription and Geographies of Nineteenth Century Musical Reception," *Journal of the American Musicological Society* 52, no. 2 (1999): 284.

[11] Richard Leppert, "Sexual Identity, Death, and the Family Piano," *19th Century Music* 16 (1992): 114.

[12] Joseph August Lux, *Die Moderne Wohnung und ihre Ausstattung* (Vienna: Wiener Verlag, 1905), 116.

center of a hut) and in many respects anchors it; desks, books, and tables for needlework seem subaltern and purely ornamental next to a piano.

The piano similarly lords over and engages all the inhabitants of the building it occupies. In contrast to other pieces of furniture, it is not intended for a sole user, a single sex, or a particular kind of use. Rather, it involves a whole spectrum of social operations, which never concern just one family member, but for better or for worse involve all of them. When, in 1867, Hanslick fulminated against the veritable "piano plague" that was raging among his contemporaries, he did not simply have in mind the fact that a piano now stood in every single house. The "piano plague" also involves the fact that people assemble around it like no other part of the home. Christensen's image of the "sonic hearth" also refers to this: the family cowers around the piano, hungering for domesticity, warmth, and security. Walter Benjamin described the piano as an "item of furniture that, in the apartment of the petit-bourgeoisie, forms the actual dynamic core of the sadness that predominates here, the center of all catastrophes."[13]

Ulrich, the protagonist of Robert Musil's *Man Without Qualities*, looks at his friends' piano with utter hatred, describing a gluttonous Moloch that terrorizes everything: "Ulrich never could stand this piano, always open and savagely baring its teeth, this fat-lipped, short-legged idol, a cross between a dachshund and a bulldog that had taken over his friends' lives, even as far as the pictures on the wall and the spindly design of their arty reproduction furniture."[14] Walter Benjamin described the "interior of the nineteenth century" as a place where "objects slowly take possession of the apartment,"[15] like corals slowly colonizing a sunken ship. The "sonic hearth" was an imperialist of interior space, a vengeful, black-and-white demon that lays claim to the interior like an infernal kraken.

Nineteenth-century writers frequently took note of the depths of devotion this idol could demand of its worshipers. In a piece from 1881, the humorist Friedrich Schlögl described how life in impoverished Viennese households could not make do without a weekly piano evening:

> With effort, one maintains the honor of the house and, each week, offers an evening of performance; one is amiable and witty, discusses the newest artistic and literary events, offers clever remarks, and does impersonations. Because everyone requests that they do so, the daughters of the family play a little *Faust* waltz by Liszt, to universal applause.[16]

---

[13] Walter Benjamin, *Moskauer Tagebuch* (Frankfurt: Suhrkamp, 1980), 41.
[14] Robert Musil, *The Man Without Qualities* (New York: Knopf, 1995), 45.
[15] Walter Benjamin, *The Arcades Project*, ed. Rolf Tiedemann (Cambridge, MA: Harvard University Press, 1999),
[16] Friedrich Schlögl, "Die Saison der Wurst," in *Wienerisches* (Vienna: Prochaska, 1883), 91.

Adalbert Stifter complained, too: "In a thousand houses, they're hammering away at the pianoforte."[17] In a similar fashion, Charles Sealsfield (a pseudonym for Karl Postl) described a typical Sunday in Vienna at mid-century:

> From three o'clock in the afternoon until eleven at night, the whole city is in a regular uproar of music and amusement. Up and down the street, all one hears is music. In every burgher's house the piano is the first thing one sees. The guest has scarcely sat down and refreshed himself with the watery wine and Preßburg *zwieback* before Miss Caroline, or whatever her name may be, has followed her parents' enjoinder to play something for the group.[18]

The piano is simultaneously a hearth (it unifies the family), an object of social representation (it presents the family to the outside world), and a passageway—for the performance of "Miss Caroline, or whatever her name may be," offers an initiation into the family circle.

The piano was the first thing that "the guest" caught sight of, and it was the best way for Miss Caroline and her family to make a good first impression. It functioned as a point of connection that allowed the family to integrate new members; conversely, it operated as a means by which outsiders could wheedle their way into the family nucleus. Contemporary accounts make it clear that "Miss Caroline, or whatever her name may be," exerted herself for art's sake alone. One could make matches at the keyboard, forge familial alliances. Men meanwhile could play their way to status and honor—like, for example, the Viennese gentleman named Freund, of whom Karl Kraus cruelly claims that he "became government counsel... when people discovered his aptitude for playing four hands with an archduke."[19]

Hanslick's *Geschichte des Concertwesens in Wien* cites the following report made by a correspondent of the *Leipziger Musikzeitung* in 1808; the report describes the "sedulous, impassioned music-making" in Vienna:

> To provide an idea of the number of musical amateurs here: every girl of a better family, whether talented or not, must learn to play piano or sing; in the first place, it's fashionable; secondly, it's the comfortable way to present oneself to society and thereby—if fortune smiles—to make a match worthy of notice. The boys must learn music, too—in the first place, because it is only proper and fashionable, and, secondly, because it acts as a recommendation in fine society: experience has taught that a few of them

---

[17] Adalbert Stifter, *Aus dem alten Wien: Zwölf Studien* (Frankfurt: Insel, 1906), 235.

[18] Charles Sealsfield (Karl Postl), *Österreich, wie es ist, oder, Skizzen von den Fürstenhöfen des Kontinents* (Vienna: Schroll, 1919), 189.

[19] Karl Kraus, *Schriften* (Frankfurt: Suhrkamp, 1987), 1:170.

have played their way to the side of a rich wife or into a very profitable relationship.[20]

If music happened within the family circle, it happened at its outer edge, at the point where inside and outside intersected. This becomes clear when we look at paintings of the period: pictures of young women in particular, practicing with their piano teacher or in a duet (whether the two people are playing a piano together or a piano and a violin) were so numerous in the eighteenth and nineteenth centuries that they essentially constituted a genre unto themselves. They are fairly generic depictions of domestic life, but many of them feature a person at, near, or watching the piano who is visually marked as an outsider. Which is to say that, in most cases, this person is a man—often overdressed for the family salon or wearing street shoes. The fine arts, in particular, depicted music lessons as "an opportunity for the seduction of a virgin who was nonetheless commonly presented as sexually curious." As the nineteenth century wore on, according to Leppert, pictures of this kind grew "less comic, more voyeuristic."[21]

Literature, too, turned these delicate maneuvers involving the private realm of the family and the somewhat more public sphere around the piano into a ready motif, to either comic or voyeuristic effect. Here, the figure of the piano teacher was paradigmatic. We can assume that Ossip Schubin (a pseudonym for Aloisia Kirschner) employed a well-known *topos* when introducing in a short story "a girl from a good family who, scarcely sixteen-years-old, ran off with [her] piano teacher"[22]: "half a child, she was or wasn't interested in him—what do I know!"[23] The most famous literary example of the intrusive music teacher is Troukhachevsky in Leo Tolstoy's *Kreutzer Sonata*. In less melodramatic form, the almost fateful necessity—mostly social recognition and advancement—that requires the protagonist Pozdnyshev to bring the violin player Troukhachevsky into the house, the erotic dimension of the music itself, and the (homo)erotic investments that slowly push the triangular relationship to its catastrophic finale must have taken place at the keyboard in bourgeois parlors across Europe.[24]

The painter René-Xavier Prinet (1861–1946) depicts this story as a cataclysm of domestic space (fig. 1.2). His *Kreutzer-Sonata* (1901) shows Troukhachevsky and Pozdynshev's wife in an almost violent embrace, which disorders the entire space around them. The cover on the piano looks like a crumpled bedsheet or a garment discarded in haste. The curtains are drawn and the window behind the lovers

---

[20] Quoted in Hanslick, *Geschichte des Concertwesens in Wien*, 1:67.

[21] Richard Leppert, *The Sight of Sound: Music, Representation and the History of the Body* (Los Angeles: University of California Press, 1993), 161.

[22] Ossip Schubin, *Toter Frühling* (Braunschweig: Westermann, 1893), 39–40.

[23] Schubin, *Toter Frühling*, 190.

[24] Leppert, *The Sight of Sound*, 153–75.

Figure 1.2 Kreutzer-Sonata (1901), by René-Xavier Prinet.

is exposed, its blackness leaving the domestic sphere disturbingly perforated. The paintings above the piano seem to dissolve into a blur, as though agitated by what is happening in front of them. And yet, not everything that is disturbing about this interior can be laid at Troukhachevsky's feet: why is the right curtain missing, why the dark night glowering through the window panes? Why is the corner so barren, and why is the instrument relegated to such an exaggeratedly marginal position? We know what a domestic scene with the violinist would look like, a single woman basking in the glow of the lamp before the piano. But this is clearly not that scene independent of Troukhachevsky's existence in it. Troukhachevsky disorders domestic space, but that domestic space was crying out for someone to fill it with action.

Prinet's painting picks up on the ambivalence with which Tolstoy's story treats Troukhachevsky's entrance into Pozdynshev's home. The intruder who destroys the domestic sphere enters as "dangerous supplement"[25] : the household perceives him as a threat, but grants him entry as if it were a matter of destiny. Pozdynshev *wants* the intruding teacher in his house, after all—and he *needs* him as a sign of his social ascent. He not only sexualizes the relationship between his wife and the

---

[25] Jacques Derrida, *Of Grammatology* (Baltimore: Johns Hopkins University Press, 1997), 149.

piano teacher but also, strangely, the person of the teacher himself. The air of inevitability Pozdnyshev gives events in retrospect actually points to something objective: events "must" follow this course inasmuch as the story traces the necessary contact between two spheres that stand in a relationship that is just as antagonistic as it is ambiguous—and just as dangerous as it is necessary.

Piano playing was a way of turning outsiders into family members, but at the same time many contemporaries suspected that the obsession with domestic music making amounted to making private matters (unduly) public. The family tried to display its wealth, its class, its cohesion, its refinement, but often enough probably managed to communicate just the opposite. The piano pedagogue Johanna Kinkel wrote in her *Eight Letters to a Friend about Piano Lessons* (1852):

> An educated house, in which no piano stood, would be impossible. Girls who cannot properly recite a poem learn to sing all the same. It is hardly possible to attend a gathering without having to endure music—and what horrible music! Music-lovers and music-haters alike are terrified when they enter a salon for a little rest only to stare into the open maw of a piano with two candles on it.[26]

The family's need for self-representation, and its frequent ineptitude at doing the same, of course allowed in the outside world in a very different way: as diagnostician of the domestic life of the family.

If there was something demonic about the domination the piano exercised in the domestic sphere, it also by its nature telegraphed more about the domestic sphere than the family might have wished or intended. After all, the piano—by sound alone—can command even the largest home (and this is what makes it the domesticated descendant of the church organ). Anyone who has ever lived in an old building under the music room of an old apartment knows that this piece of furniture does not only lord over the space in which it is properly housed; it can also terrorize neighboring floors and even adjacent properties, making courtyards and staircases reverberate with badly timed Beethoven and endlessly repeated false notes. Hanslick called it "piano-playing to public detriment" and the "vampire with keys next door."[27]

Skill and clumsiness, playing habits, repertory, and the like are not private matters (as is, for example, the case with television programs today). Unlike those who claim to watch documentaries when, in fact, they are watching soap operas, piano players display shortcomings of ability and knowledge at least semi-publicly.

---

[26] Johanna Kinkel, *Acht Briefe an eine Freundin über Clavier-Unterricht* (Stuttgart: Cotta, 1852), 37–38.

[27] Eduard Hanslick, "Gemeine, schädliche und gemeinschädliche Klavierspielerei," in *Aus neuer und neuester Zeit* (Berlin: Allgemeiner Verein für Deutsche Literatur, 1900), S:106.

Channeling the dyspeptic Ulrich, Musil's narrator once again comments on this little-loved aspect of domestic piano playing: "the house made the piano resound, forming one of those megaphones through which the soul cries into the cosmos like a rutting stag, answered only by the competing cries of thousands of other lonely souls roaring into the void."[28]

Four-Hand Playing as Fault Line

The location of the piano at the intersection between home-sweet-home and the great-big-world—its lonely, monomaniacal dominion, which guaranteed that the status of the "sonic hearth" would be that of *primus inter pares* in the bourgeois interior—held implications both for the status of playing with four hands and for the view that the home and the world cast on four-hand playing. In an article from 1906 on "Schubert's Pieces for Piano Four-Hands," one reads: "Unfortunately, the piano is all too often condemned to solitude; it has entered a closer bond only with the violin and the voice. Still, even in trios and quartets people complain—and not wrongly—that it stands too far from the [feeling of] community."[29]

Especially when it comes to four-hand playing, the question of community is made both more urgent and more complicated by the instrument's peculiar status within the home. Since the piano stands apart from other ensembles, the two players experience far more autonomy than people playing in other groupings of instruments, and they are allied particularly closely. They form an ensemble that does not readily permit expansion, reduction, or combination with others. It is as compact as musical communities come, but at the same time, it does not need an opening to the outside, and at any rate can't really achieve it, either. Although practitioners may dispute this characterization in empirical terms (many did even in the nineteenth century), this understanding seems to have set the tone for nineteenth-century perspectives on two partners at the piano.

The keyboard played four-handed in a private home is marked by one of the fault lines Jürgen Habermas has described. "The line between private and public sphere extended right through the home," Habermas writes, "the privatized individuals stepped out of the intimacy of their living rooms into the public sphere of the *salon*; but the one was strictly complementary to the other."[30] Thus, in the nineteenth century, in the German-speaking world one typically referred to piano four-hands as *Hausmusik*, *Kammermusik*, and *Salonmusik*. "Home," "chamber," and "salon" all have

---

[28] Musil, *The Man Without Qualities*, 46.

[29] Hermann Wetzel-Stettin, "Schuberts Werke für Klavier zu vier Händen," *Die Musik* 6 (1906), no.7:37.

[30] Jürgen Habermas, *The Structural Transformation of the Public Sphere* (Cambridge, MA: MIT Press, 1991), 45.

to do with the domestic sphere, but none of them is as securely and exclusively situated in that sphere as, say, the kitchen or the boudoir. Adorno observes: "Better than all others, this music befitted the home. It was brought forth from the piano, a piece of furniture, and those who went at it without fear of faltering and false notes were part of the family."[31]

While its relationship to the home and to domestic life was strong but vexed, the nineteenth century treated the association between piano four-hands and the family as unproblematic. Playing together at the same instrument expressed close familial unity. For example, there are two books by Henri Bertini (1798–1876) featuring "four small duos": one is called *Frère et soeur*, another *Mère et fille*. Winifred Wagner—if her correspondence is to be trusted—achieved her position in the Bayreuth clan thanks to her four-hand playing of the master's works. The process was just as intimate as it was ruthless: her sister-in-law, Winifred remembered, "was so overweening in nature that she claimed about three quarters of the piano for herself, and there I was, sitting up at the top, with barely a quarter for myself."[32] The roles performed at the keyboard are familial—although Bertini leaves it open whether his etudes were conceived for players who were already "frère et soeur," or if one became like "brother and sister" by playing them.

If in general the keyboard functioned as an axis between inside and out, between the family and the outside world, then piano four-hands epitomized this function like few other practices. When people played together, new—and sometimes unwelcome—members joined the family; alternatively, through four-hand playing domestic energies yield a public product. In literature, four-hand playing became almost a byword for strangers worming their way into a family or wheedling one susceptible family member away from it. Adolph L'Arronge, a writer for the Berlin theater, depicted this constellation in a scene where the piano teacher makes advances on the young daughter of the family without anyone being in the least surprised. Anna reports to her mother the "tricky overtures" (*verfängliche Anspielungen*) made by her piano teacher Mehlmeyer during four-hand playing. The German can make it sound as though Anna were simply talking about risqué "allusions," but it turns out neither the "overtures" nor their "trickiness" is meant metaphorically, for Mehlmeyer's "overtures" are a matter of manual dexterity, not language:

> Recently, when we were sitting and playing a piece together, he made all kinds of tricky overtures. Whenever my right hand was busy playing high notes, his left hand reached for a low note, and when I used my foot on the damper pedal, his foot always pressed the sustaining one. Just watch: he'll propose to me next.[33]

---

[31] Theodor W. Adorno, "Four Hands, Once Again," *Cultural Critique* 60 (Spring 2005): 1.

[32] Quoted in Brigitte Hamann, *Winifred Wagner: A Life at the Heart of Hitler's Bayreuth* (London: Granta, 2005), 9.

[33] Adloph L'Arronge, "Mein Leopold," in *Dramatische Werke* (Berlin: Stilke, 1908), 1:8.

In his autobiography Franz Grillparzer described this initiation ritual in reverse (and with markedly Freudian undertones). Not the external world that influences the cosmos of the family, but the familial dynamic that holds effects in store for the public. Here the keyboard provides the stage for the sublimation of incestuous energies into productive social work. A fixation on the mother is transformed into exogamic eroticism, which in turn provides the basis for social activity.

The episode goes as follows. Grillparzer "often [played] with [his] mother compositions by great masters that have been arranged for four-hand piano." In the process, he is struck by the "embryonic thoughts" of his great Golden Fleece trilogy (*The Guest, The Argonauts, Medea*): "during all the symphonies of Haydn, Mozart, and Beethoven, I thought constantly of my *Golden Fleece*, and the embryonic thoughts merged with the notes, forming an indistinguishable whole." However, his mother's suicide interrupted the ritual and the trilogy's "embryos" were not carried to term, as it were. Only when he played piano with the daughter of a lady friend did his projects resume their growth: "Suddenly, I once again knew what I wanted."[34] The transference from the familial rite into the most public of arts (heroic theater) underscores a rerouting of libido: the transformation of domestic energies into a public product. The transformation only works when Grillparzer replaces his mother with another woman (at least as a partner at the piano). At the same time, his productivity seems to be a function of the pieces he plays with his mother and his acquaintance: "It then happened that we reached those symphonies that I had played with my mother, and all the thoughts came to me that I, half unconsciously, had put there the first time."[35] It is these thoughts that make it possible for him to overcome his personal crisis and "get back to work."

So proto-Freudian was this scene that it proved irresistible to early psychoanalysis. Four-hand playing was a frequently discussed phenomenon in early analytic writing—nary a disciple, opponent, or colleague of Freud did not turn to it as a theater of libido at one point or the other. But the episode from Grillparzer's autobiography became a veritable evergreen in the pages of psychoanalytic books and journals. When Sigismund Rahmer (1863–1912) published a "psychological-physiological study" entitled *From the Work-Bench of the Dramatic Genius* (*Aus der Werkstatt des dramatischen Genies*, 1906), the episode became a prime piece of evidence. Wilhelm Jerusalem discussed it in *The Function of Judgment* (*Die Urtheilsfunction*, 1895), and Frieda Teller mentions it in the pages of *Imago*, one of the most important psychoanalytic journals edited by Freud himself.[36] What drew these men and women

[34] Franz Grillparzer, *Grillparzer's sämmtliche Werke* (Stuttgart: Cotta, 1871), 9:118.

[35] Grillparzer, *Grillparzer's sämmtliche Werke*, 9:118.

[36] Sigismund Rahmer, *Aus der Werkstatt des dramatischen Genies- Musik und Dichtkunst- eine psychologisch-phyhsiologische Studie* (Munich: Reinhardt, 1906), 16; Wilhelm Jerusalem, *Die Urtheilsfunction: eine psychologische und erkenntniskritische Untersuchung* (Wien und Leipzig: Wilhelm Braumüller, 1895), 10f; Frieda Teller, "Musikgenuß und Phantasie," *Imago: Zeitschrift für Anwendung der Psychoanalyse auf die Geisteswissenschaften, Band IV*. (Leipzig und Wien: Heller, 1916), S:13.

to Grillparzer's story was not four-hand playing, but its location: it functions as a perfect pivot between the privacy of the family and attachments to things outside of the family, between the privacy of the individual psyche of the author and the published work.

The piano's position within the bourgeois household created a historically specific way of spectating the goings-on there, which is especially interesting as soon as two pairs of hands meet at the keyboard. The standardization and industrialization of piano manufacturing in the first half of the nineteenth century made the instrument a "sonic hearth." Of course, the instrument kept evolving throughout the nineteenth century; the sorts of piano we can buy today did not emerge until fairly late in the century. The iron frame, for instance, was an innovation of the 1860s, and it entailed a wholesale shift in the instrument's sound. In terms of range, however, much earlier the instrument attained the shape we are familiar with today. In the 1820s Goethe still made music on a grand that had a five-octave range (something that would not have been unusual in a harpsichord), but by mid-century eighty-eight keys had become standard.

This evolution of the instrument was necessary to make playing *à quatre mains* as attractive as it became: there had to be enough space for two people (and two pairs of hands) at the keyboard.[37] The late eighteenth and early nineteenth centuries had witnessed any number of pianos—all of different dimensions, lengths, and registers, and often with entirely different sounds.[38] In the music that was composed specifically for the piano, however, the fortepiano quickly gained the ascendancy.[39] The instrument envisioned for pieces for four hands was most often either a baby grand or a simple upright piano. Moreover, we can guess that many arrangements for four hands were not simply written for any piano, but, more specifically, for a "pianino." This term referred to the upright version of the instrument—which is still ubiquitous today—as opposed to the grand piano.

One example is the arrangement of Anton Bruckner's Seventh Symphony: the strings' *tremolando*, which produces a wonderful, floating quality in the first bars, is reproduced on the piano by a quick *tremolo*. The score demands that the *tremolo* be played *pianissimo*, which forces the player to perform a difficult balancing act between speed and volume. On a grand piano, a layman can scarcely achieve this effect: as soon as enough pressure is applied to produce the *tremolo*, the volume has already far surpassed the volume of *piano*. And even when one reduces the pressure, the two notes of the *tremolo* are separately audible and the wonderfully glistening-and-swimming character of the overture is lost altogether. Only the

---

[37] Pascale Vandervellen, *Le Piano de style en Europe des origins à 1850* (Liège: Mardaga, 1994).

[38] C. F. D. Schubart, *Ideen zu einer Ästhetik der Tonkunst* (Vienna: Degen, 1806), 287.

[39] For the nineteenth-century view of the same process, see, for instance, Edgar Brinsmead, *The History of the Pianoforte* (Buren: Frits Knuf, 1879), 117f.

thinner volume and reduced scale of resonance in a pianino or otherwise smaller instrument can achieve this effect.

The expansion and thorough standardization of the keyboard enabled the adaptation of orchestral and chamber music for the instrument: "The expansion of range" is the reason "why it is only at the turn of the [nineteenth] century that the regular arrangement of orchestral works for four hands begins."[40] In the process, the piano—which was already *the* furnishing in bourgeois interiors—became *the* instrument of the bourgeoisie, permitting people to gain access to the musical canon, to experience and possess it, and to educate themselves and their children.

The Outsider's Gaze

There would seem to be a world of difference between the grand piano and a boudoir piano, a small commode-like instrument that also could be used as a *toilette*.[41] But, as Leppert has pointed out, the grand retains the "semi-private"[42] of its diminutive ancestor. The boudoir piano had often been equipped with a mirror. The woman playing—for the boudoir piano was clearly conceived for women—was supposed to gaze upon her own reflection while playing, as if in a *vanitas* painting. But even when no mirror had been installed, pianos relied on mirror effects for regulating play: François Couperain's *L'Art de toucher le clavecin* suggests to his aristocratic (and again predominantly female) audience that in order to avoid "making facial grimaces," players should "correct" themselves by means of a "mirror on the music rack of the spinet or harpsichord."[43] Portraits of women at the piano frequently included an allegorical mirror image (a family picture placed on or near the piano, for instance), or the female player is actually mirrored in the shining lacquer of the instrument itself—for instance, in Walter Sickert's painting *Gladys at the Piano*.[44]

The gender dynamics of the scene are clear: like the *vanitas* of the visual arts, this self-reflection gave license to a controlling (and usually masculine) gaze from outside. The woman seated alone at the instrument is presented as though on a platter for all to see. And everyone had a look: novelists for their depictions of customs, painters for their portraits, psychiatrists for their diagnoses, and family fathers for purposes of surveillance. Myriad pairs of eyes were fixed on the hands on the keyboard, with myriad different intentions. Especially when four hands played on it,

---

[40] Max Wilhelm Eberler, *Studien zur Entwicklung der Setzart für Klavier zu vier Händen von den Anfängen bis zu Franz Schubert*, dissertation, LMU Munich, 1922, p. 3.

[41] Leppert, "Sexual Identity, Death, and the Family Piano," 114.

[42] Leppert, "Sexual Identity, Death, and the Family Piano," 116.

[43] François Couperain, *L'Art de toucher le clavecin (The Art of Playing the Harpsichord)* (Los Angeles: Alfred Music Publishing, 1974), 30.

[44] Wendy Baron, *Sickert: Paintings and Drawings* (New Haven, CT: Yale University Press, 2007), 405.

observation was permitted and even desired. A scene that Gisela Andretzi depicts in her novel *Frauenherzen* (1890) may count as paradigmatic: "Lischen and Agnes played four hands. Leo accompanied them on the violin. Behind the two girls stood Hans, who whispered a joking word every now and then; it seemed he was more entranced by the two players than by the music."[45]

To identify the essence of this gaze—and the nature of its object—more fully, it is instructive to compare and contrast them with representations of *individual* parties (normally women) at the piano—a comparison that must take both the pictorial arts and literature into consideration. Did painters and poets look in the same way at the individual at the piano and at a couple playing together? In figure 1.3, we find, once more, the perspective we encountered in Coppée's "Morceau à quatre mains." The image, which is based on a drawing by C. S. Reinhart, appeared in *Harper's Magazine* (1885), where it accompanied a short story by Eustace Clare Grenville Murray (1824–1881).[46] The picture shows a young woman in evening attire, playing the piano under the watchful eyes of a young man. The latter is a guest in this world, for he is wearing a cavalry uniform (the accompanying story mentions a "hussar's uniform"[47]), and his boots even have spurs. One learns in the story that the young man is not just any officer: he is the crown prince. His military attire connotes publicity, history, and masculinity—in contrast to the self-contentment, the classical calm (witness the bust on top of the piano), the ahistoricity, and the pervasive femininity of the domestic scene.

Grenville Murray's story is entitled "His Royal Highness's Love Affair." It is what is known as a "Ruritanian romance"—strictly speaking, it is one *avant la lettre* inasmuch as the fantastic land of Ruritania was only invented in 1894 (by Anthony Hope). Ruritanian romances were set in small, fictitious, German-speaking Central European countries—here, the land is called "Gothia." The British family Chowery has settled in Gothia and become entangled in the highest matters of state; it so happens that the crown prince of the land falls in love with the pretty daughter, Mabel. Reinhart's drawing illustrates his romantic efforts. The subtitle of the picture—taken from Grenville Murray's tale—reads, "If she went to the piano, he followed her, and turned her music." Needless to say, the crown prince does much more than turn her music: the picture suggests that his eyes do not remain on the sheet music for long, but soon focus on the girl—although it is hard to tell whether he is looking at her hands, her head, or her *décolleté*. Nevertheless, there is tension between text and image, since he is not doing what the words say he is doing. One can assume,

---

[45] Gisela Andretzi, "Frauenherzen—Roman," *Oesterreichische Lesehalle* 10, no. 112 (April 1890): 108.

[46] *Harper's Magazine* 71, no. 322 (July 1885): 227–40; the story was reprinted in Eustace Clare Grenville Murray, *Imprisoned in a Spanish Convent with Other Narratives and Tales* (London: Vizetelly, 1886), 149–91.

[47] *Harper's Magazine*, 230.

Figure 1.3 "When she went to the piano, he followed her and turned her music" (1885). Drawing by C. S. Reinhart, *Harper's Magazine*. (New York Public Library)

then—and the expression on his face suggests as much, too—that his intentions are not entirely honorable. The girl, on the other hand, senses nothing of this—and for the same reason that we already know from Coppée's poem. "For their eyes are cast down onto the keys": the player cannot recognize that her suitor is interested in something other than music. Her gaze is self-contained, lowered onto the keyboard; she is either looking at the notes, at her own hands, or flitting bashfully between the two. Grenville Murray's text reads:

> There were times when she was really frightened by the pertinacity of the Prince's attentions. She dared not raise her eyes lest they should meet his. If she shifted her position, he changed his. If she went to the piano, he followed her and turned her music. At table he scarcely ate, but sat devouring her with his eyes.[48]

[48] *Harper's Magazine*, 230.

Of course, the scene discloses its full meaning (both in Reinhart's illustration and in Grenville Murray's narrative) only to the outside viewer—and not least of all because only the observer can read the caption, which makes explicit the dissonance between the supposed intentions of the crown prince and the way he is in fact behaving. Once again, the woman, forgetting herself and lost in a sunken gaze, is only an object: the unknowing object of the prince's advances and equally the unsuspecting object of the observer/reader. Still—as is often the case in visual art—the object, although unaware of the observer, strikes a pose. Her lowered head turns to the left and exposes her even features; only because she assumes this position can the viewer see her eyes, lowered decorously. The eyes and the expression on her face amplify the coquettish quality of the way she holds her head—she is flirting, Reinhart's picture seems to suggest, without wanting to do so or even knowing that she is doing it.

This is not uncommon in the nineteenth century: female piano players innocently offer themselves to the gaze of the observer, and thus become complicit in their own objectification. Fair Mabel Chowery avoids the gaze of the crown prince, but she does so only to offer an even more compliant object for his gaze and desire. This is true—almost exclusively—of women. For when the nineteenth century diagnosed a piano plague—and this is of central significance for our discussion of piano four-hands—it regarded it as a sexually transmitted disease affecting above all women. It was (supposedly) women who were addicted to pianos; conversely, a man acquired feminine traits when he succumbed to this addiction. As Edmond de Goncourt puts it in his novel *Chérie*, music is "the hashish of women":

> As she grew older, the physical caresses of the sounds filled her with a mysterious drunkenness. It exalted her state of well-being, gave her fullness of life, whipped up her imagination mercilessly, enhanced her senses, and, finally, provided a little bit of the supernatural pleasures that men obtain from intoxicants: perhaps music is nothing other than hashish of women?[49]

The keyboard formed a feminine space, a temple of art. At the same time, this place required constant supervision. Victorian painting, for example, prefers lascivious female figures alone at the piano, in erotically charged poses; often, bare arms and legs peek out from underneath their dresses.[50] Playing itself resembles masturbation, or at least awakens the suspicion—Edmond de Goncourt, for example, made an explicit connection between (female) solo playing on the piano and onanism.

When Thomas Mann has young Hanno Buddenbrook sit down at the piano and improvise at the end of a long and harrowing school day toward the conclusion of

---

[49] Edmond de Goncourt, *Chérie* (Paris: Charpentier, 1884), 105.
[50] Leppert, *The Sight of Sound*, 153ff.

his novel *Buddenbrooks* (1903), he turns to a very similar set of *topoi*. Hanno, an only child and his mother's favorite, is an effeminate, impractical, and ineffectual daydreamer, and the sudden vigor, even excess, he builds up on the keyboard is rendered in highly suspicious, and vaguely moralistic, tones by Mann's narrator:

> There was also something insatiable and depraved beyond measure in the way [the melody] was savored and exploited. It sucked hungrily at its last sweet drops with almost cynical despair, with a deliberate willing of bliss and doom, and it fell away in exhaustion, revulsion, and surfeit, until finally, finally, in the languor that followed, all its excesses trickled off in a long, soft arpeggio in a minor key.[51]

Hanno's playing is aesthetically suspect (accomplished, yes, but far from inspired) and Mann's description imbues Hanno's improvisation with a clear autoerotic tinge—in a tone that suggests a disease is being diagnosed here. Indeed, after Hanno's "excesses" have "trickled off," the chapter ends and the next chapter opens with a textbook discussion of typhoid fever. Only at the end of it do we learn that the disease has claimed Hanno's life. The narrator is nearly clinical in his scrutiny of Hanno's piano playing, and he lapses into medical jargon immediately after relating the scene in the piano room. There is something here that requires diagnosis, supervision. And, as the novel implies, Hanno is insufficiently supervised: someone else other than the ethereal realist narrator ought to be watching him, and whoever it is ought to be intervening.

This is where a schoolboy from Lübeck and the Victorian *vanitas* at the piano intersect: they all call for diagnosis, for scrutiny, for control.[52] *Vanitas*, courtesan, *inverti*, "masturbating girl"[53]—they must all be controlled; and yet they defy those who would know their secrets. The observer becomes a doctor, a diagnostician, and also a voyeur—Marcel at the window of Odette de Crécy, which is always the wrong window. But if playing solo at the piano always arouses the suspicion of autoeroticism, what happens when a second pair of hands joins in? Mann's narrator also has (homo)erotic traits appear in Hanno's friendship with his fellow student Kai, who says he "knows why [Hanno is] playing" the piano.[54] What if Hanno and Kai were to have played together on that fateful afternoon? Would that scene be perceived, observed, and interpreted in the same way?

---

[51] Thomas Mann, *Buddenbrooks: The Decline of a Family* (New York: Knopf, 1993), 641.

[52] Gerald Izenberg, *Modernism & Masculinity: Mann, Wedekind and Kandinsky Through World War I* (Chicago: Chicago University Press, 2000), 111.

[53] Eve Kosofki Sedgmick, "Jane Austen and the Masturbating Girl," *Critical Inquiry* 17 (1991): 818–37.

[54] Mann, *Buddenbrooks*, 638.

Fanny zu Reventlow was the muse for the artists of bohemian Munich at a time when Mann wrote *Buddenbrooks*. An accomplished writer in her own right, she achieved fame as an eccentric, the "Countess of Schwabing." Her satirical novel *The Money Complex* (*Der Geldkomplex*, 1916) features the following scene: three friends discover that the bride of their acquaintance Balailoff ("our friend, so to speak") is cheating on him with his (male) secretary. The couple inhabits the same building as the friends—"the pavilion of the bride lies near our wing; all evening long, one hears her playing piano." Although the friends have no view of the apartment's interior, it is the instrument itself that tattles on the bride's affair:

> That evening we were in peaceful conversation. Henry had fetched some wine from the office, and Baumann, who had tied one on, suddenly said pensively: "Just listen, that's really strange ... she's playing with four hands." We fell silent and entertained our private thoughts while Baumann's girlfriend tried to convince him, in all seriousness, that it was impossible to play four hands alone. Of course, in her presence we did not wish to voice our suspicions, but once she had left, we turned the light off and waited nervously at the window until the piano playing fell silent. Shortly thereafter, we saw the secretary creeping through the garden.[55]

In terms of humor, it is a very effective "curiosity" when a single woman plays with four hands; at the same time, the humor depends on a precise understanding of what "playing with four hands" on one's own might mean. Here, the text points to amorous entanglements; in later chapters, we will encounter texts in which the same paradoxical configuration entails suspicion of an entirely different kind—excessive self-confidence, for example, or an overly dramatic mode of performance. In every case, playing with four hands points beyond the private sphere, affording others insight into the contours of this sphere and, thereby, making possible an even more unrestrained form of voyeurism than is provided by piano playing alone—and not least because it offers the voyeur so many more possibilities for interpretation.

What is striking is the uncommon certainty with which the friends at dinner know exactly what to make of four-hand piano playing wafting in from across the way. The four hands at the piano are, as Reventlow describes the scene, only too legible—and consequently, the incomprehension of Baumann's girlfriend seems unspeakably naïve. It is irrelevant how realistic Reventlow is being—whether, in the first place, a music aficionado could recognize, across a courtyard, if four or only two hands were at work; and whether, second, this party would know what to make of a performance *à quatre mains*. The nineteenth century viewed the keyboard—and

---

[55] Franziska von Reventlow, *Der Geldkomplex/ Herrn Dames Aufzeichnungen* (Munich: Biederstein, 1958), 63.

especially when it was played with four hands—as eminently decipherable. Baumann's girlfriend and people like her looked unspeakably naïve, but for those in the know the scene was an open book—provided one possessed the right way of looking (be it musical, medical, or psychological). In fact, it was more readily comprehensible for the voyeurs in the neighboring apartment than for those who, like Balailoff's bride, sat at the piano and imagined that no one would catch onto them, or that they were doing nothing that anyone else could catch onto.

Here, the strange mixture of holiness and lasciviousness that characterized lonesome female figures at the keyboard is transferred to duets: the unbridled autoeroticism becomes a constant suspicion of unseemly alloeroticism. In cluelessly pointing out "that it is impossible to play four hands alone," Baumann's girlfriend actually points to the fundamental problem that the phenomenon posed and the endless wellspring of phantasms it provided. One never plays four-hands alone; it involves a couple seated together—and in the next room, others sit and wonder who is playing and why. In the eyes of the observers, the second party at the piano becomes almost by necessity the co-conspirator of the solitary player—not a guarantor that nothing is going on but, rather, a signal that something absolutely has to be going on. When a second player joins *vanitas* in front of her notes, that player in some way becomes the mirror of the first: the semiprivate space between player and instrument becomes the semiprivate space between the bodies.

Representations of four-hand playing in the visual arts are at first glance quite a bit tamer than those of single pianists, especially if those single pianists were women. The moment a painter or draughtsman adds a second pair of hands, representations of four-hand piano playing could be altogether un- or anti-erotic. The drawing *Ellen and her Grandmother* by Paul Helleu (1859–1927), a friend of the brothers Goncourt, is defiantly innocent (fig. 1.4); Walter Sickert, himself an avid painter of solos and duets at the piano, excoriated the picture as "pretentious, superficial and vulgar."[56] Paintings of four-hand playing, like Frank Huddlestone Potter's *A Music Lesson* (fig. 1.5) or John Constable's painting *The Bridges Family* of 1804 seem squeaky-clean, free of any of the suggestiveness that was *de rigueur* in visual representations of single players.

The artist (1776–1837) shows the family assembled around the piano, upon which the two older daughters have placed their hands (fig. 1.6). The hands of the eldest seem almost to reach for the keys. If one compares Constable's family, which occupies almost the entire pictorial space—or even Helleu's attentive, upright, and chaste figures (whose relationship is immediately clear, even without the title)—to paintings like Frank Huddlestone Potter's *Girl Resting at a Piano* (fig. 1.7), the iconographic contrast can hardly be missed. The solitary girl at the piano isn't playing

---

[56] Walter Sickert, "The Royal Society of Painter-Etchers," *The Complete Writings on Art*, ed. Anna Gruetzner Robins (Oxford: Oxford University Press, 2000), 50.

Figure 1.4 Ellen et sa Grandmère, by Paul Helleu. (New York Public Library)

the piano. She gazes into the distance, her pose is unsuited for piano playing, and the fan lends her pose a coquettish air. She is quite visibly up to no good—most certainly not piano playing—and the reader is called into the picture to supervise her mischief.

Helleu's drawing, on the other hand, shows the two figures thoroughly wrapped up in an activity that, because it is disinterested, contains no dangerous attention or energy. The direction of their gazes has no reference to anything outside of or alien to the family. The gazes of the Bridges family likewise are either directed toward the notes or turned to other members of the family; this family is self-sufficient, and knows nothing of Potter's girls dangerous daydreams. There is not really an outside; at the far right of Constable's painting is a window, and Helleu puts an extremely schematic picture at the opposite end of the piano. Unlike the pictures of women alone at the piano—such as, for example, Potter's girl with the fan—there is nothing external here that might comment on, contradict, or allegorize the scene at the piano or provide an object for roving and unbridled female desire. Whereas a

Figure 1.5 A Music Lesson, by Frank Huddlestone Potter. (Tate Gallery, London)

Figure 1.6 The Bridges Family (1804), by John Constable. (Tate Gallery, London)

Figure 1.7 Girl Resting at a Piano, by Frank Huddlestone Potter. (Tate Gallery, London)

cloud of ambivalence enshrouds the solitary figure at the piano, piano four-hands, it seems, is insistently single- and even simple-minded.

At the same time, a certain ambivalence also creeps into these seemingly airtight idylls. It creeps into Helleu's work through a strange displacement of perspective: he draws the figures with great precision, but renders the instrument on which they play only schematically. Furthermore, the piano is not drawn in proper perspective; it almost seems that the piano is taller in the background than in the foreground. The reason for the conscious distortion of the image seems to be that this trick pushes both the faces and the hands into the extreme foreground. The hands, in particular, are rendered with extraordinary detail—as if there were something to be read here, something to be compared and recognized. Indeed, the players' hands are very different from one another, and not just because one of the two players is so much older than the other. There is information to be gleaned here that cannot be picked up elsewhere in the picture; the following chapters will suggest what exactly that information might be. At any rate, it is clear that this detail—the hands that are so insistently foregrounded for our perusal—interrupts the seeming self-containment of the scene. Their placid faces may suggest that these two women are in a bubble all by themselves. But in fact this scene is intended for an observer, an interpreter—and his presence, at least in terms of perspective, is no coincidence; indeed, it provides the *raison d'être* of the drawing.

The hands of the Bridges sisters, on the other hand, cannot be seen. The picture doesn't seem to contain any reference to an observer who might interpret and analyze—and thereby control—the scene. All the same, there is an intruder in the family circle; however, unlike Reinhart's prince who was so quick to butt in and turn the music, he does not enter the picture. The intruder is Constable himself. Sometimes, the gaze of the intruder simply belongs to the painter. Constable, it seems, fell in love with one of the two sisters playing piano together in the painting, and "his visits were in consequence discouraged."[57] His sketches and studies for the picture show Mary Ann—the eldest of the Bridges daughters, who was clearly the main object of his visual and erotic interest—playing four-hands.[58]

On a literary terrain, Frank Wedekind, in the short autobiographical narrative "I am bored" ("Ich langweile mich," 1883), depicts what happens when a second pair of hands is added to the implicitly autoerotic event of solitary piano playing. The narrator (as a result of the boredom that gives the piece its title) wants to seduce the piano teacher Wilhelmine, who for her part has turned the image of a star tenor into a fetish of sorts. Wilhelmine carries the picture with her wherever she goes and treats it like a religious relic. When playing the piano with a partner, she places the picture she worships on the music stand; "as we play, she plants a kiss, at every quarter note, on the features she so adores."[59] Here, the image of the *vanitas* at the piano is transformed alloerotically: instead of sunning herself in self-abandon in the reflection provided by the mirror or the music, this *vanitas* contemplates the picture of a love object on the piano.

The mirror of *vanitas* has the covert function of admitting a masculine gaze, and so the tenor's picture disturbs the narrator's gaze in its contemplation. By emphasizing the fact that she is erotically invested in her playing, but that that investment does not involve her musical partner, Wedekind highlights the uncanny dimension of the four-hand scene: the self-oblivious female onanist at the piano requires (at least as far as the voyeur is concerned) a man, no matter who, who might replace the music for her, wean her from it. Wedekind's story raises the question: What if vanity had a love object and it wasn't you?

> At the end of the etude she succumbs to complete agony, collapses at the corner of the sofa, and allows me to caress her without resisting in the least. Only now and then she stammers in a dying voice: "Oh, you are so unappetizing, so unappetizing!"[60]

---

[57] D. S. MacColl, "Constable as a Portrait-Painter," *Burlington Magazine* 20 (1912): 286.

[58] Anne Lyles and Robin Hamlyn, *British Watercolours from the Oppé Collection with a Selection of Drawings and Oil Sketches*. Exhibition catalogue (London: Tate Gallery, 1997), 194.

[59] Frank Wedekind, "Ich langweile mich," in *Mine-Haha und andere Erzählungen* (Hamburg: Rowohlt, 1955), 82.

[60] Wedekind, "Ich langweile mich," 82.

The beloved can only maintain an erotic relationship with the narrator through the picture of the tenor; only in exchange with the object on the music stand does he not seem "unappetizing" to her. The question about the sexual relationship is always present in interpretations of four-hand piano playing in the nineteenth century. But suspecting that sex stood behind the exertions at the piano tended to raise more questions than it answered: Could two subjects really achieve the oneness that playing together at the same keyboard suggested? Or was there always an element of illusion involved—a dream image, like the portrait of the tenor?

That experience of intoxicating unity—a perfect relationship at the keyboard—seemed always to belong to someone else. Only in the eyes of the observer did the fantasized harmony actually exist; the act itself, then as now, probably never quite lived up to this impossible goal for the two actual players. A contribution by Wilhelm Reich in Magnus Hirschfeld's *Zeitschrift für Sexualwissenschaft* from 1924 relates the following dream told him by a patient: "A young man comes to my sister, they sit in the next room and play piano; I grow jealous and want to play on my own piano. I look for notes, and they take them away from me."[61] It does not require much psychoanalytic acumen to decode the meaning of this and similar scenes: the word "jealousy" is clear enough. What gives the voyeurism and the unattainable eroticism in the next room an interesting spin is the fact that the dreamer is not a male patient, but a female one.

The young woman dreaming finds herself in the same position as Reventlow's company of diners, but she wants, for herself, the sex that she witnesses (if in a coded manner). She is forced to play "with her own piano" (which Reich duly interprets as a masturbatory desire[62]), but none of this works because "they" take the notes away from her. Therefore, the dream pits, on the one hand, the fantastic fulfillment of sexuality in piano four-hands against the concomitant sense of lack in the party observing the activity (if the dreamer had been a man, Reich would certainly have spoken of "castration"). The voyeur is denied even playing by—or with—herself. The (seeming) perfection of the relationship in the "next room" snatches the symbolic phallus away from her.

The situation facing this observer—namely the fact that she lacks what the observed parties enjoy without knowing what they possess—is probably not to be understood only in psychoanalytic terms. The phenomenology of four-hand piano playing in the nineteenth century constantly returns to this dynamic: the more rapturous an observer (or an author, a painter, a poet) in his or her presentation of four-hand playing, the more the texts display a certain hesitation, perhaps even shame. They seem embarrassed that they are forcing something to speak

---

[61] Wilhelm Reich, "Der psychogene Tic als Onanieäquivalent," in *Zeitschrift für Sexualwissenschaft* 9 (1924–25): 307.

[62] Reich, "Der psychogene Tic als Omanieäquivalent," 308.

(representing and objectifying it in verbal, visual terms) that is interesting first and foremost because of the mute, tactile communication between players.

Observing four-hand playing, in other words, necessarily means experiencing it in an entirely different register than the one in which the players encounter one another. Unlike in a quartet where the view from cello to first violin is not altogether different from the audience's view of the same, the four-hand scene thrives on a radical distinction between the experience itself and the experience *of* the experience: the experience itself is what Martin Heidegger called "present-at-hand," and the other is "ready-at-hand." The view from outside reproduces the alienation that the viewer believes is being suspended in the act itself. The narratives about piano four-hands are, so to speak, indices of this alienation; for although we have already encountered figures (de Bernard's Gerfaut, for example) who play piano four-hands with ulterior motives, the main attraction of playing piano four-hands is probably to be sought in the fact that two people sit alongside each other, touch each other, and move together without it having to mean anything in particular.

For the onlooker there is a scandal inherent in this utopian attempt to achieve meaninglessness, and he or she responds by investing the scene with ever more latent meanings. Yet what an outsider might take for potential eroticism is in itself nothing more than a way of making music in which the gaze plays no role (apart from the obligatory one that one casts on the notes), in which all signs from one player to another must be tactile or whispered. And the self-sufficiency of the piano players, which generates the many analogies to marriage, friendship, and sexual love, is simply due to the fact that the two players, unlike the members of a quartet, cannot see their public, but are entirely absorbed by the microcosm that exists among the bench, the keyboard, and the music stand. It is not just that the players don't care whether the onlookers have long since left the room, or what kind of gazes the remaining observers cast on them—all of this is, for better or worse, invisible to them. The self-containment of the dyad at the piano makes the observer supplementary, who becomes a voyeur who must somehow justify himself.

The four-hand scene in the nineteenth century is determined by a tension between the eroticism that is projected into the scene and the experience of actual four-hand playing. The relationship between eroticism and bald fact is not determined primarily through misinterpretation; rather, it designates a point at which both—eroticism and being-together—come into contact. Just because four-hand piano attracted a certain voyeurism in the nineteenth century, that does not mean that the nineteenth century understood the phenomenon as only erotic. What people thought they saw had to do with the physical closeness, verging on oneness, that one could observe as four hands rushed up and down the keyboard. They understood this closeness in terms in which eros, work, and community reflected each other.

Four-hand piano could reflect a whole spectrum of kinship systems. Sometimes, the texts or images themselves are not entirely sure which one they think they are looking at. What kind of being-together is this, then, which needs no one else and seems to admit no third party into the alliance? Piano four-hands was, as Hermann Wetzel-Stettin wrote in 1906, "by its nature an ensemble destined for unity."[63] It almost by necessity drew comparisons with other forms of intimacy—especially ones occurring in the realms of eroticism, family, and school. The way that the relationship at the keyboard is understood and represented—whether as a love affair, a family bond, a working relationship, or instruction—will be addressed in the next chapter.

Hanslick emphasizes that, in playing together, one must become what an impassioned dilettante once, in his company, called a "four-handed person"; it is necessary to "negate personality entirely and stress only musical utility."[64] A "four-handed person," according to Hanslick, "increases in value the less he pretends to be two-handed."[65] Therefore, in four-hands playing there lies a harmony that comes from within; yet at the same time, the activity involves giving up individual claims to power and, often enough, checking one's own ability. In this context, Adolf Bernhard Marx observes:

> When practiced with four hands, piano-playing is deprived of one of its greatest merits: that is, the complete freedom of performance that occurs through an individual player left entirely to his own devices, under whose sole rule, really and truly—not "so to speak" and "almost"—everything comes from a single spirit and heart.... Four hands do not double skill; rather, they deprive, also for outsiders, both of the players crowded together of a significant portion of their effectiveness.[66]

As in Hanslick's comment, playing with two hands is associated with unfettered power, whereas four-hand playing entails the partial abandonment of precisely this power. It's unification and voluntary self-restriction, renouncing effectiveness in the name of community with another. Just like the family, the two players were complete unto themselves. Just like marital partners, the two players at the piano undertook a parallel risk of submitting to another's skill and whims. Wordless communication, physical harmony, complete union of personalities, and the partial renunciation of individual will—in the nineteenth century, this describes the way both marriage and piano four-hands were understood. But could a good marriage teach good four-hand playing? Or was four-hand playing key to a good marriage?

---

[63] Wetzel-Stettin, "Schuberts Werke für Klavier zu vier Händen," 37.

[64] Eduard Hanslick, *Aus dem Concert-Saal: Kritiken und Schilderungen aus 20 Jahren des Wiener Musiklebens* (Vienna and Leipzig: Braumüller, 1897), 459.

[65] Hanslick, *Aus dem Concert-Saal*, 460.

[66] Adolf Bernhard Marx, *Die Lehre von der musikalischen Komposition, Dritter Teil* (Leipzig: Breitkopf und Härtel, 1845), 573.

In a letter to Georg Friedlaender from 1893, the novelist Theodor Fontane poked fun at the apparently widespread notion that piano for four hands could save marriages: "It is nonsense to believe that one might become happy by playing a sonata with four hands. Marriage is founded on other things."[67] Fontane's ironic observation illustrates the immense suggestive power that emanated from piano four-hands. He might declare it "nonsense" to believe that piano four-hands can provide the basis for a marriage, but it also seems that many people believed this nonsense. In the chapters to follow, we will encounter more than a few of them—for example, a couple that cannot achieve togetherness because they can't keep rhythm together; or another couple that only functions when the spouses play piano.

Marriage offers only one model to describe the partial renunciation of subjectivity when playing piano four-hands. Another can be found in Friedrich Bodenstedt's comedy, *Wandlungen* (1875), when the friends Irma and Emma are talking. Irma declares: "Even playing piano isn't really fun for me anymore, since we no longer play together." Emma responds: "I, too, have grown so used to playing together that I'm always missing two hands when I play alone—as if I had been born with four hands!"[68] Here, then, it is friendship that functions as the analogue of piano four-hands. In piano four-hands, as in friendships, one gives up a little of oneself in the name of the greater whole. At the same time, Emma's feeling that she "had been born with four hands" points toward an entirely different dimension: in playing piano four-hands, one is de-individualized; the moment the four hands set about their secret ministry, the individual subject is no longer intact.

If four-hand playing could effect something of a deconstruction of the individual subject, it shared this effect with certain philosophical approaches of the late nineteenth century—among others, with the philosophy of the passionate four-hand player Friedrich Nietzsche. Nietzsche's own compositions are few in number, but a good many of them were for four-hand piano. The one he seems to have been proudest of was titled "Hymn to Friendship."[69] Nietzsche addressed questions of friendship and love in his writings of the same era (in particular, the seventh book of *Human, All Too Human*). He argues that friendship is to be esteemed more highly than love—as in music, friendship is supposed to have, at its core, a "shared higher thirst for an ideal that stands above the individual."[70] For Nietzsche, then, passing beyond the *principium individuationis* was more a matter of friendship than of love,

---

[67] Letter dated March 1, 1893; Theodor Fontane, *Briefe an Georg Friedlaender* (Heidelberg: Quelle & Meyer, 1954), 213. Fontane's skepticism notwithstanding, his novels, especially *Irretrievable* and *Stechlin*, nevertheless feature many scenes of four-hand playing.

[68] Friedrich Martin von Bodenstedt, *Kaiser Paul / Wandlungen* (Berlin: Grotem, 1876), 167.

[69] Friedrich Nietzsche to Malwida von Meysenburg, January 2, 1875, in Friedrich Nietzsche, *Nietzsche: Briefwechsel (KGA II)* (Munich: Hanser, 1954), 48.

[70] Friedrich Nietzsche, *Die fröhliche Wissenschaft, Werke* (Munich: Hanser, 1954), 2:48.

so it was only fitting that Nietzsche dedicated his most significant composition for four hands to friendship.

In less spiritual terms, when Bodenstedt's heroine thinks that she "was born four-handed," she suggests that four-hand playing turns two players into what Edward T. Cone called "a single four-handed monster." Cone's phrase comes from the twentieth century, but the idea was also employed on multiple occasions in the nineteenth, and it brought to bear some pet obsessions of the nineteenth century—ideas about degeneracy and descent, ideas about norm and abnormality—to bear on its favorite form of music making. The image suggests that the melting of individuals in four-hand playing must be so complete that ultimately there remains just one body with two hearts; or, as *Newsweek* wrote in 1943: "two minds must work as one; twenty fingers must strike as ten."[71]

Of course, marriages, friendships, and monstrous births always are other people's business, too. Observers of four-hand piano playing often interpreted it in terms of its public consequences, be that as a problem, an opportunity, a piece of evidence, or a symptom. This enabled a politics of playing four-hands. Two people freely uniting and renouncing part of their independence, without seeming to mind doing so, is appealing, not just in terms of intimacy; it may also hold promise for social and political life. The player who is prepared to share his instrument, enter compromises with others, and renounce his own claims to power is, in other words, not just a good marriage partner or friend; he is also a good citizen.

In his study *Duo Pianism* (1950), Hans Moldenhauer compares four-hand players with a "republic" in which all questions of feeling, communication, and compromise are resolved. "Thus, no absolute or *a priori* authority is ever invested in any one … but all leadership becomes incidental." Playing four-hands therefore opposes the autocratic dimensions that the subject assumes in playing solo or submitting to a conductor in an orchestra. It represents a form of self-renunciation, not discipline. It is no surprise that Moldenhauer (1906–1987), who fled Nazi Germany in 1938, as well as many of the great duettists he interviewed, who likewise fled the Nazis for America, stressed the absence of "absolute leadership"—the absence of the "Führer principle"—as one of the most attractive aspects of "duo-pianistic" praxis (that is, two people playing together at one or two pianos). As Moldenhauer viewed it, the four-handed republic is most strongly threatened by "dictatorial practices," which have "no place in duo-pianism."[72]

The position of the piano at the threshold between inside and outside—the status of playing four-hand as the point of connection between family and society—produces a perspective constituted by transfers from one domain to the other. Private matters are translated into public codes; conversely, the public sphere

---

[71] "Twenty that Strike as One," *Newsweek*, December 27, 1943, p. 84.

[72] Hans Moldenhauer, *Duo Pianism* (Chicago: Chicago Musical College Press, 1950), 193.

offers a model for private praxis. In both cases, the household and the subject are opened to something that is always already different, which guides and motivates the exchanges. Whether this opening is understood as necessary but dangerous or as a political-utopian matter, either way the strange organic "melting" of horizons in four-hand piano playing and the autonomy of the unity that results constitute scandal, opportunity, and/or danger.

The utopian "politics of piano four-hands" will not concern us immediately; instead, our attention will fall on the judgment of the family unit by the outside world that occurs in scenes of piano four-hands. Despite its frequent idealization, the unity of four-hand playing cannot escape the outside view that the piano seems to invite, inasmuch as it forms the hinge connecting the household and the public sphere. The next chapter explores the connection between the private and public spheres that piano four-hands makes possible—the fact that, in the nineteenth century, the family could bring into the home the entirety of classical music in the form of arrangements for four hands. Music for four hands was an article of consumption—an inherently "public" attempt to domesticate music and musical praxis. At the same time, as a commodity, it demanded that the domestic sphere constitute itself by way of imports from the outside: four-hand music was almost entirely mediated through publications.

2

Four-Hand Piano Playing between Parlor Music and the Culture Industry

In the fall of 1863, nineteen-year-old Friedrich Nietzsche wrote from boarding school to his mother, Franziska. He complained about the "piteously thin" goose he had been served for the feast of St. Martin, but rejoiced at his approaching visit home for Christmas. Then he appealed to a tradition that might be familiar even to parties who know nothing about geese prepared for St. Martin's Day or boarding-school kitchens: he itemized his Christmas wishes. For Christmas, he wanted: "(1) The *Grand Duo* by F. Schubert, arranged for four hands; (2) Düntzer's edition of Goethe's lyric poems."[1] Music for piano four-hands was music that a young man could ask for as a Christmas present—something he could proudly bring back, along with "Goethe's lyric poems," to boarding school at Pforta. If teenagers ask for CDs and MP3 players today, their counterparts in the nineteenth century requested scores for four hands.

Piano four-hands belongs to the bourgeois interior of the nineteenth century. The piano was the *primus inter pares* of bourgeois furniture, but playing that instrument *à deux* structured the phantasmagoric "dream world" that Walter Benjamin evoked in his *Arcades Project* like few other activities. What that world was like, what comforts it could offer, and what insecurities it had about itself all were on display here. Theodor W. Adorno called four-hand piano music one "that one could handle and live with—before music's progress commanded isolation and secret craft."[2] In other words, works for four hands are commodities. During their hundred-year heyday (from Haydn to Brahms), four-hand scores were produced so that the bourgeois public could entertain itself instead of buying tickets in order to be entertained. This chapter addresses the peculiar kind of consumption associated with four-hand piano

---

[1] Friedrich Nietzsche, *Sämtliche Briefe (KSA), Band 1—Juni 1860-September 1864* (Berlin: de Gruyter, 2003), 266.

[2] Theodor W. Adorno, "Vierhändig, Noch Einmal," in *Gesammelte Schriften 17*, ed. Rolf Tiedemann, Gretel Adorno, Susan Buck-Morss, Klaus Schultz (Frankfurt: Suhrkamp, 1971), 4:303.

music: consumption that demanded a good deal of activity by consumers, consumption that was collective by necessity. The next chapter will discuss what people did with arrangements for four hands after they had bought them; the complementary question—what four-hand arrangements did to those who played them—is the topic of chapter 4.

The music critic Eduard Hanslick described a situation that was likely repeated thousands of times in nineteenth-century Europe, whether in Germany, England, or Russia, whether among the high bourgeoisie or among impecunious students:

> A package of new scores lay on my piano, unopened—just like the instrument itself, for some time now. With no small joy, we went about our little preparations; one of us opened the package, the other the piano. It was self-understood that we would begin with a piece for four hands. That, after all, is the most intimate, the most agreeable, and, within its limitations, the fullest way to make music in the home.[3]

This episode indicates the economic aspect of the four-hands phenomenon: that in the nineteenth century there existed in Europe a reading public for scores. Members of this reading public behaved like literary consumers: they awaited publications from certain authors; they ordered new releases from catalogs or bought subscriptions; they sought to establish complete collections. We can see how closely four-hand music and publication were linked on the basis of a seemingly unremarkable—but still telling—fact about Schubert's works, to which Maurice J. E. Brown has drawn attention: while much of the composer's output was published only after his death, and many pieces were made available only with the publication of the *Gesamtausgabe*, every single four-hand composition by Schubert was published commercially during his lifetime.[4] More than any other kind of music, it seems, pieces for four hands were written to be published, intended to make money through sales rather than performance, and were marketed to collectors.

Because, as a "sonic hearth," a piano was part of the basic furniture of the bourgeois household, the reading public preferred piano scores. Increasingly, it preferred *Auszüge*—that is, arrangements of chamber music, opera, orchestral pieces, or choral compositions for two or four hands.[5] Commercially, piano four-hands made the

---

[3] Eduard Hanslick, *Geschichte des Concertwesens in Wien* (Vienna: Braunmüller, 1869), 405.

[4] Maurice J. E. Brown, *Essays on Schubert* (New York: St. Martin's, 1966), 85.

[5] In lists like this one, the term "four-hand arrangement" designates a very specific thing, but the pragmatics of the concept don't always line up with the terminology deployed by music publishers and periodicals. Just as today, in the nineteenth century it could mean two different things when it called a score a "piano transcription," a "piano *Auszug*," or a "piano arrangement": first, in arranging an opera, the arranger can hand over the role of the orchestra to the piano but maintain the singers' voices in their entirety; alternatively, the transcriber can hand over the entirety of the piece, including the human voices, to two- or four-hand piano. These two forms of arrangement were, of course, used

most sense since it permitted a more precise reproduction of the sound and textures of the original, and demanded comparatively little skill on the part of the user (in comparison to arrangements for a single pianist). In his *Lehre von der musikalischen Komposition* (1845), the composer and musical theorist Adolf Bernhard Marx (1795–1866) wrote:

> Four-handedness has the self-evident advantage of making easier to execute—or, indeed, possible in the first place—many things that two-handedness is denied. Such full chords, such bass notes rolling over octaves, such polyphony that is clear, easily represented, and readily recognized in performance—what player has not taken joy in them?[6]

Marx's contemporaries time and again remarked on the incredible victory march of music for four hands—and, especially, transcriptions for piano four-hands. They were not always altogether happy about it. In 1832, for example, the Leipzig *Allgemeine musikalische Zeitung* described the "innumerable arrangements with which the public is flooded, so to speak."[7] Indeed, documentary evidence, as far as it is available, confirms that the journal was not necessarily hyperbolic in invoking the images of inundation.

To be sure, many traces of this musical practice are lost to history; often enough, advertisements for transcriptions and transcriptions reviewed in the periodicals of the age don't match up. In many cases, what was advertised were probably unauthorized arrangements—possibly pirated editions, and in any event not the kind that would be recognized or reviewed by the periodicals.[8] What is more, many composers arranged works by their colleagues as acts of friendship; naturally, these were accessible only to a limited circle. And only a few composers who supplemented their income by arranging wrote about work conditions with the frankness of the composer and *Kapellmeister* Franz Gläser (1798–1861): "For the arrangement of

---

quite differently and are addressed to fundamentally different consumers. The first is intended as a practical aid for practice or study for professionals, reviewers, or those engaged in publicly performing the arranged work in its nonarranged form. The second is intended for those who want to bring the arranged work onto one instrument, who wish to reproduce the piece without too much work or too much manpower. Almost all of the transcriptions advertised in the *AmZ* or listed by Hofmeister fell into this second category—after all, only they could effectively be marketed as *Hausmusik* (cf. Helmut Loos, *Zur Klavierübertragung von Werken für und mit Orchester des 19 und 20 Jahrhnuderts* (Munich: Katzbichler, 1983), 16.

[6] Adolf Bernhard Marx, *Die Lehre von der musikalischen Komposition, Dritter Teil* (Leipzig: Breitkopf & Härtel, 1845), 573.

[7] *Allgemeine musikalische Zeitung* (hereafter *AmZ*), (November 14, 1832): 752.

[8] Loos cites the following example: Brahms's Serenade no. 1, op. 11, first appeared in a four-hand transcription with Breitkopf & Härtel; an identical version later appeared under a different name with Simrock (Loos, *Klavierübertragung von Werken für und mit Orchester*, 24).

an entire opera, I received twenty Viennese guilder.... I would have been quite happy to receive many commissions of this kind. But I had to busy myself a great deal with copying on the side."[9] In his autobiography, Richard Wagner does not mention that, during his lean years in Paris, he tried to make ends meet by working on opera arrangements for four hands. Although otherwise given to sharing too much rather than too little, his statements about his arranging activities were so scant that there is still controversy today about which arrangements actually came from the pen of the future Master of Bayreuth; the material appeared either anonymously or simply with the last name "Wagner," and there were several Wagners in the music world at the time.[10]

The composers' discretion places some limits on our knowledge of the marketing machine surrounding four-hand scores—how many scores existed, how many were printed, how they were marketed and publicized. All the same, one can get an idea of the market, the product, and the consumers from Adolph Hofmeister's *Handbuch der musikalischen Literatur*, a "General, Systematically Organized Register of Musical Works Appearing in Germany and Neighboring Lands." These volumes appeared annually in Hofmeister's own Leipzig publishing house. Just looking at the number of publications Hofmeister recorded tells part of the story already. In 1880, the "Yearly Register" noted 322 newly published or reprinted scores for four hands (four hands at one piano); in 1890, the number is 287; in 1900, 163; in 1913, still 134; in 1925, only 27; finally, in 1960, the figure stands at 26. The number of works for four hands sinks rapidly after the First World War, and the number of works for two pianists at two pianos climbs—though not by much. However, these figures suggest already *how* the four-hand era ended. Works for two pianos are no longer parlor music; they are clearly conceived for a concert hall (cf. chapter 8).

Such a sampling is, admittedly, rather unscientific. Hofmeister's meager notes do not distinguish between new publications and reprints. Moreover, our count does not differentiate between, for example, an entry for a small waltz for four hands and an entry for Bruckner's collected symphonies. It also seems that original compositions are relatively overrepresented—especially when one compares Hofmeister to advertisements of new publications in music periodicals. Nevertheless, the sheer mass of publications (and especially arrangements) is striking. In some annual registers, the same operas by Lortzing, Wagner, and Meyerbeer, or the same symphonies by Haydn and Mozart, appear in multiple adaptations. Within a single year, different publishers thus either published or republished four-hand arrangements of the same piece of music! The same edition of the *Handbuch* lists no fewer than seven competing versions of Mozart's symphonies—by André, Bagge, Brissler, Conradi, Gleichauf, Markull, Mockwitz, and Czerny.[11]

---

[9] Cited in Loos, *Klavierübertragung von Werken für und mit Orchester*, 24.
[10] See Richard Wagner, *Sämtliche Werke—Band 200, IIa* (Mainz: Schott, 1874). In his memoir *My Life*, Wagner does mention a few original works for four hands that he wrote as a student around 1830.
[11] Friedrich Hofmeister, ed., *Handbuch der Musikalischen Literatur* (Leipzig: Hofmeister, 1860), 5: 95.

In addition to strict adaptations and original compositions, one finds in the pages of Hofmeister's almanac many potpourris and variations on famous melodies. Between 1852 and 1859, the following potpourris of famous opera melodies were credited to one "G. W. Marks," who worked for the Hamburg publishing house Cranz: Meyerbeer's *Robert le Diable, Les Huguenots, Il Corciato*, and *Le Prophète*; Donizetti's *La Fille du Régiment, Lucia di Lammermoor*, and *Maria di Rohan*; Mozart's *Don Giovanni, The Magic Flute,* and *Clemenza di Tito*; Rossini's *Siège de Corinthe* and *Otello*; Verdi's *Rigoletto, La Traviata,* and *Luisa Miller*; Beethoven's *Fidelio*; Wagner's *Tannhäuser*; and finally, the interlude from Mendelssohn's *Midsummer Night's Dream*.[12] Marks's exceptional productivity may be credited to the fact that he was probably not a real person. Rather, "Marks" was an identity that a number of nameless hirelings—among them, in all likelihood, a young Johannes Brahms—assumed when writing arrangements and potpourris for Cranz.[13] The pseudonymous hack's career extended for the better part of the first half of the century: Brahms used the pseudonym for his potboilers, but "Marks" had already been active when the composer was still an infant. Consumers seeking potpourris of *Tannhäuser, Rigoletto, La Traviata, Fidelio,* and *Lohengrin* did not need to rely on the various "Marks." They had many options: Beyer, Cramer, Diabelli, Krug, Östen, Horr, and Onslow all adapted the same operas in the same seven years!

The lists of recent publications compiled by the Leipzig *Allgemeine musikalische Zeitung*—which the journal ran four times a year, with brief annotations—show that this volume of output was not new to the second half of the century. These lists also make clear that original compositions constitute a small subset of new works for four hands. The editors remarked again and again on the fact that the greatest part of works sent to them consisted of arrangements, potpourris, and adaptations. They kept meticulous score, both in tabulating the number of compositions that were published and in keeping count of how many of these works were arrangements—a number they present with palpable chagrin. In the second half of 1840, the journal registered "58 compositions, mostly arrangements."[14] From "1 April until *Johannisfest* [24 June],"[15] there are "51 publications—that is, 14 more than at last count." "From *Johannisfest* until *Michaelisfest* [29 September],"[16] the sum stands at "forty—that is, eleven less than in the previous count." Here, one finds the same commentary: "as usual, mainly arrangements."[17]

---

[12] Hofmeister, *Handbuch der Musikalischen Literatur*, 5: 94.

[13] Kurt Hofmann, "Brahms the Hamburg Musician 1833-1862," in *The Cambridge Companion to Brahms*, ed. Michael Musgrave (Cambridge: Cambridge University Press, 1999), 3–30, here p. 18. For an opposing view on the identification of "Marks" and Brahms, see Karl Geiringer, *Brahms* London: Allen & Unwin, 1947), 41.

[14] *AmZ* (January 20, 1841): 51.

[15] *AmZ* (March 31, 1841): 267.

[16] *AmZ* (July 14, 1841): 540.

[17] *AmZ* (October 6, 1841): 813

The primary reason for the boom in music for four hands lay in their use and collection value. Often, classical symphonic works existed in a dozen competing four-hand versions. Music publishers employed in-house transcribers. (This, as mentioned, is how Brahms began his career.[18]) Thomas Christensen lists the following examples: Theodor Kirchner and Hugo Ulrich (Peters), August Horn (André), Robert Keller (Simrock), Otto Singer (Universal).[19] The publishing house Breitkopf & Härtel in Leipzig regularly had new adaptations performed to see whether they suited the "spirit" of the composer or the tastes of the public. If the adaptation strayed too far from the original, or if it was deemed too daunting for the lay public, the manuscript was sent back—usually without consideration for the transcription's own aesthetic quality. (Chapter 4 analyzes one such example.)

The arrangers seem to have been quite adept at striking a balance between the spirit of the original and the new piece's playability—often, only a few months elapsed between the composition of an opera or a symphony and its adaptation for piano four-hands. Franz Schubert himself, well known for original compositions for four hands, also had a go at variations on popular pieces. Just how fast adaptation and distribution occurred can be seen in the case of his variations on a theme from Hérold's *Marie* (op. 82, no. 1, D. 908). Hérold's opera had its Viennese premiere on December 18, 1826; by February the following year, Schubert had already completed his arrangement. The variations were printed in 1827, and the first reviews (for example, that of G. W. Fink in the Leipzig *Allgemeine musikalische Zeitung*) appeared at the beginning of 1828.[20] But the classics in particular—for example, the symphonies of Haydn and Mozart—were adapted time and again. The *Allgemeine musikalische Zeitung* commented with some concern that "without interruption, a hundred professional—and unprofessional—hands were busy bringing these works to the sonically impoverished, but harmonically rich instrument of everyday life."[21] Carl Czerny, who is mostly remembered today for his etudes (cf. chapter 6) was a veritable one-man factory—among other works, he adapted all of Mozart's and Beethoven's two-hand piano sonatas for four hands.

It is remarkable how industrial this all sounds—and contemporary observers did not hesitate to remark on it. With evident disapproval, the *Allgemeine musikalische Zeitung* spoke of transcriptions of this type as "factory work."[22] However, in the nineteenth century—well before the invention of the radio and phonograph—there

---

[18] Robert Kamaiko, *The Four-Hand Arrangements of Brahms and Their Role in the Nineteenth Century*. Dissertation, Northwestern University, 1975, 15.

[19] Thomas Christensen, "Four-Hand Transcription and Geographies of Nineteenth-Century Musical Reception," *Journal of the American Musicological Society* 51, no. 2 (1999): 267.

[20] Dallas A. Weekley and Nancy Arganbright, *Schubert's Music for Piano Four-Hands* (London: Kahn & Averill, 1990), 67.

[21] *AmZ* (November 14, 1832): 753.

[22] *AmZ* (November 14, 1832): 753.

were far fewer opportunities to experience live music, and one did not acquire knowledge of classical music by listening to it so much as by playing it. A musical education almost necessarily proceeded by way of arrangements for piano.[23] How else could a moderately well-to-do music lover in a provincial European town come to know Haydn's *Seven Last Words*, Mendelssohn's symphonies, or Wagner's operas? Other than travel, four-hand transcriptions were his or her only option. Four-hand piano playing, as Hanslick puts it, was an indispensable means of acquiring, "in one's own parlor, the best possible knowledge of orchestral music."[24]

Publishers were mindful of that indispensable function of their product. In some cases their scores explicitly assembled entire programs, combining different works in one volume the way a symphony hall might on a playbill; the four-hand transcription was the only way to attend a concert in a faraway metropolis. When the Universal-Edition published four-hand versions of Bruckner's unfinished Symphony no. 9 (arranged by Bruckner's pupil Ferdinand Löwe, and Joseph Schalk, who was instrumental in making Bruckner a household name), the editors combined it with a transcription (by Josef Venantius von Wöss) of the *Te Deum*. As the editors make clear, this is only secondarily owed to the fact that the ailing Bruckner may have considered joining the *Te Deum* to the Ninth as a choral fourth movement; primarily it is owed to the fact that these two works received their posthumous premieres together, and the Universal-Edition attempts to replicate this particular concert.

It is altogether probable that many nineteenth-century aficionados knew the majority of the classical-music canon only in piano versions; that when they heard a piece of music for the first time, they were gathered around a piano and not in a concert hall. Arthur Schnitzler's short story "Frau Bertha Garlan" features a heroine who is a former piano virtuoso now living "in a small city, where occasional amateur concerts were the highest form of artistic enjoyments ever offered." Schnitzler describes her disillusionment with her provincial town in terms of transcription: Bertha Garlan moves from evenings at the symphony or the opera to evenings playing four-hand piano. "The first year she was here, she participated in such an evening at the 'Red Apple' inn—that is, she and another young woman from town played Schubert's two marches together."[25]

Another document from the same time—also from the Austro-Hungarian Empire—offers a much more positive view than the story of Schnitzler's heroine, for whom four-hand playing seems to be identical with the limitations of the provinces. Nicholas Goldschmidt, who became famous in Canada as a music teacher, opera director, and conductor, was born in Moravia. In a conversation with his

---

[23] On "life before recordings," see Robert Philip, *Performing Music in the Age of Recording* (New Haven, CT: Yale University Press, 2004), 4–25.

[24] Hanslick, *Geschichte des Concertwesens in Wien*, 405.

[25] Arthur Schnitzler, *Gesammelte Werke—Die erzählenden Schriften* (Frankfurt am Main: Insel, 1961), 1:399–400.

biographer, he recounts the following episode from the first decades of the twentieth century. Goldschmidt grew up in the small town of Tavíkovice, and his parents, who were interested in music, had to rely on four-hand piano playing to share the classical canon with their sons:

> The nearby city of Brno boasted a notable lending library, a private business, containing a large section devoted to the world's great musical literature all transcribed for piano four hands. Symphonies, opera, chamber music, they were all available. Every month or so the boys ordered a new selection from the catalogue, often not sure of what to expect when it arrived. Schubert's *Trout Quintet*, a Bruckner symphony, whatever was on the list that looked appealing or was recommended by their teacher, they tried them all.... The boys went eagerly to the local post office to pick up the parcels of music, at least one of which was especially impressive. "I remember one that was so huge we could hardly lift it; they had sent us the four-hand version of Wagner's *Götterdämmerung*. You can imagine how long it took us to play it!"[26]

Goldschmidt's reminiscences point to how commodified the trade in four-hand arrangements was in the nineteenth century, but they also show just how strange a commodity those arrangements really were. Not only do these boys get much more than they bargained for in ordering scores by the sound of their titles; we can also see the sensual promise inherent in the sorts of lists compiled by the likes of Hofmeister, the *Allgemeine musikalische Zeitung*, and the Brno lending library: the children order fetishes, knowing only their names; the objects of desire arrive at the post office, where they wait to be played. Even if it seems foreign to us today, we all know the magic that catalogs exercise on children's imaginations. One can easily conceive how the phrase "Twilight of the Gods" could excite the fantasy of a boy, how he might feverishly seek to apprehend its mystery—that is, the musical-sensory reality that lies hidden behind it—and how a massive tome, as big as a telephone book, materialized to both satisfy and frustrate that fantasy.

Despite the shock it involved, the Goldschmidt brothers seem to have ended up playing *Götterdämmerung*. For years to come, they probably associated the opera with the massive package they had to drag home from the post office, not with performances they may have subsequently attended. In an interview, the Dutch composer Marius Flothuis (1914–2001) described this kind of relationship to the musical work:

---

[26] Gwenlyn Setterfield, *Niki Goldschmidt: A Life in Canadian Music* (Toronto: University of Toronto Press, 2003), 13.

One day, my brother brought Gustav Mahler's First Symphony home, in the version for piano four hands. Of course, the piece's opening sequence cannot be realized on the piano. Still, it gave us the opportunity to get to know the work [and others]. And I must say: when I came to a concert house for the first time and heard Haydn and Mozart, I heard things that I had known for a long time. Only the instrumentation was unknown to me.[27]

The philosopher Frithjof Rodi observes that he "got to know most symphonies by Mozart, Beethoven, and Schubert through piano abridgements, which [his] father, together with one of [his] sisters, played, for the most part, in arrangements for four hands." In the same way, he was acquainted with the "preludes to Wagner's operas, concerti grossi by Händel, and parts of the *Matthäus-Passion*."[28]

Naturally, this mode of consumption also changed the strategies of those who wrote music and made a living from its sale. The emergence of a reading public for scores entailed corresponding changes in the relationship between composers and publication. As the eighteenth century drew to a close, the court composer who wrote for a living, but did not need to publish what he wrote, increasingly became a thing of the past. Now, composers had to secure a regular income as teachers, conductors, or freelancers, composing or arranging for a public they never confronted directly.[29] At the same time, as chapter 1 has shown, the pianoforte began its victory march across Europe, and publishing houses began to make their money selling transcriptions as well as original works, giving rise to a new category of work: pieces that became part of the canon as printed matter, not as concert pieces. For example, Dvorak's *Slavonic Dances* were first bestsellers in print. They became classics because people played them for themselves; only later did they hear them in their concert versions. Max Reger (who adapted several of Richard Wagner's operas for four hands) wrote to his editor in 1896 and advised him that it was "absolutely, urgently necessary" that "the suite [in E minor, op. 16] appear for four hands" for reasons of what we would today call publicity:

> There are so many people who play piano four hands, and they have a burning hunger for new works; the suite, in four-hand adaptation, is perfectly suited to make my works more accessible to them. I remind you only of [Joseph Gabriel] Rheinberger's organ sonatas—they came out [in the

---

[27] Hans Ester and Etty Mulder in conversation with Marius Flothuis, in Hans Ester and Etty Mulder (eds.), *Fliessende Übergänge: Historische Studien zu Musik und Literatur* (Amsterdam: Rodopi, 1997), 51.

[28] Frihtjof Rodi, *Das Haus auf dem Hügel* (Würzburg: Königshausen & Neumann, 2006), 81.

[29] Douglas Townsend, Program notes for the Musical Heritage Society recording MHS 3911/12/13.

original and] for four hands at the same time and helped his name become known.[30]

Piano transcriptions made the repertory of concert halls available for bourgeois collecting. Veritable libraries of beautifully designed volumes could be obtained—for example, the symphonies of Mendelssohn-Bartholdy that were printed by Breitkopf & Härtel in Leipzig.[31] Just as today some music aficionados show off CD collections (or, more impressively, record collections), these volumes made it possible to possess the canon of classical music in physical form. Frithjof Rodi remarks that his "father's collection of sheet music"—"which was scattered to the wind years ago"—might be used to "measure the spectrum" of what "a musically trained layman knew of the musical canon around 1920."[32] Transcription determined what one could have and what one had to have. Piano arrangements offered a means to familiarize oneself with the musical canon; at the same time, what was adapted and what wasn't determined what belonged in the canon at all. As Thomas Christensen has observed, adaptation for piano was "a principal means...by which a coalescing canon of musical 'masterworks' was constituted and experienced."[33]

Of course, not all the *Auszüge* that were distributed by the big publishing houses were made for piano, and when they were, they were not necessarily for four hands. Adaptations of great orchestral works were made for string quartet, for solo piano, and for piano and accompanying instrument. At the same time, arrangements for four hands clearly had a special status: they could claim to capture more of the original—and claim to make this surplus much easier to play. We have already quoted Marx's observation: "Four-handedness has the self-evident advantage of making easier to execute—or, indeed, possible in the first place—many things that two-handedness is denied."[34] Eduard Hanslick describes how, within a generation, adaptation literature transformed into a piano monoculture:

---

[30] Letter dates July 21, 1896; Max Reger, *Der junge Reger: Briefe und Dokumente* (Wiesbaden: Breitkopf & Härtel, 2000), 54.

[31] There was no reason for an enthusiastic collector to stop with just Mendelssohn's symphonies. In December 1848, Breitkopf & Härtel began advertising the composer's collected works. (Mendelssohn had died the year before.) The ad noted that almost all of the works represented in the collected works were available as four-hand arrangements—among them the Quartet no. 2, op. 13; the Octet op. 20; *A Midsummer Night's Dream*; the Third Symphony; the Trio in C minor, in the composer's own arrangement; the *Hebrides Overture*; the concert overture *Meeresstille und glückliche Fahrt* in Baldenecker's transcription; the *Capriccio brilliante*, op. 22; the Trio in D minor, op. 49, transcribed by E. F. Richter; the Piano Concerto no. 1, op. 25; the *Melusine Overture*, op. 32; the organ sonatas; as well as the *Rondo brillante* in an arrangement by F. L. Schubert. The *Sechs Gesänge*, op. 19, as well as the Piano Concerto no. 2, op. 40, had been transcribed by that inveterate stakhanovite Carl Czerny.

[32] Rodi, *Das Haus auf dem Hügel*, 81.

[33] Christensen, "Four-Hand Piano Transcription and Geographies," 256.

[34] Marx, *Die Lehre von der musikalischen Komposition*, 573.

If one reads through the catalogs of music from Haydn's and Mozart's time until the middle of Beethoven's fame, one hardly encounters a single arrangement for four hands among the dozens of adaptations for three, four, and five different instruments. Beethoven's first symphonies were also arranged for string quartet long before anyone started to arrange them for four hands. These days, our concert halls offer no overture, no symphony, that one cannot taste in advance—or enjoy again, afterward—in four-hand arrangement.[35]

Without a doubt, the uncrowned king of the four-hand piano arrangement was Brahms. He transcribed his four symphonies for piano duo, both on one and on two keyboards. Moreover, Brahms arranged the majority of the rest of his *oeuvre*, though usually only for four hands on one keyboard: the overtures (*Akademische Festouvertüre*, *Tragische Ouvertüre*), the *Hungarian Dances*, the Haydn variations, the Serenade, op. 11, and all manner of chamber music (for example, the String Quartets nos. 1 and 3 and the String Sextets nos. 1 and 2). The composer even arranged his Piano Concerto no. 1 and the *German Requiem* for four hands.[36] From the beginning, Brahms offered his publishers a new score together with its adaptation for four hands. For example, in August 1860, he sent P. J. Simrock the Serenade no. 2, op. 16, and noted: "As payment for the work and the four-hand transcription, I request 16 *Friedrichsdor*."[37] In 1861, he offered another sextet (op. 18)—once again, "together with a good four-handed arrangement I have prepared."[38] The same game was repeated in 1865 with the Sextet no. 3, which Brahms delivered, together with the piano arrangement, in exchange for twenty *Friedrichsdor*.

Interestingly, when requesting the standard free copies to which he was entitled, Brahms frequently specified that he wanted the arrangements for four hands. It is entirely possible that the composer, like his buyers, had only these versions at his disposal. It strikes one as odd today, of course, but it does make sense that Brahms might not wish to lug about the parts for individual instruments.[39] Nevertheless, it does seem bizarre that, when Brahms undertook the adaptation of his piano quartets for four hands, he had to ask the publisher for the scores of his own pieces, "since I do not own them."[40] Brahms, in other words, collected his own works and acquired them in exactly the same way as his "readers" did. The same occurred with

---

[35] Hanslick, *Geschichte des Concertwesens in Wien*, 405.

[36] See, e.g., Walter Frisch, *Brahms: The Four Symphonies* (New Haven, CT: Yale University Press, 2003).

[37] Letter dated August 13, 1860 to P. J. Simrock; Johannes Brahms, *Briefwechsel* (Reprint Tutzing: Schmieder, 1974), 9:20.

[38] Letter dated July 1861; Brahms, *Briefwechsel*, 9:31.

[39] Letter dated December 28, 1865; Brahms, *Briefwechsel*, 9:44.

[40] Letter dated April 1870; Brahms, *Briefwechsel*, 9:93.

Meyerbeer, who noted in a letter that, "to my great sorrow," the score of an overture "is not in my possession."[41] The reason, once again, was commercial: "at the request of my publisher, I entrusted them to an artist who was to arrange the piece for two hands, for four hands, and for two pianos." Consumerism, then, democratized the relationship between composer and public; and authors acquired, collected, and owned their works in much the same form as did their audience.

That said, the absolute best sellers among Brahms's piano works for four hands were not transcriptions. Here, Brahms proceeded differently, orchestrating, after the fact, compositions that had originally been written for piano four hands. This was the case with the *Hungarian Dances*, which were longtime best-sellers for Breikopf & Härtel, as well as Simrock, in Leipzig. These dances remain among the most popular pieces for piano four-hands today and can probably found in many living rooms from which Brahms's transcriptions have otherwise long since disappeared. To capitalize on the success that the *Hungarian Dances* had enjoyed, the publisher Simrock commissioned the *Slavic Dances* from the young—and, at the time, unknown—Antonin Dvorak.[42] Max Reger, in the 1890s, tried his hand at the same game, writing *Waltz Caprices* (op. 9), *German Dances* (op. 10), and *Six Waltzes* (op. 22), which took Brahms and Dvorak as their model.

Increasingly—especially with Brahms and Dvorak, but also in the case of Reger's *German Dances*, Grieg's *Norwegian Dances*, and many others—collectors did not compile personal libraries so much as put together *national* libraries. In this way, the *furiant*, the polka, the *ländler*, and the *dumka* could reenter salons from which, as actual dances, they were otherwise largely excluded. The bourgeoisie, which also preferred its fairy tales and legends in the form of high literature, could thus admit folk culture into their parlors by way of musical bibliophily. Only in this way, it seems, was folk culture introduced to salons in which otherwise folk culture had little business. In the case of Dvorak, titles such as *From the Forests of Bohemia* and, of course, *Legends*, announced a project that was not unlike that of the Brothers Grimm: to mine a national essence that supposedly lay outside written language, but that the bourgeoisie felt it needed to keep in touch with. As J. Barrie Jones has shown, the main interest of musical nationalism in the nineteenth century involved genres that were based on language or at least had recourse to language as a program (*Lied*, opera, and symphonic poem); transcriptions, because of both the way they were marketed and the way they were consumed, helped constitute and define a national canon.[43]

---

[41] Letter dated April 10, 1852; Giacomo Meyerbeer, *Briefwechsel und Tagebücher, Band 6*, ed. Heinz Becker and Gudrun Becker (Berlin: de Gruyter, 2002), 291.

[42] Letter from Dvorák to Brahms dated March 23, 1878, in Antonin Dvorák, *Korrespondence a Dokumenty (1871-1884)*, ed. Milana Kuny (Praha: Editio Supraphon, 1987), 1:140.

[43] J. Barrie Jones, "Nationalism," in David Rowland (ed.), *The Cambridge Companion to the Piano* (Cambridge: Cambridge University Press, 1998), 176.

It is no coincidence, then, that Theodor Adorno refers to the bibliophily of literature for piano four-hands.[44] In the nineteenth century, the piano represented something like a transcendental *point de capiton* for what was recognized as music. Whether a choral work or chamber music, symphony or string quartet, *Volkslied* or opera, everything was arranged for piano (for two hands or four). As Richard Leppert puts it in his commentary on Adorno: "If it was music, the piano could (re)produce it."[45] Piano music not only had privileged access to all kinds of music, it also determined—like an encyclopedia—what counted as music and what did not, what one should know and what wasn't worth the effort. (In the canonization of music through the piano there also lies an element of "knowledge as power"—Foucault's *pouvoir/savoir*; a desire for control underlies this encyclopedism.)

Of course, robust sales and a perfect marketing machine don't tell us the true extent of the social phenomenon. After all, one aspect of bibliophily is that those who collect books do not necessarily read them, and consuming a transcription for four hands demands greater effort than, say, enjoying a lithograph that hangs on the wall. But where music for four hands is concerned, things seem to have been different: the scores and arrangements served not only the mania for collecting but also the mania for playing. Piano arrangements of symphonic works, in particular, seem to have been played with the same fervor with which young people of the 1960s listened to records and those of the 1980s made mix tapes.

At the same time, the comparison to bibliophily is not perfect for another reason: four-hand scores were, for all their ubiquity and utility in the arsenal of bourgeois education, looked down upon in ways that books and reproductions of visual art were not. The bourgeois could fill his house with luxury editions of Schopenhauer and with Beethoven scores, too. But when he bought transcriptions—to be played one after the other in succession—he invited mockery from his contemporaries. Even those parties who dutifully provided the market with adaptations for four hands were aware of their subaltern nature. Thus, Brahms himself, who displayed a downright mercantile mentality in serving this niche market, told publisher Fritz Simrock in a letter: "I would prefer it if my name were not directly featured on the title page as an arranger."[46] Later the same year, the composer put it more gruffly, requesting "that now—as soon as possible—you delete my name as the arranger for four hands from the 'Concerto' (op. 15) and *Requiem*. I cannot behold the *Requiem* without anger."[47]

Even today, most editions of Brahms credit him only as composer and not as arranger. Although he had mastered the art of the transcription for four hands and

---

[44] Adorno, "Vierhändig, Noch Einmal," 303.

[45] Richard Leppert, "Four Hands, Three Hearts—A Commentary," *Cultural Critique* 60 (Spring, 2005): 7.

[46] Letter to Fritz Simrock dated April 1870; Brahms, *Briefwechsel*, 9:95.

[47] Letter to Rieter dated October 15, 1870; Brahms, *Briefwechsel*, 14:190.

practiced it enthusiastically ("If only I understood composition as well as arrangement…," he lamented in the same letter), Brahms did not wish to be identified in this way. His disciples still observe his will piously: the transcriptions do not appear in all the registers of his works and bibliographies.[48] For Brahms himself it was the repetitive, subaltern, and unnecessary character of the four-hand transcription that made it less than a "real" work: in a letter he turns to a zoological metaphor and complains "how ridiculous it is to ruminate one's own works!"[49]

It does not seem that it was the tawdry repute of the marketplace that occasioned this reserve. Brahms had no problem delivering his arrangements along with his scores, yet something in the way the transcriptions were consumed embarrassed him. This defect was somehow associated with four-handedness. Whenever the mandarins of the music world mocked the inauthenticity of piano arrangements, they magnanimously gestured toward counterexamples—for example, Liszt's transcriptions of Wagner's and Beethoven's music, which were extremely difficult arrangements for two (virtuosic) hands. In this spirit, Brahms told Simrock that he "[would have] considered an arrangement for two hands interesting, if a particular virtuoso had done it."[50] But Brahms was of another mind where piano four-hands was concerned.

As we saw earlier, the *Allgemeine musikalische Zeitung*, which compiled new musical editions four times a year in the 1840s, also treated the pure quantity of new releases for four hands (and especially arrangements for four hands) as an embarrassment. Whereas the sheer number of new publications for two hands was thought to indicate the genre's importance (even though there were numerous adaptations and arrangements among them, too), the editor seems altogether dismayed by how much material had been produced for four hands: "Under this heading," he comments, "one rarely finds much with a name, because most of it is arranged."[51]

Elsewhere in the register (which otherwise maintains a neutral tone), the editor launches into a tirade against the boom of piano four-hands on the musical market: "For some time now, bravura pieces have been produced just so that compositions might also accessible to piano players who are not well practiced." This might be "advantageous for publishers at first," he continues, but this democratization of the musical canon has him concerned: "It is disadvantageous for virtuosos, because soon there will be hardly a use for pieces of which every beginner can claim, 'I play that, too!'"[52] Moreover, the tone of the (comparatively few) reviews of publications for four hands in the music press alternate between indifference and condescension: "There will be no lack of moderately accomplished dilettantes drawn to these

---

[48] Komaiko, *The Four-Hand Piano Arrangements of Brahms*. Edwin Evans's *Handbook to the Pianoforte Works of Johannes Brahms* also lists the four-hand arrangements (New York: Scribners, 1936).
[49] Letter to Rieter dated October 15, 1870; Brahms, *Briefwechsel*, 14:191.
[50] Letter to Fritz Simrock dated March 1880; Brahms, *Briefwechsel*, 10:143.
[51] *AmZ* (July 1841): 540.
[52] *AmZ* (July 1841): 540.

entertainments, which are melodically and rhythmically easy to grasp."[53] Many of the most prolific arrangers achieved success, above all, as writers of etudes (for example, Czerny, Bergmüller, and Bertini); for this reason, critics often treated arrangements for four hands as if they were higher-end forms of piano training with "as much content as is bearable for not-yet-particularly-practiced students" who need to be encouraged to "direct their attention to technical matters in an enjoyable way."[54] For them, the consumers of four-hand music were dupes, hoping for Wagner, but unknowingly doing mere finger exercises.

In a 1906 article on Schubert's piano music for four hands, Hermann Wetzel-Stettin took on the task of defending the composer's music for four hands. "Compared to the accomplishments of soloists, playing with four hands seems to many to be something of lesser value"; it is "more an item of curiosity than an artistic achievement to be fully honored."[55] Wetzel-Stettin attempts to vindicate Schubert's music for four hands as an "artistic achievement," but at the same time, he promotes compositions for four hands at the expense of arrangements for four hands. He begins with a question that—in view of the plague or flood that his contemporaries so often lament—is striking: "Who even plays piano four hands today?" Wetzel-Stettin explains what he means with a qualification: "Not rushing through the great orchestral works and a few pieces of chamber music, in a hurry and in haste with a friend."[56] Playing *Auszüge* is not the same as playing four hands in the vulgar sense; the writer banishes commonplace "rushing through" from the domain of true and proper works for four hands. The very fact that four-hand "rushing through" is so ubiquitous means for him that "real" four-hand playing is actually something very rare. Herein lies Schubert's significance: "What he intended for four hands is never an arrangement. He viscerally objected to putting the children of his spirit in an ornamental gown that did not suit them."[57] Music for four hands is redeemed as something artistically meritorious, then, only insofar as it is not an arrangement. In his rescue operation, Wetzel-Stettin once again demotes adaptations for four hands to mere fashion—they are modish, not artistic.

Such contempt is a bit surprising, given how widespread the phenomenon was. Therefore, we should seek to cast some light on the factors that served to make piano four-hands embarrassing when it left the sphere of pure (private) consumption and entered that of (public) social *performance*. Why, in a century when the "private vice" (as Mandeville had so famously put it) of consumption came to be largely recoded as "publick benefit,"[58] did this particular form of consuming suddenly seem

---

[53] *AmZ* (November 1841): 898.

[54] *AmZ* (November 1841): 898.

[55] Hermann Wetzel-Stettin, "Schuberts Werke für Klavier zu vier Händen," in *Die Musik* 6, no. 7 (1906): 38.

[56] Wetzel-Stettin, "Schuberts Werke für Klavier zu vier Händen," 37.

[57] Wetzel-Stettin, "Schuberts Werke für Klavier zu vier Händen," 39.

[58] Bernard Mandeville, *The Fable of the Bees: Or, Private Vices, Publick Benefits* (London: Tonson, 1724).

suspect? This is particularly surprising given the fact that four-hand playing, unlike so many other forms of cultural consumption, yielded real use-value for consumers and bystanders alike. Why was the obsessive piano player ridiculous in a way that model-train enthusiasts and stamp collectors were not? And why, once again, was a distinction made between piano four-hands and playing solo?

The previous chapter already provided one answer: piano four-hands, which occupies a position between the concert and the solo, was deeply tied to the bourgeois utopia that goes by the name of private sphere. For Theodor Adorno, four-hand piano playing was part of the *intérieur* as much as the etchings that might hang over the commode, or indeed, the upright. One of the most famous such etchings itself came to embark on a long odyssey across different media, an odyssey that sheds light on the strange position piano transcription—and four-hand transcription in particular—occupied within the culture of nineteenth-century domesticity.

The picture in question is *The Isle of the Dead* by Arnold Böcklin (1827–1901). Böcklin painted the five different versions of *The Isle of the Dead* between 1880 and 1886. It depicts a small rocky island with dark cypress trees playing off against a bone-white cliff, and an tiny rowboat ferrying a coffin, an oarsman, and a mysterious figure clad in white onto the island. The motif became a runaway success as an etching, and soon became a fixture in the domestic *intérieur* throughout Central and Western Europe. Reproductions of it hung in Freud's study, Hitler's summer residence at Berchtesgaden, and, or so it seemed, every bourgeois parlor in between.

Given its remarkable career in the domestic sphere, it should not surprise that Böcklin's painting was quickly turned into *Hausmusik*—the Vienna composer Karl Weigl (1882–1949) composed a musical ekphrasis for the piano. But the painting's most enduring musical legacy took place outside of the home, in the concert hall—Heinrich Schulz-Beuthen, Max Reger, and most famously, Sergei Rachmaninov all wrote tone poems inspired by Böcklin's painting. When the Berlin composer Otto Taubmann (1859–1929) arranged Rachmaninov's lush tone poem (op. 29) for piano four-hands, he in some sense completed Böcklin's long voyage from medium to medium: Böcklin's famous painting had given rise to Sergei Rachmaninov's tone poem, a musical ekphrasis of visual art. But that image itself had become popular only when Max Klinger's etching made the motif commercially available. Taubmann's transcription thus constituted simply one more translation into yet another form.

Each of these successive translations of *The Isle of the Dead* had reshaped the original motif, especially with regard to its relationship to the public and the private. Böcklin's paintings had all been commissioned by private collectors—Marie Berna, who bought the second version of the painting, had asked Böcklin for "an image to dream by." Thanks to Klinger's print, this emphatically private image quickly became an item of mass circulation and mass response; it, and other Böcklin prints, appear in novels, stage directions for plays, and even opera libretti around the turn of the century. The image had become so ubiquitous that it emerged as a kind of shorthand for bourgeois domesticity. Rachmaninov had retrofitted this emphatically domestic painting for the concert hall, but Taubmann's transcription returns it to its origin, the bourgeois interior.

In a strange turn, however, the painting's zigzag trajectory across media is inscribed in Taubmann's arrangement. More starkly than necessary, Taubmann juxtaposes an objective and regulating element dominated by chords with a melodic and subjective element, giving one entirely to the secondo-player, the other entirely to the primo. The interplay between the two players thus seems to mirror *The Isle of the Dead*'s position between the public and the private. Taubmann has the secondo open with low chords; the primo first chimes in with the simple three-note figure four bars in. Even then, the primo has only one note to play at a time; the primo, the subjective side of the four-hand arrangement, very hesitatingly and very provisionally claws its way into the piece, only to slowly disappear again by the end of it.

It seems Taubmann is not just concerned with reproducing the textures of Rachmaninov's tone poem; he also provides something of a reading of Böcklin's painting: the painting derives its power from the tension between the towering stillness of the rocks and cypress trees (which loomed larger with each successive version of the painting) and the tiny rowboat with the white figure, the only dynamic element in an otherwise almost oppressively still canvas (especially in the third version, immortalized by Klinger, in which the seawater is completely placid). Taubmann reflects this preponderance of the objective and static by having the secondo dominate the primo, especially early in the score. The primo has to establish itself over and against the secondo, and it is ultimately unsuccessful in that endeavor. Individual and cosmos, private and public come into conflict in Taubmann's arrangement, which manages to comment both on the *The Isle of the Dead* itself and on the fact that in the nineteenth century no one came to the painting independent of its checkered intermedial history.

If the intermedial fate of *The Isle of the Dead* reflects some of the form's own anxiety about its place in the domestic sphere, it also points to another aspect of the institution of four-hand piano playing: it wasn't as safely domestic as other nineteenth-century pastimes; the possibility of publicity and of the public forum clung to it as either bad conscience or latent threat. The piano as "sonic hearth," on the one hand, and as a "universal instrument,"[59] on the other, also forms the point where inside and outside change place. Performance in private, as Jürgen Habermas has shown, always presupposes a minimal amount of public, too—that is, somebody for whom one must *represent* it, someone to whom it is shown. This somebody comes from outside the family; either he is to be brought inside or the inside is to be brought out to him. This fact makes consumption deeply ambiguous: it mediates

---

[59] Adolf Bernhard Marx, *Die Musik des neunzehnten Jahrhunderts und ihre Pflege* (Leipzig: Breitkopf & Härtel, 1955), 273.

interpersonal relationships both within the family and on the larger level of society. Consumption, that is, is a point that leads from one sphere to another, in which public problems can become attached to the private realm: sickness, decadence, pettiness, philistinism, sexual nonconformity.

In this way, the perspective of the outsider resembles the attitude that one found (and today, in many ways, still finds) in discourses about sickness, hygiene, or drug use. The observer is obliged to provide a diagnosis that judges players from a position of power. Instead of personal or shared enthusiasm, the spirit of *impassiblité* predominates. In general terms, what makes the consumers of music for four hands (and normally, this means the consumers of *arrangements* for four hands) so suspicious is the fact that they are fetishists—in both senses the two figures who invented the discourse of fetishism in the nineteenth century gave the term. On the one hand, adaptations reproduce the "fetish character of the commodity" that Karl Marx had first made an object of critique in *Das Kapital*; on the other, as acts of substitution (or, as the music journal *Cäcilie* put it, "surrogates"[60]) for what always escapes the player, worries about four-hand music in many ways anticipate Freud's descriptions of fetishism.

Though they didn't use that word, critics of the four-hand phenomenon thought that it turned consumers into fetishists. Indeed, and as we will see, Marxian and Freudian conceptions of the fetish seem causally linked on this point: *because* the arrangement for four hands lacks something essential, it must be consumed compulsively and in repetition. Commentary in the Leipzig *Allgemeine musikalische Zeitung* confirms that condemnations of scores for four hands resemble typical discourses about addiction (or the addictive consumption of novels, which was frequently imputed to women[61]) in common circulation in the nineteenth century:

> Playing four hands has achieved such immense popularity among amateurs that (despite the numerous, more-or-less useful arrangements of all significant music, old and new, for instrument and voice) eager players, who are used to process a half-dozen symphonies, quartets, and so on in a single afternoon or evening, can hardly find enough new material.[62]

Hanslick, too, compares playing four-hands to addiction—not to drugs, but to gambling: "we pick up the notes like a deck of cards."[63] It doesn't matter what we play, he seems to mean; the main thing is to get more stuff—and anything in the package of scores will do. That the *Allgemeine musikalische Zeitung* was hardly

---

[60] "Über Klavierauszüge überhaupt und insbesondere," *Cäcilia* 3 (1825): 25.

[61] See Pamela K. Gilbert, *Disease, Desire, and the Body in Victorian Women's Popular Novels* (Cambridge: Cambridge University Press, 1997), 65f.

[62] Cited in Christensen, "Four-Hand Piano Transcription and Geographies," 258.

[63] Hanslick, *Geschichte des Concertwesens in Wien*, 405.

exaggerating the speed with which bourgeois families flew through musical literature can be seen by looking into Arthur Schnitzler's diary. Schnitzler, who preferred to play four hands "with mama," provides a very detailed inventory of their shared repertory. On March 3, 1905, he noted that he "played Mahler's Second with Mama." (Mahler, incidentally, he qualifies as "the greatest living composer."[64]) On March 5, Beethoven's Quartet op. 130 was the featured item. January 7, [1906], it was Mahler's Fifth, and January 10, "a quartet by Glazunov." January 14 featured Schumann's Second Symphony. Even if the rate of consumption in the Schnitzler household seems to be less intense than the "half-dozen symphonies" suggested by the *Allgemeine musikalische Zeitung*, one should note that more than forty years elapsed between the article's publication and the diary entry. Also, of the works Schnitzler mentions, two (namely, Mahler's Second and Fifth) are a good ninety minutes long—a duration that equaled several symphonies and quartets of the mid-nineteenth century.

The *Allgemeine musikalische Zeitung* does not just view the sheer *mass* of arrangements for four hands with suspicion, but also the quality of works—after all, the operative terms in the passage quoted above are "usefulness" and "material." Not only does the eagerness of amateurs have something inauthentic about it; this inauthentic something penetrates deeper than reception or distribution, and instead has a correlate in the logic of the music itself. If contemporaries felt some embarrassment at the proliferation of four-hand music in particular, this was to some extent because four-hand transcription threw a spotlight on much broader developments in music history.

The journal entries quoted above involving Arthur and Mama Schnitzler suggests that transcriptions sometimes ran entirely counter to the logic of music and instrumentation, increasingly by necessity. Whereas a Glazunov quartet or Schumann symphony is readily suited to be arranged for four hands, the musical form runs up against its limits in a piece like Mahler's Second. (The composer himself registered disappointment at Max Singer's adaptation.[65]) One could even say that this is part of Mahler's project—to write music that resists easy commodification, the kind that can be removed from an orchestral context and symphonic space only with difficulty. Adorno already argued as much: the monumentality that is often ascribed to Mahler basically represents a struggle "against the bourgeois-private, conventional constriction of music,"[66] which piano arrangements epitomize.

All the same, the Second Symphony—a piece that, at several points, calls for *ppppp* and, in the third movement alone, offers passages *col legno* (the striking of

---

[64] Arthur Schnitzler, *Tagebuch, 1903–1908* (Vienna: Verlag der Österreichischen Akademie der Wissenschaften, 1991), 111.

[65] Henri-Louis de la Grange, *Gustav Mahler, Vol. 3: Vienna: Triumph and Disillusion (1904-1907)* (Oxford: Oxford University Press, 1995), 23.

[66] Theodor W. Adorno, "Wiener Gedenkrede," in *Gesammelte Schriften* 16:327.

strings with the bow), *glissandi*, and frequent *pizzicato*—was adapted for piano. Moreover, Mahler's symphonies employ instruments placed behind the stage or audience; arrangement for piano, then, amounts to a destruction of symphonic *space*. Even with more traditional orchestration, every piano arrangement runs the risk of falsifying the original to the point of unrecognizability. Thus, Adolf Bernhard Marx observes: "The sounds of certain other instruments—for example, those of the strings (or the prolonged notes of the wind section), are, in part, impossible to execute on the piano; other passages remain without effect—or have a different or lesser effect."[67]

The fact that this point, which applies after all to all transcriptions no matter for what instrument, was most frequently raised with regards to four-hand transcriptions similarly has its basis in the logic of the form. This is because four-hand transcription is different in intent, in function, and in logic from, say, an arrangement for a single piano player. The latter is much more a case of *interpretation*—the arranger extracts a melody, casting aside the majority of the accompanying figures and chords, and replaces them with those native to the piano. Piano four-hands, in contrast, is supposed to be more complete: the second pair of hands at the keyboard expresses the wish to capture orchestral or chamber music more fully and in its own native textures—that is, in greater detail; consequently, details that are not depicted are more conspicuous than when adaptation is made for only two hands. In the arrangement for four hands, it is more evident that the emphatic multidimensionality of Mahler's symphonic compositions, the extreme dynamics, and the manipulation of space and sound are missing. Whereas the adaptation for two hands can only be counted an approximate sketch, four-hand arrangement makes much more immodest claims, and when it falls short of those claims, the judgment of music theorists is far less forgiving.

Just how acutely aware arrangers were of this problem can be seen in transcriptions such as the one Josef Venantius von Wöss (1863–1943) made of Gustav Mahler's Symphony no. 3 for the Universal-Edition. Wöss, an old hand at transcribing, seems determined not to rob Mahler's symphony of its, well, symphonic textures. His arrangement demands extreme dynamism from the two players—notations such as *ppppp* and "barely audible" abound in the score; the pedaling is compulsive. But Wöss's demands on his readers do not end there: especially in the symphony's titanic first movement, he replicates Mahler's dynamic shifts between full orchestration and extremely sparse solo parts to the extent that, at some points, only a single note is played among all four hands. In general, Wöss is at pains not to rely on recognizably pianistic textures (dissolving rows into chords, for instance); rather, his reduction is uncompromisingly orchestral. It deliberately telegraphs that

---

[67] Adolf Bernhard Marx, "Klavierauszug," in *Encyclopädie der gesammten musikalischen Wissenschaften oder Universal-Lexikon der Tonkunst* (Stuttgart: Köhler, 1837), 136.

it is not fully at home on the keyboard. It is, in the terms Walter Benjamin invented for the "task of the translator," an othering translation—one that always reminds the listener that this piece was not written for this instrument, that when played in the parlor it is really a piece in exile.

A piece that we will discuss at greater length in the next chapter parodies four-hand music's ambition to pull the orchestra into the domestic sphere in much the same terms. Camille Saint-Saëns's *Carnaval des Animaux* presents a great menagerie of exotic animals and adds among them two *pianistes*. These unusual beasts perform a series of scales in unison, which are only momentarily interrupted by loud chords from the orchestra. Saint-Saëns's joke is clear: four-hand players want to be orchestral, but they are (as the *Allgemeine musikalische Zeitung* also seems to see it) basically exalted piano students. Saint-Saëns seems to single out true music for the home, but that music consists of mere finger exercises. And he grants this music its moment in the spotlight only to make fun of it.

His mockery relies on a strict division between domestic and symphonic music that also characterizes Mahler's Third and Wöss's adaptation of it. Saint-Saëns brings the embarrassingly schematic nature of *Hausmusik* into the concert hall, and he underscores the line of separation by transgressing it; Mahler's symphonic composition draws the same kind of division by systematically undermining its possibility for adaptation into any other form. Under such conditions, it is only fitting that Saint-Saëns mocks *two* pianists and not one. Saint-Saëns denounces the shameless presumption to recreate symphonies and symphonic space in the domestic sphere.

Hans Gál has observed that, at the turn of the century, the reigning symphonic style made the transfer of sound "onto the black-and-white of the keyboard"[68] more and more problematic. Adorno similarly notes that music after Brahms, seeking to "glorify tone color,"[69] increasingly shrank away from easy adaptability. For thinkers like Adorno, the fact that Schumann's music was far more easily adaptable than the recalcitrant sound of Mahler was a mark of progress in nineteenth-century music—something that nineteenth-century propagandists of aesthetic autonomy would have largely agreed with.

The irony is that from a historical standpoint, adaptation occurred more and more frequently in the late nineteenth century. The growing resistance to adaptability parallels an increasing tendency to adapt—as music resisted being used commercially, commercial use became more frequent and almost automatic. When arrangements for four hands began invading the bourgeois household, symphonic music increasingly sought to escape the confinement of practical application. Thus, whereas Schubert only adapted the ballet sequences and overtures of his operas, there are full-scale adaptations of entire Wagner operas; these works are much less

---

[68] Hans Gál, *Franz Schubert and the Essence of Melody* (London: Gollancz, 1974), 146.
[69] Adorno, "Vierhändig, Noch Einmal," 304.

suited to this purpose. The more poorly modern music was fit for transcription, the faster market forces processed it.

But if Saint-Saëns's *Carnaval des Animaux* ridicules its duo pianists for violating the border between private music and concert music, this is not the only reason they are presented as objects of derision. The duettists play scales without inflection or development. What they take for music is really protomusic; and what they take for music making is something less than that—sound production it may be, but proper music making, the piece seems to imply, is something different. Part of what marks these duettists as nonmusicians is the fact that they replace development with repetition, psychology with compulsion. When the critics of the *Allgemeine musikalische Zeitung* express their concern about the four-hand boom, they often remark on the oddly compulsive, excessive character of piano four-hands. The eager players, who make their way through "a half-dozen" pieces only to hungrily seek new material, seem to have little to do with the exalted and decorous figures of Mozart and Maria Anna at the piano that one sees in the painting by de la Croce. It may be that this uncanny repetition compulsion lies within all trends, but the intensity with which piecework, need, and addiction manifested themselves in the bourgeois salon does seem remarkable.

Theodor Adorno, in an English-language piece he wrote on the subject of the "radio voice" (which remained unpublished in his lifetime), describes the change that orchestral music underwent when it was heard (at the time, still in mono) in a radio transmission. Adorno compares the phenomenon to photography: transmitting music in this way is like taking a picture of it.[70] A telling image—for just as a photo must reduce phenomenal reality to a small, purely visual section of space, radio must abstract away all sonic elements that are too soft or too loud for transmission, to say nothing of the dimensions of performance that have nothing to do with sound. Something similar might be said of arrangements for four hands, for they propose to transfer groups of instruments onto a single instrument; there are sounds that cannot be simulated, even approximately, and there is also a nonsonic element, an aesthetic topography (in the sense of *aisthesis*—sensory perception not just of the beautiful, but also of what is given to the senses *tout court*): the spatial experience of the concert hall (or church) that must by definition disappear in adaptation.[71]

Where Adorno's comments reflect on the form that succeeded four-hand piano playing as the go-to mode of musical transmission, similar comparisons were made at the very beginnings of the four-hand boom, when early nineteenth-century critics likened arrangements for four hands to lithography, which preserves form but fails to capture color. The *Allgemeine musikalische Zeitung* observed that "an arrangement

---

[70] Theodor W. Adorno, *Current of Music (NS 3)* (Frankfurt: Suhrkamp, 2006), 520, 523.

[71] Cf. Adrian Daub, "Adorno's Schreker—Charting the Self-Dissolution of the Distant Sound," *Cambridge Opera Journal* 18 (2006), no. 3: 247–71.

for four hands stands in approximately the same relationship to the original score as an engraving to an original painting, with its living colors."[72] E. T. A. Hoffmann made an analogous point: "the pianoforte points to the great work like a sketch that evokes a great canvas; fantasy animates [the lines] with the colors of the original."[73] Although some critics intended the comparison in a positive way, it was normally made to point to a defect of the form. (Hoffmann himself noted that he was "not particularly in favor of arrangements."[74]) Democratization and education in art, the critics argued, come at the price of inauthenticity. The aura of the work goes missing when one subjects it to transcription of any kind—and particularly when it is subject to adaptation for four hands on the piano.

There was good reason why German critics were particularly leery of four-hand transcriptions' distorting or abstracting tendencies. Starting in the late eighteenth century (probably with Gotthold Ephraim Lessing's famed essay on the *Laoköon*), German philosophy had become convinced that different artistic contents demanded different forms, that each art had its own logic, and that transitioning from one form to the other was often a fraught proposition. Other thinkers, like Johann Gottfried Herder and G. W. F. Hegel understood the relationship between the arts as part of an organic and historical process—contents transitioned from, say, Greek statuary to renaissance painting with some sort of logic. Skipping steps in this transition by necessity produced bad art. That meant that nineteenth-century Germans were if anything less than willing to countenance the idea that an original piece and its four-hand transcription were somehow just two different pieces, although they shared melodies and harmonies. Organicist notions of the arts and their relationship predominated, and transcription was usually seen as a disruption of that relationship, rather than as a continuation of it.

Although it was by no means standard practice, there was nevertheless the tendency to indicate the roles played by instruments in the original score—for example, "first violin" or "trombone." Hugo Ulrich's arrangements of Beethoven's symphonies indicate the instruments above the notes (although only when those instruments are actually carrying melody). This is not always the case, but it raises an interesting question: What is the player supposed to do with this information? How can the player modulate his playing when "Vcello" or "Clar.Fag." is indicated? This practice seems to have stemmed from the fact that arrangements for four hands were the phonographs of the nineteenth century, and were addressed as much to players who enjoyed recreating the piece in their own four walls as they were to *readers* of scores who were interested in both the melodies and the timbre of the music. More generally, however, the significance of such notation—which is of no

[72] *AmZ* (November 14, 1832): 757.
[73] E. T. A. Hoffmann, *Sämtliche Werke in Sechs Bänden* (Frankfurt: Deutscher Klassiker Verlag, 2004), 1: 552.
[74] Hoffmann, *Sämtliche Werke in Sechs Bänden*, 1:551.

consequence for playing itself—is that it pays tribute to the spirit of the original composition. The supplementary character of the piano arrangement can be seen right away; the note "Vcello" documents nothing other than the shame inherent in arrangement, making a copy of the original.

This shame principally affects piano and adaptations for piano—the piano, after all, is both a "transcendental yardstick" and an "everyday instrument"[75] with an everyday sound; as Max Weber observed, one "automatically compares it to an orchestra and finds it wanting."[76] This, the nineteenth-century philistine found embarrassing—or was supposed to, at any rate. Thus, at a soirée at the Verdurin's house, Proust's narrator hears a motif that will not let him go. When he inquires about the piece, he is told it is the andante of the viola sonata by the (fictitious) composer Vinteuil; the young pianist is performing an arrangement. The boorish Mme. Verdurin offers the following remark: "You didn't know that the piano could achieve that. It's not even a piano playing, I swear! Every time, I am astounded, I think I'm hearing an orchestra. It's even more beautiful than an orchestra, more complete."[77] The greatest compliment that the philistine can pay the piano is that it doesn't sound like one.

Hugo Wolf employs a related *topos* in a review. His commentary does not refer to music that is set for four hands in order to facilitate play or to make money; he worries about orchestral pieces that require what he terms four-hand surrogates in order to be brought before an audience in the first place. In particular Wolf is concerned with Anton Bruckner's symphonies, which, owing to limited interest and their own massive scale, have to be debuted stripped of their "instrumental attire"[78] in four-hand performance, naked and out of place. In his review of a "Bruckner Evening" in December 1884, Wolf points out the "regrettable nature" of the situation. The way he laments the absence of Bruckner's orchestral sound, it sounds as though the "titanic" composer has been castrated.

On the whole, Wolf is extremely satisfied with the music and the interpretation of the pianists (none other than the arrangers Joseph Schalk and Ferdinand Löwe). Wolf seems disturbed by one thing: that Bruckner's symphonies only reached the public on piano. "Bruckner, this titan, must now make himself intelligible to the public on piano; truly a regrettable matter, but still better than not being heard at all."[79] How did this regrettable situation arise? "The tribunes" of the orchestra where

---

[75] *AmZ* (November 14, 1832): 753.

[76] Max Weber, *Die rationale und soziologischen Grundlagen der Musik* (Tübingen: J.C.B. Mohr, Paul Siebeck, 1972), 77.

[77] Marcel Proust, *Du Côté de chez Swann* (Paris: Editions de la Nouvelle Revue Française, 1929), 293.

[78] Max Kallbeck, "Feuilleton: Pastoral—Oder tragische Symphonie," *Neues Wiener Tageblatt*, January 7, 1907.

[79] Hugo Wolf, *Hugo Wolfs musikalische Kritiken*, ed. Richard Batka and Heinrich Werner (Leipzig: Breitkopf & Härtel, 1911), 126.

the piece was supposed to have its premiere "vetoed the decision of the conductor."[80] What stands in the way of Bruckner, blocks his path to the concert hall, and necessitates a premiere via four-hand piano comes from the ruse and resistance of an "orchestral body" (as Wolf puts it). Its head (conductor) is willing, but the flesh is weak. The metaphor is an extremely interesting one: the orchestral body is both the body that mutinously stands in the composer's way and the body that eludes his grasp because of this same insubordination. The arrangement for piano is disembodied, and poor Bruckner—to whom even Wolf, who is deeply sympathetic to the composer, ascribes a certain fecklessness—cannot lay hold of the orchestra itself.

Comparisons with lithography also highlight the fact that arrangements for domestic use made a certain form of bodily-sensory experience impossible by annulling and privatizing the public space of the symphony hall. Interestingly, none of the critics seems to have fully sounded out this aspect of the equation between adaptation and graphic reproduction: the concept of private vs. public never became the basis for their evaluation, even though it objectively underlies it. The problem, in other words, was not just the loss of color but rather the privatizing of a masterwork that is actually supposed to explode the frame of the purely domestic. Here, the comparison to lithography is perhaps inadequate. The *Auszug* is more like a photograph, which can be magnified or reduced at will.

If arrangements for four hands are also in a certain way photographic music, then this is so because what they cannot convey is always already inscribed within them as a lack. As Christian Metz once remarked, every photo, in showing a rectilinear visual section of reality, necessarily points to the awareness that something else is not there and could not be included. Metz calls this absence *hors-champs*.[81] The landscape beyond the picture frame is a metonymy for what photography must abstract out of existence if it is to constitute itself as a medium in the first place. Metz links this moment of cutting, in which reality is destroyed and consigned to oblivion—even though a trace of it remains in the surviving picture (or sound, in our case) as a kind of vaccinating germ—with the Freudian moment of castration, and equates the memory of what has been lost with the fetish.

The analogy to the score for piano four-hands is impossible to miss: here, too, one honors the imitation of an experience that can only ever be incompletely reproduced in its sym-phonic (literally, sounding together), communal, and phenomenal (that is, spatial) dimensions. In arrangements of orchestral, choral, or larger chamber works for piano, this character of lack is always already part of the form—it pushes away certain sonic and phenomenal values (voice, timbre, audience etc.), but at the same time it makes a display of what has been omitted. What is missing is always present in its missingness; the music, then, is also private in the sense of the

---

[80] Wolf, *Hugo Wolfs musikalische Kritiken*, 125.
[81] Christian Metz, "Photography and Fetish," *October* 34 (Autumn 1985): 81–90.

ancient etymology of *privatio*: deprivation.⁸² The fetish character of the score for four hands is not just indebted to the dictates of exchange, then; the abstraction that occurs is also always a lack *in the object itself*—that is, a fetish in the Freudian sense.

The *Allgemeine musikalische Zeitung* says as much in its condemnation of addictive piano playing with four hands: repetition compulsion is not based solely on the commodity nature of the score but also on the fact that, even when one holds it in one's hands, one never possesses the thing itself. The household that rushes through multiple symphonies in a single afternoon is in a hurry because the next object is always supposed to compensate for the lack of the object at hand. Yet this next score can only renew desire for another one, and so on. The *Allgemeine musikalische Zeitung* gestures toward the following: the phenomenon of piano four-hands is overdetermined; it can never be sufficient for the libido that is invested in it— the drives attached to the phenomenon of piano four-hands always overshoot, are always excessive, and are always disappointed.

But must we necessarily subscribe to nineteenth-century judgments? From the nostalgic perspective of the twenty-first century, there arises another possibility: perhaps it is the fetishism displayed by four-hand players that gets to the beating heart of the four-hand piano phenomenon, and not the misgivings and suspicions of the professional artists. Adorno, for example, points out that the symphonic repertory could be adapted for four hands only "all too well"—so well that "I cannot escape the feeling that it was only retrospectively elevated from the realm of the monochrome, tragically intimate duet to instrumental multiplicity."⁸³ In the nineteenth century, music for four hands was insistently associated with either a "foretaste" or a "savoring" that only occurred afterward. It came too early or too late, but was never the main course.⁸⁴ Behind Adorno's "all too well" there lies the suspicion that talk of adaptation for four hands as something inauthentic actually represses the possibility that piano arrangements could be "the real thing" or, perhaps, that "the real thing" never existed in the first place—that music and its enjoyment, whether at home or in the concert hall, only consists of before and after. When we consider that, in empirical terms, this was often the case—for example, a four-hand version might precede the orchestral version; alternately, a four-hand version could replace an orchestral score that was never performed or went missing—then the hasty talk of coming "too soon" or "too late" has something questionable about it.

Johannes Brahms's Piano Quintet in F minor (op. 34) was originally...well, what was it originally? Brahms wrote the piece as a string quintet, but since the music provided "stubborn, passive resistance,"⁸⁵ he arranged it as a sonata for four hands (admittedly, for two pianos); ultimately, it became a piano quintet. That

---

⁸² Hannah Arendt, *The Human Condition* (Chicago: University of Chicago Press, 1998).
⁸³ Adorno, "Vierhändig, Noch Einmal," 305.
⁸⁴ Hanslick, *Geschichte des Concertwesens in Wien*, 405.
⁸⁵ Max Kalbeck, *Johannes Brahms* (Berlin: Verlag der Brahms Gesellschaft, 1908), 2:52.

this back-and-forth between musical forms occurred over the "ether" of four-hand music should hardly be surprise us.[86] However, perhaps we should be surprised that we find ourselves talking about "ether"—for why should it be that the piece in its arrangement for four hands "only" has the character of a "medium," a vehicle for the "original" that then assumes its "proper" or "valid" form? This question stands behind Adorno's "all too well": what makes the version for four hands secondary? Is it possible to speak of a primary text—an original and copy? The fetishist is someone who commits the error of assuming of something mediated that it has been given without mediation. Where, then, are we to seek fetishism in piano four-hands? Does it lie with parties always hurrying to the next arrangement, or does it belong to those who think they must no longer do so because they have seats in the concert hall?

---

[86] Marie Agnes Dittrich, "Tradition und Onnovation im Klavierquintett in f-Moll op. 34," in Gernot Gruber (ed.), *Die Kammermusik von Johannes Brahms* (Laaber: Laaber, 2001), 175f.

3

"At Best an Intruder, at Worst a Voyeur"

Four-Hand Piano Playing and the Family Unit

> The fact that the St. Matthew's Passion is now available arranged for four-hand piano will no doubt be welcomed by some, who either can't manage the piece with just two hands, or don't know how to read the full score or the piano transcription, or who are such besotted [*enragiert*] four-hand players that the need to play everything in that form.
> —*Allgemeine musikalische Zeitung*, March 29, 1865

This passage opens a review of new four-hand arrangements in the *Allgemeine musikalische Zeitung* in 1865, that is, at a time when the tsunami of four-hand transcriptions had been washing over Europe for decades. Nevertheless, the reviewer finds it necessary to rehearse once more the reservations the musical cognoscenti expressed about the inundation. Four-hand transcriptions are for amateurs, for people who don't have the means or the talent to understand the full score—so far, so familiar. But what of the last type of four-hand player the reviewer describes? The "besotted four-hand player" who seems to have no practical reason for his or her obsession other than a "need to play everything in that form"? What drove that person to four-hand scores? The writer seems to throw up his hands; some people just can't be helped.

Throughout the nineteenth century, critics, authors, and even composers regarded four-hand piano playing as somehow lacking vis-à-vis more established genres, but that lack was not just a matter of four-hand music's being more commercialized and market-driven than other forms of music. Instead, it seemed to inhere in the *use* that the family unit made of these objects. There was something troubling about the flood of four-hand scores, but it was not their proliferation itself, or the way they bowdlerized the concert experience; nor was it just a matter of the obsessiveness with which their audience hungered for them and consumed them. What troubled musical professionals about these scores and their audience was the rite of four-hand playing itself, as opposed to habits of collection, ownership, and self-representation. The promise that drove Mother Schnitzler and her son Arthur to the piano every three days—what drove eager amateurs to play "half a dozen symphonies, quartets, and the like"[1] in the course of a single afternoon—involved the act of playing itself. For its practitioners, four-hand playing contained the fantasy of a joint enterprise: work without work or an end-product, underpinned both by a sensible division of labor and by a sensual promise of happiness.

All this feeling was emphatically private, yet somehow four-hand playing always attracted comments from outsiders. It may be true that Arthur Schnitzler and "Mama" practiced the art as a "conversation without words, harmony beyond language."[2] But in practice their wordlessness provoked an all the more vigorous discourse in the public sphere: when the arrangement for four hands poked beyond the threshold of the domestic sphere, it was mocked. The thoroughness with which piano four-hands was relegated to the world of domesticity (or pushed back into that world) provides the focus of this chapter. At the same time it will be clear that, also within the private sphere, the status of playing four-hands was extremely ambivalent. On the one hand, the piano played *à quatre mains* provided the bourgeois household with a place of assembly second to none; on the other hand, it is always suspicious to the members of the household. At least in literature, it stabilizes the family and threatens it, too.

Schnitzler's Invisible Duettists

Mother and Arthur Schnitzler were conspicuous four-hand players, and it is easy to suggest meanings behind their fervent devotion to the hobby. When it comes to Schnitzler the writer, four-hand playing is harder to spot, as are the meanings behind its relative invisibility. *Fräulein Else* is a text with no four-hand piano playing, but it's worth asking why and, somewhat more counterintuitively, how it isn't there. The story, presented as a stream of consciousness, unfolds over a single day at an Italian spa. Young Else receives a letter from her parents beseeching her to ask the wealthy art dealer Dorsday for a loan of thirty thousand guilders to save her father—an attorney bankrupted by his own shady business dealings—from prison. Dorsday agrees to provide the loan, but on one condition: he wants to see Else naked. The novella consists primarily of Else's inner monologue as she tries to decide whether she is ready to sacrifice her self-respect to her parents' self-serving

---

[1] Quoted in Thomas Christensen, "Four-Hand Piano Transcription and Geographies of Nineteenth-Century Musical Reception," *Journal of the American Musicological Society* 52, no. 2 (1999), S. 258.

[2] Ulrich Weinzierl, *Arthur Schnitzler: Leben, Träumen, Sterben* (Frankfurt am Main: S. Fischer, 1994), 31.

schemes. At the end, Else disrobes in the music salon of the hotel, in the presence of Dorsday and other guests; then, in her room, she commits suicide.

Fräulein Else has all the elements of the four-hand scene as laid out in the previous two chapters: the voyeuristic gaze Mr. Dorsday casts on an innocent girl, the objectification of the female body, the way that body eventually becomes complicit in its own "feminization," up to the fact that Else eventually submits to Mr. Dorsday's prurient designs in a music room.[3] The one element that is missing is four-hand piano playing itself. Provided we don't let a simple absence inconvenience us and postulate that if it is not there, it is because it is conspicuous in its absence, then where would we look for this conspicuous absence? If piano playing *à quatre mains* were to be featured in the text, where would it occur?

Would Mr. Dorsday demand to be allowed to play with Else? He does not desire physical contact; instead, he wants to observe. No, the absence of playing four-hands seems to be of a piece with the family's absence. In its absence, piano four-hands contours the family dynamics of the novella: Else's family catalyzes the catastrophe by asking for money, but no family member ever makes an appearance. Else is absolutely alone as she faces her decision ("How alone I am!" she cries out at several points[4]). Unlike the vast majority of texts considered until now, the family in *Fräulein Else* is present only in spectral form—as a telegram, as the voice of memory, or as an element of internal monologue. There is no family unit into which piano four-hands could provide entry, or about which it might provide information.

What hints we do get about the distant family suggest that it isn't the epitome of intimacy and interpersonal warmth that many other texts with four-hand scenes describe. Else seems devoted to her distant father, but she is aware that what she calls her degradation into a "strumpet," a "slut,"[5] is not just carelessly caused by her parents. She assumes that they were counting on Dorsday's perversity, and that the barter Dorsday proposes, or something like it, was their plan all along. It is not just the *absence* of the family unit that distinguishes *Fräulein Else* from the other texts involving piano four-hands—it is also the fact that in this novella the family is quite different. Far from a warming hearth of private happiness, the family unit instead emerges as something distant, cold, and exploitative. It's not the advances and threats of the aged libertine that have four-handed dimensions; rather, the menace involves the family unit that mendaciously hands over its own daughter to him. Better perhaps to keep a piano away from this kind of family.

Indeed, the conspicuous absence of piano four-hands is no coincidence: rather, its absence is a matter of holding back, of censorship. In fact, piano four-hands

---

[3] Susan C. Anderson, "The Power of the Gaze: Visual Metaphors in Schnitzler's Prose Works and Dramas," in Dagmar Lorenz (ed.), *A Companion to the Works of Arthur Schnitzler* (Rochester, NY: Camden House, 2003), 314.

[4] Arthur Schnitzler, *Fräulein Else* (Berlin and Vienna: Zsolnay, 1924), 31.

[5] Schnitzler, *Fräulein Else*, 65.

did occur in *Fräulein Else* in an earlier draft, except that Schnitzler did not include the relevant passage in the final version of the novella. In a typescript with drafts intended for the middle section, the father is characterized as follows by the heroine's internal monologue:

> Obviously, once again difficulties for Father. For how long had it been this way? She loved him greatly. Recently just managed to avoid prosecution; in the evening, they played together at the piano.⁶

Schnitzler incorporates almost all the elements of this fragment into the final text, only four-hand piano playing goes missing along the way. What conscious or unconscious motives might lie behind this act of censorship, especially given that piano four-hands was such a common activity for Schnitzler's own family? Astrid Lange-Kirchheim suggested that Else's playing with her father functions as a "cover fantasy" "for Schnitzler's relationship to his mother—which could also explain why Schnitzler omitted the motif of piano four hands from the final novella."⁷

Taking Schnitzler's omission as an occasion for psychoanalyzing the author himself is tempting, but ultimately not that instructive. However, one thing seems relevant to our reading of the text: in the middle of a narrative work that is principally concerned with nakedness, exposure, and making the private public, we encounter an act of censorship that—whether it is conscious or unconscious—seems to have a basis in the author's private life. What motivates this censorship is less interesting than its form: a marker of private life (four-hand playing) is omitted for reasons of privacy. It seems as though speaking, expressing, "publicizing," four-handedness is somehow a fraught question both in the plot of *Fräulein Else* and in the process of its composition.

What is more, Schnitzler's omission seems designed to keep certain questions about the family as such at bay. The absence of piano four-hands produces a secure distance between the family unit and the events in the novella. It is difficult to imagine a lost version of the text in which Else and her family are staying at the same hotel. A bourgeois family actively pimping out their daughter at a resort? Even for a scandal-happy writer like Schnitzler that would have been a tall order. Moreover, the reader runs less risk of having to decide whether Else's family is the exception or possibly the rule. Since neither mother nor father ever takes the stage, readers

---

⁶ Arthur Schnitzler, "Fräulein Else" (draft), Arthur Schnitzler Archive Freiburg i. B., box C, XL, folder 140, p. 3. The author is grateful to the estate of Arthur Schnitzler for permission to quote from the draft.

⁷ Astrid Lange-Kirchheim, "Die Hysterikerin und ihr Autor: Arthur Schnitzlers Novelle Fräulein Else im Kontext von Freuds Schriften zur Hysterie," in Thomas Anz and Christine Kanz (eds.), *Psychoanalyse in der modernen Literatur: Kooperation und Konkurrenz* (Würzburg: Königshausen & Neumann, 1999), 129n.

can assume with some relief that *Fräulein Else* depicts a broken family, not a normal one—let alone the family as such.

That would be undermined by an episode with piano four-hands; the symbolic power of the *topos* would be too great, to say nothing of the role it plays in the ideology of domesticity. If Else were to play four-handed with her father, then the separation between home and economy could not be preserved. That is the family secret that Schnitzler's strange act of censorship seems intended to guard: although it is supposedly a matter of emotions and divorced from economic concerns, the family unit (embodied by the four-hand partners Arthur and Mama, Else and Papa) turns out, in reality, to be steeped in matters of money and economy. The family sends the daughter out to make money through de facto prostitution because, in the universe of *Fräulein Else*, the safely self-contained family unit, beyond money and economy, simply does not exist. Whether—and how—this insight is to be located in Schnitzler's life and work, and how he felt about that insight need not concern us. It is enough that the familial praxis and the domestic ideology of four-hand playing are deeply allergic to any traces of money, work, and commerce.

Of Privacy and Privation

Leaving behind the world of the four-hand transcriptions that Arthur and Mama (and probably Else and Papa, too) played, and turning to a much stranger creature—namely four-hand playing in an orchestral context—we find a similar dynamic at work. Camille Saint-Saëns' *Carnaval des Animaux* parodies piano four-hands by acknowledging its value only as a form of private practice and denying it all public usefulness. Saint-Saëns' *Carnaval* is a musical commodity, and it is conscious of that fact. It has little of the carnival in the sense of Mikhail Bakhtin,[8] but instead smacks of circus and spectacle. Instead of embracing confusion and parody, it parades calculated vignettes through the ring. The proceedings have something museum-like: the *Carnaval*'s birds do not fly free but occupy a *volière*, a birdcage; the fishes swim in an aquarium; and one vignette even puts fossils on display. In the middle of this exhibition the listener encounters an even more unusual species: *les pianistes*. The vignette consists of nothing but two pianos performing a rudimentary series of scales, only occasionally interrupted by orchestral chords.

Is it a coincidence that Saint-Saëns makes fun of *two* pianists? In contrast to the *Hémiones* or the *Éléphant*, for example, the humor does not lie in the fact that a well-known melody is set to the wrong tempo or instrument—Offenbach's *can can* in slow motion or Berlioz's graceful *Dance of the Sylphs* adapted for scratchy contrabass. In the case of the pianists, it seems that the genre itself is unfitting—unfitting

---

[8] Mikhail Bakhtin, *Rabelais and his World* (Bloomington: Indiana University Press, 1984), 15.

for a concert hall, unsuitable for the stage. Saint-Saëns's score provides the following instructions: "The players have to imitate the playing of a beginner and its *gaucherie*." In this *gaucherie*, it seems, playing four-hand piano resembles playing a scale: both have the job of making stage performance possible, yet neither scales nor practicing at a grand piano belong in a concert hall. Saint-Saëns places an embarrassing private matter on stage: the stupid repetition that underlies virtuosity, shameful and unavowed (like naked Else in the music salon). The fact that it is two pianists playing seems to be *part* of the awkwardness. One only plays piano together in private; put onstage, the activity risks being embarrassing.

It's not that in the nineteenth century four hands were explicitly barred from performing together at concerts. In 1882, Saint-Saëns himself played publicly with none other than Franz Liszt in Zurich. As the *Musikalisches Centralblatt* reports, the two composers performed the latter's second *Mephisto* waltz (which was originally written for a single player) in an arrangement for four hands at the gathering of the Allgemeiner deutscher Musikverein.[9] However, this double performance by two virtuosos is not something we find in the *Carnaval*: here, it is students and players of mind-numbing finger exercises, people taught along the lines suggested by Carl Czerny, slaves of musical scales, who stand in as representatives for piano four-hands in general—indeed, people recognized a parody of Czerny in the *pianistes*; chapter 6 will suggest another possible model.[10]

Writers for the musical journals similarly tended to place arrangements for four hands alongside works written for practice. As they saw it, the canonic status of famous works for four hands was sugar that made the bitter medicine of finger exercises easier to swallow. Saint-Saëns's parody also makes this point: the two pianos rehearse what is supposed to be raw material, later to be covered with the glaze of melody, and thus to be made appetizing and suitable for the public. And of course it mocks the pianists by pointing out the labor that stands behind the artistry. Saint-Saëns shares this line of attack with sneering remarks in the *Allgemeine musikalische Zeitung* and elsewhere: simplified transcriptions are catnip for piano students with a slight megalomaniacal streak. And they are no longer art—they drag sweat and toil into the sphere of art, which is supposed to be free of both. Here, Saint-Saëns strikes at a neuralgic point: labor and four-hand playing are supposed to be related, but the former is supposed to lead in an organic way to the latter; what we see in the *pianistes* is the reverse: four-hand piano is just playing finger exercises while imagining yourself as a concert pianist.

Four-hand playing held a very particular promise in the nineteenth century, and it was based on the relationship between piano four-hands and labor. Four-hand playing was, in short, collaboration in the absence of need. On the one hand, four-hand

---

[9] *Musikalisches Centralblatt* 32 (August 10, 1882): 301.

[10] See, for instance, Brian Rees, *Camille Saint-Saëns—A Life* (London: Chatto & Windus, 1999), 261.

piano playing is one of those activities by means of which the bourgeoisie sought to banish from the home the labor upon which its wealth was based (to wit: the labor of others). Walter Benjamin, in *Berlin Childhood Around 1900*, mentions the glass mine he was allowed to play with in his aunt's house. He points out that this was something special at a time when "a child from a wealthy bourgeois household" could no longer "look at places of work and machines."[11] This time was, of course, also the era of piano four-hands. Like Benjamin's mine, four-hand piano playing is profoundly phantasmagoric: it represents processes of labor, and even communal processes of labor, all the while mystifying the actual labor required for its creation.

The four-hand score qua use object has the peculiarity that its mere acquisition does not in any way fulfill its promise. It is therefore quite different from buying a CD, for example. If the customer wanted to make good on the sensory promise offered by the ornate title pages from publishers like Simrock or Schott (with motifs that slowly transitioned from neoclassicism to art nouveau as the century wore on), he or she had to make an effort; or rather, an effort alongside one other person, a person one was close to. Four-hand music was, to use Roland Barthes's term, "muscular music" in which the body must "itself... transcribe what it reads." Music for four hands is also *musica practica* insofar as it is normally played by (sometimes very skilled) amateurs and hearing it "does not produce contentment in us, but rather the wish... to *make* music ourselves."[12]

This music and its sensuous quality are, as Adorno says, things one experiences "entirely in private." Music for four hands is a form of collaborative production and it unfolds its true essence only in the act of playing. That made it significant in an age when elsewhere in the economy labor and its products were ever more alienated, as was one person's effort from that of all the others. Four-hand playing, by contrast, involved a collaboration in which the whole being on which and toward which the collaborators worked is entirely and immediately sensible. The inanimate thing that one had bought requires a human being to manifest its true substance, or what is commonly called its "value." Playing arrangements for four hands made this value concretely tangible, even pleasurable. Its magic depended on a community determined by a division of labor a good deal more fulfilling and meaningful than the one people tended to encounter in nineteenth-century labor processes.

As the shared labor of a community that defines itself primarily through the absence of labor, there is an aching and unacknowledged contradiction at the heart of four-hand playing. A political desire is transferred back into the bourgeois private sphere: in truth, the fantasy of a better division of labor is talking about society at large, but four-hand players seek to realize it only in the private sphere and in the name of a particular familial community. Four-hand playing aestheticizes a political

---

[11] Walter Benjamin, *Gesammelte Schriften* (Frankfurt: Suhrkamp, 1980), IV.1:249.

[12] Roland Barthes, "Musica Practica," in *Image/Music/Text*, ed. Stephen Heath (New York: Hill and Wang, 1977).

idea, but at the same time it robs that idea of its political teeth. The strange labor of four-hand playing poses a challenge to the social division of labor; but since it is emphatically familial labor, the promise of happiness becomes private instead of public. Pain at wrong notes becomes mere neurosis; yearning for a better state of affairs transforms into incestuous interplay.

Playing four-hands is private, but nevertheless communal. The individual "was not allowed to modify the tempo and dynamics according to capricious inclinations, as he was accustomed to do with the lyrical pieces by Grieg. Rather he had to orient himself according to the text and the instructions of the work, if he did not…want to lose the connection with the partner."[13] As Adorno emphasizes, playing with four hands involves a force field of desires and prohibitions. Desire is bundled, and it is this bundling that ensures that, however they relate to each other, the two domestic players belong "to the family," as Adorno claims. Just like being in a family, this bundling can be momentarily joyous and complete, such that the two drives coincide; but then the dictates of the score intervene and the "drives" must be reined in. The mysterious unity of the partners can only occur through the division of labor.

This is readily visible in observing four-hand playing: the four hands reach for each other; they graze and caress in a space between the bodies that is almost invisible to the onlooker. The two players' eyes are locked on the same score, their wrists sometimes rest one on the other. The two pianists inhabit their own world together, seem to be tenderly united—politely but clearly separated from the outside. However, their unity is only momentary: as if struck by lightning, the hands rush apart again and play at opposite ends of the keyboard. The eroticism of playing four-hands lies in the back-and-forth between this moment of fulfillment and the moment of self-denial. At times, it seems as though even the players cannot be altogether sure which of them is producing which note; then, suddenly, each one is again responsible for his (or her) own proper sphere—almost ashamed at the fleeting indiscretion. As Edward T. Cone put it, "Such a performance is…a peculiarly intimate affair, and when it is undertaken in public, the auditor may feel at best an intruder, at worst a voyeur."[14]

What Is a "Four-Hander" For?

Four-hand piano playing both solicited erotic investments and restricted them. Michel Foucault warned us "other Victorians" ("nous autres, victoriens"[15]) against

---

[13] Theodor W. Adorno, "Four Hands, Once Again," *Cultural Critique* 60 (Spring 2005): 2.

[14] Edward Cone, *The Composer's Voice* (Berkeley and Los Angeles: University of California Press, 1974), 135.

[15] Michel Foucault, "We Other Victorians," in Paul Rabinow (ed.), *The Foucault Reader* (New York: Pantheon, 1984), 292ff.

seeing only repression behind the prudery of certain social arrangements rather than different means of productively channeling eroticism and sexuality. Indeed, as far as piano four-hands is concerned, the private sphere was always erotically charged, albeit often in a less than straightforward way. One reason for this erotic charge was simply "the near approach of the hands of the different persons,"[16] as the composer Charles Burney had remarked in the eighteenth century. Piano four-hands represented a safe space in which touching and nearness were permitted or even desired—something that was otherwise unusual at the time. "Playing four hands allowed, in the tête-à-tête of the hands—and, moreover, under the protection of art—proximity that was not customary in married couples, a welcome and unassailable pretext for more frequent meetings."[17] What is more, the instrument itself was figured as somehow feminine, as was music in general; making music on a single keyboard thus carried erotic connotations from the moment one sat down on the bench.

But, of course, those connotations weren't clear, uniform, or predictable. Instead, the positions that the inhabitants of the private sphere assumed vis-à-vis each other on the keyboard were overdetermined. On the keyboard the two players became, and the family witnessed, a couple, but only in rare cases a married one. Instead, it could assume any number of guises, suggest all manner of relationships, or oscillate unsettlingly between different kinds of relationships. Schnitzler's transubstantiation in *Fräulein Else*, the ease with which mother-son turned into father-daughter, points to that fact. And the alchemy didn't end here: "parent-child, teacher-student, pursued-pursuer"—all these relations could unfold at a keyboard at which four hands played.[18]

In one of his essays, the music critic Eduard Hanslick reports a question that strikes modern ears as highly unusual: "Who is your four-handed person?" Hanslick presents question in a way that lets one know that he himself considered it a little odd. It sounds strangely *indiscrete*: you almost want to tell him it is none of his business. There is something lewd and prying in the question, and the term "four-handed person" (*Vierhändiger*) presumes an intimacy and monogamous loyalty within the relationship that leaves it strangely suspended between friendship, love, marriage, and family.

> "Who is your four-handed person?" I was once asked by an impassioned amateur.... Not everyone can call a wife, a beloved, a bosom-friend his

---

[16] Quoted in "Piano Duet," *The New Grove Dictionary of Music and Musicians* (New York: Macmillan, 1980), 14:680.

[17] Gunilla-Friederike Budde, *Auf dem Weg ins Bürgerleben* (Göttingen: Vanderhoek & Ruprecht, 1994), 140.

[18] Philipp Brett, "Piano Four-Hands: Schubert and the Performance of Gay Male Desire," *19th Century Music* 21 (1997): 154.

own, but every mortal should have a "four-hander," as if this person were a dance partner for one's musical lifetime.[19]

The example of the British composer Sir Arnold Bax, whose duet partner left him in 1914, makes it clear that the monogamy between "four-handers" was not entirely unlike that expected of husbands and wives. "Do you know I have not played a piano duet since you left—because nobody will do after yourself for that form."[20] But, given such enraptured declarations of fidelity, is a "four-hander" more like a wife, a beloved, or a bosom friend? In Schnitzler's "Frau Bertha Garlan" (1901), the widow of the title is not entirely sure: the piano keyboard for her becomes a place at which roles constantly blend into one another. Her young nephew reminds her of her lover; the piano virtuoso she adored in her youth melts together with her departed husband, for whom she never felt much more than respect. Hanslick seems to think that a "four-hander" should move beyond these categories, whereas Schnitzler suggests that these categories not only cannot be banished from four-hand playing but that the activity instead makes each of these categories unstable, gives it shades of all the other possible constellations.

Observers can be if anything less sure which of these constellations they are beholding, a fact that for many spectators of piano four-hands seems to have been part of its charm. The Russian pianist Rosina Lhevinne performed exclusively with her husband Josef for almost forty years. She claims that concert organizers often suggested that the married couple employ different last names. "They thought it would stimulate interest if the public were to speculate who he is to her—and who she is to him."[21] This form of observation (which Tolstoy makes the subject of *The Kreutzer Sonata*) has certain voyeuristic aspects; at the same time, it also always represents an attempt to "discipline and punish"—it involves a gaze that forces the body into a semiotic corset, commands obedience, and seeks to ferret out possible infractions. In general, it is a matter of observing the body, classifying it, and diagnosing it. Whether—as the musicologist Philipp Brett has shown—Schubert and Josef von Gahy are figured as a homoerotic couple, or whether the reader of Schnitzler's diary is inclined to divine too close a relationship between the writer and "Mama," the partnership "comes under scrutiny from other members of the household in interesting ways."[22]

Such scrutiny occurs in paradigmatic form in the works of Gerhart Hauptmann. In his play *Friedensfest*, the father, succumbing to paranoia, believes that his wife is entertaining a "bad relationship" with his son's friend just because she is playing

---

[19] Eduard Hanslick, *Geschichte des Concertwesens in Wien* (Vienna: Braumüller, 1869), 405.

[20] Quoted in Lewis Forman, *Bax: A Composer and his Times* (Rochester, NY: Boydell, 2007), 132.

[21] Quoted in Hans Moldenhauer, *Duo Pianism* (Chicago: Chicago Musical College Press, 1950), 187.

[22] Brett, "Piano Four-Hands: Schubert," 154.

piano four-hands with him—although his children declare this "beyond the shadow of a possibility."[23] Of course, the diagnostic gaze need not be jealous or controlling; often, the diagnosis supposedly has the players' best interests at heart (especially when those players happen to be female). In *Maria Regina* (1860), a novel by Ida, Countess of Hahn-Hahn, a physician recommends that Count Windeck carefully observe his daughters Corona and Regina while playing four-hands, something he had not previously paid much mind to. Regina (who, like the author herself, has recently converted to Catholicism) is in the throes of a crisis of faith that neither her father nor her doctor knows how to interpret. And thus they decide to turn to four-hand playing as their diagnostic tool:

> He entered his daughters' room. Both sat at the grand piano and played together Beethoven's *Symphony in C-minor*. They wanted to interrupt their performance when he came in; but he told them to continue and sat down across from them to observe and compare. Corona's little face was glowing from eagerness and attention; as she played the first movement, her bright-pink cheeks, her slightly parted lips, the focused gaze with which she read the notes, revealed how immersed she was in her task. Regina played with much greater ease, skillfully yielding, here and there, to her sister, turning the pages, and displaying no strain at all; why, then, did such a sharp, pronounced red burn on her cheeks? And why did her eyes have such a striking glow? I hope she isn't frantic, the Count mumbled in fear.[24]

What precise meaning really lurks behind the "red on her cheeks" is almost beside the point. Indeed, Regina's father and the doctor he calls in spend a whole chapter exchanging different diagnoses, both of which turn out to be wrong. What is more interesting is the gaze itself, which two authority figures—a father and a physician—cast on two women playing four-hand piano. Interestingly, it is not just a certain *fact* that this gaze must espy but, rather, the epistemological status of that playing itself. For not only are father and doctor not in agreement about the diagnosis; the father seems to assume that he is diagnosing something of which his daughter herself is not aware (he thinks she is ill), whereas the doctor seems to think that it is a secret that Regina knows very well but is concealing from the outside gaze (he thinks she is in love). The two men therefore also puzzle over the question of whether the two girls are only a passive object of scrutiny or are actively opposed to their controlling-diagnostic gaze.

In a striking scene from *David Copperfield* (1850), Charles Dickens foregrounds this disciplining gaze and makes it more complex. Here, four-hand piano playing

---

[23] Gerhart Hauptmann, *Das Friedensfest: Eine Familienkatastrophe* (Berlin: Fischer, 1904), 55–56.
[24] Ida Countess Hahn-Hahn, *Gesammelte Werke* (Regensburg: Habbel, 1900), 1:407.

functions as the connector between different and sometimes competing masculine authorities, on the one hand, and female seducibility/seductiveness, on the other. Headmaster Dr. Strong is married to a much younger woman named Anne, who has a relationship with the shifty Jack Maldon. David Copperfield, the first-person narrator, realizes this fact only when he sees Anne Strong playing four-hands with the kindhearted Agnes Wickfield and notices the reaction of Agnes's father, Mr. Wickfield.

> The Doctor was very fond of music. Agnes sang with great sweetness and expression, and so did Mrs. Strong. They sang together, and played duets together, and we had quite a little concert. But I remarked...that Mr. Wickfield seemed to dislike the intimacy between her and Agnes, and to watch it with uneasiness.[25]

The unease in the paternal contemplation first prompts David to take a closer (and diagnostic) look at the homey scene offered by the "little concert." It is not his own observations that make David suspicious. Instead, he observes the observers; their reactions allow him to interpret the scene at the piano "correctly" and thereby share in the observers' unease. The young man appropriates for himself the gaze the elder man casts on the women. Indeed, David immediately sees what Mr. Wickfield sees—what unsettles him so much about the "intimacy between Mrs. Strong and Agnes."

> And now, I must confess, the recollection of what I had seen on that night when Mr. Maldon went away, first began to return upon me with a meaning it had never had, and to trouble me. The innocent beauty of her face was not as innocent to me as it had been; I mistrusted the natural grace and charm of her manner; and when I looked at Agnes by her side, and thought how good and true Agnes was, suspicions arose within me that it was an ill-assorted friendship.[26]

Four-hand piano playing—or rather, its observation—unmasks the "innocent beauty" as mere appearance. On the one hand, the true depravity of Mrs. Strong becomes legible only in this situation; on the other hand, the danger exists that this depravity could affect "good and true" young Agnes. After all, Mrs. Strong's depravity appears to be contagious: the suspicion shared by David and Mr. Wickfield does not concern the relationship between Mrs. Strong and Jack Maldon so much as the

---

[25] Charles Dickens, *The Personal History of David Copperfield* (London: Bradbury & Evans, 1850), 199.

[26] Dickens, *David Copperfield*, 199.

relationship between the two women. They are concerned that Mrs. Strong could corrupt Agnes and could seduce her into seductiveness.

The scene does not stage desire between two women so much as the relationship of the two to each other, and to desire as such; and these relationships unfold in perfect legibility before the eyes of a gaggle of male observers (Dr. Strong, Mr. Wickfield, David). It is not insignificant, either, that the very Agnes Wickfield about whose innocence and constancy David worries becomes his wife at the end of the novel. The scene stages a transfer of the paternal gaze to the future husband, and of the title to its object. Masculine distrust of woman represents a shift of masculine authority from one generation to the next.

We find a similar constellation in *Goldelse*, a novel by Eugenie Marlitt that was first serialized in 1866 in *Die Gartenlaube*, probably Germany's first mass periodical. Six years after Hahn-Hahn's novel, and sixteen years after Dickens's, Marlitt's staging of playing *à quatre mains* departs from these antecedents by presenting the activity not as the epitome of bourgeois life but rather as one characteristic of aristocratic privilege. Despite the unusual class dynamics at play around the four-hand keyboard in Marlitt's novel, Mr. Wickfield's suspicions about four-hand playing—and the careful surveillance it necessitates—remain unchanged.

Marlitt's novels were intended for an extremely large audience of mostly bourgeois readers (about two hundred thousand copies were sold of each *Gartenlaube* around the time Marlitt's novel appeared in its pages). They tended to hew closely to a fairly simple schema intended to flatter its readers, especially when it came to their depictions of family life. Not by accident, the *Gartenlaube* described itself as a "family magazine" and was intended to be read aloud or together within the home. In *Goldelse*, a daughter of the bourgeoisie falls in among nobility; she is led into temptation by their way of life, but she manages to avoid disaster thanks to her moral strength. What makes her temptation interesting is that Elisabeth ("Else") is a piano teacher, and that her seduction comes by way of an invitation to play at four hands.

The bourgeois Ferber family moves into an ancient castle called Gnadeck, an estate where Elisabeth's uncle works as a forest warden. Right away, the family begins to make the eerie old edifice bourgeois—to transform it from a castle into a home: "The sinister door that led to the larger wing had been walled up; the lofty oak wings with brass locks and bolts covered the masonry and hid the fact that, beyond it, there was nothing but wilderness."[27] The Ferbers suffuse this stark and forbidding structure with warmth, modernity, and humanist charm. The cherry on top of the domestication of the old rulers' residence is represented by—what else?—the acquisition of a piano: "a beautiful, table-shaped instrument that was carried without further ceremony into the foyer and placed, in the tapestry room above, beneath the bust of Beethoven."[28]

---

[27] Eugenie Marlitt, *Goldelse* (Leipzig: Ernst Keil, 1875), 64.
[28] Marlitt, *Goldelse*, 65.

Marlitt describes this domestication of the rambling aristocratic space into a compact and family-friendly one as a process of containment and unification: she plays with the fact that the same German word, *Flügel*, can refer to the separate wings of the impracticable old structure and to the instrument the Ferbers bring in to rejuvenate it. The piano transforms the forbidding aristocratic space into an inviting bourgeois one, and it also transforms the castle's dwellers into a family. Almost as soon as it is brought in, the family gathers around the instrument. The daughter of the household pays musical homage to the bust of Beethoven, and they enthusiastically watch "as the wondrous melodies rush forth from under the fingers of the young girl." The classics function as a hearth around which the family assembles: "the little family took seats in the niche of the broad arching window and fell into the master's [i.e., Beethoven's] ocean of thoughts, whose portrait looked down from the wall at the enthusiastic player."[29]

Their musical idyll is disturbed by a messenger from Castle Lindhof, the foreign building in the valley, "a monstrous structure in the Italian style that pushed up fairly close to the foot of the mountain where Gnadeck lay."[30] The messenger brings Elisabeth a letter from the Baroness Lessen. "She began by telling the young girl many flattering things about her magnificent piano-playing, which she claimed to have heard on walks through the forest for the last few evenings, and she added the question whether Miss Ferber was inclined—under conditions to be determined beforehand of course—to play four hands a few times every week with Miss vom Walde."[31]

Marlitt's choice of words is anything but neutral: there seems little doubt for the reader that the letter is less than sincere. The flattery and the Baroness's claim to have overheard the piano playing by chance (coupled with the narrator's strange doubts about the latter) give the whole thing a whiff of seduction. Certainly the family seems to understand it as that, as evidenced by the family members' reactions. Her uncle in particular angrily objects to the idea, "because Elisabeth—now and forever—does not fit in among the trash down there!" Concern surfaces, as it did in *David Copperfield*, whether something "unsuitable" might make its way in through four-hand playing. "Do you want to see what you have carefully built disappear under poisonous mildew or frost—then just go ahead."[32] Family, castle, piano evenings—all three are under threat from the creeping rot that lurks down in the valley.

Even though the class relations that Marlitt depicts are rather atypical (piano four-hands, after all, is characteristic of the bourgeoisie or of nobility that has become culturally bourgeois), and even though the *topos* of the seductive aristocrats prying

---

[29] Marlitt, *Goldelse*, 66.
[30] Marlitt, *Goldelse*, 52.
[31] Marlitt, *Goldelse*, 67.
[32] Marlitt, *Goldelse*, 68.

on unassuming burghers is more native to the eighteenth century, the text nevertheless seems quite concerned that playing four-hands might be accompanied by moral "poisoning"—a concern it shares with Dickens's novel. But whereas Dr. Strong, "as a great music-lover," guilelessly brings piano four-hands into his house, both Marlitt's characters and the narrator make a sharp distinction between playing four-hands and playing solo. Whereas performing Beethoven solo crowns the process by which the ruined old castle becomes a comfortable home, playing four-hands represents a clear threat to this (newly) bourgeois residence.

When the characters rush to defend the bourgeois sphere against aristocratic attempts at corrupting it, the menace posed by Lindhof and the defense mounted by the father figures are tinged with nationalism. It is not just dwelling places that are threatened and need to be protected, but Germanness itself is under attack. The strange chiasm in the plot—the fact that the burghers move into the medieval castle whereas it is the nobles who occupy the "Italian" villa in the valley—stresses the connection between German essence (the knightly castle) and the bourgeoisie. The burghers are the better nobles, and thus become the bearers of national identity. And the piano is, of course, part of it.

Playing four-hands, which for Else's uncle (who, as a forest warden, represents the native soil and its protection) belongs to the nobility, also belongs to the "foreign" terrain of Schloss Lindhof. Previous chapters of this book have shown how four-hand piano playing could function as a vehicle of nationalism. In Marlitt instead, the exclusion of playing four-hand piano is what constitutes a properly "German" sphere. The forest warden (like David and Mr. Wickfield) guards the virtue of his niece; still more, however, he defends the virtue of his homeland against foreign encroachment. Schnitzler's plan for *Fräulein Else* likewise makes it clear that Herr Dorsday, who menaces the family, is emphatically alien: "Interesting, but bad breeding. A Hungarian Jew."[33]

Unlike the women in Dickens, Marlitt's Elisabeth is drafted into the defense effort when faced with foreign encroachment upon home, nation, and family. *David Copperfield*'s Agnes seems to have no idea of the dangers posed by playing four-hands with Mrs. Strong. Elisabeth, on the other hand, knows perfectly well what the danger is, and she is on her guard as she heads down into the valley: "Every person must have a little trust in both her lucky star and herself; and so I wouldn't despair at all, even if, as soon as I entered that strange world, I should fall into an abyss of Egyptian darkness and hideous reptiles." Instead of shielding herself from all danger in the abstract, Else proposes, as it were, a series of moral experiments (or perhaps even a kind of moral homeopathy) in order to test her own character. Marlitt's heroine is active and self-confident in the way that she encounters the threats posed by piano four-hands. For all that, *Goldelse* does not depart from the

---

[33] Schnitzler, "Fräulein Else" (draft), p. 2.

sexist convention of making sure that the girl is monitored and supervised—not least of all supervised by herself—as though she were particularly inclined to yield to seduction at the keyboard. She, too, needs guidance from the "members of the household," even if Marlitt is kind enough to include the heroine herself among these members.

But how exactly do these "members of the household" see four-hand piano playing? In all three novels just discussed, characters view it with distrust, but they desire it fervently nevertheless, and even regard it as necessary. It's not that four-hand piano playing is simply accepted as a necessary evil; much rather, in Marlitt, Dickens, Hahn-Hahn, and Schnitzler this supposedly risky situation is sought out on purpose, be it as a status symbol, a social requirement, or simply an activity too enjoyable to forgo. David Copperfield learns from the older men to scan the goings-on at the piano for potential dangers, he does not, therefore, doubt the doctor's love of music; and even Marlitt's novel, which attaches negative connotations to playing four-hands like few other works of bourgeois realism, seems to find testing Elisabeth's character by duet necessary and positive. Agnes and Else *must* expose themselves to the danger that comes from playing four-hands, even though the members of the household (chiefly men, of course) are only too aware of the risk. Such is the dialectic of bourgeois music making: it is a matter of *bon ton* among those who can afford to come into contact with the autonomous sphere of art to let themselves be infected[34]—even if such contacts always entail the risk of surrendering to this realm entirely and thereby bringing about the decline of the family.

The Piano and/as Organ: Four-Hand Playing and the Psychoanalytic Gaze

Max Weber, as we have seen, contrasted the "moderately large interior space" that is the natural habitat for the piano (and thereby for four-hand piano playing, as well) with the "colossal interior space"[35] required by the organ. In this new space the piano takes on a role analogous to the one that the organ plays in church: it gathers people, binds them together into a congregation or family. Organ and four-hand piano are cousins because the organ is another one of the few instruments that can be played jointly and also because, at a time when bellows were needed, it usually required at least two people to operate it. At least in the nineteenth century, there was even a flourishing industry devoted to churning out organ arrangements of famous works, though on a far smaller scale than those for four-hand piano—the reason had to

---

[34] Gerald Izenberg, *Modernism & Masculinity—Mann, Wedekind and Kandinsky Through World War I* (Chicago: Chicago University Press, 2000), 117–19.

[35] Max Weber, *Die rationalen und soziologischen Grundlagen der Musik* (Tübingen: Mohr/Siebeck, 1972), 77.

do once again with the perceived adaptability of the instrument. Romantic organs in particular were designed to reproduce orchestral textures (for example, the *Sauerorgel* in Berlin).

If piano four-hands assumes characteristics of the organ and transfers them to the domestic sphere, then this transfer greatly changes what can be gleaned from the instrument and the way in which one gleans it. Four-hand piano is the organ in bourgeois music religion, even though the small congregation views the "sonic hearth" with much more suspicion (especially when played by four-hands) than worshipers view the organ at church. Music making at home was thought to teach women and children very valuable things and very dangerous things—and valuable and dangerous were often difficult to separate. The household needed music to worship at the altar of privacy, but music always already threatened it and its privacy.

In *Papers on Psycho-Analysis* (which was published in 1918, although the text reproduces a lecture delivered in 1911), Ernest Jones, Freud's biographer and a psychoanalyst himself, reports the analysis of a dream in which an organ and a piano appear together—even though (and this is hardly surprising given that Jones's text dates from 1911) the contrast between organ and piano hardly merits mention in his eyes. The patient in question suffers from exhaustion and lack of energy, which affect her playing the piano in particular: "a feeling of powerlessness, amounting to a complete paralysis in both arms. This was at first manifested only while playing the piano, a recreation of which she had been particularly fond."[36]

In his analysis, Jones understands the piano as an instrument of instruction. It provides a place of transmission of moral doctrines and codifications of intimacy. Just as in the four-hand scenes in literature, the keyboard as a medium of transmission is overdetermined—it is a place where one can instill virtue, and where one can encounter the contagious power of vice. Jones's diagnosis relies mostly on a dream that his patient reports:

> She dreamed she was in a large hall. At one end, opposite to her, was a maroon coloured church organ. There were several upright pianos, and one baby grand piano, at which she was playing. Her boy was kicking at it from the side, and she reproved him saying, "You ought not to abuse such a beautiful instrument."[37]

Jones immediately notes that the dream unambiguously plays with the double meanings of the words "organ" and "instrument": "organ" means both the musical device and a body part. As is the case with the term "instrument," "organ" can be a euphemism for genitals. Therefore, the dreamer is playing with an (her?) organ;

---

[36] Ernest Jones, "The Relationship between Dreams and Psycho-Neurotic Symptoms," in *Papers on Psycho-Analysis* (London: Wood, 1918), 264.

[37] Jones, "Dreams and Psycho-Neurotic Symptons."

at the same time, she tells her son "not to abuse such a beautiful instrument." The abuse the dreamer cautioned her son against was really self-abuse—that is, masturbation. Jones remarks: "It was not hard to infer that the acts of masturbation and piano-playing had become unconsciously associated in her mind." Indeed, the patient declares: "When I woke from the dream I found I had been doing it in my sleep."[38]

The connection between masturbation and piano playing is anything but new. Alain Corbin points out that, long before the birth of psychoanalysis, Edmond de Goncourt established the connection between piano playing and (female) masturbation. What is new in the case of Jones's patient is the passing-on of the prohibition: the dream is about forbidding the son the abuse of his instrument—in fact, Jones points out, the patient had given this very instruction to her child in real life. But why the large array of instruments that stand at the analysand's disposal? She recollects an "organ," "several upright pianos," and, finally, the "baby grand" on which she plays. The signifier "baby," in view of the autoerotic themes of the dream, cannot be a coincidence: the "baby grand" refers to sexual reproduction. The fact that the young boy is kicking it symbolizes, therefore, a turn away from alloerotic sexuality, on the one hand, and a renunciation of productive (non-masturbatory) sexuality, on the other—he kicks the "baby" with his feet.

One of the complaints that made Jones's patient seek psychotherapy was paralysis in her arms, which first manifested itself in a certain lack of energy in her piano playing. The piano, then, is not just a dream symbol but a symptom as well: the piano conveys sexuality; conversely, sexuality determines piano playing. The fact that a lack of energy, ever since Tissot's *Onania*, has been seen as a primary symptom of excessive masturbation is significant in this regard. Whatever power medical horror stories about neurasthenia caused by masturbation had held in the nineteenth century, it had all but dissipated by the time Jones's analysand sat down on his couch; however, Jones assumes, the patient's subconscious may have made this very connection: "Roughly put, her loss of power in piano-playing, which gradually extended to other functions, was in a way a punishment for playing with her fingers in another, forbidden direction."[39] The piano is where the analysand's own moral instruction from childhood resurfaces. After all, the analysand does not seem to believe that masturbation is bad for her; but she certainly was taught that it was as a child, and on the keyboard those teachings still hold a totemic power.

Once again, then, the piano is strongly overdetermined. On the one hand, the piano is simply a piano, the instrument on which neurasthenia can be gleaned and diagnosed; on the other, piano playing points toward the sexual organ. The same seems true of the other instruments in the dream (to which Jones pays relatively

---

[38] Jones, "Dreams and Psycho-Neurotic Symptons," 265.
[39] Jones, "Dreams and Psycho-Neurotic symptons," 265.

little attention). The "organ," which is emphatically marked as a "church organ," does not simply mean "(sexual) organ"; rather, it signifies the church and, by extension, the promulgation of prohibitions (for example, the prohibition of self-abuse) that occurs there. One could say, therefore, that the dream reflects the secularization and domestication of morality: organ and church, as well as their function of passing on conceptions of morality, have been relegated to the background; the instrument that the small boy defiles—the "baby"—is an instrument associated with the domestic sphere.

The dream is about education, the passing along of (moral) instruction—especially, of course, instruction on how the "beautiful instrument" is to be used and not abused. Therefore, it involves two doctrines: first, how the libido is to be managed; second, how the actual instrument is to be employed. Whether this occurs autoerotically (by playing on one's own instrument) or alloerotically (by playing with the "baby" instrument), the regulation of the drives that the mother prescribes here is realized by music. Because music teaches the one (how to employ the instrument), it implicitly teaches the other, too (how to use the "instrument" of euphemism). As was already the case in Dickens, the keyboard is the site for transmitting certain messages, some of which are conscious and others unconscious—and playing four-hands, as an action involving two parties at the same "instrument," is, as we have seen, particularly risky in this regard.

Schnitzler's *Fräulein Else* also points to this vital yet unsettled function of four-hand piano playing. The piano plays host to some kind of instruction; however, what exactly is taught is uncertain. And what is being transmitted may be as uncanny as what Agnes learns from Mrs. Strong—as threatening as what Elisabeth might learn from playing with Miss vom Walde. For Schnitzler's Else, too, the teachings that occur at a piano played by four hands do not involve virtue in general or particular virtues—what one learns here seems far more opaque and disturbing. For playing four hands functions, in *Fräulein Else* as the expression (and, as Schnitzler's fragment makes clear, as the seed) of the unique mixture of profound love and wild contempt that Else feels for her father: "Suddenly, she hates her mother. Only her father does she still love, like a child."[40]

Schnitzler's text makes clear that Else's "education"—and, in particular, the part involving her father—basically involved integrating her into the deceptive economy of a deeply dysfunctional family: "they only raised me to sell myself, one way or the other,"[41] she realizes. Basically, therefore, Schnitzler censors not just what is private in piano four-hands—not just what is dysfunctional in the family unit, which is structured by piano playing—but also the profound uncanniness that lies within the Oedipal transmission of conscious and unconscious values by musical means.

---

[40] Schnitzler, "Fräulein Else" (draft), p. 6.
[41] Schnitzler, "Fräulein Else," 87.

The missing episode of four-hand playing represses the unspoken secret that dominates Else's family and, Schnitzler implies, all families—namely that they are structured by dominance, commerce, and essentially pimping by more polite means.

In the nineteenth century, the dangerous role of mediating between art and the reality principle normally fell to the mother. This was particularly pronounced in Victorian culture. Ruskin lists the paradigmatic responsibilities of the mother: to "clothe" children, to "induce them to love order," and to "instruct" them. According to the bourgeois ethos, she is not permitted to have anything to do with breadwinning or running the household; therefore, almost against her will, she becomes the high priestess of art, and it is her duty to minister to her children. The children taste the fruits of art the mother offers, even as the premonition of paternal prohibition clouds the proceedings. Hanno Buddenbrook comes to the piano through his "southern" mother. Thomas Mann's own mother Julia played four-hands with one of her lovers, a violinist from the opera,[42] thereby inspiring a whole series of maternal and female figures in her son's early works.[43]

One day, clearly, the son will need to free himself from the maternal sphere of art—and, as Suzanne Cusick has shown, the daughter must also not surrender entirely to the "homosocial triangle";[44] she, too is subject to prohibition. This means, on the one hand, that the realm of art is only ever open to the adult son as a sphere of melancholy—as when, for example, tears are in his eyes at Bayreuth; on the other hand, it means that what is taught there has always already had something secret and taboo about it. No matter how little the mother shares of this forbidden yet necessary sphere, it is always already too much, too dangerous, too intimate.

In the nineteenth century, (bourgeois) woman is by definition a private, stationary being; if she is not, then class preservation is *semiotically* at risk. Man, on the contrary, is active and public; he must not yield to the private madness of genius—and if he does so, class preservation is *materially* impossible. The path the son follows in this schema is eccentric: in order that the family not suffer a demotion in class status, he must mature as a private being and, later, grow alienated from the private sphere; otherwise, once again, the family is automatically *déclassé*. The fact that it is a sphere to be left behind hovers over its security and weighs down its supposed immediacy. That is to say, in the event of an overdose, separation from the aesthetic-private sphere is impossible—generally, this condition is referred to as "decadence." Peter Gay has called it "the dirty little secret" of the Victorian

---

[42] Klaus Harpprecht, *Thomas Mann: Eine Biographie* (Hamburg: Rowohlt, 1995), 42–43.
[43] Izenberg, *Modernism & Masculinity*, 107ff.
[44] Suzanne G. Cusick, "On a Lesbian Relationship to Music: A Serious Effort Not to Think Straight," in Philip Brett, Elizabeth Wood, and Gary C. Thomas (eds.), *Queering the Pitch: The New Gay and Lesbian Musicology* (New York: Routledge, 1994).

household: on the one hand, femininity is always supposed to be restricted to women; on the other hand, "men needed it and without it could not become men."[45]

The forbidden teachings of the mother could only be permitted (very) conditionally by the father; like the four hands hidden and moving between two bodies, they are just as necessary as they are feared. The father watches both to make sure he catches sight of nothing, as well as to ensure that there is something there for him to not catch sight of. Slavoj Zizek notes that the scandal of *Madame Bovary* does not stem from the fact that she "represents the irresistible charm of adultery"; instead, the scandal is that she "deprives" us of "even this last refuge." "A passionate extramarital liaison not only does not pose a threat to conjugal love but also functions as a kind of inherent transgression that provides the direct fantastic support to the conjugal link and thus participates in what it purports to subvert."[46] The "inherent" or "internal" transgression is also very important in the way the pairs of hands play together: the form demands transgression (leaving one's allotted, "proper" space, crossing hands, touching thighs). This transgression is not an accident that might impede playing together; rather, it belongs to the form itself.

From the perspective of the observer (be he intruder or voyeur), too, it is only through transgression that the spectacle of piano four-hands comes into being. Four-hand playing presents itself to observers openly (almost coquettishly) as hermetically sealed. Picture a salon in which a quartet is playing. The reluctance on the part of the observer to stand up, to wander behind the violinist in order to catch a glimpse of the music, is clearly much greater than the hesitation he might feel to approach two people playing piano and to look at over their shoulders (and at their hands), whether approvingly or critically. The four-hand players, meanwhile cannot survey the room (cannot return the gaze, as it were) as the members of a string quartet might.

In such a scene, censorship and visual pleasure are almost impossible to tease apart. The spectacle of two pairs of hands playing thrives on eroticism that must remain invisible. Only through the suspicion that something exists between Agnes and Mrs. Strong can David Copperfield make the paternal gaze his own: the performance at the keyboard is necessary to structure power relations in the household. Whether any mistrust is merited in the first place is utterly beside the point.

It is one of the rules of the game here that we see nothing, even though we must assume that something there is something to not see. After all, the two players rushing through a score by Brahms in fits and starts, with furrowed brows and panicked expressions, are probably not thinking of sex, desire, or transgression at all. But that does not change the fact that our desire, as spectators, must be able to suppose a desire behind the tense, often awkward movements, and that to some extent our

---

[45] Peter Gay, *The Cultivation of Hatred; Vol. III, The Bourgeois Experience: Victoria to Freud* (New York: Norton, 1993), 299–300.

[46] Slavoj Zizek and Mladen Dolar, *Opera's Second Death* (London: Routledge, 2002), 134.

enjoyment of the spectacle depends on that supposition. How much more beautiful, and how much stronger, must this illusion have been when a practiced team shared the keyboard, relaxed, confident, with a sphinxlike smile dancing around each player's lips? Their elation is probably just as meaningless as the panicked expression the amateurs wear, yet it provides pleasure to the viewer all the same—because the smiles convince him that there is something not to see here.

Small wonder, then, that the piano keyboard became a fixation for nineteenth-century observers, all the more when four hands attended to their secret ministry on it: the hands performed desire and yet concealed it from the viewer. They are the only aspect of the performance that one is permitted to gawk at outright. The movements of legs or the posterior are, if at all, only accessible to the gazes of children. The composer Carl Orff, for example, reports: "Already when I was one-year-old, I was drawn to every kind of music. Most gladly, I sat under the piano, at my mother's feet, as she played."[47] Everyone else who wanted to know what the feet were doing was barred from expeditions under the piano—what they wanted to look for in the feet, they instead had to espy in the hands.

This is why the hand emerges as the crucible of the observation of four-hand playing. Any habitual duettist will point out that the hands are only one small part of what makes the form compelling and enjoyable, but the observer is far more restricted in what he or she is allowed to pay attention to. The face and the hand were the only body parts a woman was allowed to show in the presence of others—and the only body parts that others were allowed to interpret. At the same time, these hands had to speak for everything that was not directly open to the diagnostic gaze. The wealth of connotations the nineteenth century attached to four-hand playing had to be funneled, as it were, through this tiny eye of a needle: the hand as the nexus of interpretations that would strike us as abstruse today will be the topic of the following two chapters.

As we have seen, the piano is a central place in the family for assembly, education, and activity that, however, is explicitly *not* considered work (indeed, it even counts as anti-work). Yet as Saint-Saëns's mockery makes clear, this centrality makes playing with four hands exclusively *private*—and in public space, it is ridiculous. Making four-hand playing ridiculous has something to do with familial eroticism: playing four-hands serves yearnings, advances claims, and promises things that seem absurd outside the domestic sphere. Such privacy and subtle eroticism are, of course, matters that result from the fact, discussed in the first chapter, that the two players must necessarily come close to each other; indeed, they must fuse with each other. (Just how far this fusion extends, we will see in the next chapter.) It is fed less by the close contact between the players than by the fact that this contact, from the perspective of the observer, is extremely difficult to classify.

---

[47] Quoted in Lilo Gersdorf, *Carl Orff* (Reinbek bei Hamburg: Rowohlt, 1981), 12.

Nevertheless, the nineteenth century obsessively tried to figure out where the activity belonged, which is also the result of the fact that piano four-hands was often conceived as the epitome of the domestic sphere and the site of its imperilment. It is probably this very paranoia that permits and makes possible the various familial operations at the piano played by four hands: how could David Copperfield ever learn to view his (future) wife as a patriarch does if the anatomical theater of four-hand playing did not exist? If, in four-hand playing the keyboard represents a place of assembly, education, and activity, then in a certain sense—whether in Dickens, Marlitt, or Hahn-Hahn, or in Ernest Jones's dream analysis—it is always a matter of debate what that assembly, education, or activity really consist of.

4

Four-Handed Monsters

> "I am in Lady Agatha's black books at present.... I promised to go to a club in Whitechapel with her last Tuesday, and I really forgot all about it. We were to have played a duet together.... I don't know what she will say to me. I am far too frightened to call."
>
> "Oh, I will make your peace with my aunt.... And I don't think it really matters about your not being there. The audience probably thought it was a duet. When Aunt Agatha sits down to the piano, she makes quite enough noise for two people."
>
> — Oscar Wilde, *The Picture of Dorian Gray*

At first glance, the passage from Oscar Wilde's *The Picture of Dorian Grey* is little more than a trifle: the image of Lady Agatha making enough noise to convince her listeners that she's playing a four-hand duet is indeed a deft, and amusing bit of characterization. But we have encountered the image on which this characterization relies too often now to leave it at that. Franziska von Reventlow relied on the same joke in a different version: in her novel, playing four-hand piano by yourself meant having a secret affair with the other pair of hands. Wilde's joke implies something else: the fact that Lady Agatha is loud enough by herself to convince her listeners she is two duettists points to something monstrous—what by rights, by nature, should take two, for her takes only one.

Playing four-hands means being monstrous—either merging one's own ego with another or else inflating one's own ego to the point that it can pass for two. There is something unnatural in either process. Lady Agatha represents these two discomfiting processes in personal union: her solo four-hand playing is part of her bluster, her liking to take up enough space for two. But she also usurps (and here Wilde's joke coincides with von Reventlov's) both roles at the piano, and unites the latent sexual division of labor Reventlov relies on in one person. Aunt Agatha transcends, or perhaps transgresses, her status as single individual; she is somewhere between being one person and being two. Her four-hand playing doesn't so much transform the music as it transforms the player. All humor aside, Wilde's description of this piano amoeba has something demonic about it. Eve Kosofsky Sedgwick has pointed to the fact that fathers and mothers are rarities in Wilde's comedies, and that uncles, and in particular aunts, seem to be everywhere. They are non-mothers and non-fathers, parents only around the corner. And there is some of this in Agatha's four-hand playing: she is matronly without being motherly; in the play, as on the keyboard, rather than assert authority she asserts dominance.[1]

But what exactly makes Lady Agatha a monster? What makes an organism a monster in the first place? In the case of Lady Agatha it seems to be her usurpation of an activity that is intended for two subjects. But is a single person playing four-hand really still a single person, and are two people playing four-hand really still two? Edward Cone answers that question as follows: "The aim of four-hand music should be to invoke a single persona, not by the interaction of two agents, but by the blending of the two players into a single four-handed monster."[2] Indeed, four-handed Agatha and Cone's "four-handed monster" may point to a preliminary definition of monstrosity: from the quasi-theological theories of monstrosity offered by Ambroise Paré (1510–1590) to the nineteenth-century interest in the "Elephant Man" Joseph Merrick, monstrosity has to do with too much or too little body. Either the monster was lacking organs or extremities, or those organs and extremities expanded past the bounds of the "normal" bodily schema.[3]

Consider the example of a four-handed creature depicted in figure 4.1: "Fipps, the Monkey," protagonist of German humorist Wilhelm Busch's picture poem of the same name, which appeared in 1879. A monkey, granted, is not a monster, but rather the rule. And Busch's musical monkey goes through a number of positions at the piano that would be impossible for a human in his place, but that seem eminently reasonable for a monkey. He eats an apple while playing the piano, uses his tail to depress the keys during a moment of laziness, or plays flute and piano at once. But in another picture, which accompanies the following lines about "Kattermäng" (Busch's semi-serious Germanization of *quatre mains*), is different:

All *Kattermäng* requires two,
But for himself he alone will do.[4]

Fipps successfully manages in reality what Lady Agatha's domineering behavior accomplished on metaphorical grounds alone: he plays four-hands by himself.

---

[1] Eve Kosofsky Sedgwick, "Tales of the Avunculate," in *Tendencies* (Durham, NC: Duke University Press, 1993), 52–72.
[2] Edward Cone, *The Composer's Voice* (Berkeley and Los Angeles: University of California, 1974), 135.
[3] Marie-Hélène Huet, *Monstrous Imagination* (Cambridge, MA: Harvard University Press, 1991), 1.
[4] Wilhelm Busch, *Werke (HKG)* (Wiesbaden: Vollmer, 1959), 2:331–36.

Figs. 4.1 "Fipps, the Monkey" (1879), from the picture poem by Wilhelm Busch.

And yet the picture of the feat that Busch provides has something rather disturbing about it (fig. 4.2): unlike in Fipps's other exertions at the piano, there really isn't a monkey visible at all here. If it weren't for the title, if it weren't for the other pictures in the series, the observer would be left to wonder what strange horrific creature is digging into the keys here. The monkey's body is obscured by the back of his seat, and the gaze upon the keyboard reveals only two isolated, almost disembodied-seeming pairs of hands. It's clear that they all hang together somehow, but there's no bodily schema that would make sense of them. The whole thing seems unnatural in pose and position, even for a monkey. A creature that is self-sufficient in playing "Kattermäng," we gather, is a good deal more uncanny than a monkey that eats an apple while playing piano with his feet.

From E. T. A. Hoffmann's mouse king to the real-life Elephant Man, the monster was that which undercut or transgressed the still-emerging identity of subject, body and person. As such monsters were a constant source of fascination for the nineteenth century. Monstrous births, mixed creatures were a frequent and popular subject in the press and in literature. They were photographed, sketched, exhibited in traveling shows. There exists since St. Augustine an etymological connection between the Latin terms *monstrum* and *monstrare*—monstrosity and its display were linked in the West for millennia.[5] Whether the monster was a (divine or

---

[5] See, for instance, Augustine's *The City of God* (*De Civitate Dei*), ed. Whitney Jennings Oates (New York: Random House, 1948), 577.

Figure 4.2 Fipps plays piano all by himself.

natural) sign, or whether it was simply a curiosity its discoverer endeavored to share with the rest of the world, the monster had, or needed, a public which analyzes and interprets the monster.

In the first chapter we quoted Robert Musil's description of the piano as a pagan idol, "a cross between dachshund and bulldog."[6] But Musil thought the piano monstrous because it brutally subjugated the bourgeois *interieur*. It wasn't monstrous in the sense explored above. For the physical schema of the piano had, if anything, gotten firmer in the course of the nineteenth century: the carnavalesque carousel of forms of the turn of the nineteenth century gradually stabilized into the one, the true, the reliable pianoforte. Far from being monstrously unstable in its shape, then, the piano's contours if anything got more stable and pronounced as the century wore on. It is the four hands playing on the piano that became monstrous, became one monster. It was the players whose bodily schemata suddenly seemed to fail, who seemed to fall somewhere between being a self-possessed subject and being an executing organ of someone else's body; who seemed to oscillate wildly between polite collaboration with another and Fipps-like dissolution. Four-hand players are somewhere between being one and being two: the boundary dissolves, but not entirely. They play duets, but they are not as safely dualistic as, say, a singer with an accompanist six feet away.

[6] Robert Musil, *The Man Without Qualities* (New York: Knopf, 1995), 45.

The second chapter asked what the bourgeoisie did with the thousands of transcriptions, potpourris, and arrangements they could buy from catalogues, could collect in matching sets, and could rush through in various configurations in an afternoon. This chapter will turn that question on its head: what did those scores (and particularly the transcriptions) do with those who played them? It deals with different forms of monstrosity in four-hand piano playing, different configurations of "not fully one, not fully two." In the first configuration, it is the merging of hands, arms, and wrists that constitutes the monstrous element of four-hand playing. As we shall see, the transcription and composition practices of the nineteenth century in many cases provoke or at least necessarily create such moments of monstrosity. The second configuration concerns the monster "behind" the hands: the hands remain distinguishable, but the bodies behind them seem to merge in often obscene ways. This leads to a third configuration, the equally obscene chiasmus of two players in one voice. If four-hand piano has a voice, it is one in which the body producing the sound is not simply bisected down the middle but, rather, one in which one party controls and manipulates the voice of the other. Finally, we will turn to the configuration that constitutes the reverse image of the obscene imbrication described earlier: the fact that the two bodies also give each other a law, and that not just transgression but also censorship function according to the principle "not fully one, not fully two."

Transcribing for Monsters

Franz Schubert composed his Rondo in D major (op. 138, D. 608) in 1818, but it wasn't published until 1835. It is, according to Ernest Lubin, "hardly one of Schubert's more serious compositions,"[7] but its subtitle is significant, "Notre amitié est invariable," often understood as a dedication to Schubert's frequent duet partner Josef von Gahy (1793–1864). We have already remarked on the close connection the nineteenth century postulated between friendship and four-hand playing; the analogy between the two had to do with the melding of the subjects in four-hand playing (a melding that Schubert remarked upon repeatedly, both when it came to duets generally and four-hand duets in particular). As Dallas Weekly and Nancy Arganbright have pointed out, at the end of Schubert's Rondo the two players' hands are supposed to cross—and in fact they finish the piece interlocked with one another.[8] Here, then, the surrender of subjectivity (under the sign of *amitié*) is equated with the surrender of personal space on the keyboard. If there is something

---

[7] Ernest Lubin, *The Piano Duet* (New York: Grossman, 1970), 59.
[8] Dallas A. Weekley and Nancy Arganbright, *Schubert's Music for Piano Four-Hands* (London: Kahn & Averill, 1990), 67.

monstrous about the new being created in this way, it has to do with the way hands and arms interlace on the keyboard.

A twenty-first-century film pushes this strange corporeality of four-hand playing, in which limbs and bodies seem to meld, much further. Still, as we shall find, it only makes more explicit a way of viewing four-hand playing that was already prevalent in the nineteenth century. Tim Burton's animated film *The Corpse Bride* (2005) tells the macabre story of young Victor, who is married of to a princess of the underworld, the corpse bride of the title, and is whisked away into a sort of Hades by her. Even though he rebuffs the advances of his supposed wife, Victor quickly develops an understanding for the tragic situation his cadaverous mate finds herself in. She is madly in love with him, still lingers in romantic girlhood fantasies of a white wedding, but nevertheless has the one problem that she doesn't have a pulse, or a lot of skin left. In a remarkable scene, Victor surprises his postmortem fiancée at the piano, sits down next to her, and begins picking up her melody (fig. 4.3). Before long, the two are playing the same theme *à quatre mains*, and their newfound understanding, their newfound affection for one another becomes evident when one of her hands comes loose and sprints down the keyboard toward his hands (fig. 4.4). First it caresses his hand, then it climbs up his arm, and finally nestles in on his shoulder. She bats an eyelid and would probably blush if she weren't dead. "Pardon my enthusiasm," she says, and he replies "I like your enthusiasm"—and tenderly returns her hand (fig. 4.5).

The "four-handed monster" is the heraldic animal of our investigation of what exactly four-hand transcription does to the body that performs it. In four-hand

Figure 4.3 The four-hand scene from Tim Burton's *The Corpse Bride* (© 2005 Warner Brothers Pictures)

Figure 4.4 "Pardon my enthusiasm": From Tim Burton's *The Corpse Bride* (© 2005 Warner Brothers Pictures)

Figure 4.5 "I like your enthusiasm": From Tim Burton's *The Corpse Bride* (© 2005 Warner Brothers Pictures)

playing, primo and secondo form a single Gordian knot—like a single kraken, they lay into the keys; their hands, wrists, and arms entwine. But the visual interlacing is only one way in which the two players seem to erase the boundaries between each other. After all, the four hands follow a law that, for the observer, remains obscure but for the mere listener, is completely unintelligible. Primo and secondo have roles to play, which refer them back to one another as two aspects of the same phenomenon, neither of which can be experienced in isolation. These kinds of roles, and the characteristic crossing of the hands, have their origins in particularities of nineteenth-century composition and transcription practices. The two players are not just physically interlaced; they are also inextricably cross-linked by virtue of the roles that they take vis-à-vis one another. Neither these physical crossings nor the cross-linked roles are primarily or usually owed to the whimsy of individual composers or arrangers but, rather, cut to the very formal core of four-hand piano music in the nineteenth century.

This formal core becomes visible when one leaves behind the two players at their keyboard and the suspicious "members of the household,"[9] and instead turns to the anonymous producers of that musical yard ware called transcriptions. While much of the repertoire that entered the bourgeois household was original rather than transcribed, the moment of translation from one medium to the other shines a spotlight on those aspects of a work that only an orchestra can create, and conversely those that only appear when the same piece is set for the piano. For in each transcription, transposition and interpretation have to somehow balance each other out: which sound figures, which instruments are transposable to the keyboard. How such transposition and interpretation work exposes the dynamics that four-hand transcriptions found around the instrument in the nineteenth century, and which they in turn institutionalized.

We do not know very much about how commercial transcribers working for the big music publishing houses went about their business. Many of them are unknown to us or hide behind pseudonyms. If they are famous, they are famous for other work, and their biographers are tight-lipped about their work as arrangers. Even letters, diaries, or memoirs, which would shed light on their solitary craft, are hard to come by. A lot of the transcribers who have survived as household names were also famous for writing etudes. But even Carl Czerny's memoirs make hardly any mention of his transcription work. Henri Bertini (1798–1876) likewise was a prolific four-hand transcriber and composer of etudes, and he is, if at all, remembered today only for the latter. The many diligent scribes who labored to sate the public's hunger for new arrangements, variations, and potpourris—Hugo Ulrich, Frédéric Kalkbrenner, August Stradel, Friedrich Mockwitz, Robert Wittmann, and others—left few testimonials about how they went about their work.

It is therefore a true stroke of luck that one of those scribes became world famous as a composer. Young Johannes Brahms earned his keep doing transcriptions before he became famous with his own compositions, and he kept transcribing his works

---

[9] Philipp Brett, "Piano Four-Hands: Schubert and the Performance of Gay Male Desire," *19th Century Music* 21 (1997): 154.

even once successful. In January 1855, Brahms, then still completely unknown, sent a four-hand transcription of Robert Schumann's Quintet op. 44 to the publisher Breitkopf & Härtel in Leipzig.[10] Clara Schumann seems to have made the introduction. The publisher play-tested the piece, checking on its spirit and its playability; two music professors performed the piece for the publisher and his staff. In February, the publisher decided not to publish the manuscript: "Unfortunately listening to and watching the performance has convinced us that the piece cannot and must not be published in this form." For "two very seasoned players, who are very interested in Schumann's music, encountered such difficulties that we have to assume the wider public would be scared off [by the arrangement]."[11]

This episode makes clear how publishers scrutinized the four-hand scene: four-hand arrangements were supposed to hew to the spirit of the original—and that spirit was largely the composer's intent. This, it seems, is why Breitkopf & Härtel turned to professors "interested in Schumann." At the same time, the publisher insisted on observing play. The reason was that the public, even those with an interest in Schumann, might be scared off by the difficulty of the arrangement. Though he seems to have missed the mark in this arrangement, Brahms himself had similar aims in transcribing his own work: in letters to his various publishers, he makes clear that he cares more "about the pianistic, about playability than about whether the integrity of each part has been maintained."[12] And to the publisher Rieter he writes that he made the transcription of his piano concerto (op. 15) "for playing and not (as is the fashion these days) for reading"[13])—for, as he writes to Simrock, "I really hope people like playing it."[14] Ease of play and appropriateness for the piano were thus central coordinates in Brahms's transcriptions of his own works. A few decades later Max Reger would write to the publishing house of Lauterbach & Kuhn that he wanted to transcribe a work for piano four-hands, and that his aims were threefold: "(1) that it be fully *pianistic* and fully four-handed, (2) that it *sounds* good, (3) and that it becomes easy to play and becomes 'house-music.' After all, that's what this kind of 4hand arrangement is supposed to be."[15]

However elusive the spirit of a piece or a composer, it is no accident that it came to play such a large role in four-hand transcriptions. As Theodor Adorno pointed out, only four-hand piano can seriously attempt to simulate the sym-phonic qualities of the orchestra. And even Franz Liszt wrote in the foreword to his 1839 (two-hand) transcription of Beethoven's Fifth Symphony: "Within the compass of

[10] Johannes Brahms, *Briefwechsel* (Tutzing: Schneider, 1974), 14:17.

[11] Brahms, *Briefwechsel*, 14:18.

[12] This is according to a report by Hentschel, quoted in Max Kalbeck, *Johannes Brahms* (Berlin: Deutsche Brahms-Gesellschaft, 1911), 3:80.

[13] Brahms, *Briefwechsel*, 14:86.

[14] Brahms, *Briefwechsel*, 9:23.

[15] Max Reger, *Briefe an die Verleger Lauterbach & Kuhn* (Bonn: Dümmler, 1993), 70f.

its seven octaves [the piano] can, with very few exceptions, reproduce all aspects, all combinations, and all formations of the most thorough and deepest sonic creativity. It leaves to the orchestra no other advantages than the wider palette of tonal colors and mass effects."[16] While Liszt praises the piano in general, nineteenth-century observers emphasized that Liszt's encomium of pianistic sound applied *a fortiori* to four-hand piano. *Grove's Dictionary of Music and Musicians* of 1879 writes that four-hand piano can "reproduce the characteristic effects of [orchestral] works more readily and faithfully than arrangements for pianoforte solo."[17]

Purely in terms of anatomy, the two pairs of hands can play twenty different notes at the same time. That means that quantitatively all the notes of the Schumann quintet that Brahms transcribed for Breitkopf could be transposed, one to one. Any restrictions are not logistical in nature but, rather, depend on the ability and ambition of the duettists themselves. This means, on the one hand, that four-hand arrangements can ensure that a good deal more of the spirit (Liszt's foreword speaks of "the inspiration of the master"[18]) survives in translation than in other forms of transcription—even though this made the choices, transpositions, and omissions the transcriber *did* include all the more significant. The compositional spirit had to do with the orchestral sound of the original, which, as far as many nineteenth-century observers were concerned, many two-hand transcriptions could not simulate sufficiently. A musical encyclopedia from the 1860s remarks that four-hand transcriptions were "more complete in reproducing details, and richer, stronger and more differentiated in their sonic effects"[19] than those for two hands.

Composers were keenly aware of this. Hector Berlioz, notoriously recalcitrant when it came to the piano, wrote as one of his few piano works a four-hand transcription of *L'Enfance du Christ*.[20] Entrusting the fullness and differentiation of his orchestral sound to a mere ten-fingered mortal seems to have been anathema to him. And in 1825, Ludwig van Beethoven found himself in the position of having to defend the spirit of his original composition against an unauthorized transcription. In a Viennese music journal, he wrote: "I take it as my duty to alert the musical public against a four-hand piano transcription of my recent overture, which misses the mark entirely and departs completely from the original score." Instead, Beethoven recommends the "absolutely faithful" transcription which "will soon appear in a legitimate edition with B. Schott's Sons in Mainz," which, as it happened, had been

---

[16] Cited in Zsuzsanna Domokos, "'Orchestrationen des Pianoforte': Beethovens Symphonien in Transkriptionen von Liszt und seinen Vorgängern," *Studia Musicologica Academiae Scientiarum Hungaricae* 37, nos. 2–5 (1996): 250.

[17] *Grove's Dictionary of Music and Musicians* (London: Macmillan, 1879), 79.

[18] Quoted in Domokos, "Orchestrationen des Pianoforte," 250.

[19] Arrey von Dommer, *Musikalisches Lexikon* (Heidelberg: Mohr, 1865), 172.

[20] Berlioz never finished the transcription. *L'enfance* eventually appeared in a transcription by Méreaux and Ritter (Albi Rosenthal, "Music Manuscript in Basle," *Musical Times* 116, no. 1588 [1975]: 537).

arranged by none other than Czerny.[21] The sound available to four-hand playing thus allowed the public, the publishers, and the composers to insist on greater fealty to the spirit of the orchestral original.

At the same time, Breitkopf's letter to young Brahms makes clear that four-hand transcriptions are objects of use, and therefore have to be useable for their consumer (rather than scaring them off). It was above all the *playability* of four-hand transcriptions that made them such runaway successes. In his 1906 biography of Tchaikovsky, Edwin Evans (1874–1945), music critic and the author of the guide *How to Accompany at the Piano* (1917), welcomed the fact that more of the composer's works were available in four-hand arrangements than for piano solo. "A few exist also for piano solo, but generally speaking, they are almost unplayable in this form. For instance, to the ordinary pianist only one movement of the 'Pathetic' symphony, the last, is accessible. The 'Casse Noisette' suite is an easy and effective solo, but in most arrangements the waltz is stripped of the varied counterpoints which are one of its principal charms in the orchestral version."[22] In the interest of playability, orchestral sound normally had to be reduced somehow: harmonies were transposed, parts were combined or left out entirely. This is mostly required by the partition of the keyboard or, rather, the transposition of the orchestra onto the keyboard. In order to simulate orchestral sound, the keyboard is subdivided: the lower registers are given to bass and tenor, the middle and upper registers to alto and soprano.

But the sonic reduction of the orchestral score doesn't just require a parceling out of the keyboard, but also of the score—in other words, the arranger has to decide what is melody and what is mere accompaniment. While the melody is, of course, the epitome of what Breitkopf in his letter to Brahms calls the spirit of the piece, the accompaniment can and has to be reduced. Priority was normally given to counterpoint, then instruments were left out that were essentially impossible to simulate on the piano; the rhythm they created had to be retained, which meant that the parts of certain rhythmic string or wind instruments had to be included. They are usually given to the secondo, since the primo is usually given fewer voices to bundle.[23] In classical transcriptions, the divisions of score and of keyboard are performed in a way that keeps melodic lines as intact as possible.

That means that both players usually busy themselves in their own corner of the keyboard, but the logic of the melody drives them again and again into the center of the keyboard. It is just as impossible to divvy up the spheres of activity of the individual players as it is to hand one motif or one melody fully to one player. Crossings of the hand are thus completely inevitable, as is the handover of a melody from one player to the other. Arrangers frequently tried to avoid crossings in the interest

---

[21] Quoted in Albert Dreetz, *Czerny und Beethoven* (Leipzig: Kirstner, 1932), 24.
[22] Edwin Evans, *Tchaikovsky* (London: Dent, 1906), 189.
[23] The author is indebted to Tim Ribchester for this point.

of playability, but this was where the composer's spirit raised its recalcitrant head. Anton Halm adapted Beethoven's *Grand Fugue* (op. 133) by consistently keeping primo and secondo in separate spaces, which required sacrificing musical logic to avoid crossings.[24] This aroused Beethoven's ire, who heavily criticized this disregard for the composer's spirit, and eventually went so far as to draft his own four-hand version of the piece, which only resurfaced a few years ago in manuscript form.

Just as Beethoven criticized Halm's reduction of his score for supposedly disregarding the spirit of the composition, there were music critics who had the opposite problem and who charged that transcriptions did not separate enough chaff from the wheat. While Beethoven's letter to the editor praised Czerny's arrangement of his overture for its accuracy, Czerny's student Louis Köhler (1820–1886) criticized his teacher's Beethoven arrangements only a few decades later in *Dwight's Journal of Music*. Czerny, Köhler charged, overburdened all four hands, leaving the players little room to put their own spin on the music. No note could be emphasized, the intimacy of individual moments was drowned in a constant fullness of sound, and the scherzos, according to Köhler, felt hulking and massive, miles away from the elegance and frailty of the originals. In general, Köhler argued, Czerny strove to keep all hands and all parts of the keyboard busy (so that none of the four hands had too much downtime), which departed rather starkly from the true Beethoven sound, since the master didn't constantly lean on piccolo flutes, the highest registers of the violin, and the lowest of the basses.[25]

Adolf Bernhard Marx expressed a similar view of Czerny's four-hand transcriptions of Beethoven. He generally applauded Czerny's achievement, but criticized the "play mania" (*Spielseligkeit*)—Czerny's tendency to keep every part of the keyboard busy at all times:

> We cannot approve of the fact that he, in order to make room for figures and fullness of parts [*Stimmfülle*], or also in order to humor the play-mania of the piano in order to find replacements for the irreplaceable orchestral effects [of the originals], changes and transposes registers, loses himself in the highest registers and in general sacrifices the orchestral quality of the original and the loyalty to it, up to the point where the player may well get an entirely wrong impression of the original work.[26]

The user experience of four-hand transcription was that of holding an orchestral work in one's own four hands. At the same time four-hand reduction, precisely

---

[24] Alexander Wheelock Thayer, *Thayer's Life of Beethoven* (Princeton, NJ: Princeton University Press, 1967), 975.

[25] *Dwight's Journal of Music* 4, no. 6 (November 12, 1853): 41.

[26] Adolph Bernhard Marx, *Die Lehre von der musikalischen Komposition, Dritter Teil* (Leipzig: Breitkopf und Härtel, 1845), 574.

because it had to keep all four hands busy at most (if not all) times, tended to spread out the textures of the original over the length of the keyboard like so much chewing gum.

For this reason, the tendency to split *unisono* passages by doubling the octaves was both central to transcription practice and not without its detractors. There were debates as to when it was appropriate enough, which intersected (though it by no means coincided entirely) with the debate over whether playability or spirit were to be treated as paramount.[27] Whatever the case, there was no denying that doubled octaves often rather drastically altered the character of a piece. When Mendelssohn's *Hebrides Overture* (op. 26) was arranged for four-hand piano—first by the composer himself, later by Gustav Friedrich Kogel for Peters publishing house—the strikingly tender woodwind solos were usually doubled. The effect surrenders the naturalism, the pictorial quality of the original; we do not hear "Fingal's Cave," we do not hear the sea and its birds; the pianistic sound becomes both more abstract and more arbitrary than the orchestral textures.

The logic of orchestration that predominates in classical music necessarily pushes the melody to the primo-player, while the secondo is usually more of an accompanist. The secondo is the one determining the rhythm—in particular, in the many dances that dominated the four-hand repertoire in the nineteenth century. So long as the arrangement doesn't rely on a contrast between the two players (for instance, if an etude has the teacher provide simple chords to guide the pupil's play), the secondo of course won't play just rhythm and accompaniment. In most arrangements, depending on how complex a field the primo has to attend to, the secondo might be asked to take over for bass, cello, and viola—strange the piece that would relieve all of them of melodic duties!

But especially in the comparatively less complex pieces discussed in the second chapter (the marches, waltzes, potpourris, and variations), the two players were rather starkly divided: the primo got to "show off the crystalline shimmer of the upper registers of the piano" while "the lower register (played by the secondo) was generally relegated to playing uninteresting and inferior accompaniment figures."[28] This schizophrenia predominated not just among the musical day laborers who churned out the endless stream of arrangements and dances but also among some of the most renowned composers for four-hand piano. Kathleen Dale, for instance, has pointed out that in Schubert's "simpler pieces," such as the dances and the marches, the secondo is often little more than an accompanist, "while primo luxuriates in the cream of the melodic and decorative passages."[29]

---

[27] Domokos, "Orchestrationen des Pianoforte," 273.

[28] Douglas Townsend, Program notes for the Musical Heritage Society recording MHS 3911/12/13.

[29] Kathleen Dale, "The Piano Music," in Gerald Abraham (ed.), *The Music of Schubert* (New York: W.W. Norton, 1947), 124.

The secondo keeps rhythm, comments on the melody, and also does the bulk of the pedaling. Generally, then, the secondo is responsible for sound and rhythm—that is to say, he or she takes on a more orchestral function compared with the soloist-like role of the primo. When concertos were arranged for four hands, the soloist's part was often almost entirely handed to the primo. When it came to the transcription of songs, the primo usually took over the role of songbird, whether it was a song written for soprano or alto.[30] When it came to translating the human voice—its continuity, its subjectivity, and its personality—to the keyboard, four-hand arrangements invariably turned to the primo.

Far from an equitable side-by-side, the two pairs of hands thus often presented something far more lopsided. They busied themselves not just in distant parts of the keyboard but they also did very different work there. The secondo was the accompanist, and was tasked with regulating and modulating; he or she more frequently strayed into the contested territory at the center of the keyboard. The secondo determined the voice, both his or her own and that of the primo—the secondo in many respects was the public face of the "four-handed monster." The primo, meanwhile, stayed fairly content in the soprano range. He or she left its proper sphere only rarely, and depended on its voice and its rhythm on the other. The primo player thus carried the subjective melody, while the secondo took up a position of collectivity—in the first instance, the collectivity of the orchestra, but also the collectivity of citizens, of humanity as such.

In transcribing his own Symphony no. 2, Johannes Brahms seems to have interpreted his orchestral score with this kind of division of labor in mind. In the first movement ("Allegro non Troppo"), the second lyrical theme (Walter Frisch calls it a "lullaby"[31]) is introduced by the secondo (in measure 82) and picked up by the primo. During this first run-through, the secondo plays the theme and the primo plays the accompanist. But the primo doesn't provide a rhythm; rather, the primo luxuriates in a coloratura (which is repeated once more in measure 156). The moment the two switch roles, this playful accompaniment drops out and the secondo simply keeps the beat. In the orchestral score, melody and accompaniment simply switch sides in a kind of chiasmus.[32] This symmetry vanishes in the four-hand arrangement. The primo, it seems, is not allowed, or is incapable of keeping the beat; it has to flutter around the melody with a songbird's playfulness. The secondo, conversely, is not permitted any such playfulness; the moment the secondo lets go of the melody, it is condemned to take control, to keep measure, to create order. The relative symmetry of the orchestral version thus gives way to two starkly divided

---

[30] On the gendered imaginaries of the "songbird," cf. Susan Rutherford, *The Prima Donna and Opera, 1815–1930* (Cambridge: Cambridge University Press, 2006), 47.

[31] Walter Frisch, *Brahms: The Four Symphonies* (New Haven, CT: Yale University Press, 2003), 70.

[32] Reinhold Brinkmann, *Late Idyll: The Second Symphony of Johannes Brahms* (Cambridge, MA: Harvard University Press, 1995), 147.

roles. To some extent this division is born of the necessities of transcription—but not entirely. There are other reasons why Brahms leaves out rhythmic chords that could easily be transposed into the primo's sphere of influence, or lyric passages that ought to go to the secondo-player—reasons that have little to do with pragmatism and more to do with ideology.

What is the nature of this ideological charge? It may bear pointing out that in English, primo and secondo were long known as "top" and "bottom" (even though it was common practice to print the two parts on opposite pages). Composers, arrangers, players, and observers understood primo and secondo as gendered actors. Common transcription practice turned the secondo's control over rhythm and voice into a cypher for masculinity—the secondo becomes the head of the musical household. The primo, meanwhile—highly subjective, far more tender, and of a kind of fragile privacy—occupies the kind of domestic position the nineteenth century usually assigned to women.

This sexual dichotomy seems to have enabled a whole chain of associated pairs of concepts. Charles de Bernard's novel *Gerfaut* describes a keyboard-bound flirtation and runs through a number of them: heroic Gerfaut plays the manly "basse," the pretty baroness plays "le chant"; the narrator takes care to note that his play is full of aggressive "énergie," while hers is characterized by "une légère indécision." Her indecision is amplified when his hands begin to "imprison" hers. At last his hands, and his role, are turned into a "bass clef" while she becomes a "treble clef." If writers like Charles de Bernard neatly separate roles, each element of these pairs clearly depends on the other; they are not just distinct—the two pairs of hands are complementary. Neither of them makes sense without the other—something else that would have reminded the nineteenth century of the sexual relationship.

This understanding of the complementary roles of songbird and accompanist as a kind of code for the relationship between the sexes, as well as the relationship between publicity and privacy, drew on another form that thematized these two pairs of concepts: the *Lied*. Franz Schubert wrote to his brother Ferdinand: "The way in which [Johann Michael] Vogl sings and the way I accompany him, how we seem to be *one* in such a moment, that seems to strike people as something new, something remarkable."[33] What makes the configuration of singer and accompanist remarkable in this manner is the way in which two people seem to be unified and referred to one another in their activity. This same ideology of unification and latent eroticism seems to have been projected onto the four-hand keyboard, where the logic of song and accompaniment was less natural and thus more visible.

So fraught was this dichotomy in the nineteenth century that we can trace it even into the philosophy of music. In the third book of *The World as Will and Representation*, Arthur Schopenhauer equates melody with the intentional striving

---

[33] Quoted in Heinrich Kreissle von Hellborn, *Franz Schubert* (Vienna: Gerold, 1865), 124.

of the will, and thus individual subjectivity.[34] This "highest objectivation of the will" finds its expression in the soprano's voice. But if Schopenhauer seems to assign the highest dignity to a vocal range usually associated with women, he is sure to temper his praise: the soprano's melody objectifies the will without being conscious of it, and Schopenhauer genders this unconsciousness as female. "Just as a magnetic somnambulist explains things that she has no idea about when awake," so the soprano "expresses the many different forms of the striving of the will."[35] Schopenhauer relies on oppositions and associations that crystallize into the roles of primo and secondo: soprano, subjectivity, and melody on the one hand; lower registers, objectivity, and harmony, on the other. The primo is subjective, private, individual, while the secondo is objective, legislating, public, and collective. Only together, according to the ideology of four-hand pianism, can they create the unheard-of oneness of which Schubert speaks—to create *sym*-phonic music in their tiny intimate community.

The way the gender dynamics play out in the tiny keyboard household is anything but accidental. Given how the nineteenth-century ideology of domesticity thought of gender almost made it necessary. From Rousseau onward, conceptions of community, and especially those accounts of community that contrasted it with more elective and looser forms of human coexistence, were inspired by and closely linked to the sexual relationship. The reason Rousseau, for instance, insisted on normative gender roles was not primarily that he held certain prejudices or preconceived notions (which in other areas he was able to demolish like no other); instead, he was guided by the idea that men and women are naturally referred to one another, naturally depend on one another, and that this kind of interlocking complementarity of roles has to be true for any community.[36] Since then, the sexual relationship was almost obsessively adduced as the paradigm for human community. This was as true for Rousseau as for the propagandists of organicist states, the Romantic generation, and finally Ferdinand Tönnies, who first introduced into the discourse of sociology the distinction between the closeness and intimate "community" and the elective and far looser "society."

In this context, the fact that the differential roles that structured four-hand playing in the nineteenth century were gendered is anything but surprising. The four-handed monster was thus not just an individual; it was also a kind of embryonic community. For nineteenth-century thinking, the kind of co-dependence that transcription and composition practice brought to the keyboard was never fully separable from questions of sex and gender. The moment you put a community to work on the keyboard, you sexualized it to some extent and you created a community only insofar as it had an erotic component, however sublimated.

---

[34] Arthur Schopenhauer, *The World as Will and Representation* (Cambridge: Cambridge University Press, 2010), 288.

[35] Schopenhauer, *The World as Will and Representation*, 288, translation modified.

[36] Penny A. Weiss, *Gendered Community* (New York: New York University Press, 1993), 46.

But matters were more complicated still. After all, the way four-hand transcription created a community on the keyboard, and the way this community was shot through with erotic concerns, was a matter of how four-hand music was written or written about. But it says nothing about how it was actually played. We have no evidence that women usually played the primo part or that men tended to regard the secondo part as their prerogative. Literary couples (such as de Bernard's Gerfaut and his baroness) certainly tend to shake out in this way, but whether this springs from writerly conceits or from an unwritten law is not clear. Here, too, the analogy to the *Lied* is instructive: songbird and accompanist are likewise coded in gendered terms. But as the example of Schubert and Vogl shows, there is little to suggest that this gendering has practical consequences in performance. After all, the relative positions in both singing and four-hand playing have primarily to do with the relative skill level. For instance, it is unlikely that a female piano teacher (or a mother) assigned her charges the secondo position or if a correpetitor took over the melody.

And this is where a second complication arises. Any accompanist knows that if the soloist drives or drags, he or she can easily dictate rhythm to the accompanist. While the subjective "voice" of the soloist indeed falls to the primo, and its objective frame falls to the secondo, the question of who leads and who follows depends much more on the individual players. And unless the duettists are a well-seasoned team (and even then only if they are equally matched in their abilities), there will be one player who leads and one who follows. The keyboard plays host to a veritable tug of war which can concern minutiae like speed or expression, but can also touch on deep questions of interpretation. Ossip Schubin (Aloisia Kirschner, 1854–1953) includes the following episode in her novel *Im Gewohnten Geleis* (1901): Countess Klotilde tries to avoid playing four-hand piano with her cousin. "For it was rather tiring to play four-hands with Leontine. [Her cousin] constantly referred to 'her sense' of a piece, in particular of Beethoven's Ninth Symphony. It was certainly a very good sense—but it was nevertheless tiring."[37]

The "very good sense" is in some ways a distant echo of the composer's spirit that Beethoven and others so insisted on. By reference to the spirit of the composition, the composer claims power over the work as it threatens to dissipate in moving between the different media; by reference to her sense, cousin Leontine claims power over a performance that threatens to get lost in the space between the players. Richard Hoffmann, a student of Arnold Schoenberg and his assistant during his Californian years, reports that he played four-hands with the master, "until I hurt him. Well, he played the primo part—what else could Schoenberg have played?—I was the secondo, and at some point I bruised his thumb with my little finger, during some crossing or other. So we stopped."[38]

---

[37] Ossip Schubin, *Im Gewohnten Geleis* (Stuttgart: Engelhorn, 1901), 59.

[38] Markus Grassl and Reinhard Kapp, eds., *Die Lehre von der musikalischen Aufführung in der Wiener Schule* (Vienna: Böhlau, 2002), 95.

There is something wonderfully catty about Hoffmann's recollections: on the one hand, Hoffmann seems to remember Schoenberg as a bit of a tyrant ("what else could Schoenberg have played?"), but on the other, his insistence that he "bruised [Schoenberg's] thumb" with nothing less than his little finger makes the composer come across as quite prissy. Four-hand playing, it seems, is always also about struggles for superiority; on a space as fraught as the four-hand keyboard, even a couple of serious and professional musicians like Hoffmann and Schoenberg readily slip into the cattiness of Klotilde and cousin Leontine. Of course, the categories Hoffmann uses to poke fun at his teacher are themselves thoroughly gendered; the statement that "what else" other than primo Arnold Schoenberg could have played reads differently in light of previous chapters than it might to the uninitiated.

The gendered code the nineteenth century applied to the relationship of primo and secondo was, by necessity, overlain with another, one that tried to answer Humpty Dumpty's question from Lewis Carroll's *Through the Looking—Glass*, "which is to be the master—that's all." Primo and secondo are about masculinity and femininity, but femininity is not the same as subservience, nor is masculinity the same as dominance. The four-hand keyboard is strongly charged with sexual signification, but this signification is quite unstable. The man might find himself as a primo and has to let himself be voiced by a woman; or he plays the secondo part but still is dominated by his songbird. Men and women may try on each other's traditional roles or they may forgo such roles entirely; they may be impossible to place in gendered binaries in much the same way as a more alluring monster with a long tradition in the West, the androgyne.

Monstrous Bodies

Until now we have sought the monstrosity of the four-hand monster primarily in the play of the hands: the androgyny with which the two sets of hands meld together, the embryonic community they form, and the way the two pairs of hands manage to both become one and remain separate. But this monstrosity also concerns the part of the body that doesn't have a voice, that doesn't bespeak its meanings on the keyboard. Four-hand playing isn't just structured by means of gaze and hand—that is to say, by the interactions of two separate automata that sometimes seem to blend. What Edward Cone describes as the aim of four-hand playing is a "blending of two players."[39] This "blending" is not just motivated by the score. After all, while players may occasionally find themselves crossing hands, or complementing one another's exertion, their bodies interact far more continuously, and in fact start doing so the moment they sit down at the instrument. Their torsos will touch, their shoulders

---

[39] Cone, *The Composer's Voice*, 135.

may rub against each other, and they will sense each other's breath from the first measure on.

This kind of bodily interaction almost by necessity had something monstrous for the nineteenth century. After all, while the body was allowed to spread itself like an amoeba before the piano, it was forced into ever tighter corsets off the keyboard. The impetuous corporeality of four-hand playing, the excess of body which was allowed to splay itself across the keyboard, was a local antidote to the sublimation of physicality elsewhere. Reports of Schubertiades, Liszt evenings, and the like from the first half of the nineteenth century again and again remark on the relationship between four-hand playing and dancing. The many four-handed waltzes that were sold early in the century were not exclusively intended for communal playing and listening, but also were meant to allow an audience to dance. Eliza Wille, for instance, relates how she danced to an "orchestra" composed of Liszt and Chopin: "I happily remember an evening when Liszt and Chopin played waltzes four hands, for a small, intimate circle, and us young girls were allowed to dance to the music."[40] Similarly, the Schubert evenings that took place in the home of the Spaun family didn't just feature four-hand playing, but also frequent dancing.[41]

Interestingly, this is a constellation we largely seek in vain in nineteenth-century literature: four-hand playing abounds in literature, but no one dances to it. One possible reason is that most of these scenes come from the second half of the century—that is to say, a time when scenes of dancing to four-hand music disappear from diaries, memoirs, and letters as well. As the piano got larger, as it started to move into the center of the parlor, and as it colonized more of the domestic sphere, it became harder to dance in the piano room. The morality of the age must have done its part to drive dance from the parlor, and to divorce four-hand piano playing from bodies moving across a dance floor. The fact that within one generation the dancing body disappeared from the four-hand scene (in particular the emphatically physical waltz) must have been recognized—perhaps with a sense of nostalgia, perhaps with a sense of guilt. By 1884, in Edmond de Goncourt's *Chérie*, the analogy between dance and four-hand playing has become simply that—an analogy. "Grand-father promised me that every Sunday we'd dance on the piano together."[42] Literal dance, once an organic relationship between bodies, has become mere metaphor. The melding of limbs, the close bodily embrace of the dance becomes the even more persistent closeness of the two players sitting side by side at the piano. In the figure of the four-handed monster, the body gets its revenge: banished from the social pursuits around the piano, it instead hijacks the instrument itself. The

---

[40] Eliza Wille, *Richard Wagner and Eliza Wille—Fünfzehn Briefe des Meisters nebst Erinnerungen von Eliza Wille* (Leipzig: Breitkopf & Härtel, 1912), 58.

[41] Arthur Loesser, *Men, Women and Pianos: A Social History* (New York: Dover, 1990), 161.

[42] Edmond de Goncourt, *Chérie* (Paris: Charpentier, 1884), 196.

decorporialization of the listener finds its analogue in the corporeal overdetermination of the players.

Cone's "four-handed monster" is thus monstrous not because of its four hands but, rather, because of the body that lies behind them. *Monstrous* here also means "obscene." After all, in the nineteenth century, hands and faces had the right to speak about women or for women, while the rest of the body most certainly did not. Obscenity lies in the fact that a body part appears without being animated by the subject, without being used by the subject to communicate; rather, it appears for its own sake, creating meaning without the subject having any say in it.[43] Face and hand, in other words, are *media* or *means* of communication, while a bare breast, a carelessly exposed leg, or even a carefully covered backside signify with brute immediacy and without the subject's input.[44]

In Adolph L'Arronge's comedy *Mein Leopold* (1873), young Anna is certain that her piano teacher "will propose to me" because he keeps invading her space while they play four-hand piano. And it isn't the motion of his hands that has Anna convinced: "When my right hand was busy in the discant, his left hand found the bass, and if I pushed the pedal with my foot he too found the forte pedal with his other foot." Her mother responds that none of this "is particularly decent," but she too is unconcerned with the hands: she is upset "that you don't just play four-hand, but also four-foot."[45] But the feet are not the only body parts that may find each other in four-hand playing, although a good bourgeois daughter might be forgiven for not mentioning them. The feet, the arms, the legs, the torsos, and the backsides—all of them are in close proximity in four-hand playing, and all of them may touch, often for extended periods of time.

Enter Sandman

But there is another body the two four-hand players share, a body that is at once more physical and more metaphysical. This is the body bespoken by the voice. Of course, the pianists themselves do not vocalize; they do not produce any bodily sound themselves unless they breathe loudly or whisper to one another. But the two bodies that find themselves in such obscene agreement on the piano stool communicate through a third body—a metaphysical, transubstantiated body of sound. And the two players partake of this third, shared body in a manner that is itself obscene. The form of four-hand playing forces upon the players certain kinds of

---

[43] Hans-Peter Duerr, *Der Mythos vom Zivilisationsprozess, Band 3: Obszönität und Gewalt* (Frankfurt: Suhrkamp, 1995),

[44] Richard Leppert, *The Sight of Sound—Music, Representation, and the History of the Body* (Berkeley and Los Angeles: University of California Press, 1993), 153–88.

[45] Adolph L'Arronge, *Mein Leopold*, in *Dramatische Werke* (Berlin: Stilke, 1908), 1: 8.

bodily communication: on the one hand, insofar as body parts that aren't supposed to speak have to communicate, but on the other, because the body that produces the piano's sound is a shared one.

This is because four-hand playing doesn't just distribute notes, chords, and roles between the two players; it distributes a whole array of ancillary activities. Some of them are contingent and can be performed by either one of the players (for instance, turning the pages), but there is one activity that four-hand piano practice to this day usually assigns to the secondo—pedaling. Unlike turning pages, pedaling turns out to be anything but ancillary; for what we earlier referred to as the subjectivity and the voice of the piano is centrally determined by the pedals. What is paradoxical about this situation is that the player who usually plays the role of songbird (*le chant*) doesn't actually get to determine what this voice sounds like.

The fact that primo and secondo share the same pedals, and the fact that the secondo usually controls them, isn't strictly speaking a dictate of the score. Still, it is clear that the modulations demanded in the score can be created only through this strange arrangement. Even professional pianists require some practice to pedal for another person. And indeed, pedaling in four-hand playing is a unique configuration, as a comparison with the configuration singer/accompanist makes clear. Of course, the pianist "determines" the singer to a certain point, but this determination is entirely external and mostly a matter of rhythm and speed. The primo, however, surrenders far more to the secondo. Imagine a singer whose sound could be manipulated by the accompanist just by pushing down a pedal! This is the role of the primo: a songbird, but a mechanical songbird. When it opens its mouth, the other player determines what kind of sound emerges. The fundamental uncanniness of this arrangement was thematized by E. T. A. Hoffmann in "The Sandman," where the automaton Olimpia plays duets by herself in a more uncanny anticipation of Wilde's Aunt Agatha.[46]

Olimpia, it turns out, is a gifted pianist and a unique vocalist. Her preferred means of expression is no accident, for Hoffmann seems to have given much thought to the uncanniness of the piano's voice. Four-hand scenes are very rare in his oeuvre, but Hoffmann is almost obsessive in investigating the central terms that make the four-hand voice so strange. The question of how body, voice, and subject relate is central to much of his work. And again and again, Hoffmann's investigations proceed by multiplying one of these factors—that is to say, Hoffmann asks what happens if one body has several voices, or one voice has several bodies, or one body houses multiple subjects. And it is precisely this kind of asymmetrical multiplication (two subjects, one voice) that creates the strange vocality of four-hand piano playing.

---

[46] E. T. A. Hoffmann, *Poetische Werke in sechs Bänden* (Berlin: Aufbau Verlag, 1963), 2: 371f.

The fact that the inventor of creatures like Olimpia himself wrote music for piano suggests that for Hoffmann the doppelganger was linked to the mechanical voice of the piano. Consider the famous scene in "The Sandman," in which little Nathanaël hides in his father's study in order to witness his father's nighttime meeting with the mysterious sandman. Nathanaël witnesses his father and evil "Master Coppélius" hunched over a "work."[47] The boy cannot see what their four hands are working on, but the narrative suggests that it is indeed Olimpia, the "lifeless doll" who ensorcels grown-up Nathanaël, and who bedevils him with her mechanical voice. The scene in which Nathanaël fully falls in love with her unfolds at a piano evening: "Olimpia played the grand piano with great facility, and sang a bravura aria with her bright, almost cutting glass bell of a voice."[48] "The Sandman" presents Cone's four-handed monster as a robot woman: the mechanical songbird accompanies herself on the piano. The unification of Schubert and Vogl is realized here as a technological feat— melody and accompanist enter a personal union, just without a person.

Hoffmann was quite familiar with the process of transcribing and arranging pieces for piano; most of the works Hoffmann reviewed for the *Allgemeine musikalische Zeitung* were either piano transcriptions or piano *Auszüge* with additional parts for voice. And he was particularly well versed in four-hand transcriptions. In the summer of 1810, he not only reviewed Beethoven's Symphony no. 5, but also its four-hand transcription.[49] Hoffmann, one of the promulgators of what Carl Dahlhaus has called the "romantic metaphysics of instrumental music,"[50] consistently emphasized the importance of the voice as opposed to the semantic content of song, and tried to apply this logic to musical instruments. And yet, the voice does not function in Hoffmann's fictions as a sort of *unisono*—it is never an index of the unity or singularity of the individual or of its body.

Another story of Hoffmann's which deals with mechanical constructs come to life (as well as one such construct that turns out to be a human being under a spell) is "Nutcracker and Mouse King" (the basis for Tchaikovsky's *Nutcracker*). On Christmas Eve, the nutcracker commands his armies in the living room, in a war not against a four-handed monster but against a seven-headed, and thus fourteen-handed one—the mouse king. This mouse king is a variation on an old German legend, the rat king. This mythic creature was supposed to consist of an entire mischief of rats whose tails and hind legs have grown together. The mouse king thus consists of one body that is shared by several individuals. The mouse king reverses the uncanny corporeality of the doll Olimpia: instead of several bodies with

---

[47] Hoffmann, *Poetische Werke*, 2:378.
[48] Hoffmann, *Poetische Werke*, 2:400.
[49] E. T. A. Hoffmann, *Sämtliche Werke* (Frankfurt: Deutscher Klassiker Verlag, 2003), 551.
[50] Carl Dahlhaus, "Studien zur romantischen Musikästhetik," *Archiv für Musikwissenschaft* 42, no. 3 (1985): 163.

one voice, the mouse king has one body, but several voices: "Squeaking in triumph from seven throats, the mouse king approached."[51]

Can a creature that "squeaks from seven throats" speak with one voice? And wouldn't a multiplicity of voices raise the question of which one squeaks for the creature as such? These were the questions that occupied an author like Hoffmann, fascinated as he was with subjects who were not quite identical with themselves. In a letter he wrote to Carl Schall in 1822, Hoffmann complains about the kind of mechanical writing he has to do:

> You'd have to have four hands like a flea, and since four hands require two heads, it would be necessary that the head appoint a vice-head as its vice-roy, as its lieutenant, or at least as its careful director of a department.[52]

This letter points to a central aspect of Hoffmann's characterization of four-handed monsters generally: four hands require two heads. Four-handed monsters, as much as they are about unification and indistinction, have something schizophrenic, since the head has to "appoint a vice-head" as its "viceroy, lieutenant." Just as in Lady Agatha's bizarre four-handedness monstrosity, it is a question of power; but in Hoffmann, that question is far more vexed than in Wilde, for all the comparisons Hoffmann invokes in his letters imply an asymmetry of power between the four hands and their two heads. In reporting on a concert by the pianist Sigismund Thalberg from 1838, the *Allgemeine musikalische Zeitung* invokes many-handedness as a sign of the subject's mastery over its own body, as well as the body of the instrument (and by extension of music itself): "Parisian news claimed that he was four-handed, but we should be inclined to concede to him six—so awesome and amazing his ability."[53] Hoffmann by contrast insists that four hands need two heads: many-handedness doesn't symbolize the omnipotence of the subject; instead, it points to the internal fracture of this subject. After all, who is head, who is vice-head? Who is whose "lieu-tenant," who stands in for the other as a mere placeholder? Who is to be master—that's all?

In a fairy tale included in *Prinzessin Brambilla*, Hoffmann raises the question of what exactly happens to the subject when it sits as a four-handed mouse king before a piano sonata. There, a princess gives birth "to two most darling princelings, although they were twins [*Zwillinge*], should have been called ones [*Einling*], for they had grown together at their bottoms."[54] The way the narrator vacillates between twinning and oneness in many respects encapsulates the scandal of the four-handed

---

[51] Hoffmann, *Poetische Werke*, 3: 272.

[52] Letter from E. T. A. Hoffmann to Carl Schall, January 19, 1822; quoted in Peter Faesi, *Künstler und Gesellschaft bei E.T.A. Hoffmann* (Dissertation, University of Basel,1975), 84–85.

[53] *Allgemeine musikalische Zeitung* 41, no. 1 (January 2, 1839): 12.

[54] Hoffmann, *Poetische Werke*, 5:734.

monster. What is particularly vexing in the fairy tale is that the four-handed monster is a prince, or perhaps two princes. Just as a pianist, a successor to a throne ought to be single, a soloist; sharing the instrument of state with another seems to play havoc with sovereignty. When the king grows "a bit concerned with this double blessing," his ministers try to calm him down by positing that "in general the entire governmental sonata would sound fuller and more magnificent when played *à quatre mains*."[55] Hoffmann took the figure of the double prince from a parable by Georg Christoph Lichtenberg (1742–1799), who had intended it as a commentary on the absolutist state.[56] Hoffmann turns them into a psychological cypher; two princes of exactly opposite disposition become a symbol for the *a priori* split subject.

The composer Carl Reinecke (1824–1910) wrote a piece that brought this entire menagerie together: a suite about the seven-throated monster for the four-handed monster and its governmental sonata "*à quatre mains*." His suite "Nutcracker and Mouse King" for four-hand piano based on Hoffmann's fairy tale (op. 46) appeared with Breitkopf & Härtel in 1865 (the overture appeared separately in 1855). Reinecke's success as a composer was mixed, and he was active mostly as a piano pedagogue and as an author of piano transcriptions. Reinecke's suite follows Hoffmann's plot quite closely and thus also depicts the climactic battle between the mouse army and the automata of Godfather Drosselmeyer.

Reinecke includes an interesting joke in the piece. For much of the piece, primo and secondo together simulate the mechanical stride of the army of automata, but toward the end of the piece the automata wind down and run out of energy. Primo and secondo slow down in unison, then slow down further, and then pause for a moment altogether. The primo stays silent for two full measures while the secondo plays five identical groups of four quick (*molto piu animato*) sixteenth notes—we are listening to the mechanical tin soldiers being rewound. Once the secondo's wind-up work is done, the two players return to the main theme and to the old tempo. The piano, or perhaps better, the four-handed monster *at* the piano, becomes for a moment a wind-up toy that needs to be rewound. And it should no longer come as a surprise that it is the secondo who has the job of rewinding it. In assigning the roles in this way, Reinecke mixes the content of the piece—the automaton—with the form of the piece: four-hand playing. The rewinding of the automaton is at once a rewinding of the piano, a rewinding by the party that controls the voice. Reinecke equates the uncanny march of the automata with the relationship between primo and secondo—and thus musicalizes the way of thinking four-handedness Hoffmann had pioneered in his prose.

Hoffmann's uncanny mechanical doublings—the songbird who accompanies herself, the automaton that rewinds itself—point to the central scandal in

---

[55] Hoffmann, *Poetische Werke*, 5:734.
[56] Gerald Bär, *Das Motiv des Doppelgängers als Spaltungsphantasie in der Literatur und im deutschen Stummfilm* (Amsterdam: Rodopi, 2005), 231.

four-hand vocality: there is simply no other musical arrangement where one subject intones a melody while the other gets to decide on the intonation. The primo opens its mouth and moves its tongue, but it is the secondo who decides what comes out. This arrangement dislodges and unsettles what Roland Barthes has called "the grain of the voice." This grain is to be found at the intersection of voice and speech: it cannot be reduced to either the expression of the subject, the lexicon of the language it uses to express itself, or to the phonemes of the voice. Rather, the grain refers back to the materiality of the body; it is "the body in the voice as it sings."[57]

Mladen Dolar has put the same idea in a similar way: the voice, he writes, "is the material element recalcitrant to meaning, and when we speak in order to say something, then the voice is precisely that which cannot be said."[58] When Theodor Adorno undertook a physiognomy of what he calls "radio voice," he meant something analogous: just as the physiognomy of a face has as its objects that part of the face that doesn't intend to mean (an extension of the body parts that do not mean in themselves), so Adorno's physiognomics of the voice focuses on that which isn't supposed to be intrinsically meaningful, that which is just supposed to be a vessel for information, communication, or melody.[59] As Adriana Cavarero has shown, the reason why this vessel is traditionally understood as secondary is that it is tied to the animal *zoe*, while whatever is carried depends on *logos*.[60] Dolar's conception of the voice, Barthes's *grain*, and the Greek *phone* are all physical—they speak the body.

In four-hand piano playing, one player thus manipulates the grain of the other's voice. And because this is an unusual arrangement for pianists, even seasoned players tend to switch roles only rarely—one usually acts as the manipulator while the other is manipulated.[61] It would go too far to claim that there is something emphatically sexual about this. But it is clear that the monster into which the two players meld concerns the shared voice of the instrument as well; once again, there seems to be something uncanny, something threatening about the way boundaries between individuals break down in four-hand playing, something monstrous about the way the new entity behaves.

The two young duettists Elizabeth Joy Roe and Greg Anderson have put a characteristically ironic spin on this configuration. These two Julliard graduates are one of the most successful piano duos active in the United States at the moment, mostly because of their inventive, frequently pop-inflected repertoire (a few years ago they premiered a four-hand transcription of the *Star Wars* soundtrack), and their ironic

---

[57] Roland Barthes, "The Grain of the Voice," in *Image/Music/Text*, ed. Stephen Heath (New York: Hill and Wang, 1979), 188.

[58] Mladen Dolar, *A Voice and Nothing More* (Cambridge, MA: MIT Press, 2006), 15.

[59] Theodor W. Adorno, "Radio Voice," in *The Current of Music* (Frankfurt: Suhrkamp, 2007), 499–559.

[60] Adriana Cavarero, *For More than One Voice* (Palo Alto: Stanford University Press, 2005), 33–36.

[61] I am indebted to Jeffrey Kallberg for this information.

emphasis on the eroticism of four-hand performance. In 2007, the two first performed their arrangement of Astor Piazzolla's *Libertango*, which the composer had originally written for the Octeto Nuevo de Buenos Aires. The danger in transcribing a piece like *Libertango* is that the sound of the guitar cannot be translated for the piano and that its characteristic vulnerability is hard to reproduce on a grand piano. Anderson and Roe sidestep these pitfalls by means of a fascinating trick: the primo plays both guitar and accompanying instruments; the secondo's contributions on the keyboard are comparatively meager. That is because the secondo is busy in the piano itself, in the sounding body of the instrument. While the primo takes charge of the keys, the secondo reaches into the belly of the instrument and muffles those piano strings that would correspond to guitar notes in the original score. This indeed creates a sound strikingly reminiscent of plucked guitar strings.

Anderson and Roe take the idea of the secondo as voice-giver and voice-regulator to the extreme. The primo is responsible for almost all the notes in the score, but the sound of the instrument is created by the secondo. The scandalous way in which the secondo interferes with the primo's sound is pushed from the twilight of the pedals to the main stage. The secondo disappears into the instrument up to his elbows—like the protagonist of David Cronenberg's film *Naked Lunch*, whose hands disappear into his typewriter. In each case, the boundaries of the subject dissolve, but so do the boundaries of the work of art this subject creates. Instead, the work itself becomes scandalously physical; it impinges on the creative subject in ways that feel improper, immodest, monstrous.

The implicit eroticism of this arrangement is heightened by the two duettists themselves—helped by the fact that they are both quite good-looking. They present the manipulation of the other's embodied voice not just as a scandal of sound but also as visually scandalous. That is because the secondo has to lean rather closely over the primo's hands in order to cover the "guitar" notes quickly enough. The pose at times actually resembles tango moves: the two sets of arms and hands interlock, the bodies almost at a right angle. The metaphoric dance of the hands on the keyboard becomes literalized into an actual tango. The artists themselves have remarked that they "were struck by the parallel qualities" between tango and four-hand piano playing, "the elements of sensuality, intimacy, and drama, and thus we created our arrangement... to demonstrate this connection."[62]

Machine Voices

The previous sections of this chapter have celebrated the four-hand arrangement (both as an arrangement on the printed page and as an arrangement in domestic

---

[62] Interview with Gerg Anderson and Elizabeth Joy Roe, 2008.

space) as an instance of anarchy, as a melting away of boundaries of all kinds. But even in this blooming confusion of genders, subjects, and subject positions, there is a censoring agent. This is all the more remarkable since, on first glance, it would seem like mutual censorship and regulation are much more prevalent in other arrangements. What soloist and piano accompanist, or members of a quartet, negotiate by means of glances and nods, four-hand players seem to adjudicate in a far more organic and instinctual fashion. But if visual regulation falls away in four-hand playing, the question of how to coordinate the two sets of hands becomes all the more important when a rhythmically complex orchestral piece—a piece that is, after all, premised on the possibility of visual coordination—makes the awkward transition onto the piano keyboard. The orchestra relies on its flamboyant visual reference point, the conductor; where does he go when a symphony is transcribed for four hands, but its complexity is maintained?

Given the gendered dynamics of four-hand arrangements and four-hand playing, it is actually surprising that it is not the masculine pole of the duo—that is to say, the secondo—who is usually entrusted with the task. For one thing, both players get to slow down or rush through the proceedings; and for another, speed is not the same as complexity. For what would a leader-follower arrangement do with triples, syncopation, or *tremolando*? Instead, it is clear that both players have their own internal conductor, a kind of musical superego. Adorno points to the fact that in playing four hands, "tempo and dynamics" cannot unfold freely subject only to "capricious inclinations"; instead it must be regulated by "text and instructions."[63] But how are these instructions communicated? Unlike in the quartet, where visual intuition can register swaying instruments or the movements of players' feet, this superego cannot be communicated visually at all. The moment the other's hands move, it is already too late.

If, for instance, the initial chords of Beethoven's *Eroica* are supposed to sound crisp in a four-hand arrangement, the duettists, especially if they are not professionals, cannot rely on visual cues to coordinate. They will most likely rely on breathing to communicate rhythm. The "inner conductor" gets the body to communicate with another, but it bypasses the hands in doing so. The torso moves, the lungs inflate, the spine straightens, and by the time the hands move, all the important information has already been shared. They arrive late to their own party.

That is, if the players have good timing. Adorno claims in his essay that in many ways the lack of such timing is characteristic of four-hand playing. "All four-hand playing is unreliable and fallible." Even "two piano soloists with the highest rhythmical training will find it more difficult to play precisely than an average orchestra."[64] Adorno is not alone in his assessment; we have encountered similar

---

[63] Theodor W. Adorno, "Four Hands, Once Again," *Cultural Critique* 60 (Spring 2005): 2.
[64] Adorno, "Four Hands, Once Again," 3.

judgments again and again in earlier chapters of this book. Mistakes were part of the program for this quintessentially dilettantish form of music, and Adorno's assessment in the rearview mirror not only celebrates the utopian moment of togetherness and communal movement but also points to the opposite moments, in which the other's movements are reminders that we are messing up, are indeed bound to mess up.

Not only the voice is shared in four-hand playing; so is the agent of control and censorship. The four-handed monster does not constitute itself simply by way of a scandalous and libidinous manipulating and being manipulated. Somewhere between the bodies lies a metronome, a code, maybe even a law. Just as four-hand playing almost by necessity creates moments of transgression only to punish them forthwith, so the perverse melding of the four-hand voice always also carries in it a moment of accommodation to an external law. It's a law that comes, like the four-hand voice, from nowhere, but that nevertheless demands complete adherence from both players, even if it does not originate with either of them. Four-handed monstrosity thus is not just something alluring and scandalous, it's something that would need to be domesticated and controlled from the outside. It also has a petite bourgeois element; it accommodates itself to the world as it is, without questioning or chafing. The pedantic utopia of absolute synchronization is both a fantasy of complete community and a desire for total mimicry.

Tracing this pedantic utopianism requires turning to a piece that isn't really four-hand music in the strict sense, and it also requires a leap outside of the timeframe of this study. For while the fantasy of absolute synchronization is in evidence throughout the nineteenth century, it was the late twentieth century that brought it to a head. What if two pianos played an absolutely identical melody? Two pianists face one another, or sit side by side, and press the same keys at exactly the same moment. On the one hand, such an arrangement gets rid of the concrete corporeal strangeness of the four-handed monster; a piece like this requires perfect, almost machine-like automatism, not the careful sifting of signals and motions. On the other hand, the uncanny corporeality of the four-hand voice is finally completely realized here—the two duettists share one sounding body, albeit on two instruments.

Steve Reich composed his *Piano Phase* for two pianos in 1967, an example of so-called process music. The piece starts with precisely the configuration just described, with two pianos repeating the same short fragment of melody. But the "phase" that gives the piece its name derives from the fact that, with each repetition, the two pianos separate ever so slightly from their *unisono* figure. Difference enters into repetition. Reich discovered this technique by accident when trying to loop two tapes with the same sound fragment synchronously. One of the two tape decks slowed down and the "phase effect" was born. In the final composition, two tapes play the same brief sound bite ("It's gonna rain," a snipped Reich recorded from the tirade of a San Francisco street preacher) synchronously, until one of the tapes slows down.[65] The two initially synchronous voices start sliding vis-à-vis the other, at first imperceptibly but soon creating a whole range of interesting sound effects.[66] Eventually the slower tape has fallen back enough that the canon-like relationship between the two voices stops and the two tapes repeat "It's gonna rain" in unison.

In interviews, Reich claimed that he at first thought it impossible that instruments and actual musicians could create this effect. He proved himself wrong with his *Piano Phase*, which applies the same idea to human players and a simple melody. Two pianos repeat the same twelve-note figure in unison, then one of the two players will "accel. very slightly." The two sound figures begin their canonic slide; they pass each other almost tectonically, until eventually the slower piano has fallen back enough to restore unison. Reich first experimented with the concept by recording himself playing the little melody fragment, looping the tape, and playing a duet with his recorded loop—an idea he would later repurpose in a piece called *Video Phase*. In this piece, a marimba player duets with a video image of himself in a similar technological canon.

Piano Phase in many respects represents the terminal moraine of the voice of four-hand piano playing. As the composer notes, in the piece it doesn't matter "whether a musical process is realized through live human performance or through some electro mechanical means."[67] Whether we are hearing two pianists, a single pianist paired with a audio or video tape, or two tapes looping, it doesn't make the voice we hear any more or less impersonal. *Piano Phase* is an echo of the scandal embodied by Hoffmann's doll Olimpia: a machine that accompanies itself on the piano, mechanical playing and a "glass bell of a voice."

For *Piano Phase* doesn't have two different parts or voices at all. The acoustic effect is quite the opposite: before the phasing starts, the audience hears only one voice—*unisono*. As the shift begins to become perceptible, it does not create an impression of polyvocality but, rather, seems to change the resonance, as though the acoustics or even the shape of the room had suddenly changed.[68] Once the two parts separate further, this resonance effect is replaced with a veritable echo. Only fairly late in the phase does an actual rhythmic effect set it.

Piano Phase is not really a duet, with two parts. It is not a dialogue of any kind but, rather, a monologue that is technologically replicated and manipulated vocally. But, all of the differences notwithstanding, the voice that the two pianos share is essentially that of four-hand players. In both cases, one player manipulates the voice of the other (by simulating effects of resonance, of echo, of rhythm); and in

---

[65] Keith Potter, *Four Musical Minimalists: La Monte Young, Terry Riley, Steve Reich, Philip Glass* (New York: Cambridge University Press, 2000), 169.

[66] Paul Epstein, "Pattern, Structure and Process in Steve Reich's 'Piano Phase,'" *Musical Quarterly* 72 (1986), no. 4:496.

[67] Steve Reich, "Music as a Gradual Process," in *Steve Reich: Writings on Music*, ed. Paul Hillier (New York: Oxford University Press, 2002), 35.

[68] Epstein, "Reich's 'Piano Phase,'" 498.

both cases, it is hard to tell apart the voices or to speak of one apart from the other. Four-hand playing and *Piano Phase* really know only one voice, albeit one that is co-produced by two players.

But there is another element that four-hand piano playing and the two keyboards of Reich's *Piano Phase* have in common—that of training. In the interview mentioned earlier, Reich seems genuinely surprised that two tape players can be simulated this easily by two human beings. In *Piano Phase*, humans simulate what machines have done before. And as human being duets with machine, adjusts to and emulates the machine, all semblance of expression, subjectivity, and emotion falls away. The point of Hoffmann's characterization of Olimpia is that the mechanical doll cannot express anything either by playing or by her voice—she can merely spit out what has been fed into her. And in extreme cases, four-hand players can only regurgitate the dexterity, the practice that he or she has been fed over the years, rather than something that would count in a deeper sense as his or hers. Four-hand playing, on one extreme, does not express or celebrate communication, emotion, and content, but simply what nature and incessant drills have wrought. Four-hand playing as a display of natural dispositions, and of gymnastic dexterity, will be the topic of the next two chapters.

5

The Semantics of the Hand

> It is obvious that you can no more be certain of a good offspring than you can be certain of a good tune if you play two fine airs at once on the same piano.
> —G. K. Chesterton, *Eugenics and Other Evils* (1922)

In his fragmentary memoirs (*Erinnerungen aus meinem Leben*, 1842), Carl Czerny tells the story of how he became Beethoven's pupil. "On a winter day my father and I hiked from the Leopoldstadt into the center of town, into a street called the *Tiefer Graben*, then climbed high, perhaps into the fifth or sixth floor, where a rather filthy-looking servant took us to see Beethoven." In Beethoven's apartment, "a very disorderly-looking room," the master bid little Carl sit "on a rickety chair at the fortepiano built by the Walter Company," and to play some music.[1] "Since I felt self-conscious about starting with one of his own compositions, I started off with Mozart's Concerto in C-Major."[2] Beethoven sat down next to the boy "and began playing the orchestral melody with his left hand whenever I had only accompanying parts." Czerny withdrew into the accompaniment—a rather unusual primo-secondo relationship. The friendship between these two musicians, which would last until the older man's death, was thus formed over a kind of four-hand flirt.

Eventually, Czerny worked up the courage and played an actual Beethoven piece, namely the *Pathétique*, which had only recently come out. Beethoven watched him carefully and then declared, "The boy has talent, I'll teach him." But not just Beethoven scrutinized young Carl's playing in that disheveled room in the Tiefer Graben; the boy turned the tables on the master and in turn sized up the older man. Not his playing, of course, but his hands: "His hands were overgrown with hair and the fingers were very broad, especially at the tips."[3] While Beethoven probably paid attention to Czerny's technique and quickness, little Carl Czerny was looking for

---

[1] Carl Czerny, *Erinnerungen aus meinem Leben* (Baden Baden: Heitz, 1968), 13.
[2] Czerny, *Erinnerungen aus meinen Leben*, 15.
[3] Czerny, *Erinnerungen aus meinem Leben*, 13.

something else in Beethoven's hands: he was looking for the essence of the genius pianist in the narrowest sense; he wanted to discern the *natural* forces that stood behind the master's mastery. And while only a Beethoven gets to judge potential pupils from on high, even a ten-year-old boy is allowed the reverse gaze, the one that scrutinizes the master's hand with help from the categories of the observation of nature.

We find a similar form of observation in the childhood recollections of Felix Moscheles (1833–1917), son of the famed pianist Ignaz Moscheles. Moscheles recounts a visit to their London home by his father's friend Felix Mendelssohn-Bartholdy. Little Felix seems to have been too young to be much impressed by Mendelssohn's virtuosic playing, but he remembers paying special attention to the composer's hands. "As a little boy I was mainly impressed by his long chord-grasping fingers, contrasting as they did with my father's small velvety hand." Just like young Carl Czerny on the Continent, little Felix Moscheles in London seems to have categorized the famous musician's hands, and that means he compared them to others. And while Czerny's memoirs do not explicitly name his motivation in applying these categories to hands, Moscheles gets quite specific: he looks at the hands "to lie in wait for the outward manifestations of [Mendelssohn's] genius."[4]

This is the basic experience at the heart of this chapter: for us twenty-first-century readers, the shape and appearance of Beethoven's hand may be interesting as curio or trivia. But at the time when Czerny and Moscheles made their observations, and even more so at the time when they set those observations to paper, that same phenomenon was taken to reveal much more. Any analysis of the popularity of four-hand piano playing in the nineteenth century has to be cognizant of the fact that the hand was for the nineteenth century what the double helix is for us: not just a carrier of meanings, but also an index that puts the entire individual on display, at least for those able to decode nature's secret language. This bio-gnostic sort of thinking was practiced in many musically interested households—the Wagners in Wahnfried are only the most prominent example—and it stands to reason that the two *topoi* were at least unconsciously connected. And even those who refused the premises of this kind of attention to the hand, or who were at least skeptical, knew full well what others thought one could read in a hand. August Strindberg wrote in 1908: "A lot of people pay a great deal of attention to the appearance of the hand, but I have never done so. Be it that I was just trying to be respectful of the secrets of my acquaintances, or that I just resisted looking at hands. I was married to a woman, and I cannot recall ever having looked at her hands."[5] Strindberg himself often turned to scenes of four-hand playing in his works, and he must have been

---

[4] Felix Moscheles, *Fragments of an Autobiography* (New York: Harper & Brothers, 1899), 26.

[5] August Strindberg, *Das Buch der Liebe: Ungedrucktes und Gedrucktes aus dem Blaubuch von August Strindberg* (Munich: Diederichs, 1989), 132.

aware that four-hand playing was the most socially acceptable way of inspecting a woman's hands prior to marrying her.[6]

This chapter thus deals with the question of whether the nineteenth-century mania for four-hand playing is related to the nineteenth-century mania for hands—and whether four-hand playing specifically solicited a diagnostic and physiognomic gaze that was employed by wider and wider circles as the century wore on. Under this kind of gaze the two pairs of hands once again tell a story—but that story is no longer about flirting, desire, and renunciation; rather, it is about descent and dynasty. This is why it is once again in literature where this connection is made most clearly. In particular, we will deal with the literature of naturalism. We will find that Gerhart Hauptmann, for instance, used four-hand piano playing in order to talk about sexuality and heredity among classes that were not naturalism's usual subjects. Hauptmann moves away from pure visual positivism—that is to say, the hand in its pure materiality is not his primary focus—but the hand as executing organ demarcates, via gesture and interaction, a network of descent and heredity for him. While he doesn't follow the physiognomics of Lombroso and his ilk, Hauptmann nevertheless insists on the eminent readability of the hand: just as the "chirognomists" thought they could deduce the human being from its hand, so in Hauptmann's play *Das Friedensfest* the hereditary outlines of the "family catastrophe" (as the play's subtitle describes it) are to be read in hands.

As we saw in the first chapter, nineteenth-century observers witnessed piano playing spread throughout Europe like a plague; and scrutinizing such playing was another favorite pastime, often with diagnostic intent. This scrutiny could occur over long distances (when cultural and music critics weighed in on what people did in their parlors), from a polite medium distance (when guests of the house were treated to a performance) or, as it were, in extreme close-up, when friends, family, or those hoping to become either stood right behind the players, turned pages for them, or leaned on the piano. But what did such eyes see, trained as they were to understand hands as clues, when the daughter of the house played Beethoven? What made her parents proud if her teacher remarked that their child had the right hands for the piano? "Before the invention of sound recording, music was something *seen* as much as heard," Lawrence Kramer writes.[7] The aesthetically minded average citizen of a mid-size European city owned the Beethoven symphonies as transcriptions that could be visually displayed, and he knew the great virtuosos, singers, and classic opera stagings through lithographs and, later, photographs.[8]

---

[6] Strindberg refers to four-hand playing several times in *Taklagsöl* (The Topping Out Party, 1906) and his memoir *Tjänstekvinnans son* (Son of a Servant, 1886).

[7] Lawrence Kramer, *After the Lovedeath: Sexual Violence and the Making of Culture* (Los Angeles: University of California Press, 1997), 129.

[8] Richard Leppert, *The Sight of Sound—Music, Representation and the History of the Body* (Los Angeles: University of California Press, 1993), 1–14.

This visual component had, as we saw, a fetishistic aspect. Music lovers tended to absolutize the visual because they were unable to lay hold of the actual music. The fact that the nineteenth century was obsessed with pictures of the great opera divas (for instance, the *carte-de-visite* renditions of Adelina Patti[9]), who were often shown with their mouths silently agape, makes sense only in a world in which most people who owned such representations would never actually get to hear the voice that went with that open mouth. The same goes for the great theater actors and actresses: Proust's *petit Marcel*, a born fetishist, forms an image of "la Berma" this way, long before he gets to hear her in the theater: "My acquaintance with these lines of Racine's was in black and white, as mere print on the pages of books; but now my heart beat faster at the thought that I would soon see them in the warm, sunny glow shed on them by the Golden Voice."[10]

Such was the fetishistic desire that the nineteenth century lavished on the visual representation of great pianists, whether this was in the shape of drawings of actual concerts or of caricatures. But, of course, the same problem arose: one couldn't capture Thalberg's celerity, Liszt's brilliance, Rachmaninov's genius. The fetishist's solution to this problem is hypostasis. Take that what you can lay hold of and render it absolute. This is how three strands of nineteenth-century culture—the cult of genius, positivism, and the veneration of images—came to intersect on the keyboard. If one wanted to lay hold of Beethoven's genius, one dug up his skull and measured it. And because one couldn't transmit a lifelike impression of what a virtuoso like Rachmaninov did with his hands at the piano, one made plaster casts or photographs of those hands.

From its inception the new medium of photography helped isolate hands, and helped those hands speak in their isolation. Not just the ubiquitous lithographs of "Liszt at the piano" or similar scenes were collector's items; so were photo volumes that brought together the hands of great writers, musicians, conductors, and painters, usually seen from above. But even the famous hand sculptures, such as the cast made by Jean-Baptiste Auguste Clésinger of Chopin's hands (along with a death mask) immediately after the composer's death, became popular pieces of home decoration. The (usually twentieth-century) photo volumes suggest that such casts existed for most of the great musicians of the nineteenth century—many appear to have been made while the artist was still alive.

This is particularly odd if one considers what exactly a bourgeois household was supposed to do with such a book of photographed hands—or with Chopin's hands in bronze on the commode. Hardly any of these hands are actually aesthetically pleasing—and in any event, theirs isn't a kind of beauty one usually knows what to do with. It seems, then, that they were training wheels by means of which the

---

[9] Andrew Wynter, *Curiosities of Toil and Other Papers* (London: Chapman and Hall, 1870), 199.
[10] Marcel Proust, *In the Shadow of Young Girls in Flower* (New York: Penguin, 2002), 13.

members of the household learned and sharpened the gaze that little Carl Czerny and young Felix Moscheles trained on the great pianists they met. These fetish objects want to be approached diagnostically; they teach a gaze that understands the hand as an index toward the natural disposition of the whole person. One could even imagine a guessing game: I show you a hand, and I cover the legend. Can you guess whether it's Gerhart Hauptmann, the Kaiser, or a murderer? And if you guess correctly, how did you do it?

At the same time this seemingly cold, diagnostic gaze always had its erotic element. It is after all among the most sacred duties of the diagnostician to look even when every layperson would avert his eyes in embarrassment or disgust. It is thus not too far from the voyeur's gaze—and phenotypically indistinguishable from it. Only voyeur, fetishist, and diagnostician are permitted a gaze that, as Jean Baudrillard once put it, "cannot get enough of the body," a gaze that gets so close to the body that its corporeal schema dissolves into a plethora of disconnected details. A book full of hands severed by means of photography was intended for, and indeed called forth, such a gaze: that of the diagnostician and the voyeur; or the voyeur who fancies himself a diagnostician; or the voyeur who disguises himself as diagnostician.

In the nineteenth century, the hand was one of the few body parts that men and women were allowed to display to one another and to which they were allowed to pay attention in one another—and if such attention could be camouflaged as diagnostic, and thus in some way scientific, then there were in principle no limits to the devotion to hands. Just as Adalbert Stifter fusses over the "little faces" of his protagonists, the hems of their dresses and their hands, while leaving out the body that connects all these body parts in his descriptions, so a man was allowed to devote himself to a woman's hands, was allowed to look down on them from up high and study the play of her muscles, with an intensity that would be scandalous if devoted to her shoulders, say, or her legs.[11] As we saw in the introduction, our male observer is usually not alone in this view from up high: large gatherings followed along like in an anatomic theater as a body opened itself up before them like a book. Just as in the anatomy books of the seventeenth and eighteenth centuries, in which cadavers pull off their own skin in order to give the viewer a glimpse at their inner organs, so the hands disrobe before the diagnostic gaze, conspiring in their own absolute legibility.[12]

Music thus made possible the fetishist's favorite pastime: lingering with the object, perhaps a little too long, to devote to it attention that may seem unwarranted to the uninitiated. Carl Czerny wrote a series of *Letters of Instructions at the Pianoforte* (*Briefe über den Unterricht auf dem Pianoforte*) to "Little Miss Cäcilie," whom he was

---

[11] Cf. W. G. Sebald, *Die Beschreibung des Unglücks—Zur österreichischen Literatur von Stifter bis Handke* (Salzburg: Residenz, 1985), 29–30.

[12] Cf. Claudia Benthien, *Skin: On the Cultural Border Between Self and the World* (New York: Columbia University Press, 2002), 64f.

unable to teach personally "because of how far away she lived," and whom he thus taught in epistles. In his letters, he guided the "Little Miss" through a whole gamut of topics, from the first steps, via rhythms and striking the keys with precision, all the way to "preferred compositions" for beginning pianists. It is striking how frequently Czerny's letters imagine the hands that they guide across the keyboard by remote control: "What is more, your tender little fingers and hands have all the natural properties that are so important for the Fortepiano."[13] Czerny's imagination does not stop at the hands: While advising little Cäcilie on the ideal posture at the piano his inner eye wanders underneath the piano: "If your little feet are unable to touch the ground, then get a small footstool."[14] And not just the "little feet" are subjects of Czerny's missives; in order to impart perfect posture and technique to his charge, he touches on elbows, armpits, neck, the back of Cäcilie's head, and again and again "your small, tender, but already quite powerful fingers."[15]

This rapturous puppetry of an imagined female body is deeply disturbing for the modern reader—even if one leaves aside the fact that Czerny's puppet was at the time barely twelve years old.[16] But the male gaze from the outside is, as always, carefully legitimated: Czerny selflessly shoulders the responsibility of scrutinizing and disciplining Miss Cäcilie's hands.[17] Czerny is absolutely certain that such disciplining is woefully necessary, for with "such a young, lively little person as my dear Miss Cäcilie" the fingers are "little, disobedient creatures, which, if not reined in, will gallop off like a young horse."[18] To keep in check these little disobedient creatures, to save them from themselves and their self-destructive impulses by keeping them, against their instinct, on the keyboard, that is the paternal task Czerny selflessly sets for himself.

Domesticating the girl's wild hands also means taming her body. That is because her body's movements are supposed to serve those of the hands, and aren't allowed to have any purpose besides: "When both hands have business in the highest or lowest octaves, then a calm inclination of the torso is as necessary as it is appropriate. If difficult pieces require short powerful chords or little jumps, we have to allow our hands a little bit of appropriate leeway. And since you have to look at the notes, and at other times at your hands, a little movement of the head, if not necessary, is at least excusable."[19] Czerny's gaze may strike us as prurient and Victorian; but

---

[13] Carl Czerny, *Briefe über den Unterricht auf dem Pianoforte* (Straubenhardt: Antiquariat-Verlag Zimmermann, 1988), 1.

[14] Czerny, *Briefe über den Unterricht auf dem Pianoforte*, 3.

[15] Czerny, *Briefe über den Unterricht auf dem Pianoforte*, 9.

[16] Grete Wehmeyer, *Die Einzelhaft am Klavier: Die Kunst der Fingerfertigkeit und die industrielle Arbeitsideologie* (Kassel: Bärenreiter, 1983), 95.

[17] Ruth A. Solie, *Music in Other Words* (Berkeley and Los Angeles: University of California Press, 2004), 89; Matthew Head, "'If the Pretty Little Hands Won't Stretch': Music for the Fair Sex in Eighteenth-Century Germany," *Journal of the American Musicological Society* 52 (1999): 203–54.

[18] Czerny, *Briefe über den Unterricht auf dem Pianoforte*, 25.

[19] Czerny, *Briefe über den Unterricht auf dem Pianoforte*, 33.

what is more striking perhaps is the way in which stillness and clarity of boundaries are moralized Otherwise, the rule seems to be: stay still, keep your head fixed, don't move your torso. At least Czerny's attempts at directing an absent female body is limited to one seated at the piano; a few decades later, Hugo Riemann would demand that the dedicated teacher meddle even more in the pupil's life: "It is the teacher's responsibility to attend himself to the bodily health of his pupil, and to ensure that [the pupil] takes care of his or her health by means of long walks, cold baths, etc."[20]

In the first chapter, we pointed out that the woman at the piano is a kind of *vanitas*: she is lost in herself, looks at herself in the mirror of the score, which allows those around her (in particular, the men around her) to make her the object of their gaze. But the naked *vanitas* we know from the history painting can never behold herself in anything but the tiny excerpt offered by the inevitably diminutive mirror she holds before herself. She is privy only to a small subset of her form, while the observer gets to luxuriate in the totality of her beauty. The eroticism of Czerny's letters works much the same way: even though every letter tells "Little Miss Cäcilie" to force her fingers to do this or that, to pay attention to this part of her anatomy or another, Czerny insists at the same time that her play be "natural." In other words, she is not to scrutinize herself too much—her fingers should move as though she were not paying attention to them. The girl at the piano is sexy because she cannot have herself as an object in the same way, or to the same degree as the man has her as his object. That means, above all, that she is not allowed to pay the same kind of attention to her hands, which are objects of Czerny's obsession: "You must get in the habit of looking more at the notes than at your fingers," Czerny reminds her.[21]

But for everyone but Miss Cäcilie, it seems, the opposite maxim holds true: they have gotten into the habit of looking more at the fingers than at the notes. But what are they supposed to look for there? Dexterity or maladroitness? Elegance or mechanics? The two examples we have drawn from Czerny's life point to two different gazes: the one young Carl directs at Beethoven, and the one that grown-up Czerny directs to his "Little Miss Cäcilie." There is the little boy who attempts to espy the master's genius in the physical hand; and the teacher who attends to his charge's hands. The question in what follows is: Czerny describes two gazes that belong to one individual and are directed toward another individual. But what happened when two pairs of hands share a keyboard? What would Czerny have imagined, had he written his letters to two young ladies rather than one? Or if he had put Cäcilie's local teacher, whom he frequently mentions in his letters, on the piano stool alongside her, and thus within reach of her inclined torso, her elbows, and particularly her "little, disobedient" fingers?

---

[20] Hugo Riemann, *Vergleichende theoretisch-praktische Klavierschule*, op. 39 (Leipzig: Kistner, 1890), 3.

[21] Czerny, *Briefe über den Unterricht auf dem Pianoforte*, 33.

In the nineteenth century, in which makeup and fashion conspired to make life and death resemble one another, as Walter Benjamin writes, the hand had to express what face, mien, gesture, and posture could suppress or dissimulate. Slavoj Žižek has called the hand the "ultimate partial object." The hand belongs to us, but not in the way our sense organs do. It is the prosthesis in ourselves. The hand can turn on us, it can fail to heed us, and it can even betray us. In a horror film from 1946, *The Beast with Five Fingers*, starring Peter Lorre, the hand of a brilliant pianist escapes from his coffin and takes revenge on those who have wronged its erstwhile owner. In the course of its bloody campaign the hand does two things: it plays Bach arrangements (for one hand, since the pianist had only one good hand prior to death) and it murders. *The Beast with Five Fingers* is the second Peter Lorre film with homicidal pianists' hands. In *Mad Love* (1935), a remake of *Hands of Orlac* (1924, based on Maurice Renard's novel *Les mains d'Orlac*), Lorre performs transplant surgery on the pianist Stephen Orlac. The hands turn out to belong to an executed killer, which turns Orlac's musical virtuosity homicidal.

Even though the nineteenth century bequeathed to us techniques by which individuals can be identified—above all, of course, fingerprint analysis—the main focus in the interpretation of hands was elsewhere: the hands of Orlac are not interesting because they belong to Orlac, but because of what they tell us about Orlac. The hand is thus not a means of identification but, rather, of classification, subsuming the individual under a *type*. The hermeneutics of the hand weren't meant just to discover data points for identification; rather, they allowed for conclusions about the hands' owner. The pianist Orlac knows that his new hands aren't his much earlier than does the gendarmerie, who insists on running his fingerprints (which, of course, aren't his). That's because rather than measuring them, he has compared his hands with a plaster cast à la Clésinger (fig. 5.1).

The nineteenth century thought it could recognize the criminal, the pervert, the *crétin* by his or her hands—for instance, in Cesare Lombroso's "positivist criminology." Hands could be checked for "atavistic stigmata," which inevitably betrayed the "born criminal" or the nymphomaniac. In Lombroso's *L'uomo delinquente* (*Criminal Man*, 1876), we find a table that puts the length of a person's hand into correspondence with different crimes: firebug, pugilist, adulterer—all of these are supposed to be diagnosable by means of the hand. Tables like Lombroso's postulated a "normal hand" (without fail that of a white bourgeois male) and then interpreted any physiological deviations from that norm as a cause (rather than consequence) of a characterological abnormality; in Lombroso's table, the normal hand shows up in the right corner while the bulk of the table compares it to the averaged measurements of each class of perpetrator.

According to Max Nordau, who coined the term *degeneration*, "Degeneracy betrays itself among men in certain physical characteristics, which are denominated 'stigmata,'" primarily, Nordau claims, "deformities, multiple and stunted growths

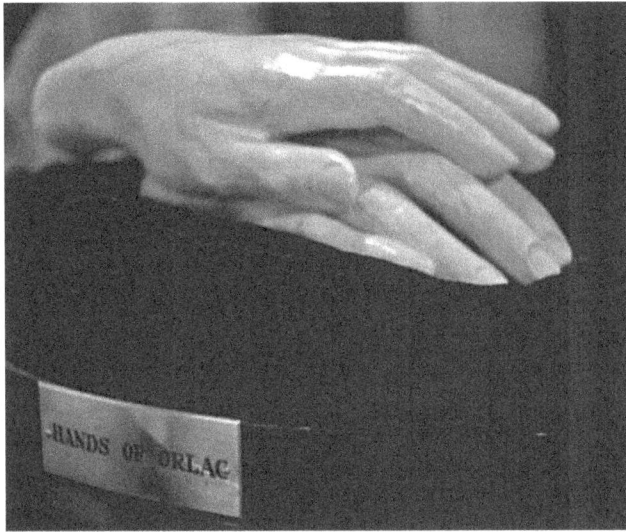

Figure 5.1 A sculpture of the hands of the pianist Stephen Orlac, as it lies on his piano. (From the 1935 film *Mad Love*; © Metro-Goldwyn-Mayer)

in the first line of asymmetry."[22] And Otto Weininger, in his influential *Sex and Character* (1903), proposed that certain physical deformations indicated homosexuality, when, for instance, a person's physiology looks more like that of the opposite sex: "Sexual inversion never occurs without an anatomical approximation of the other sex."[23] How fortunate that Czerny paid close attention and passed along the fact that Beethoven had hirsute hands!

This sustained interest in the hand as a social and hereditary indicator probably had reasons in social history, as well. The stench of the long climb up the social ladder could be purged from faces and dress, but the hand betrayed those who had done physical labor. For even though the hand catalogues of the early twentieth century presented, say, "peasant hands" and "worker's hands" as *biological* types, what their photographs actually depicted, under the guise of biology, were the traces of labor, and thus of social status. And "peasant hands," it goes without saying, couldn't play piano. Putting your hands on the keyboard was the same as submitting to an inspection for unemployment. In the eighteenth century, François Couperain's *L'art de toucher le clavecin* had pointed out to his readers that "men who wish to attain a certain degree of perfection should never do any rough work with their hands."[24] Somewhat paradoxically, the same age apotheosized labor. Four-hand piano playing was useful because it held dual citizenship

---

[22] Max Nordau, *Degeneration* (New York: Appleton, 1895), 17.

[23] Otto Weininger, *Geschlecht und Charakter* (Vienna: Braumüller, 1903), 54.

[24] François Couperain, *L'Art de toucher le clavecin/The Art of Playing the Harpsichord* (Los Angeles: Alfred Music Publishing, 1974), 32.

in this paradoxical world: it was intellectual and physical labor that presupposed unemployment; it was a consciously unproductive form of industry, the opposite of business—art, not handiwork.

But there is a fundamental ambivalence at the center of this art. The hands that meet on the keyboard (and that others watched meet on the keyboard) contained in themselves a semantic component. But since they didn't rest but, rather, raced up and down the keys, this semantic component was visible only in action; and reading hands on the keyboard was different from performing palmistry on a still hand. It was, in other words, a matter of interpreting the actions of the hand, even though those actions did not occasion any product by which the action could be judged. The ambivalence arose because four-hand playing was supposed to be, on the one hand, nonreproductive and asexual but, on the other hand, was covertly resexualized by the supposedly scientific gaze that the nineteenth century cast on hands. Under this gaze, which was in some sense a necessary consequence of the era's relationship to work, the innocent play of the hands becomes a wedding waltz.

August Strindberg remarked that he had been "married to a woman, and I cannot recall ever having looked at her hands."[25] But the idea of looking at the hands of one's spouse, or potential spouse, in order to divine her secrets seems to have been fairly widespread. A writer for the *Leipziger Musikzeitung* suggested that it was the hope for a husband that drove many women to make music in the home: "firstly, it's all the fashion, and secondly, it's the easy way of, if luck be willing, making a match."[26] Strindberg was probably correct in supposing that looking at hands had a match-making component. A woman's piano playing was meant to communicate more than just skill; her swiftness on the keyboard was meant to telegraph her "nature" to potential mates. Her hands fretted and strutted for that very gaze that young Carl Czerny trained on Ludwig van Beethoven.

These techniques of observation anticipate photographic technologies. The gaze they require is already that of a camera. It dismembers the body, renders every detail autonomous.[27] Joëlle Bollock speaks of this effect as a photographic "synecdoche":[28] a part of the body is supposed to contain all there is to know about that body. It is thus not that surprising that, immediately after the actual invention of the camera, the new technology supported and stabilized this preexisting gaze by freezing the object, by making it measurable and commensurable. On the other

---

[25] August Strindberg, *Das Buch der Liebe: Ungedrucktes und Gedrucktes aus dem Blaubuch von August Strindberg* (Munich: Diederichs, 1989), 132.

[26] Quoted in Eduard Hanslick, *Geschichte des Concertwesens in Wien* (Vienna: Braumüller, 1869), 1:67.

[27] Ute Eskilden, ed., *Der Fotografierte Mensch in Bildern der Fotografischen Sammlung im Museum Folkwang* (Göttingen: Steidl, 2004), 61–63.

[28] Joëlle Bolloch, *The Hand* (Paris: Editions Musée d'Orsay, 2007), 7.

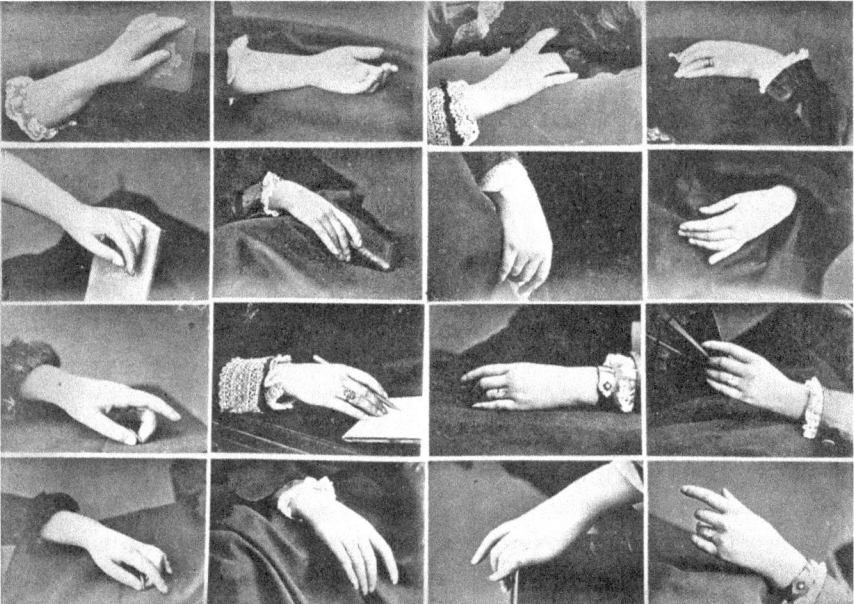

Figure 5.2 One of Jean-Louis Igout's studies of hands. (Musée d'Orsay)

hand, the question of what this new form of documentation was actually supposed to document remained variable: the early pioneers of photography were very interested in movement and gesture. Most famous, perhaps, are Eadweard Muybridge's attempts to capture the "visual unconscious" of human hand movements—in 1887 he used several cameras simultaneously to trace the "Movement of the Hand Drawing a Circle".[29] But other photographers were interested in the organ itself, and they tended to abstract from whatever action a hand was engaged in. The photographer Jean-Louis Igout, for instance, created an almost encyclopedic panel of human gestures, but the gestures are in each case frozen, removed from action (fig. 5.2)—like the gestural vocabulary of the visual arts, each gesture corresponds to one single meaning. Unlike in the case of Muybridge, how a particular pose comes about is left out of the picture. Igout drew upon living subjects for his pictures, but Adolphe Bilordeaux went a step further and created an image of an image: he photographed plaster casts of hands.[30]

But, of course, it was possible to abstract even further: one could cleanse the hand of all traces of gesture and present it to the spectator like a butterfly wriggling on a pin or a cell culture under a microscope. Two distinct traditions tended

---

[29] See, e.g., Jennifer Blessing, ed., *Speaking with Hands: Photographs from the Buhl Collection* (New York: Guggenheim Foundation, 2004), 23.

[30] Bolloch, *The Hand*, 11.

toward this way of looking at bodies, both looking for the hand "in itself"—that is to say, beyond what it did or how it communicated intentionally—but both understanding that "in itself" in fundamentally different ways: positivism, which sought to apprehend the "in itself" statistically and quantitatively, and physiognomy in the style of Johann Kaspar Lavater, which proceeded descriptively and qualitatively. Both of these traditions came to inform the nineteenth century's point of view on hands. And whether observers approached the hand as a statistical datum or an object of intuition and contemplation, what they looked for in a hand remained strikingly constant. The first of these two chirognomic discourses is exemplified by Lombroso's *L'uomo delinquent* (1876); the second one asserts itself in a "Collection of Hand Pictures of Great Men and Women Living and Dead" by Rudolf Voigt. The ways of reading hands employed in both texts strikingly resemble Czerny's way of looking at pianists' hands.

This is not entirely surprising because piano playing generally, and the piano praxis of the nineteenth century specifically, isolated the hand in exactly the ways that the hermeneutics of men like Lombroso and Voigt depended on. Even on a purely optical level, the tables and schemas relied on by the would-be interpreters of hands frequently resemble the scene of four-hand piano playing. In many cases the position of the hands seems directly inspired by the way a hand looks on a keyboard. The graphics in Lombroso's books typify the outline of the human hand, as well as the lines on the palm. Their positions resemble those of pianists at a keyboard, as though the numbered "types" Lombroso compiles were indeed players seated next to one another playing only with their left hands. But Lombroso also focuses on the *palm* of the hand, which of course is one part of the hand that has to remain invisible on the keyboard.

Voigt's coffee table book, simply titled *Hands* (*Hände*), was published almost a half-century after Lombroso's work—it appeared in 1929, and thus after the piano four-hand boom had receded. But it remains relevant for our discussion for several reasons. Most of the pictures of hands Voigt gathers in his volume are nineteenth-century photographs, or else are twentieth-century photographs of plaster casts. In any event, most of the personages Voigt brings together in his book hail from the heyday of four-hand piano playing. That means that although Voigt's perspective may be of slightly later vintage, the raw material he relies on is owed to analogous obsessions in the nineteenth century. For the images Voigt systematizes were almost entirely photographed, drawn, or sculpted in the nineteenth century— his encyclopedism may be new, but the gaze his pictures depend on is that of the time when the pictures were made.

Voigt's volume gathers architects, scientists, but overwhelmingly musicians— and the way he presents them once again recalls hand positions in piano playing. Many of the pictures—for instance, the picture of Franz Liszt's hand (fig. 5.3), Felix Mendelssohn-Barholdy's (fig. 5.4), and Richard Wagner's (fig. 5.5)—suggest the perspective of a person leaning over a piano keyboard. In other representations— for instance, in the picture of Clara Schumann's hand (fig. 5.6)—the hand

The Semantics of the Hand

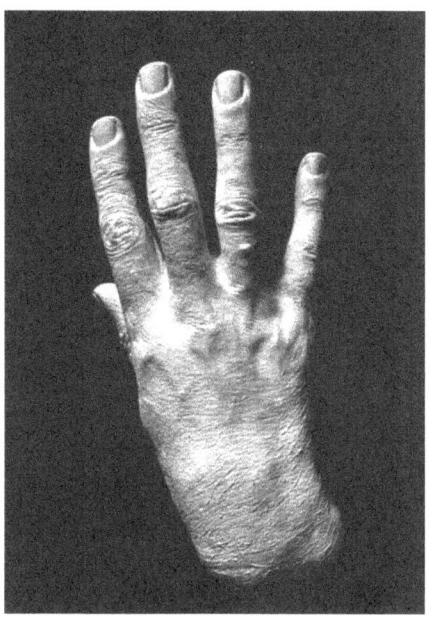

Figure 5.3 Franz Liszt
Photographs from Rudolf Voigt, *Hände—Eine Sammlung von Handabbildungen Grosser Toter und Lebender* (*Hands: A Collection of Hand-Pictures of famous Living and Dead*), 1929.

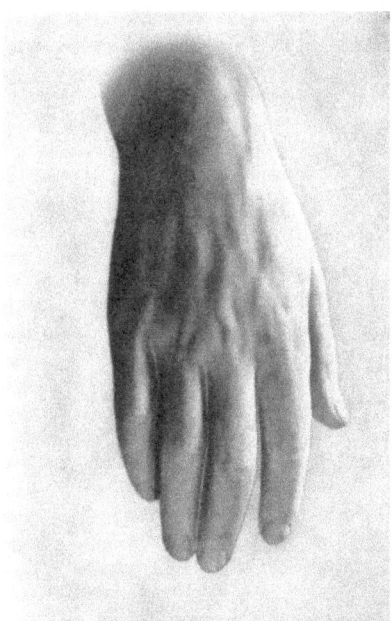

Figure 5.4 Felix Mendelssohn-Bartholdy
Photographs from Rudolf Voigt, *Hände—Eine Sammlung von Handabbildungen Grosser Toter und Lebender* (*Hands: A Collection of Hand-Pictures of famous Living and Dead*), 1929.

148 FOUR-HANDED MONSTERS

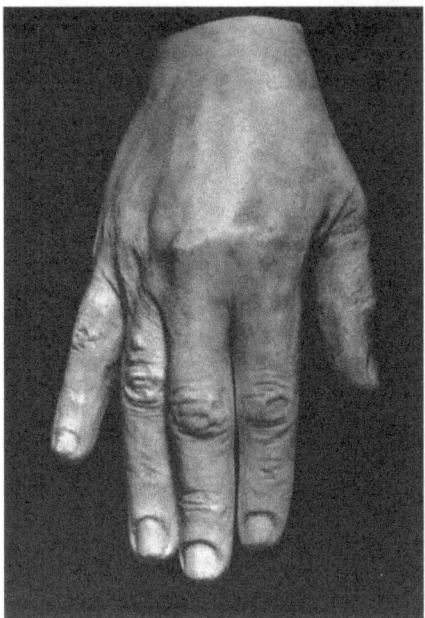

Figure 5.5 Richard Wagner
Photographs from Rudolf Voigt, Hände—*Eine Sammlung von Handabbildungen Grosser Toter und Lebender (Hands: A Collection of Hand-Pictures of famous Living and Dead)*, 1929.

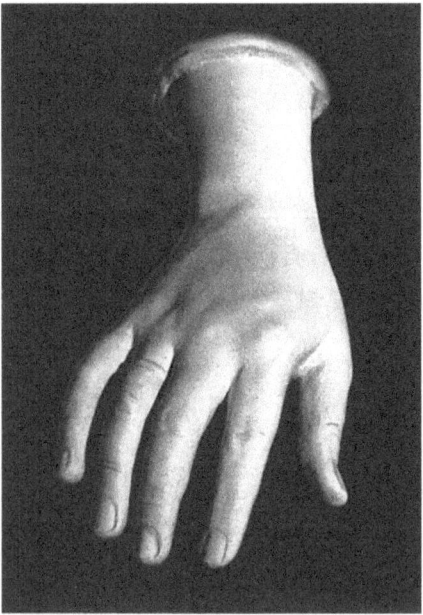

Figure 5.6 Clara Schumann
Photographs from Rudolf Voigt, Hände—*Eine Sammlung von Handabbildungen Grosser Toter und Lebender (Hands: A Collection of Hand-Pictures of famous Living and Dead)*, 1929.

gesture suggests piano playing but the perspective, with the fingertips closest to the vantage point, simulates an impossible perspective, namely that of the piano itself. The picture thus encourages the viewer to identify with the perspective of the instrument—another moment of abstraction in which the gaze is supposedly liberated from subjectivity and instead becomes a god's-eye view.

Almost all of the pictures Voigt presents look like this—as though the keyboard had been removed in postproduction. Unlike Lombroso's panels, for instance, none of Voigt's hand pictures allows a glimpse at the palm of someone's hand or a balled fist. Just as in Lombroso's work, Voigt's primary interest is what another physiognomist, Casimir Stanislas d'Arpentigny, called "les forms de la main"—that is to say, the proportions and outlines of the hand. The hand lines, central to traditional palmistry and still a part of hand analysis for Lombroso, are deliberately left out. That means that what is worth noting about a hand, and what is visible in observing piano playing, is absolutely identical—no hand lines, no fingerprints.

Even the piano techniques taught by Czerny and others almost flattered this gaze. When Czerny describes to his pupils the appropriate position of the hand on the keyboard, he might as well be describing the pictures in Voigt's volume. "The forearm (from elbow to the fingers) has to make a horizontal line; for the wrists should neither bounce up like little hills, nor drop off downwards."[31] What the coffee table book accomplishes by means of photography, arresting the object in time, turning it into an exhibit and specimen, Czerny manages through technique. The palm of the hand and the arm are immobilized; only the fingers move. But as Czerny makes clear in the second volume of his influential piano school, even they are never allowed to obscure one another—"no finger may be attached to the other"[32]—nor are the thumbs allowed to come to rest on a black key, which would tilt the view of the hand.[33] Both Czerny and Riemann emphasize the supposed "naturalness" of this position, but in describing it they talk again and again of visibility and perspective. Riemann remarks, for instance, that "very common mistakes include dipping down the hands, tilting the hand to the side of the little finger; the middle fingers attain a completely skewed position, and the distance between the knuckles of the second finger and the middle joint of the thumb is enlarged beyond what nature intends."[34]

As Grete Wehmeyer has shown, the piano textbooks of the era focus almost entirely on the movement of fingers, leaving arm and shoulders entirely aside. This has to do with the evolution of playing styles on the new instrument. The eighteenth century bequeathed to the nineteenth a technique that was primarily score

---

[31] Czerny, *Briefe über den Unterricht auf dem Pianoforte*, 4–5.

[32] Riemann, *Vergleichende theoretisch-praktische Klavierschule*, 3.

[33] Carl Czerny, *Vollständige theoretisch-practische Pianoforte-Schule*, Theil 2 (Vienna: Diabelli, 1839), 4.

[34] Riemann, *Vergleichende theoretisch-praktische Klavierschule*, 6.

based, and intended for the much narrower width of a harpsichord. This relatively static way of moving at the keyboard only gradually gave way to a more virtuosic and more anatomically oriented practice, in which shoulder girdle, wrists, and lower arm had a role to play in creating sound. The earlier technique keeps the fingers very much exposed, observable and readable; Clementi, for instance, suggests that the student using his etudes put a coin on the back of his hand; Couperin proposes a wooden cane for the same purpose.[35] Visibility was only part of the intent, however; as we shall see in the next chapter, the new style popularized by Liszt and others had erotic connotations, since it kept the body mobile, uncontrollable, and obtrusively present. The earlier style transfixed the player under the gaze of the teacher or observer, like a creature petrified by the flash of a camera.

If technique was by itself not sufficient to keep the body still, there were a number of technologies that we tend to associate with photography rather than piano playing—for instance, the so-called *Handbildner*. Particularly extreme in this regard was the contraption Johann Bernhard Logier made part of his teaching technique. Since Logier wanted to provide affordable instruction to a large number of pupils at once, he attached a rail to each piano and affixed the students' wrists to it. The fingers were put in individual grooves that, on the one hand, kept them apart from one another and, on the other, made it impossible to hit the keys with anything but the fingertips.[36] At the same time, it kept the hands extremely immobile and restricted their reach, especially because Logier usually chained more than one pupil to a piano. This arrangement was admittedly extreme (and it was controversial even at the time), but it makes clear just how close piano playing strayed both to experimental arrangements and to photographic practices—like butterflies wriggling on a pin, the hands squirm before the gaze of the teacher.

The violence exerted by contraptions like Logier's has much in common with the clamps, clasps, and rods by means of which photography controlled the twitchy bodies during the enormous exposure times of early cameras.[37] And their violence was exerted to the same ends. "Motionlessness was one of the central criteria for the selection of the subjects of early photography," one historian writes, "and where motionlessness wasn't automatic the subject was forced into it."[38] Roland Barthes, for instance, speaks of the headrest used during portrait photography as "the pedestal of the statue I would become, the corset of my imaginary essence."[39] The "chiroplast" (*Handbildner*) was a means of making hands static and stable—and the cast of Chopin's hand on the piano

---

[35] Thomas Fielden, "The History of the Evolution of Pianoforte Technique," *Proceedings of the Musical Association*, Vol. 59 (1932), 39.

[36] W. MacDonald Smith, "The Physiology of Pianoforte Playing with a Practical Application of a New Theory," *Proceedings of the Musical Association*, Vol. 14 (1887), 50.

[37] Georges Bataille, "Figure humaine," in *Oeuvres Complètes*, ed. Denis Hollier (Paris: Gallimard, 1970), 181–82.

[38] Eskilden, *Der Fotografierte Mensch*, 10.

[39] Roland Barthes, *Camera Lucida* (New York: Farrar, Straus and Giroux, 1981), 13.

was the in same way just a physical rendition of the process of photographic staging described by Barthes. The body is supposed to prostitute itself to the camera's gaze, whether at the photo studio or on the keyboard. In both places it was a matter of "forcing the heaving mass of humanity into a form that fit all, a uniform," by means of immobilization.[40]

Outside of the "five finger exercises" Logier forced on his students, movements of arm and hand are almost unavoidable, in particular if the hands are supposed to cover the extreme registers. But here, four-hand arrangements provided surcease: two pairs of hands do not need to move as much, and in transcriptions that placed emphasis on ease of play, the hands didn't have to move too quickly. What is more, as we saw, the two pairs of hands were supposed to fulfill very different roles on the keyboard and could thus be observed performing very different activities. The compositional practice of the day made it possible for primo and secondo to accentuate different aspects of hands and hand movements. The primo, who normally takes over the melodic duties, tends to have the more mobile hands; the secondo-player, by contrast, usually has to play many more chords, which affords ample opportunity to display the hands' reach and span. The Barcarole in Rachmaninov's *Six Morceaux* of 1894 represents an extreme example of chirognomic difference: the middle part of the piece has the primo play a compressed lyrical piece, which the secondo accompanies with almost brutal chords, which require extreme reach and a powerful hand. The primo, by contrast, luxuriates in finely meshed arpeggios that require a deft touch and fine motor skills, but neither reach nor muscles.

Admittedly, this kind of stark binary was fairly rare; especially transcriptions usually avoided divvying up the score quite so starkly. But what matters is the gaze solicited by the way Rachmaninov's Barcarole sets up its roles. For the piece suggests—nay, forces—upon any viewer a comparison. Watching hands in four-hand situations is *stereoscopic*: the length of fingers, the position of the knuckles, the relative length of one bone compared to the other, patches of hair, the fingertips—these are not just easy to see, they are almost easier to compare. This is where four-hand playing relied on the same forms of supposed evidence (skeptics would say powers of suggestion) as the photo volumes of Voigt or the tables furnished by Lombroso—primarily juxtaposition. Here you have the hand of a conductor, here a writer's hand, here that of a peasant; here is Goethe's hand, across from it is the hand of a criminal.

Even for those who regarded the interpretation of hands with some skepticism, then, this way of presenting hands had to suggest the plausibility of comparisons. A book like Voigt's does not collect photographs of hands just as indexes; he wants to teach his readers how to interpret them. He presents his "evidence" without commentary, and even without much of a caption, but then provides an appendix that not only presents the hand's owner in more detail that is also at pains

---

[40] Bischof, *Souveränität und Subversion*, 88.

to make connections between the individual hand and the individual biography. It is remarkable what details of both hand and biography Voigt thinks are worth sharing: Voigt provides no details on when and how the photo was taken, whether it was taken while the owner was still alive, or whether it is a photo of a plaster cast. We don't learn how old the famous person was when his or her hand was photographed. Rather, the text is at pains to connect the abstract and isolated hand with a similarly reified concept of genius. Voigt considers the hands he gathers evidence only of expressions of types ("the composer," "the writer," "the pianist"), not as documents of a particular individual, of a particular age, or of a particular life situation.

Voigt is a late practitioner of a gaze on hands that was far more prevalent in the previous century. Unlike the traditional art of palmistry (chiromancy), which tried to interpret the lines of the hand as an analogue to cosmic circumstances, the bourgeois art of interpreting hands is interested in the hand as "a passive being" rather than as an organ of activity, as Hegel put it.[41] This study was called chirognomy. The two classics of nineteenth-century chirognomy were Casimir Stanislas d'Arpentigny's *La Chirognomie ou l'art de reconnaître les tendencies de l'intelligence d'après les forms de la main* (*Chirognomy, or the Art of Recognizing the Tendencies of the Intellect from the Forms of the Hand*, 1843) and Carl Gustav Carus's *Symbolik der menschlichen Gestalt* (*The Symbolism of the Human Form*). D'Arpentigny's title is already programmatic: instead of hand lines, this new "science" of the hand is interested in "the *forms* of the hand," which means the gaze wanders from the palm of the hand to its fingers and from the surface to the overall shape (*Gestalt*) and dimensions.[42]

Chirognomists were particularly interested the thumb, for anthropological as well as philosophical reasons: the thumb is what makes the human hand human; and the more pronounced the thumb, the more pronounced the humanity of its owner.I In Carus's system, this was the ability to love and the power of willing. If the first phalanx of the thumb is more pronounced (that is to say longer), it points toward an energetic person; if the second is more prominent, the person is highly logical. The other fingers are categorized as either smooth or knotty—the former are "childlike" (all children have smooth fingers initially) and point to imagination and spontaneity. The knots that develop in grown-ups point to a sense of order and philosophical reasoning.[43]

Another topic of interest were the fingertips, which chirognomy traditionally divided into three groups: "pointy" (clawlike and animalistic), "conical" (the so-called angel finger), "square" and "spatula-shaped," which point to a practical and material mindset. The longer the fingernails, the weaker an individual's

---

[41] G. W. F. Hegel, *The Phenomenology of Spirit* (Oxford: Oxford University Press, 1977), 189.

[42] Rudolf Voigt, "Einführung in die Handkunde," in *Hände: Eine Sammlung von Handabbildungen Grosser Toter und Lebender* (Hamburg: Enoch, 1929), 23.

[43] Richard Gray, *About Face—German Physiognomic Thought from Lavater to Auschwitz* (Detroit: Wayne State University Press, 2004), 113–37, 151–57.

constitution—but small fingernails point to individuals closer to the status of animals. In general, the shorter the finger, the stupider and the braver the person. If the fourth finger is longer than the index finger, the hand's owner tends toward materialism and energy; if the relationship is reversed, the owner has good taste and tends toward the artistic. Combining all these different traits, Carus distinguishes four main types of human hands: the elemental hand, the motoric hand, the sensible hand, and the soulful hand.[44] All of these traits were, of course, observable during piano playing, and especially so if there were two hands to observe and compare; the typology introduced by Carus and his ilk was thus perfectly suited to the anatomical theater of the keyboard.

The binary codes with which this complex semiotics operates depend entirely on the two spheres that were the topic of chapter 3—the domestic feminine, and the public masculine—hardness/softness, activity/passivity, reality/imagination, reason/feeling. The chirognomist Adolphe Desbarolles, for instance, claimed that the "soft hand" tended toward indolence and pointed to an otherworldliness, while the "hard hand" was a sign of activity and willfulness. The overly hard hand, however, usually showed single-mindedness, if not simple-mindedness. Even Voigt, writing decades later, interprets the hands of the great musicians according to this schema. Richard Wagner's hand, we're told, "is full of strength, but it doesn't seek nature by means of testing and grasping, but by forming it of its own strength."[45] Felix Mendelssohn is described quite differently; his hand "would be appropriate for a woman."[46]

But if chirognomy depends on a dichotomy between gendered spheres, or between the world of the aesthete and the world of the philistine, then it at the same time registers profound misgivings with this dichotomy. This is because chirognomy in Carus's mold reduces every quality of the hand to a schema that, as we saw, in nineteenth-century culture always had disciplinary aspects. In other words, the evidence Carus looked for in hands pointed to either the fear of being overly soft and otherworldly (decadence) or the fear of being overly hard and practical (philistinism). Whether in the "positive criminology" of Lombroso, the atavism discourses, or chirognomic analysis inspired by Carus, any deviations condemn the individual to an inevitable fall from middle-class respectability (in the direction of either decadence or philistinism). And since these discourses did not make a distinction between physique and character, there was nothing one could do about these inborn traits. No effort of will could offset a small thumb, conic fingers, or a "soulful hand."

[44] Carl Gustav Carus, *Symbolik der menschlichen Gestalt: Ein Handbuch zur Menschenkenntnis* (Leipzig: Brockhaus, 1858), 303–16.
[45] Voigt, "Einführung in die Handkunde," 8.
[46] Voigt, "Einführung in die Handkunde," 7.

These were, of course, the same deterministic categories that resurfaced in the context of *Hausmusik* in the bourgeois home throughout the century. The same worries the paterfamilias felt about his offspring playing the piano he could attach to their hands. It is questionable whether theories like Carus's found many followers among musicians or composers—they probably made themselves felt more acutely among consumers of four-hand music. However, Charles Gounod, who himself composed a number of four-hand pieces (although many more of them were set for four hands by a young Georges Bizet), seems to have been interested in Desbarolles, one of the pioneers of chirognomy. The British eccentric and musician Georgina Weldon relates in her autobiography that Gounod took her along to a meeting with Desbarolles, and that she was quite taken with his diagnostic acumen.[47] Gounod's feelings on the matter are not recorded. The brothers Edmond and Jules de Goncourt, on the other hand, left an extensive description of their own visits with the two Desbarolles in their "four-hand" diary (*journal à quartre mains*). They visited Mr. and Mrs. Desbarolles in January 1864.

> We recognized the chiromantic couple, the two Desbarolles. Both would take your hand, fiddle with it, turn it over, and stare deep into your eyes. Some strange feeling takes hold of you: one feels as though one is about to enter into an unknown territory, and even if one does not believe in fate, there is a kind of apprehension of finding oneself in the saddle of one's future. And the stage directions are exquisite. Nothing too theatrical. He is in all black vestments, and his only accessories are two square magnifying glasses, which husband and wife hold in hand.... Desbarolles began to tell me what my hand had to tell him. He speaks softly, slowly, in small phrases in little sips.... He does this consulting his wife, who whispers to him here and there.... Desbarolles found in me a good musical sense! But he caught himself immediately and discovered in me the nature of a nervous woman, subject to frequent neuralgic attacks, as well as a good sense of form and a rather beautiful lifeline.[48]

What Claudia Schmölders has called the "physiognomic training" in bourgeois culture extended beyond faces to the hands.[49] The educated classes were told to look at hands, not just for self-knowledge but also with a view to hereditary material, a mode of inspection not dissimilar to the ones used in animal husbandry. The

---

[47] Georgina Weldon, *My Orphanage and Gounod in England* (London: Music and Arts Association, 1882), 175.

[48] January 3, 1865; Edmond de Goncourt and Jules de Goncourt, *Journal des Goncourt* (Paris: Charpentier, 1888), 175.

[49] Claudia Schmölders, *Hitler's Face—The Biography of an Image* (Philadelphia: University of Pennsylvania Press, 2006), 70.

hereditary material was supposed to vouch for a true, natural aristocracy, an aristocracy that, in purely social terms, the practitioners of this mode of scrutiny usually lacked. The hand is not just a status symbol because its surface doesn't look like it has to do work, but it also creates a kind of biological status. That it was the length of fingers, the shape of fingernails, and the strength of the thumb that became the prime indicators of this biological status helps cast a different light on the hands rushing up and down the piano keyboard. Even today people will sometimes lament that their hands are not right for the piano; it would seem that we have not moved too far from treating the "right" hand as a patent of nobility.

The nineteenth century understood the hand as a socioeconomic and a racial-hereditary seal of quality. It bestowed hereditary aristocracy on those who hadn't inherited any actual titles. But inheriting and reproducing are usually connected. The sexual dimension of four-hand playing that was at every moment suppressed by the surveillance of the household thus nevertheless crept back into the picture: as a past one (in the shape of descent and extraction), and as a future one (in the shape of the hereditary material that meets on the keyboard). And it sneaks back in precisely because four-hand playing is scrutinized and controlled according to these criteria, rather than any other. Just as the gaze of the paterfamilias was not allowed to see a dimension that nevertheless had to exist, this form of surveillance paradoxically created the very subterranean dimension it was supposed to exorcise. The stereoscopic gaze trained on the two pairs of hands thrives on comparison. And, as is made clear by the binaries with which Carus, d'Arpentigny, and Desbarolles operated, it doesn't just look for difference—it looks for complementarity and compatibility. It understands the two players as meant for one another, as *gametes*.

Paul Heyse's novella *Moral Impossibilities* (*Moralische Unmöglichkeiten*, 1903) deals precisely with this gaze. Two pianists play together harmoniously, and their surroundings understand their harmony as extra-musical—as sexual compatibility. Granted, it is the harmony of their play, rather than of the hands themselves, that becomes the sign of compatibility; but the passage still makes clear how dynastic concerns (concerns of provenance and procreation) became manifest in interpretations of four-hand playing. In the following passage, Aunt Leopoldine wants to marry off her nephew Achim to young Agnes:

> Almost immediately the old woman concocted a clever ruse to return her un-engaged and mourning nephew back to life by means of a new love. She relied in her design on the musical talent of her cousin's daughter, which the girl had been sent to the city to develop with a respectable music teacher. Achim was sweet-tempered enough to first show an interest in the young blond Agnes's piano playing. Then, since she made rapid progress, one night he even played four-hands with her. But when Aunt Leopoldine was careless enough to remark bluntly how harmoniously the four hands

fit into one another, he recognized the web she had been weaving and stayed away henceforth with all manner of excuses.[50]

The "harmony" with which the hands "fit into one another" is owed to something very much like d'Arpentigny's "formes de la main": Aunt Leopoldine does not remark on the harmony of the music Agnes and Achim actually produce. She pays purely visual attention, and the harmony she looks for is that of the hands producing the music. Compatibility is understood almost geometrically—the two forms fit into one another, the visual provides us a trusty guide for biology. Visual attention to four-hand playing was generally understood to have ulterior motives—and if they were diagnostic and dynastic, characters in novels and real people outside of them seem to have latched onto visual cues rather than onto the music being played. What they described was less the movement of the hand, and much more frequently its shape, as though it rested on the keyboard in perfect stillness.

It, of course, didn't hurt that the division of labor on the piano was understood as thoroughly gendered in much the same way as the "formes de la main." As Edward T. Cone observed, four-hand playing "is a marriage rather than a mere friendship," even if that marriage exists primarily in the eye of the beholder. But such a marriage was a rather fraught proposition—not only because the keyboard played host to amorous advances across class lines but also because there were hereditary stakes that were imputed to the proceedings.

Max Nordau's classic *Degeneration* (*Entartung*, 1892/93) famously claimed that in surrendering to the music of his time (Nordau was mostly thinking of Wagner), young people sank below their proper biological station, that in fact they betrayed their hereditary material by giving in to this kind of art. Exposed to the "shameless sensuality" of these works, young people would sink "somatically to the level of fishes, nay to that of the arthropoda, or, even further, to that of rhizopods, not yet sexually differentiated."[51] These bad apples tumble so far down the family tree that these "degenerates" are no longer truly sexually differentiated—the sensuality of music doesn't happily unite two individuals but, rather, turns them into a kind of gelatinous pure libido. Although he himself was quite partial to four-hand playing (although he naturally preferred Beethoven), thinking like Nordau's in a way turns the promise of four-hand playing (unification with another) into a terrifying image of a degenerate backslide down the evolutionary ladder.

In literature, the deterministic theories of heredity most visibly influenced the playwrights, novelists, and poets of naturalism. We have already pointed out that the authors in the naturalist orbit frequently turn to four-hand piano playing as a motif. We have seen how August Strindberg made use of this *topos*, but there is a text by

---

[50] Paul Heyse, *Moralische Unmöglichkeiten*, in *Moralische Unmöglichkeiten und andere Novellen* (Stuttgart and Leipzig: Cotta, 1903), 177.

[51] Nordau, *Degeneration*, 556.

his German colleague Gerhart Hauptmann in which four-hand piano playing has an even more accentuated role. And even though Hauptmann was extremely critical of thinkers like Lombroso and Nordau, the scene in question clearly grapples with the theories of heredity in the ether at this time.[52]

For although Hauptmann's biological determinism asserts itself mostly in diagnostic descriptions of faces, eyes, and postures, rather than of hands (one character has "eyes that are sometimes like dead, at other moments waxy and moist, roving gaze";[53] another character's eyes "are deep-set and at times glow sickly"[54]), Hauptmann links the question of heredity, and of genetic material, to the scene of four-hand piano playing. We can assume that Hauptmann knew the meanings his contemporaries attached to hands, since Voigt's book actually includes a picture of Hauptmann's hands (fig. 5.7). Since Voigt's book was published in 1929, this picture was taken while Hauptmann was still alive—it owes its existence to Hauptmann's interest in the topic, not to someone taking a plaster cast after his death.

The Feast of Peace (*Das Friedensfest*, 1890) is set during Christmas, in a country house in Erkner, a small town near Berlin. Most of the dramatis personae consist of the members of the dissolute and fractious Scholz family (including one servant), as well as their guests—Ida Buchner, the youngest Scholz son's fiancée, as well as her mother, Marie. In the course of one evening, these unsuspecting visitors witness the "family catastrophe" of the title, a catastrophe that the play implicitly presents as a result of the genetic disposition of the family members. Every member of the Scholz family is beset by ills and complexes ranging from alcoholism and kleptomania to hysteria. The text, which again and again insists on the "family resemblance" of its characters, seems to regard these ills as heritable.

Father Fritz has run off years ago; his wife, Minna, has withdrawn into a world of hysterical self-pity, with some co-dependent help from her daughter Auguste. Robert, the oldest son, has run away as well, and makes his money as a copywriter. Wilhelm, the younger son, fled the home after a mysterious fight with his father—he tried to punch his father, and then ran off. At Ida's insistence, Wilhelm returns home for the holidays. Robert, too, has agreed to return—but suddenly father Fritz staggers in, visibly scarred by years of alcoholism and venereal disease. As the viewer has no trouble guessing, he has returned to Erkner in order to die in peace.

The father's return leads to a number of revelations—in particular, we find out what precipitated the row between father and son. When Wilhelm finally tells his fiancée the story, four-hand piano playing suddenly emerges as central to the play's plot: Wilhelm, feeling that his father keeps his mother "an unlawful captive" in the house, introduces her to a friend of his. "I brought him here to ease her mind. She played—for a week—four-hand piano with him every week." Even though there isn't

---

[52] See, e.g., Gerhart Hauptmann, *Tagebuch: 1892 bis 1894* (Berlin: Propyläen, 1985), 70.
[53] Gerhart Hauptmann, *Das Friedensfest: Eine Familienkatastrophe* (Berlin: S. Fischer, 1904), 24.
[54] Hauptmann, *Das Friedensfest*, 29.

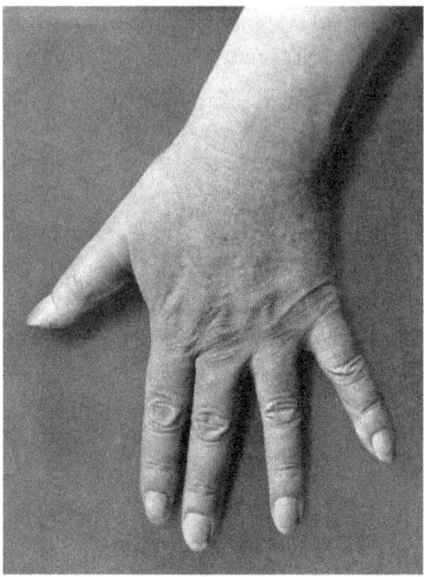

Figure 5.7 Gerhart Hauptmann
Photographs from Rudolf Voigt, Hände—*Eine Sammlung von Handabbildungen Grosser Toter und Lebender* (*Hands: A Collection of Hand-Pictures of famous Living and Dead*), 1929.

"the shadow of a possibility" of anything untoward, the servants begin talking "that she had a—bad—relationship" with the man. Angered, Wilhelm tries to find out who started the rumor, only to discover that it was his father, driven on by his paranoid delusions. "And so I punished him literally with these two hands."[55] This is the constellation that structures the rest of the play: the guilty hand raised against the father, and the innocent hand of the mother on the four-hand keyboard, in which the father's persecution complex suspects a "bad relationship." But how are these two hands related?

In general, Hauptmann's work relegates four-hand piano playing to the margins. Many among the dramatis personae of his plays sit down at the piano, but four-hand playing is rarer. Often (for instance, in *The Golden Harp*, 1933), four-hand playing appears at the beginning of a play, a symbol of the delicate balance that will come apart in the course of the play: the characters are sitting around the piano, they play piano, or can be heard playing backstage. It is the *res* of his *in medias res* openings. In a play fragment entitled *The General* (written 1915), General Otto von Beninde (who we're explicitly told is sixty-five years old) plays four-hand piano with the "nineteen-year-old pianist Eveline Lange" ("the General is playing discant"[56]). Scenes like this are not common in Hauptmann's plays, but the way

---

[55] Hauptmann, *Das Friedensfest*, 56.
[56] Gerhart Hauptmann, *Sämtliche Werke*, ed. Hans-Egon Hass (Frankfurt/Berlin: Propyläen, 1974), 9:531.

four-hand piano playing is deployed in his play *Das Friedensfest*, the suspicion it arouses, and its true innocence are anything but accidental. In Hauptmann's autobiography (*Abenteuer meiner Jungend*, written between 1929 and 1935) we find a direct model for the scene that provokes young Wilhelm's ire. A young man moves into the Hauptmann home: "You could see that he had a kind of friendship and fellowship with my aunt Julie. She sang for him, they played four-hand piano, they read books together and talked about them. My sister Johanna later spread whispers about this relationship." But Hauptmann categorically states: "But there was nothing to whisper about here."[57]

In *Das Friedensfest*, Hauptmann leaves out the shared books and the communal singing, and he reduces the "friendship and fellowship" to four-hand piano playing. Why does he do this? Why is it four-hand playing that ignites the father's paranoia, why is it four-hand playing that allays the mother's loneliness? It seems to have to do with hands. The piano episode itself is relatively marginal in *Das Friedensfest*, since it's over by the time the play starts. But the hand as such structures the entirety of the "family catastrophe" Hauptmann outlines in his play. At every turn, the hand propels Hauptmann's experimental arrangement forward: the hand symbolizes the determinism that drives these people along preordained paths, but it also symbolizes the attempt to escape from this determinism, even if only for a moment or for the time being. For the hand symbolizes the heredity of guilt: by raising a hand against his father, Wilhelm becomes part of his family's long tradition of aberrant behavior.

His brother Robert jokes that "we all have the dubious pleasure of being the spawn of a foul, fermenting swamp."[58] It is one gesture—the simple punch—that makes him a creature of the genetic "swamp" he has spent all his life trying to escape. The hand becomes an index of how far or how close one is to this swamp, whether the individual is conscious of it or not. In fact, hands seem to be indicators that function largely autonomously from their supposed owners. For Wilhelm doesn't get angry and then punch his father; the text insists several times that part of him "dies," and that it is some super-subjective force, not Wilhelm's individual subjectivity, that speaks through his hands. "My hands died off when I heard him speak about mother that way."[59] And even the mother insists: "The hand which is raised against one's father…such hands grow out of a grave."[60] Dead hands are far more active than living ones in *Das Friedensfest*; they no longer heed their owners but, rather, answer to the deterministic principles of the owners' genetic "nature" or predisposition (Robert's "swamp").

Sexuality has an ambivalent role to play in the family dynamic Hauptmann describes, an ambivalence that becomes most pronounced in the mother's four-hand

---

[57] Gerhart Hauptmann, *Das Abenteuer Meiner Jugend* (Berlin: Fischer, 1937), 247.
[58] Hauptmann, *Das Friedensfest*, 35.
[59] Hauptmann, *Das Friedensfest*, 56.
[60] Hauptmann, *Das Friedensfest*, 22.

playing and the family members' variant ways of reading it. On the one hand, all of the family members are obsessed with heredity, predisposition, and genetic material—that is to say, with past sex. But on the other, the four-hand scene turns the fixation on sexuality both into a symptom and into a cause. For it is genetic inheritance that engenders Fritz's paranoia; at the same time, everyone insists that the scene at the piano was sexual only in Fritz's clouded mind.[61] The hereditary disease that, at least in the world of the play, is passed on through sexuality (both through infection and through procreation) has as its effect that the members of the Scholz family regard everything through the lens of sexuality. This is why the two bystanders of the "family catastrophe," Mrs. Buchner and her daughter Ida, understand neither the family members' cynical view of their own heredity nor the sexual backstory that seems to have precipitated it.

It seems significant that Fritz's disease asserts itself above all when he over-interprets the play of the hands on the piano. He sees more than is there, and that is what makes him sick. But, of course, his gaze is that of the chirognomists of the nineteenth century, who likewise interpreted the two hands almost compulsively as somehow linked by (either past or potential future) procreation. Hauptmann's play isn't so much interested in making the point that this way of looking produces only illusions; rather, he wants to make the point that it is itself pathological. Only a sick brain would diagnose sexuality where the healthy one sees only four innocent hands at play. But of course that sickness is itself diagnosable—and, thanks to a rather unsubtle set of stage directions, which themselves read like a physiognomic manual, we the audience are invited to make this diagnosis. In other words, it is pathological to pathologize four-hand piano playing, but it is not pathological to diagnose this second pathology. Our own diagnostic voyeurism is not sick; we are right to diagnose Fritz, even though he is sick for diagnosing the four-hand scene. In *us*, the audience, the search for and the finding of symptoms are not themselves a symptom—in Fritz, they very much are.

If the Scholz family is caught in its own vicious circle of diagnostic narcissism, in which diagnosing symptoms is itself a symptom, its members make several attempts at escaping this circle. These attempts are aesthetic rather than sexual in nature: Wilhelm tries to become a "self-made man"[62] and to cleanse himself of the "botch-up" of his "predisposition." And his attempts to become part of the Buchner family aren't particularly erotic—it seems they've mostly tried to initiate him into normal human interaction. The other escape attempt is the mother's four-hand playing. While Wilhelm says there wasn't "the shadow of a possibility" that the episode was sexual, he also recognizes it as a "rejuvenation [*Auffrischung*] for the mother."[63] In a sense, then, father Fritz is both right and wrong: wrong because there is no

---

[61] Hauptmann, *Das Friedensfest*, 55.
[62] Hauptmann, *Das Friedensfest*, 54.
[63] Hauptmann, *Das Friedensfest*, 55.

sexual component to the four-hand playing; right because the wish for "rejuvenation" is part of a wish to escape the sexual and hereditary fate that dominates the family.

This motif of "rejuvenation" returns at the end of the drama, when Wilhelm is forced to choose whether to return to the genetic "swamp" of his milieu (to continue the family curse) or whether to take the risk of starting something genuinely new, of continuing his path as "self-made man." But this decision, too, is portrayed entirely in terms of biology and genetics. Wilhelm is afraid that his hereditary disposition would simply force him and Ida to repeat the "family catastrophe" of the Scholz family: "Think of what you've seen here! Are we just going to start this over?" Ida, on the other hand, insists that "it will be different" this time.[64] While Wilhelm is on the fence, the hand emerges yet again as a central indicator: as he oscillates between Ida and his family, he either grabs her hand or tries to let go of it. Again and again she has to beg him: "Please give me your hand again!"[65]

The hand, which initially functioned as a piece of evidence for the Scholz family's "secret"[66] (the hand raised against the father), and thus of Wilhelm's entanglement in his family's "botched-up" fate, it mutates into a symbol of trying to escape from that entanglement. Whether this escape attempt is successful remains unclear by the end of the play, but the outstretched hand ("please don't pull away your hand from poor little me," Ida begs) symbolizes the willingness to try to have things be different, to risk the genetic "rejuvenation." That means that the hand erotics of the final scene of Hauptmann's play are the same as those of the mother's four-hand piano playing: in each case, two sets of hands are engaged in a negotiation that is somehow erotic, without being particularly sexual. Throughout the play, the two fiancées don't mention love at all; they talk about trust, understanding, and promises. That may seem strange at first glance, but of course in the Scholz family, sex seems to be tantamount to blind fate. The two escape attempts are also rebellions against this sexual fate.

At his father's deathbed, Wilhelm is finally faced with the decision of whether to reintegrate himself into the hereditary complex of the family or to strike out on his own and build something radically new with Ida: "Wilhelm once again tries to pull away, but Ida once again calms him down. He wrestles down his pain, finds Ida's hand, which he clutches nervously in his own, and then walks out of the room hand in hand with the girl."[67] This final scene picks up on an idea that we discussed in the introduction: that walking "hand in hand" and playing four-hand piano aren't that different. Adolph L'Arronge gave this idea a humoristic and erotic valence; Hauptmann is deadly serious with this association, and he doesn't mean

---

[64] Hauptmann, *Das Friedensfest*, 103.
[65] Hauptmann, *Das Friedensfest*, 104.
[66] Hauptmann, *Das Friedensfest*, 47.
[67] Hauptmann, *Das Friedensfest*, 105.

for it to be erotic, either. Finding Ida's hand, walking out "hand in hand," emerges as a heroic gesture of rebellion and refusal. The same hand that Wilhelm raised against the father (which drew him into the family "swamp" to begin with) can now grasp for salvation from guilt. The hand condemns and the hand reaches for absolution. What to his father's mania looks like flirtation on the piano is in reality something far more serious: a quest for salvation.

The basic thesis of this chapter has been that there exists a connection between the hand cult of the nineteenth century and the culture of four-hand piano playing. Whether this connection plays out primarily along a visual axis (in which the hand and its activity function as an animated picture book) or primarily through the medium of the family tree (in which the hand and its activity have things to say about hereditary material and its transmission), what both have in common is that the hand is once again immensely eloquent. The hand once again has stories to tell, secrets to spill, secrets that the hand's owner may not be conscious of him- or herself. The hands on the keyboard once again point beyond themselves, are indices and signs for something outside of music. But the "four-handed monster" that becomes visible to this physiognomic gaze is not created by the two subjects in some kind of ecstatic union; rather, the monster stands already behind the two musicians, a cosmic totality, a panorama of natural history, which makes the musicians legible and interpretable. The next chapter returns to the two subjects: who are masters of their own labor, and whose collaboration creates something new, something unprecedented. But the metaphysics that so uncannily loomed "behind" the hand pairs in this chapter will resurface yet again.

6

Fordist Chords

An 1882 letter to the editor of the London *Pall Mall Gazette* lodged the following complaint: At his doctor's behest, the letter writer explained, he usually sleeps in until about 9 A.M. The other day, however, he was woken up around 5 A.M by the sound—nay, by the noise—of instruments: a "banging and slamming of musical instruments round my head." After a half hour spent half-awake, half sleeping, he realized that the noise was coming into his bedroom through an open window.

> Through this window was pouring a stream of music—oh, such music as was never before heard! I sat up in bed and listened. Bang! Slam! Thump! Stamp! It was a four-hand—*quatre-mains* they call it—piece by [Felix] Mendelssohn and [Ignaz] Moscheles arranged from Weber's "Preciosa." I recognized the airs, and remembered well that both players had arranged their own part. In other words, three ordinary hands were required by each player to get out the effects these master-players had set down on the paper. Talk about Leotard on the trapeze, and a tree full of monkeys quarelling over one cocoa-nut! Much more than this would not equal the effects produced by the agile fingers that swept that unhappy keyboard.[1]

What incensed the letter writer, evidently, was not just the sound of four-hand playing. As so often in scenes of four-hand piano playing, he found himself in the position of a voyeur. Through the half-open window he observed the following scene: "The window opposite was open, and through it might be seen two young girls being put through this *pièce à quatre mains* by a sort of female Wagner with a long stick. Up went the stick with a sort of Teufelsdrockh exclamation; down went all four hands with a terrific plunge that made piano, house, and everything in its unhappy neighborhood vibrate to the core."[2]

---

[1] Reprinted as "Piano Playing A Nuisance," *New York Times*, July 23, 1882.
[2] "Piano Playing a Nuisance."

The scene the anguished letter writer describes seems to have been an altogether common one in the nineteenth century, but the word *Teufelsdrockh* is a strange one. It sounds a little German, though it isn't, but it may well be an allusion to Thomas Carlyle's novel *Sartor Resartus* (1833–34), which remained very popular in Victorian England. The novel's subtitle is "The Life and Opinions of Herr Teufelsdröckh." The titular Herr Diogenes Teufelsdröckh lives "in the attic floor of the highest house in the Wahngasse," "the pinnacle of Weissnichtwo,"[3] where he cultivates a rather incomprehensible philosophy of "meditative transcendentalism"[4] and slaves away at his magnum opus, *Die Kleider, ihr Werden und Wirken* (roughly, *Clothes, Their Development and Effects*; the title is provided in German in the original). *Sartor Resartus* consists of the English "translation" of this fictional work, as well as a commentary by an English scholar who outlines Teufelsdröckh's philosophy with a mixture of skepticism and admiration. The novel that the nameless editor spins from these two threads is somewhere between an homage to and a parody of German Idealism. German philosophy from Wahngasse (literally, Folly Alley) meets good old British common sense. It is likely that the letter writer is thinking of this exact constellation in order to describe the doggy training of the two girls across the way.

It's not the "monkeys" with their "cocoa nut" that make the scene described in the letter so comedic—the girls' somewhat questionable talent is not its main concern. It's the "female Wagner with a long stick" "driving" the two girls through the piece who rouses the writer's satirical instincts. The two girls are being trained like circus animals, with stick and *Teufelsdrockh*. It is unclear whether the clearly Germanic flavor of the exclamation is owed to Carlyle's novel, to the teacher's Wagnerian visage, or to an English tendency to ascribe everything that smacks of excessive discipline to the Huns. At the same time, the Germans did their part to confirm the letter writer's suspicions, in that no other people devoted themselves so fiercely to physical training on the piano as did the Germans. And another association may well lie behind the *Teufelsdrockh*: the fear that someone who can play piano so well on command and with so little questioning may also do just fine marching in lockstep later in life.

The letter to the *Pall Mall Gazette* points to the flip side of the significations that came to attach to four-hand playing in the nineteenth century. To be sure, seasoned players could experience four-hand playing as a rapturous coming together, as collaboration and artistic community, but legions of others experienced four-hand playing like the two girls described in the letter. For them, four-hand playing was not about seduction and promise, about dialogue and intimacy; it was about exactitude, about norms, and about the inability to live up to either of them. Granted,

---

[3] Thomas Carlyle, *Sartor Resartus—The Life and Opinions of Herr Teufelsdrockh* (New York: Miller, 1866), 12.

[4] Carlyle, *Sartor Resartus*, 10.

most of the men and women I have cited in the previous chapters did not emphasize this part of the experience; for them, four-hand playing was a spontaneous, and frequently joyous, experience. It was an experience that requires effort and care, that can provoke frustration or disappointment, but an experience that at its best makes all of those worthwhile.

But philosophers of music like Theodor Adorno, critcs like Eduard Hanslick, conductors like Bruno Walter, and gifted amateurs like Arthur Schnitzler have one thing in common: they all love music, and they are all good at it. Taking their memories of their initiation into the Elysian Fields of the four-hand keyboard as somehow representative of nineteenth-century pianism in general would be like asking professional football players about their experiences with dodgeball in Middle School, without consulting the fat kids with thick glasses and damp circles under their arms. What to make of those who didn't relate to the piano the way Adorno did but, rather, related to it the way Adorno related to dodgeball? What did this bourgeois initiation ritual look like for those who were without much talent or interest, and who still were condemned to years of childhood spent on the piano bench?

Even those who did not show much aptitude were expected to learn the instrument, primarily because of the important social role music in general, and the "transcendental yardstick" of the piano specifically, played in the home. Secondarily, of course, because though the average bourgeois paterfamilias may not have regarded piano playing itself as inherently useful, he nevertheless regarded the virtues communicated through piano playing as transferable and found them important, perhaps even indispensable. That was because piano dressage did more than just display hereditary material; it could also speak eloquently of acquired traits. The German physiognomist Willy Hellpach in 1933 distinguished between "eugenics" and "euplastos," and while this distinction is a late one (and already clearly indebted to the Nazi years' attempts at "race science"), it captures a duality in the nineteenth-century German ideology of *Bildung*.

For *Bildung* meant two things for nineteenth-century Germans: something can be *gebildet* by being formed well by nature, or it can be *gebildet* by means of education (this second meaning survives today). Hellpach captures this duality as follows: "Our mastery of our own human nature depends on generative creation (*eugenics*) and guided formation (*euplastics*)."[5] We have thus far emphasized the former of these two: the dexterous hand understood as an index of good breeding; but if anything, the display of hands in nineteenth-century piano playing tended to show off the effort that had gone into perfecting hand motions. There is an ambivalence in the conception of aristocracy relied on by both senses of *Bildung*. On the one hand, hereditary material as expressed in the hand points to a kind of aristocracy that the bourgeois usually did not have from birth; the hand as an object

---

[5] Willy Helpach, "Der völkische Aufbau des Antlitzes," *Die Medizinische Welt* 7 (1933): 2.

sculpted and perfected by practice, on the other hand, is supposed to mark someone as being morally better than an aristocrat—because these hands have worked for their achievements, rather than blindly accepting them through their genetic code.

In the realm of music, this second, "euplastic" form of *Bildung* was mostly secured by means of etudes. These were simple pieces, meant to give fingers dexterity and a good feel for intervals and chords—in other words, aspects of piano playing that were never taken to be innate. The number of etudes on offer was vast, and it exploded as more and more households purchased pianos and now needed children capable of playing them. The most famous composer of etudes in the German-speaking world was a familiar face: Carl Czerny. Insofar as Czerny is remembered at all today, it is as a composer of etudes; but in fact, a mid-nineteenth-century piano student would have just as likely encountered Czerny through the plethora of transcriptions of famous works that bore his name—many of them for four hands. Beyond them, Czerny was a gifted, if somewhat conventional, composer in his own right; Hofmeister's *Handbook* lists no fewer than 280 compositions by Czerny for the year 1844 alone, and by far not all of them are arrangements, transcriptions, and fantasias based on other composers' music.[6] But in his own compositions, too, Czerny, who played duets with Queen Victoria and other famous contemporaries, was well disposed to four-hand music. He wrote a *Grande Sonate brilliante* in C minor (op. 10, 1821) for piano four-hands, as well as a *Grand Rondeau brilliant* (op. 254, 1832).[7] He also wrote etudes for four-hand piano.

It is no accident that Czerny composed etudes and transcribed the works of others for four-hand piano. As we saw in chapter 2, the same goes for Clementi and many others. In fact, the etude as form was promoted by much the same group of people who established four-hand playing as a kind of popular sport of the bourgeois parlor. And etude and four-hand playing emerged around the same time, too. As Grete Wehmeyer has shown, both emerge in the very first decades of the nineteenth century, and for similar reasons: the consolidation of the basic gestalt of the instrument, the industrial production and distribution that reached wider and wider audiences, and the transformations of domestic culture that put the piano front and center.

One source that four-hand piano playing and the etude do not have in common is the efflorescence of a virtuoso culture around the turn of the nineteenth century. The figures of the virtuoso and the wunderkind became patron saints of the etude form, responsible both for their popularity and for the kind of practice and mastery they pursued. The etude promised that, with sufficient and sufficiently grueling practice, any pianist may ascend to the heights of a Mozart, a Hummel, or a Czerny;

---

[6] C. F. Whistling and Adolph Hofmeister, *Handbuch der musikalischen Literatur* (Leipzig: Hofmeister, 1845), 2:77–81.

[7] *Dwight's Journal of Music* 11, no. 21 (August 22, 1857): 163.

whereas four-hand playing was, if anything, founded on the tacit acknowledgment that, without a second pair of hands to help out, this was not possible for most.

Although it struck generations of piano students as entirely natural, the etude form proceeded from a rather specific set of pedagogical presuppositions. Etudes tended to emphasize technical brilliance and public display. According to Czerny, "every degree of speed must be at [the pianist's] disposal without [the pianist] exerting force." Only once speed and movement had been mastered could a student "move on to perfecting the other forms of playing."[8] For "only the absolute mastery of the mechanics of the art" makes artistic expression possible in the first place. Normally that means that each collection of etudes presents a catalogue of important hand movements and positions in sequence (Czerny's *Kunst der Fingerfertigkeit*, op. 740, collect no fewer than fifty), and the scores give clear instructions on how many times each one of them is to be repeated. For each, Czerny gives a gloss of the point of the drill: "Mobility of the fingers while hand is still," "lower placement of the thumb," "tender pushing-off," "the thumb on upper keys with perfectly still hand."

But all of this goes for the etude form in general. Is it significant that the "female Wagner" described by the reader of the *Pall Mall Gazette* puts *two* pupils before the keyboard, and has them do four-hand drills on the same keyboard? Czerny did not just write transcriptions, fantasias, and original compositions for four-hand piano; he also published four-hand etudes. There is only one volume of them, published initially as *Exercises d'Ensemble*, but later republished as *Etüden* (op. 751, probably 1843). In spite of their name, these etudes are not really exercises for an "ensemble"; instead, the exercises rely on a much more extreme version of the primo/secondo dualism described in chapter 4. It is only the primo who exercises in them, who runs the typical gauntlet of technical challenges. The secondo is mostly concerned with accompanying the exercise, keeping measure, or polishing the mere exercise into something more like a real piece.

Czerny clearly intended the secondo part for a music teacher or a parent, while the primo is meant for the actual student.[9] There are examples of composers who took the opposite route, reversing this relationship. Ignaz Moscheles's *Daily Exercises* (*Tägliche Studien*, op. 107) were originally composed for the composer's daughter. The exercises hand to the student mostly broad chords and simple scales, while the other player (Moscheles wrote this part for himself, since he undertook his daughter's musical education) fills this rather simple scaffold with a brilliant façade; while the secondo labors through a series of chords and scales, the primo weaves a mazurka, a tarantella, a waltz.[10]

---

[8] Carl Czerny, *Schule der Geläufigkeit, Vierzig Etüden für Pianoforte*, op. 229 (Vienna: Schreiber, 1830).

[9] Klaus Börner, *Handbuch der Klavierliteratur zu vier Händen* (Zurich and Munich: Atlantis Musikbuch, 2005), 109.

[10] See also Ernest Lubin, *The Piano Duet* (New York: Grossman, 1970), 84.

In either case, then, the duo-etudes are not actually intended to teach both duettists at the same time. Instead, etudes obsessively returned to relationships of dominance and inscribed them into their very form—pupil/student, parent/child. The secondo's role once again consists of providing rhythm and of harmonizing the simple exercise through chords. One player beats the drum to which the other has to march. If the etude's project consists of what Michel Foucault has called "biopolitics," the constitution of bodies as social constructs, then four-handed etudes specialize in rehearsing bodily co-existence. Especially for the primo player, the body of the person next to you becomes the drill sergeant, the authority according to which you train your bodily movements. Wehmeyer speaks of etudes generally as a "means of disciplining," and of "sculpting drives";[11] in the case of four-hand etudes, that role falls to the person sitting beside the student. In the piano classes taught by Johann Bernhard Logier, which were aimed at families of more modest means and which will be the topic of the next section, two or even three students shared one keyboard at the same time, often on a dozen pianos at the same time. In pedagogic settings such as this one, the collective of fellow players becomes an instrument of censorship (and of self-censorship)—each player is a galley slave and drummer in one.

But arrangements like the ones propagated by teachers like Czerny, Moscheles, and Logier were not content to regulate the way in which the student's body related to music; they also intended to regulate how the body relates to itself. In a world in which most of the formal instruction that girls received involved music and the piano, the control and censorship described above were not limited to musical concerns alone. Posture and movement, what Pierre Bourdieu has called the *hexis corporel*, could be acquired and refined above all through piano playing. Bourdieu defines *hexis corporel* as "political mythology realized, em-bodied, turned into a permanent disposition, a durable way of standing, speaking, walking, and thereby of feeling and thinking."[12] "Arms and legs," writes Bourdieu, are "full of numb imperatives," which nevertheless transport political notions around social status, around sexuality, and around the interaction between classes and sexes.[13] When Arthur Loesser calls Logier's classes (which were attended mostly by girls) "boarding-school music,"[14] he is pointing to the same complex as Bourdieu: just like a boarding school, Logier's instruction did more than "just" impart expertise; they communicated a habitus, and they communicated directly to the body, bypassing the subject.

The fact that we are comparing private lessons with public institutions makes clear that the four-hand etude is much less safely ensconced in the bourgeois home than other four-hand music. This had to do with the exigencies of the market—the

---

[11] Grete Wehmeyer, *Carl Czerny und die Einzelhaft am Klavier, oder, Die Kunst der Fingerfertigkeit und die Arbeitsideologie* (Basel: Bärenreiter, 1983), 104.

[12] Pierre Bourdieu, *The Logic of Practice* (Stanford: Stanford University Press, 1990), 70.

[13] Bourdieu, *The Logic of Practice*, 69.

[14] Arthur Loesser, *Men, Women and Pianos: A Social History* (New York: Dover, 1990), 297–98.

insatiable demand for instruction, the wily teachers who sought to maximize their profits. But it also had to do with the kind of expertise the etude promoted: the point, yes, the promise of Czerny's books (and of the many others like it), was not a base level of core competencies; it was to turn the amateur into a virtuoso. Not for nothing did Czerny's *Pianoforte-Schule* have a special chapter dedicated to "producing"—that is to say, to playing piano publicly. The titles of Czerny's pieces often point to the "brilliance" of play as a goal, and this brilliance was meant less metaphorically than it may at first appear. Piano technique was intended to be clearly legible; it was intended to "garner more attention."

Piano playing should "resemble writing that you can also read from a great distance," Czerny maintained.[15] "Great distance" is not a category we have encountered much in our story of four-hand piano playing thus far. Four-hand music was music "from within your own four walls,"[16] as Hanslick wrote; the listener, however far removed he or she was physically, "was part of the family." "Brilliant" playing points decisively beyond this limited space—quite literally in the case of the "female Wagner" and her two charges who torment the reader of the *Pall Mall Gazette*. As Grete Wehmeyer has pointed out, this emphasis on brilliance "had ramifications for the style of piano playing during the decades that followed [Czerny]." That style "became far less concerned with expression and became increasingly mechanistic, characterized by a painful aggressiveness."[17] This "aggressiveness," too, shines through in the *Teufelsdrockh* exclamation with which the "female Wagner" exhorts her charges.

As was pointed out in the previous chapter, Czerny's etudes are really finger exercises—they lavish almost their entire attention on the movement of the fingers and the position of the hand, while the rest of the body (apart from very general suggestions for posture) is given short shrift. This was because the piano praxis that the nineteenth century inherited from the eighteenth was fully focused on the hand—and the tendency of certain virtuosos to use their entire body while playing piano raised some eyebrows. The worry about the corporeality of piano playing was not just owed to the prudish social mores of the Restoration era (and the Victorian era afterwards). Prior to the invention of the fortepiano and its proliferation among the bourgeoisie, there had simply been no reason to worry about this corporeality. The mechanics of clavinova, spinet, cembalo, and harpsichord, for instance, permit little beyond hand motions: there is no point in moving one's shoulders or drawing strength from one's hips while playing the harpsichord.

At first, it appears, by sheer force of habit the fortepiano was played the same way. But in the course of the nineteenth century, this praxis slowly gave way to a virtuosic praxis that hewed more closely to anatomy, in which shoulder muscles, wrists, and

---

[15] Carl Czerny, *Vollständige theoretisch-praktische Pianoforte-Schule* (Vienna: Diabelli, 1839), 60.
[16] Eduard Hanslick, *Geschichte des Concertwesens in Wien* (Vienna: Braumüller, 1869), 1:67.
[17] Wehmeyer, *Carl Czerny und die Einzelhaft am Klavier*, 102.

underarms were involved in producing and modulating sound. As Richard Leppert has shown, in debating and commenting on this shift contemporaries turned to two very different semantic fields. In order to caricature Liszt's extroverted and emphatically corporeal playing style, they portrayed the virtuoso in ecstatic poses—in describing him, they turned to the discourse of medical diagnosis. The virtuoso was understood as either a religious cult leader or as a maniac. The playing style preferred by virtuosos like Sigismund Thalberg and others, who kept their bodies fairly still and relied mostly on their hands, was portrayed as being machine-like. An anonymous French caricature from the 1830s, for instance, gives Thalberg eight symmetrical mechanical arms and hands, allowing him to cover the entire keyboard without moving his torso one bit. Leppert points out that the caricaturist even provides his Thalberg-body with extra arms in Thalberg's coat pockets.[18]

Even more strangely, there were political dimensions attached to this struggle over piano technique. The pitched battle about how to play the piano ran "parallel to the development of calisthenics and sports" in Central Europe.[19] Many of the titles and descriptors of etudes, be they for four hands or two, turned to the same vocabulary as the nascent public-exercise movement. To be sure, some titles talked academically about "studies" and about "art," but "exercise" and "school" were far more frequent appellations. Czerny, recall, had referred to his four-hand etudes as *Exercises d'Ensemble*, which was usually in the nineteenth century a term that referred to group gymnastics.

This connection was not lost on contemporary observers. Oscar Bie described in 1920 those "girl pupils who practice their healthy sport on Cramer's, Schmitt's, Czerny's etudes."[20] As Wehmeyer demonstrates, the fortunes of the new piano technique generally follow those of the calisthenics movement (above all, the so-called *Turnbewegung* in the German-speaking world): both came under suspicion in the repressive atmosphere of the restoration era, were rehabilitated by mid-century, and became pillars of the nation state by century's end.[21] Just like calisthenics, this new style of piano playing has an erotic component, but, again just like calisthenics, it is careful to sublimate that component. Both have to do with a community, maybe even a congregation gathered around a physical activity; consider, for instance, the caricature of Liszt reproduced in figure 6.1, in which the pianist's paroxysms seem to transmit themselves onto his faithful listeners.

They both invited similar anxieties and hostilities. Even by the century's end, when calisthenics was firmly anchored in the curricula of the German empire, the Catholic scholar Carl Cappellmann still associated it with the evil of self-abuse. By

---

[18] Richard Leppert, "Cultural Contradiction, Idolatry, and the Piano Virtuoso: Franz Liszt," in James Parakilas (ed.), *Piano Roles* (New Haven, CT: Yale University Press, 2002), 200–23.

[19] Wehmeyer, *Carl Czerny und die Einzelhaft am Klavier*, 158.

[20] Oscar Bie, *Das Klavier* (Berlin: Cassirer, 921), 286.

[21] Christiane Eisenberg, *"English Sports" und Deutsche Bürger* (Paderborn: Schöningh, 1999), 121.

Fig 6.1 The musical Soirée. Liszt caricature by Hermann Schlittgen (1859–1930). (New York Public Library)

virtue of the exposed bodies, he feared, calisthenics could arouse impure thoughts.[22] And while earlier opposition in the German lands and in Austria-Hungary to the movement had more to do with the fact that it tried to create a civilian force outside of the army's purview—a worrying constellation of body, class, and state—the physicality of the pursuit, coupled with the fact that it happened well outside of any state institution, was at least part of the worry. The new "natural" (which means "anatomic") piano technique propagated by Liszt and others moved away from the finger focus of earlier playing styles and instead emphasized "rotations, thrusts, throws, pushes of wrist and arms."[23] These rotations, thrusts, and throws, the clear erotic note in the duettists' bodies, was something that the traditional style of piano playing had minimized, but that the literature for piano four-hands almost necessarily had to emphasize.

[22] Carl Capellmann, *Pastoral Medizin* (Berlin: Gustav Schmidt, 1907).
[23] Wehmeyer, *Carl Czerny und die Einzelhaft am Klavier*, 158.

The etude, however, even in its four-hand incarnations, was devoted to diminishing this erotic component. Instead, it relied on repetition and a quasi-industrial work ethic. The irony was not lost on contemporary observers: as though by an unconscious compulsion, those parts of the population who didn't have to work in factories turned their pianos into conveyor belts, themselves into Charlie Chaplin trying to hit that one rivet just right each time. As Grete Wehmeyer has shown, the analogy between labor and practice emerged in the eighteenth century, and it was usually deployed to disparage excessive practicing. Even around the turn of the nineteenth century there were music pedagogues who argued that pupils shouldn't practice without supervision by their teacher, at least not at first. One look at the to-do lists that Czerny drew up in his books of etudes shows that they are no longer conceived for this purpose—for Czerny, practice meant practice in isolation. Four-hand etudes thus maintained something of the social situation that had been characteristic of the eighteenth century—the playing together of teacher and pupil—and preserved it in a time in which the etude had become an implement for what Wehmeyer so memorably calls "solitary confinement at the piano." In this way, what Max Weber called the Protestant Ethic made inroads on the keyboard: "Just like labor became a value in itself, so did 'practice' become a good for its own sake."[24]

Music critics showed just as much disdain for the drill sergeants of the keyboard as for the pervasive dilettantism among piano owners. They had little patience either for bad playing or for the attempt to get better at it. Eduard Hanslick speaks of a "cursed musical mass-dressage," which he mostly associates with the etude mania. Hanslick is especially critical of the one-sidedness of the etudes—that is, the fact that they emphasize dexterity and de-emphasize questions of comprehension and of feeling: "How much time and effort is wasted on the most thankless and most infertile bravura of the fingers."[25] Ludic—improvisational elements of piano pedagogy, which had been important in the eighteenth century—dropped out as piano instruction became more formalized.

As Oscar Bie noted in retrospect in 1920, most of the collections of etudes that appeared in Germany were called *Schulen* (schools), and that designation was barely metaphorical: "The printed schools have such elaborate systems that they resemble the organization of actual schools. There are higher schools, elementary schools, universities and private tutorials, and within each institution a set sequence of grades."[26] Johanna Kinkel's *Eight Letters to a Friend about Piano-Instruction* (*Acht Briefe an eine Freundin über den Clavier-Unterricht*, 1852) make clear that the printed "schools" were in fact meant as substitutes for actual music schools with buildings and classrooms: "This book," she writes in her introduction, "is mostly intended for

---

[24] Wehmeyer, *Carl Czerny und die Einzelhaft am Klavier*, 162.
[25] Eduard Hanslick, "Gemeine, Schädliche und Gemeinschädliche Klavierspielerei," in *Aus Neuer und Neuester Zeit* (Berlin: Allgemeiner Verein für Deutsche Literatur, 1900), 117.
[26] Bie, *Das Klavier*, 290.

musically educated mothers who either live in the countryside, or in a small town, and are therefore compelled by the dearth of capable piano teacher, to lead or at least supervise their children's piano studies themselves."[27]

The cardinal virtues in these quasi-institutional "schools" were "drill," "dedication," and "flawless playing."[28] Instead of Rousseau's Émile and Sophie, parents wanted their piano-playing offspring to become Wolfgang and Nannerl Mozart. Hanslick criticized that "nowadays we not only overstate the pedagogical value of music education, we also look for it in matters of technique alone."[29] Plenty of dissenters among the ranks of the piano instructors likewise voiced their disapproval. In her *Letters* on piano instruction, Johanna Kinkel remarks that "in my opinion all those not naturally constituted for music should just leave aside all singing and playing, lest they make martyrs of patience out of us poor teachers."[30] Patience was required even with the best of students; as Czerny's "schools" attest, constant repetition was considered the panacea of piano practicing. Czerny's *Pianoforte-Schule* of 1834 suggests "one hour of playing all 24 scales," just to get warmed up![31]

Of course, as Thomas Fielden points out, "even with [Czerny], there is no record of how he taught his pupils to cultivate the right movements and conditions." But, he adds, "one must suppose they went on till their hands ached and hoped for the best, and that the fittest survived."[32] And if four-hand playing is rather hard to spot in literature, memoirs, and letters from the time, compared to how widespread a phenomenon it appears to have been, the same goes tenfold for the etude. If pupils indeed followed Czerny's advice, they must have spent hours each day with rote repetition of a few etudes—and yet out of the novels, memoirs, and letters from the period waft only the sounds of the waltz, the aria, the sonata.

There were musicians who thematized this melodic unconscious: Saint-Saëns' *Carnaval des animaux*, for instance, brings this rote repetition onto the stage, revealing the stupefying busywork that stands behind the polished final concert. This is indicated by the final three orchestral chords of the "pianists." Throughout the piece, these orchestral chords interrupt to allow rather abrupt transitions from key to key (the pianos themselves never change key within each figure); one would therefore expect these final three blasts to provide harmonic resolution. Instead, they transition into the following vignette, *Fossiles*. Perhaps his vicious persiflage contains a bit of bad conscience: what the audience is invited to laugh at in the piece is the necessary basis of all concert performance, after all. But Saint-Saëns is not content to

---

[27] Johanna Kinkel, *Acht Briefe an eine Freundin über den Clavier-Unterricht* (Stuttgart: Cotta, 1852), 1.
[28] Wehmeyer, *Carl Czerny und die Einzelhaft am Klavier*, 91.
[29] Hanslick, "Gemeine, Schädliche und Gemeinschädliche Klavierspielerei," 113.
[30] Kinkel, *Acht Briefe an eine Freundin über den Clavier-Unterricht*, 37.
[31] Quoted in Wehmeyer, *Carl Czerny und die Einzelhaft am Klavier*, 163.
[32] Thomas Fielden, "The History of the Evolution of Pianoforte Technique," *Proceedings of the Musical Association*, Vol. 59 (1932), 47.

parody one pianist rushing up and down the scales without much musical feeling or talent. One player doing it might be preparation for great art—inappropriate for the concert hall, but necessary prerequisite all the same. Two players in the same manic pursuit is something different—it is industry, not art. The scene of Saint-Saëns' *pianistes* is based on historic models: two or more pianos in the same room, each with hapless pupils chasing up and down the keyboard in unison, were a common feature of many of the more well-organized schools of the nineteenth century. It is not entirely clear whether Saint-Saëns had these kinds of practices in mind when he decided to lampoon the *pianistes*, but the *Carnaval* clearly seems to think that there is something particularly inauthentic, and thus something particularly funny, about *two* pairs of hands stumbling through their scales.

The role of four-hand settings for piano pedagogy was controversial throughout the nineteenth century. Hugo Riemann's *Comparative Theoretical-Practical Piano School* (*Vergleichende theoretisch-praktische Klavierschule*, 1890) agitates against the very idea, arguing "that four-hand playing in the early stages of technical drills countermands the development of a clear sense of space. For the same reason it is inadvisable that a pupil only plays exercises notated in a treble clef; for no one will put the student at the center of the keyboard if he's busy only on the right side."[33] Others, however, clearly saw an advantage in four-hand instruction; Czerny's four-hand etudes were the most visible of a large crop. Other pedagogues went further yet and made a virtue of the shared keyboard, elevating it to a principle of instruction.

In the 1840s, Robert Schumann had remarked with palpable relief that "etudes now appear a little less frequently than in years prior. We greet this as a good sign, that the artists' sense turns away from the mechanical, and back towards the melodic."[34] But Schumann turned out to be wrong about the popularity of etudes; and the "mechanical" aspect of piano instruction he faulted became less and less metaphorical. Not just the endless repetitions and the one-sided focus on swift, effortless movement reeked of "mechanism"; actual mechanical devices soon invaded piano pedagogy. Saint-Saëns himself, for instance, learned to play the piano through a contraption called a *guide-mains*, first designed by Frederic Kalkbrenner.

While young Camille Saint-Saëns and his *guide-mains* may have resembled a craftsman with his workbench, the piano classes given by Johann Bernhard Logier (1777–1846) were instead inspired by industrialized mass production. Born in Germany, Logier moved to the United Kingdom around the turn of the century and established himself as a piano pedagogue. He founded a whole system of music schools, aimed particularly at the daughters of less well-heeled bourgeois families. His stroke of genius was the invention of what came to be known as the "Logier Method." Louis Spohr provided the following account of Logier's practice in an

[33] Hugo Riemann, *Vergleichende theoretisch-praktische Klavierschule*, op. 39 (Leipzig: Kistner, 1890), 2.

[34] Robert Schumann, *Gesammelte Schriften über Musik und Musiker* (Leipzig: Wigand, 1854), 4:241.

article in the *Allgemeine musikalische Zeitung* in 1820, and seems generally well disposed to it: "What first catches the eye about this method is that [Logier] lets all the children play at the same time, sometimes as many as 30 or 40 (this is not a printing error)."[35]

Another observer describes how "at not less than twenty pianos were seated nearly thirty young ladies."[36] Given such large class sizes, Logier had to create an adaptable curriculum for his students. Spohr describes Logier's etudes as follows: "He wrote three volumes of etudes for this purpose, which are built on very simple basic themes (5 notes in each hand). While the beginners play just the theme, the more advanced students practice more or less complex variations on it."[37]

Generally speaking, this is of course the principle of the four-hand etude: against objections by pedagogues like Hugo Riemann, Logier's exercises do not just ape the form of four-hand playing (since Logier places two or more students before one instrument), it even apes the musical principle of four-hand transcription. The keyboard is partitioned and parceled out to the students. No one in Logier's classrooms practiced using the entire keyboard. In general, Logier's music academies are not the opposite of the ubiquitous domestic four-hand scenes; they are more like funhouse mirror images. The unity that domestic four-hand playing celebrates is enlarged into an entire room with dozens of instruments—as is the four-hand "voice": "When the whole was put into motion," one observer wrote, "the sounds rising from so many instruments of different make and shape produced an effect rich and curious."[38] And since each group of students plays a different variation on the basic theme, even the division characteristic for four-hand etudes is maintained: with simple structure, on the one hand, and harmonic fig leaf, on the other—but it is extended to an entire room of accompanists.

But at the same time, the scene has little of the domesticity, of the secrecy, of the eroticism that clung to four-hand scenes in the domestic sphere; the rows of pianos with the pupils on their benches has something of church pews, of athletic instruction, of military drills. Just like four-hand arrangements, Logier's techniques created a kind of unity of shared voice and shared instrument, but it was synchronization dictated by circumstance; his arrangements reinterpret the meeting of the hearts in the piano parlor as a quasi-industrial process. The intimate interplay of primo and secondo turns into musical Fordism.

The ways in which Logier picked up on the domestic scene of four-hand playing and transformed it is a symptom of the wider dissemination of both the piano and of four-hand playing. It is owed to the instrument's spread beyond those segments of the population that could afford private tutors, and it is owed to the mercantile

---

[35] *Musikalisches Centralblatt* 1 (January 5, 1882): 2.
[36] William Gardiner, *Music and Friends* (London: Logmans, Orne, Brown, 1838), 647.
[37] *Musikalisches Centralblatt* 1 (January 5, 1882): 2.
[38] Gardiner, *Music and Friends*, 647.

spirit of the teacher himself, who went from poor immigrant to pedagogic "entrepreneur" (as the organist A. F. C. Kollmann calls him in 1821[39]). The structure of his instruction resembles a cottage industry, and just as Luddite anger was aroused by the norming and mechanization of work processes, so Logier's musical enclosure movement provoked ire among piano teachers worried for their livelihood.[40]

Of course, rationalization was not the main point of Logier's method. It was aimed instead at the internalization of rhythm—common playing was supposed to turn the teacher's baton into an inner metronome. Logier's method seems to have been the only instruction project for four hands that was not intended for teacher and student, but in which both players were students. The "drill," which in Czerny's four-hand etudes still segued into "solitary confinement," becomes much more universalized: the pupils perform the same exercises, or variations thereof, four- or six-handed at multiple instruments.

Logier's method attained widespread popularity and some notoriety among the musical class, but it never caught on in his land of origin. As *Pierer's Universal Encyclopedia* remarks in 1857: "In Germany, this method, which tends to emphasize the mechanical, has never gained the currency it has in England."[41] That means the letter writer to the *Pall Mall Gazette* was both right and wrong to suppose that drill practiced by the "female Wagner" hailed from Germanic origins: the ideology of the piano drill did indeed emerge from Germany (as did its prime practitioners), but its greatest success occurred in England.

In 1822, the Prussian minister of culture and schools, Karl vom Stein zu Altenstein, asked Logier to re-import his method to Prussia. As one commentator told the story in 1882, sixty years later and almost forty years after Logier's death: "The Prussian government felt compelled to lure this musical miracle teacher back into his fatherland, since it would be too bad if only the unmusical British got to enjoy the grace of his instruction."[42] The tone of the commentary is rather openly tongue-in-cheek, and the reason is clear, too: the author doesn't find it too surprising that it was the Prussians, of all people, who warmed to the idea of a mustering at the piano. The *Teufelsdrockh* yells that the irate British letter writer put into the mouth of his "female Wagner" did echo through German music schools as well. And just like the letter writer, contemporary Germans seem to have understood Logier's method as a kind of militarization of musical pedagogy. Piano practice was a form of drill, and Logier's etudes were a mustering camouflaged as music.

It was only logical, then, that the Logier method was imported into Prussia essentially like a military reform. A music journal of the time describes the project as follows: "As a consequence, Logier was charged by the minister, to instruct twenty

---

[39] *Leipziger Musik Zeitung* 12 (1821): 769.
[40] *Berliner Allgemeine Musikalische Zeitung* 4 (January 26, 1825): 25.
[41] *Pierer's Universal-Lexikon* (Alternburg: Pierer, 1857–1865), 10:469.
[42] *Berliner Allgemeine Musikalische Zeitung* 1 (January 5, 1882): 2.

teachers at the behest of the king. These teachers would then spread this method of instruction throughout the Prussian lands.... We can thus regard Logier's system of music education as officially introduced into Prussia."[43] Here four-hand piano etudes actually outpaced the calisthenics movement—both were integrated into the curriculum in Prussia and thus turned into state organs, but Logier's method arrived far earlier than the ideas of Turnvater Jahn. In either case, however, collective movement, be it at the piano or in an open field, was to be subsumed under the aegis of the state.[44]

This collectivization of a normally private transaction (independent teachers coming to individual households) proceeded by means of a form of education that was based on the principles of four-hand playing. Just as four-hand transcription democratized music consumption, the principles of four-hand transcriptions democratized piano instruction, opening it up to new segments of the population. And in each case, there was resistance to these new forms of dissemination and to the leveling of socioeconomic distinctions that went along with them.

As mentioned, Logier provided his own pieces for his unique brand of mass instruction. Adolf Bernhard Marx's *Berliner allgemeine musikalische Zeitung* reviewed the *Trio pour six mains et deux Piano Fortes*, in 1825, noting that "it can be performed four-handed as well." Logier had published it in his own musical publishing house. The reviewer opens by allowing that the arrangement of Logier's piece is primarily owed to the exigencies and requirements of his brand of piano instruction: "Logier's piano institutes, which are spreading throughout all the major cities in Prussia these days, have created an ever more urgent need for good and interesting pieces for several instruments."[45] Four or more handedness is not an accident, a whim of the composer, or owed to a desire to put teacher and student to work on the same playing field; it is, rather, a matter of method.

But Logier didn't just have a quasi-industrial solution on offer for students having difficulties with rhythm; he also applied the logic of the workshop to questions of hand position. The Logier method also covered correct hand movement and relied on a contraption called the "chiroplast" (*Handbildner*), by means of which the teacher could, as Hanslick noted with horror, literally "weld the child to the piano for hours."[46] And while Hanslick and others were properly scandalized, many of the "schools" and books of etudes published in the nineteenth century pointed interested students, teachers, and parents to mechanical means for instilling perfect posture and position. The chiroplast was only one such device on offer. (Logier patented it in 1814.[47]) There was the *guide-mains* invented by Kalkbrenner, which

---

[43] *Berliner Allgemeine Musikalische Zeitung* 11 (March 16, 1825): 2.
[44] Eisenberg, *"English Sports" und Deutsche Bürger*, 105–44.
[45] *Berliner Allgemeine Musikalische Zeitung* 34 (August 24, 1825): 270.
[46] Eduard Hanslick, *Suite: Aufsätze über Musik und Musiker* (Vienna: Prochaska, 1884), 165.
[47] Loesser, *Men, Women and Pianos*, 297–98.

Saint-Saëns relied on; "Bohrer's hand-guide" (*Bohrerscher Handleiter*) was another popular offering, as was the "Piano Dactylion"[48] or Seeber's "Finger Sculptor" (*Fingerbildner*).

The English and French terms for these devices are not as telling as those used in German; they all draw on the semantic field of *Bildung*, but in the strange sense referred to earlier, as "euplastics"—that is, the gradual molding of human anatomy into an ideal shape. The French and English descriptors (as well as the German translation *Handleiter*) portray the device as a kind of guardrail, something that convinces the hand to move a certain way. "Chiroplast," "Dactylion," and *Fingerbildner* instead suggest that they will resculpt the physical makeup of the hand, that they will work on the body without the player having much of anything actively to do with it.

In many cases, then, Logier's form of musical calisthenics was quite literally apparatus gymnastics, relying on parallel bars just like the real thing, which originated around the same time (the parallel bars are, in fact, an invention of Friedrich Ludwig Jahn). As the music historian Bernard Rainbow describes it, Logier's chiroplast was

> a wooden framework extending the whole length of the keyboard, above which it was screwed into place. Immediately in front of the player were two parallel horizontal rails between which the hands were inserted to keep the wrists at working level. Above the keys themselves was a brass rod the whole length of the keyboard. This carried the "finger-guides"—two flat brass frames free to slide along it, each containing slots into which the thumb and the fingers were to be inserted.[49]

The contraption, and others like it, aroused mostly skepticism. The 1885 edition of *Meyers Konversationslexikon* gets almost sniffy in discussing the invention, harrumphing that "the best chiroplast is a good teacher,"[50] and luminaries such as Cramer, Moscheles, and Czerny agitated against its use.[51] But other virtuosos like Thalberg and Kalkbrenner stood behind the new invention, and it soon spread throughout Europe.[52] Chiroplasts were used in music schools, but also marketed to individual learners—even late into the nineteenth century, Hugo Riemann suggests his readers acquire "Seeber's finger sculptor, available from C. F. Kahnt in Leipzig."[53]

---

[48] Robert Palmieri and Margaret W. Palmieri, *The Piano: An Encyclopedia* (London: Taylor & Francis, 2003), 200.

[49] Bernard Rainbow, "Johann Bernhard Logier and the Chiroplast Controversy,"*Musical Times* 131, no. 1766 (April 1990): 193.

[50] "Chiroplast," in *Meyers Konsersationslexikonm Vierte Auflage* (Leipzig and Vienna: Bibliographisches Institut, 1885–1892), 38.

[51] Fielden, "The History of the Evolution of Pianoforte Technique," 48.

[52] "Over den chiroplast van J. B. Logier," *Amphion* 2 (1819): 64.

[53] Riemann, *Vergleichende theoretisch-praktische Klavierschule*, 8.

There were even special etudes written for use with the chiroplast. By 1855, Logier's official *First Companion to the Chiroplast* was in its nineteenth printing, the first of its two sequels in its twelfth printing.⁵⁴ Sir George Grove claims that a full half-century after the chiroplast's invention, one could still find badly rusted specimens in London's second-hand stores.⁵⁵

The point of the chiroplast and its cousins was threefold: they fixed the hand in place vis-à-vis the keyboard; they separated the individual fingers (Riemann's *Vergleichende Klavierschule* points out that "the second finger is most vulnerable to this error"⁵⁶); and they expanded the reach of the fingers. Generally, then, they had as their objective an avoidance of touch; such devices untangled the fingers and kept the hands separate (since both hands would usually run on the same track and could not cross). Even though piano instructors claimed that using such exercises was intended to bridge distances on the keyboard, "shrinking distances as the student progresses,"⁵⁷ it of course had the added benefit that the fingers—those "little, disobedient creatures, which, if not reined in, will gallop off like a young horse"⁵⁸— are kept properly apart. In the case of Logier's classes, where two or more students shared one piano, the chiroplast also kept the pianists apart.

In the way they direct the hand and the fingers, these bizarre contraptions bear a certain resemblance to those that were to prevent childhood onanism in the nineteenth century—the corsets, chastity belts, and other machines, especially for boys. In both cases the mechanism was intended to obviate the danger that the child might touch its own body; when chiroplast and mass instruction were combined, it was also to prevent that child touching another child. Of course, in the Janus-faced configuration called "four-handed monster," the other's body is not an entirely distinct thing. In descriptions like that by François Coppée the two players related as mirror images; touching each other thus became a kind of realization of the original narcissistic fantasy, that of caressing one's own mirror image. After all, unlike in traditional four-hand playing, Logier's pupils are, if not mirror images, then at least images of one another.

Or are Logier's contraptions intended to prevent a kind of alloeroticism? If so, we can assume that it was a homoerotic relationship to an other (which in the nineteenth century was frequently understood as a form of narcissism). For the pupils gathered before the instruments seem to have been mostly single sex. William Gardiner's report from Logier's teaching workshop speaks of "thirty young ladies,"

---

⁵⁴ Cf. *Intelligenz-Blatt zur Allgemeinen musikalischen Zeitung* 8 (1826): 288.

⁵⁵ Loesser, *Men, Women and Pianos*, 300; *Grove's Dictionary of Music and Musicians* (London: Macmillan, 1879), 347.

⁵⁶ Riemann, *Vergleichende theoretisch-praktische Klavierschule*, 8.

⁵⁷ Riemann, *Vergleichende theoretisch-praktische Klavierschule*, 30.

⁵⁸ Carl Czerny, *Briefe über den Unterricht auf dem Pianoforte* (Straubenhardt: Antiquariat-Verlag Zimmerman, 1988), 25.

and Louis Spohr similarly suggests that Logier's students were predominantly female. In the discourse of early psychoanalysis, it was female patients in particular who were thought to engage in "forbidden finger-exercises" on the piano.[59] In one of his case studies, Ernest Jones notes that one of his female patients seemed to associate her dexterity at the piano unconsciously with onanism—with "playing with her fingers in another, forbidden direction."[60]

But the question is where etudes, where the workout on the keyboard in general, fit into this problem. Did pedagogues understand the Fordism of scales and chords as a way of keeping the fingers from "another, forbidden direction," or was the piano as such seen as a part of the problem? The first chapter pointed to the connection made between piano playing and masturbation during the nineteenth century.[61] Sigmund Freud claimed that "the satisfaction derived from one's own genitals...is usually alluded to by any kind of *playing*, also by *piano playing*."[62] But as Saint-Saëns makes so drastically clear in his *Carnaval*, etudes of this type stood in a very ambivalent relationship to anything we could term "playing"—anyone who has worked his or her way through one of Czerny's "schools" will attest to the fact that it is a profoundly unsexy experience.

Hanno Buddenbrook's masturbation session is staged by means of an improvisation. Robert Musil's Walter improvises obsessively and by himself, usually on Wagner (whom his wife loathes), an activity that Musil codes "almost too on-the-nose"[63] as masturbatory: the narrator seems to reach deep into the stock descriptors of nineteenth-century moral panics about masturbation when he relates how "the narcotic effect of this music paralyzed his spine,"[64] even going so far as to use the German word for "spinal fluid." The association of improvising and masturbating isn't particularly surprising, given that since the eighteenth century, onanism was understood as an excess of imagination. Fantasizing and improvising on the piano were as close as piano playing came to what Rousseau called "reading with one hand" in his *Confessions*, for both are characterized by a pathological self-fixation and boundless fantasy. This is a nexus that doesn't exist in the highly regimented, systematized, and mechanized etudes from Logier to Riemann.

At the same time, there are nineteenth-century voices who believed that piano playing was *in itself* pathological or expressive of a pathology—whether the player

[59] Sándor Ferenczi, "Weiterer Ausbau der 'Aktiven Technik' in der Psychoanalyse," in *Imago: Internationale Zeitschrift für Psychoanalyse* Vol. 7 (1921), 239.

[60] Ernest Jones, "The Relationship between Dreams and Psycho-Neurotic Symptoms," *Papers on Psycho-Analysis* (London: Wood, 1918), 265.

[61] Jones, "The Relationship between Dreams and Psycho-Neurotic Symptoms," 264.

[62] Sigmund Freud, *Vorlesungen zur Einführung in die Psychoanalyse* (Vienna: Internationaler Psychoanalytischer Verlag, 1930), 161.

[63] Jürgen Gunia, *Die Sphäre des Ästhetischen bei Robert Musil* (Würzburg: Königshausen & Neumann, 2000), 155.

[64] Robert Musil, *The Man Without Qualities* (New York: Knopf, 1995), 66.

played Czerny or improvised on *Tristan und Isolde*. The psychiatrist Emil Kraepelin (1856–1926) described a patient with "dementia precox" (what we would today call schizophrenia), whose illness made work impossible and instead drove him to piano playing and onanism. "After passing his written exams a year ago, he was exempted from the orals, since he was unable to work any more. He cried a lot, masturbated a lot, walked around without a plan, played piano without sense."[65] In Kraepelin's case study, the piano is symptom rather than therapy. Kraepelin doesn't seem to think that more or better piano playing might heal the young man; if anything, his study suggests that taking away the young man's "instrument" might be in order.

Czerny, meanwhile, seems to have thought of the etude as a way of releasing wayward energy, energy that might otherwise drive children to much more dangerous activities. Just as gymnastics was both suspect for its covert eroticism and relied on as a way of sublimate erotic energy, for Czerny the etude is a kind of homeopathic therapy. In discussing the speed and reach of his young pupils' fingers in his *Letters*, Czerny remarks: "You must not permit your fingers any caprice, or become dissolute over them."[66] Following the pull of the fingers, the place where they want to go leads to "dissolution" (*Zerstreuung*)—a word that can just mean distraction, but which, in the nineteenth century, often referred to deeper nervous or moral defects.

The innate "caprice" of the "disobedient" fingers of which Czerny speaks, and his fear that it can lead to "dissolution," anticipates in many respects an equation popular in the more salacious segments of the literary world, as well as in psychoanalytic writings—the idea that (especially female) onanism constituted "forbidden finger-exercises."[67] Insofar as Czerny understood his role as Little Miss Cäcilie's long-distance instructor, the exercises he forced his young charge to perform and repeat were intended as antidotes to more forbidden exercises. Wehmeyer similarly speculates that "practice ... was used by instructors to keep girls busy so they wouldn't get any 'foolish ideas.' "[68] In a preface to one of his piano "schools" (op. 500), Czerny remarks that "the pianoforte, especially for the weaker sex, is really the only appropriate thing, since studying it will bring with it the fewest health risks."[69]

Edmond de Goncourt makes the same point, but to the opposite effect in his novel *Chérie* (1884). A young girl studies the piano without any real enthusiasm. She practices a lot, "but without spirit, without pleasure, without love."[70] But after falling ill with scarlet fever, Chérie begins to approach her piano playing quite differently: mechanical repetition gives way to improvisation, her playing "whips up

---

[65] Emil Kraepelin, *Einführung in die Psychiatrische Klinik* (Leipzig: Barth, 1905), 24.
[66] Czerny, *Briefe über den Unterricht auf dem Pianoforte*, 25.
[67] Ferenczi, "Weiterer Ausbau der 'Aktiven Technik' in der Psychoanalyse," 239.
[68] Wehmeyer, *Carl Czerny und die Einzelhaft am Klavier*, 99.
[69] Czerny, "Pianoforte-Schule," op. 500, 3.
[70] Edmond de Goncourt, *Chérie* (Paris: Charpentier, 1884), 102.

the imaginative faculties," elicits "a feverish joy," to the point that she declares it "the hashish of women."[71] Within the confines of Chérie's boring finger exercises, this hashish was safely contained; but now her free play drives her girl into a wanton sensualism that the novel clearly marks as "decadent."[72] Decadence, hashish, masturbation—all of this becomes possible once the teacher's gaze has turned away, and once the lack of spirit, of pleasure, of love give way to the joys of improvisation.

The teachers, doctors, and pedagogues who led the charge to curb masturbation in the nineteenth century tended to understand inactivity and understimulation as the root causes of self-abuse. The excessive practice teachers like Czerny forced onto their pupils, the absurd repetitions they asked of them, and the punishing sequences they forced their hands through—these were very convenient ways of exhausting the "little, disobedient fingers"[73] enough so that "foolish ideas" wouldn't even occur to them. In the 1880s, Herbert Emminghaus, professor of psychiatry in Freiburg, suggested that if "there are suspicions that masturbation takes place," the best antidotes are "gymnastics, swimming, long walks, exercising the muscles."[74] This again reflected the understanding of the self by the calisthenics movement, which saw gymnastics as a purging of errant energy and regarded sex and masturbation as foreign contaminations of the pure German spirit.[75] Since "doing nothing," "the availability of free-floating mental energy," was the precondition for the evil of masturbation, young people's energy and attention span had to be occupied.[76]

There is another possible relationship between etude and masturbation, one that can be gleaned from one of Freud's dream analyses. Freud was never one to be hysterical about masturbation, and he once suggested to a obsessively abstinent analysand that "moderate masturbation" would be less destructive than complete abstinence. The patient in question was fixated on his mother, and told his analyst about dreams in which he and his mother endlessly ascended stairs. Shortly after Freud made his suggestion, the patient related another dream: his piano teacher admonishes him for not spending enough time with Moscheles's etudes and Clementi's *Gradus ad Parnassum*. The patient himself supplied the thought that the *Gradus* and the piano itself (since the German word for "scale" is *Tonleiter*—i.e., tone ladder) were themselves made of "steps."[77]

Freud doesn't provide a lot of commentary on his patient's dream. But this dream suggests a very different connection between masturbation and etude, and it

---

[71] de Goncourt, *Chérie*, 105.

[72] Katherine Ashley, *Edmond de Goncourt and the Novel: Naturalism and Decadence* (Amsterdam: Rodopi, 2005), 218.

[73] Czerny, *Briefe über den Unterricht auf dem Pianoforte*, 25.

[74] Hermann Emminghaus, *Die psychischen Störungen des Kindesalters* (Tübingen: Laupp, 1887), 198.

[75] Eisenberg, *"English Sports" und Deutsche Bürger*, 117–19.

[76] Peter Gay, *Education of the Senses* (New York: Oxford University Press, 1984), 306.

[77] Sigmund Freud, *Die Traumdeutung (Studienausgabe)* (Frankfurt: S. Fischer, 1972), 2:365.

is likely Freud saw this connection as well—for Freud suggests that staircase dreams are almost always about coitus. The dream teacher, who chases the patient up and down Clementi's *Gradus ad Parnassum,* is actually telling him to masturbate. In the context of the dream, the etude, the grueling ascent to the mountain of the muses (*Gradus ad Parnassum*), represents an alternative to abstinence: the compulsive repetition of the etude repeats the sexual act (be it masturbation or incest with the mother). The unwilling subject is forced not just to repeat scales and finger exercises *ad nauseam* on the piano; the young man also understands Freud's suggestion as imposing sexual Fordism, or piecework eroticism.

None of the examples cited for the possible relationship between piano practice and the erotic concerns four-hand playing. While the Logier's classes and Seeber's machines existed for duo pianists, and were often used for four-hand playing, we have no indication of how the relationship of eros and etude was understood when four hands shared the keyboard. Nevertheless, the digression into solo playing shows how the constellation of eros and work on the keyboard was configured by different observers. Was piano practice eros camouflaged as labor? Was it labor that staved off the encroachments of eros? Or was it, as Freud's analysand seems to suggest, eros as labor?

This unresolved, and probably unresolvable, ambivalence turned out to be exceptionally productive: the final two chapters of this book will show the different ways in which nineteenth-century composers, critics, writers, and pianists addressed the question of how libido and labor relate in four-hand playing. Was one of them masquerading as the other? Was one undercutting the other? And what role does the second pair of hands play, depending on the answer? The image of the "female Wagner," and her two luckless charges who raised the question of the relationship between labor and four-hand playing in the first place, suggests a flip side to the phenomenon and the questions that swirled around it. Behind the satire that the letter writer mobilizes against, the mind-numbing drill, the brutal authoritarianism, there stands a sense that a better piano praxis exists, or is at least possible. The next chapter will show that the idea of a better piano praxis was connected to the idea of a better social arrangement—and that four-hand piano playing allowed writers and musicians to sound out whatever social echoes might emanate from this practice.

The letter writer is not just astute in analyzing the scene of four-hand drill; he also knows the piece, "an arrangement from Weber's *Preciosa,* by Mendelssohn and Moscheles." He even mentions that, as he remembers, "both players had arranged their own part."[78] Why, given this context, would this be salient information? Most likely it's because the image of Mendelssohn making art communally, but independently from one another, is pretty much the exact opposite image of the two girls

---

[78] "Piano Playing A Nuisance."

who rush through the piece in a London apartment in panicked synchronization under the unrelenting baton of a "female Wagner." The piece the letter is referring to is the gypsy march from Weber's *Preciosa*, and we have a very detailed description of how this piece came about, from Ignaz Moscheles's son Felix. He relates "the marvelous way in which my father and godfather [i.e., Mendelssohn] would improvise together, playing *à quatre mains* or alternately, and pouring forth a never-failing stream of musical ideas."

> A subject was started, it was caught up as if it were a shuttlecock; now one of the players would seem to toss it up on high, or to keep it balanced in mid-octaves with delicate touch. Then the other would take it in hand, start it on classical lines, and develop it with profound erudition, until perhaps the two joining together in new and brilliant forms, would triumphantly carry it off to other spheres of sound. Four hands there might be, but one soul, so it seemed, as they would catch with lightning speed each other's ideas, each trying to introduce subjects from the works of the other.[79]

The fact that Moscheles refers to "subjects from the works of the other" points to the fact that his description, while insistent that this is a kind of game, also recognizes that there is something like a "work" being produced (a work that the female Wagner would push her pupils through decades later), that there is something worklike about this activity. Even the fact that motifs are compared to a "shuttlecock" alludes to the shuttle darting through the machines of the many cloth factories of Victorian England. But if Moscheles's description doesn't shy away from the language of industrialization, he introduces it to highlight how unindustrial, how thoroughly unconventional, was the labor he witnessed his father and his godfather performing. The shuttlecock races back and forth between two men who weave using the materials furnished by the other, two men who create a common product that unites their contributions on the fly and without "Teufelsdrockh."

This is probably what the letter writer (who comes across as quite savvy musically) meant to point to: the two "apes" with their drill sergeant play a piece that once emerged from the exact opposite type of labor, an improvisation *à quatre mains*. What the two young girls bang into the keys in their panic still bears the imprint of a musical praxis that (unlike the piecework the girls are forced to perform) doesn't have an analogue in the world of work. Two independent actors create a harmonic whole out of their own autonomous subjectivity. This isn't just a counter-image to the military-industrial complex embodied by the "female Wagner"; it is a profoundly utopian form of human collaboration, of human coexistence. The technique brought to England by Logier, and which stands behind the two girls' efforts,

---

[79] Felix Moscheles, *Fragments of an Autobiography* (New York: Harper & Brothers, 1899), 78.

is authoritarian—it alienates the subject from its own activity, from its body and from its product. But the piece the girls play points up the fact that things might yet be different, even though they usually aren't: that collaboration might involve a completely unalienated, freely chosen being-in-common. It seems possible on the four-hand keyboard—why not in society at large?

7

Musical Platonism: Four-Hand Playing Among the Philosophers

There is something in the relationship between two pianists seated before the same instrument that can comment on, spoof, or ironize labor. The last chapter dealt with the ways in which four-hand playing covertly readmitted into the bourgeois salon those labor processes that were supposed to be banished from it. Logier, Czerny, and even Freud treated four-hand piano playing (especially of etudes) as a means of sublimating or abreacting drives. What on first glance appears to be an erotic "private tumult"[1] (as Musil calls it in *The Man Without Qualities*) turns out to be analogous to industrial work processes. But it is of course possible to conceive of the relationship between four-handedness and labor in just the opposite way: rather than four-hand music reimporting the political unconscious of *Hausmusik* (i.e., Fordism, whose repression enabled *Hausmusik* in the first place), four-hand music clearly also functions as a *telos* and as an inspiration. After all, it resembles labor—but what a strange kind of labor it is!

Two people share an instrument; the average observer has no idea which player produces which sound, to say nothing of the pure listener who can barely guess. And the piece that the four hands produce together contains as much of one player as it does of the other. Everyone has heard a bad soloist with a great accompanist, or the other way around; a four-hand piece is good or bad, but without undue scrutiny we don't know which player is better. Playing four-hand piano music is a form of labor, but a form of labor that comes into view only rarely. And in four-hand playing it doesn't just come into view: you can feel it; you can hear it; you can engage in it. Four-handedness is anti-Fordism, the utopian idea of completely unalienated communal labor, one that isn't abstractly postulated but, rather, one that can be experienced by players and listeners.

The last chapter introduced Ignaz Moscheles and Felix Mendelssohn-Bartholdy as the counter-image to Logier's students, who gallop through pieces with panicked

---

[1] Robert Musil, *The Man Without Qualities* (New York: Knopf, 1995), 45.

faces in parallel tracks. While in the latter case the other player's body becomes a metronome, a timekeeper that enforces a moment of absolute heteronomy, Moscheles's and Mendelssohn's improvisations *à quatre mains* represent something like autonomy raised to the second power. The two players draw on their own spontaneity, yet create something communal; they are part of something greater than themselves without having to give up a part of themselves in the process. The two musicians seem to have been quite aware of the revolutionary dimension of this arrangement. In 1833, Moscheles wrote about their collective arrangement of the Gypsy March from Weber's *Preziosa*:

> What fun when people try to pull apart this double composition, and try to find out who made this, who made that, who wrote the primo, who the secondo-part, who invented this variation, who this modulation. I like the complete mixture of two musical spirits, and I tell you that one should divide [the piece] no more than an ice cream à la *tutti frutti*, and just enjoy it and the aftertaste it leaves.[2]

While descriptions like Moscheles's are naturally much less common than exasperated reports of overambitious, mismatched, or simply awful piano duos, there is a surprising number of these rhapsodic accounts of four-handed improvisation. In his memoirs, Eduard Hanslick describes an evening with two great pianists of the age, Julius Schulhoff (1825–1898) and Camille Saint-Saëns.

> After dinner, neither Saint-Saëns nor Schulhoff is quite ready to sit down at the piano. So Ambroise Thomas calls out: "Just sit down the both of you, and improvise something four-handed." The two, experienced musicians as well as brilliant virtuosos, oblige good-naturedly. They decide on beat and key and then start improvising in the most surprising way. One follows the other astutely, lets the other pass him or passes him by, seemingly leads him astray or lets him lead him astray, and always, though without the slightest gap in their togetherness, meeting again in effective unison.[3]

The two accounts of Hanslick and Moscheles have several tropes in common: they emphasize the now-familiar degree of integration between the two players; they insist on the organic fluidity; and they reflect the almost uncanny lack of communication with which the duettists manage to create their music spontaneously. Both accounts are haunted by the many million similar interactions that unfold entirely differently: performances in which one player leads the other astray, or when each

---

[2] Felix Moscheles, ed., *Briefe von Felix Mendelssohn-Bartholdy an Ignaz und Charlotte Moscheles* (Leipzig: Duncker & Humblot, 1888), 61.

[3] Eduard Hanslick, *Aus meinem Leben* (Kassel, Basel: Bärenreiter, 1987), 264.

element or player grates against the other. But most centrally, perhaps, the texts both acknowledge that what the audience witnesses in duo improvisation is a kind of labor, even a kind of work; however, they simultaneously emphasize those aspects that seem to set duo improvisation decisively apart from what we usually expect work (or *a* work) to look like.

Four-hand players do work, but they challenge our understanding of what it means to do work. This challenge arises in part simply because the metaphors attending to four-hand playing are much more complex than those connected to other chamber ensembles. While the nineteenth century had little trouble finding an analogy to the relationship between individual and collective in the relationship between soloist and orchestra, or in espying a fantasy of dominance in that between the conductor and orchestra, four-hand piano playing was much harder to place. If anything, four-hand playing resembled forms of community that were, much like four-hand playing itself, much harder to categorize or that actively resisted such categorization—friendship, marriage, double monarchy. Four-hand playing, as we saw in chapter 4, is monstrous—the two players are no longer truly two individuals, but they do not fully merge into one individual, either. This makes them (and their work) problematic and a fairly unstable basis for comparison; but it made them attractive to those wanting to depict a form of society or labor that no longer existed, or didn't exist yet.

Unrepresentable Labor

Moscheles's letter points to something else, as well: however commodified four-hand music was, the labor of playing itself does not produce a single thing that would be referred back to a consumer—not even in the very limited sense that there are likely to be listeners distinct from players. Four-hand playing is, rather, the production of what Marx might call a perfect use-value, the producers of which are also its consumers, living aesthetically hand to mouth. However much the nineteenth century understood four-hand playing in terms of socialized labor, it was also keenly aware that four-hand playing could model a possible, yet-to-be-realized form of social (or communal) labor. In this chapter, I will deal with four-hand playing as a figure for a different and better division of labor—or, perhaps better, a kind of labor that abstains from division and that presents this better labor concretely and sensuously.

Edmond and Jules de Goncourt are not the only "four-handed" authors of the nineteenth century, but they are probably the most famous. Edmond (1822–1986) and his younger brother Jules (1830–1870) collected, observed, and wrote together—and produced not just novels and articles but also a well-known *journal à quatre mains*, a four-handed diary. So influential was their work and their way of working that they became in many ways the model for a number of twosomes (usually brothers) practicing "écriture à quatre mains"—Paul and Victor Margueritte, for instance, or Joseph and Seraphin Rosny.[4] They understood their twinned activity explicitly as four-handedness, and they invoke the language of duo pianism to describe their activity. When they write in a letter to Flaubert that "we put our four hands cordially in your two hands,"[5] the strangeness of the gesture described is salvaged only by its musical associations. The brothers delighted in such turns of phrase that made sense only when transposed onto the keyboard.

But while it is clear that the two conceived of their activities as four-handed, it is much less clear what exactly these activities looked like. In the Revolutionary year 1848, Edmond decided to give up his profession and do something fairly unusual for a bourgeois professional of the time: "I will do nothing." Of course, the two brothers were exceedingly productive in the decades that were to follow, but they were productive in that strange way that four-hand playing is productive: they published, often enough things that their contemporaries felt ought to have remained private; they created a communal oeuvre, but their creation had nothing professional about it. This form of production (the most important result of which, the famous diary, was never actually available as an object during the brothers' lifetimes) seems to have emulated quite consciously the kind of inactivity that the psychiatrist Emil Kraepelin diagnosed as a symptom in his patient (see chapter 6). Four-handedness, even of this unmusical sort, stood in a fraught and deeply puzzling relationship to anything that was straightforwardly useful, appropriate, or healthy.

This kind of literary collective production is, of course, not without precedent. In Germany, for instance, the early Romantics—above all, the young men involved in Friedrich Schlegel's journal *Athenäum*—collectively produced a body of fragments constituting a "symphilosophy," without spelling out who contributed what. But since Romanticism, the figure of the author had become, if anything, more important in vouchsafing the meaning of a work.[6] The Goncourt brothers published precisely in genres that usually emphasize a singular author and his singular authority (the realist novel, the diary, and the essay, to name only three), while the Romantic co-authorships occurred in genres (above all, the fragment), which are about decentralized authorship to begin with. That *four* hands write a novel is far more remarkable than that four hands may bundle together some notes into a collection of fragments.

As a result, their contemporaries encountered some difficulty not just trying to classify the brothers' works but also picturing exactly *how* they worked. The brothers' good friend Gustave Flaubert used the pair as a model for his own intellectual do-nothings, *Bouvard et Pecuchet*, in the posthumous novel of the same name

---

[4] Norbert Dodille, "Goncourt colonial: Marius-Ary Leblond pour *En France* (1903)," in Katherine Ashley (ed.), *Prix Goncourt, 1903-2003: Essais Critiques* (Berne: Peter Lang, 2004), 60.

[5] Jules de Goncourt, *Lettres de Jules de Goncourt* (Paris: Charpentier, 1885), 297.

[6] Michel Foucault, "What Is an Author?", in *Aesthetics, Method, and Epistemology*, ed. James D. Faubion (New York: The New Press, 1998), 205.

(1881). At the end of the novel, after having essayed at, and largely failed in, a variety of intellectual endeavors, the two decide to turn to copying the texts of others. To that end, they build a desk for two (*bureau à double pupitre*), so they can do their work four-handed.

Since the end of Flaubert's novel devolves into a set of fragments, it isn't quite clear what Bouvard and Pecuchet have in mind with their invention, though their design appears to be novel enough to draw a local carpenter to their project. Ironically, the same kind of confusion attended to the four-handedness of the brothers Goncourt. Unlike in the case of a musician or a composer seated with lined paper at the piano, or an inspired poet scribbling away at his desk, the modus operandi of the brothers Goncourt was very hard to picture, and even harder to depict: their way of writing was four-handed only metaphorically; at no point were the brothers hunched over the same manuscript at the same time. Unlike our four-hand players, the brothers became a "single four-handed monster" only by the thaumaturgy of the printing press.

Recognizing that he cannot depict the brothers writing four-handed, in his drawing of the brothers the artist Paul Gavarni (real name Sulpice Guillaume Chevalier, 1804–1866) simply seats the two before a piano (fig. 7.1). The collaborative creativity of their four-handed writing process, which cannot be depicted, can be made visible and representable through a detour via the keyboard. The brothers, who claimed for themselves a "complete weakness and deafness for music,"[7] were not known for their music making. And as the picture above shows, the piano itself is not shown. The two brothers sit next to each other and stare at a point beyond the frame of the image. There are no notes to alibi their poses; only their hands tell us what the brothers are doing here. And yet their poses, especially Edmond's, who slouches indolently in the front, aren't exactly the kinds taught by Johann Logier and his consorts. It is even questionable whether Edmond could play piano in this pose at all.

As Richard Leppert has shown, it is a common signal in the musical iconography of the nineteenth century that the viewer is not supposed to accept the person depicted playing an instrument as *just* playing an instrument, that the busywork on the keyboard is in fact epiphenomenal.[8] The same holds true for the case of the Brothers Goncourt: Their hands appear to perform four-handed labor, but their reclined bodies are those of aestheticist dandies who want to "do nothing." Gavarni depicts a scene at the piano, but it seems he doesn't mean for it to be about the piano. The picture isn't about music; it's about four-handedness as such, and four-handedness cannot be depicted without a piano. The picture is about a communal creation, about collaboration, about community through writing and production. But all this can be depicted only when the metaphor is literalized via the

---

[7] Edmond and Jules de Goncourt, *Journal V* (Paris: Charpentier, 1888), 66 (March 3, 1862).

[8] Richard Leppert, *The Sight of Sound* (Berkeley: University of California Press, 1993), 191.

Fig 7.1 Edmond et Jules de Goncourt (1853), drawing by Paul Gavarni. (Bibliothèque nationale de France)

keyboard. Gavarni thus folds the temporality of four-handedness: the sequential harmony of the brothers' literary output becomes a true synchronous harmony when it turns musical.

While Gavarni's hands thus depict the four-handed pair of authors, the brothers paid him back by writing a (four-handed) biography of the artist after his death in 1866. The brothers express their love and admiration for Gavarni, and remark that he "showed for the younger of the two of us a kind of paternal affection."[9] In the biography, the two don't recount sitting for the drawing, but they mention in their diary that the drawing exists: "The director of the Porte Saint-Martin put on a display in the foyer of the portraits that Gavarni published in the journal *Paris*, among them the one of us."[10]

Not only were the brothers quite familiar with Gavarni's way of working, but he was quite familiar with theirs. In his drawing, he sought to portray a particular

[9] Edmond de Goncourt and Jules de Goncourt, *Gavarni: L'homme et l'oeuvre* (Paris: Plon, 1873), i.
[10] Edmond de Goncourt and Jules de Goncourt, *Journal I* (Paris: Charpentier, 1888), 66 (September, 1853).

form of collaboration—a form that he knew well, but that was hard to document, as resistant to representation as to the Protestant Ethic and the spirit of capitalism. For the co-laboration Gavarni depicts is one between two men who have decided to do nothing. Their togetherness—their very four-handedness—rests on the same anti-bourgeois axiom as Gautier's famous adage that "there is nothing truly beautiful than that which is not good for anything."[11] It is a labor characterized by self-conscious inactivity, unproductivity. The very fact that Gavarni has to move the brothers to the piano constitutes an admission that there is a contradiction between their product and its representability: the objects that emerge from the brothers' four-handed labor in no way betray four-handedness; but the four-handedness of their labor is representable only if the artist abstracts from the product and shows the brothers in an activity that does not result in a residual something.

Four-hand playing, to paraphrase an old joke about art, is beautiful, but looks like a lot of work. It also looks a lot like work. But it transposes, caricatures, or refracts that work. For in a central way the community at the piano is not a work group; it is, rather, what another pair of authors, the French theorists Philippe Lacoue-Labarthe and Jean-Luc Nancy, have theorized as a *communauté desoeuvrée*. The English translation of Nancy's book of the same name renders this title as *The Inoperative Community*, but the French original gives a better sense of what is meant when a community is inoperative: it does not have an oeuvre, a work. The two are interested in a community that would not "take place" in "a work that would bring it to completion, even less in itself as work (family, people, church, nation, party, literature, philosophy), but in the unworking and as the unworking of all its works."[12]

The inoperative community, Nancy points out, is hard to represent precisely because it doesn't rest on "objective" factors that would lend themselves to straightforward representation. In a modernity that is interested in groups mostly in terms of production, power, and prestige, the fact that it doesn't alienate itself into a work and understand itself as such a work makes the "inoperative community" nearly imperceptible. In his drawing, Gavarni wants to depict this strange kind of community: a community that shares and divides a resource, but that does not reproduce itself as a single something. There is something utopian in this kind of community: an unalienated form of labor, a nonatomistic collective that doesn't have a purpose other than itself.

A simple thought experiment points to the unique relationship between four-hand playing and work. Did Gavarni have to place the Goncourt brothers at the piano, or could he have depicted one brother singing or playing a violin while the other accompanied on the piano? After all, two instrumentalists on different instruments seem to form a small community as well, can seem intimate, and wordlessly

---

[11] Théophile Gautier, "Préface," *Mademoiselle de Maupin* (Paris: Charpentier, 1877), 22.

[12] Jean-Luc Nancy, *The Inoperative Community* (Minneapolis: University of Minnesota Press, 1991), 72.

understand each other. Such arrangements, too, can suggest a sexual relationship or a sibling relationship—indeed, the cuckolded husband in Tolstoy's *Kreutzer Sonata* is driven crazy by a relationship that unfolds between violin and piano. If Gavarni placed the brothers across a room with two different instruments, he would just as readily depict the close bond between the brothers and the community between them. But their collaboration, the fact that their strange arrangement is somehow a kind of work, would remain unrepresentable. Gavarni's decision to place the brothers at the same keyboard is not just intended to emphasize the four-handedness of their activity; it is also supposed to emphasize that somehow this activity is work, albeit a very strange kind of work.

The brothers' decision to do nothing—that is to say, to not pursue a calling or profession—just like the four-hand playing that Gavarni depicts, points beyond the purely private. It is semi-private, something domestic that has ramifications beyond the limited compass of the bourgeois home. But Gavarni's depiction of the Goncourts' project in many respects reverses the conditions of this semi-privacy. In the previous chapter we dealt with semi-privacy always as a hypertrophy, as an intrusion of public discourses and scrutiny into the private sphere, turning something private into a matter of public debate. How were the two players to be interpreted? Did they need help? Was their activity dangerous? When Gavarni begins visualizing (and musicalizing) the strange collaboration of the brothers Goncourt, the thrust is reversed: if a fraternal division of labor is capable of such close, unalienated collaboration, what exactly makes it impossible in society at large? It is not society that sits in judgment of the couple at the piano but, rather, the two brothers who sit in judgment of politics and society.

And yet, if the brothers confidently project their judgment from their own salon onto the wider world, that wider world gets to look back and gets to judge back. Their four-handedness contains a utopian kernel, but it contains it only in displaced form: Gavarni's drawing cannot show what it wants to show directly; it requires the circuitous route via the invisible piano keyboard. As Walter Benjamin argued, utopian thinking went underground in the nineteenth century. It was repressed into steel constructions, shopping malls, and world exhibition—that is to say, forms that always already understand such hopes as impossible to fulfill.

But what sets four-hand playing apart is that it connects the social utopianism—the one that dreams about the abolition of the social division of labor—with the sensuous promises of the sexual relationship. Even if four-hand music smacked of Fordism for the nineteenth century, it also always contained the opposite idea: however much the piece was cut up and distributed, it was given to the pair of players as a pair; it is work done by a small community. Four-hand playing thus momentarily instituted a thoroughly unbourgeois form of labor—one that left behind the social division of labor. And just as in Gavarni's drawing, four-hand playing made the abolition of the division of labor real and tangible, whether it be for the players or for the spectators.

Four-Hand Playing and the Critique of Alienation

The four-handedness of the Goncourt brothers was deeply anti-bourgeois, in that it was doing nothing. Analogously, the abolition of the social division of labor in four-hand playing was, at least to some extent, a critique of the world as it exists in modernity. In his *The Difference Between Fichte's and Schelling's System of Philosophy* (1800), G. W. F. Hegel (1770–1831) described the project of philosophy as follows: "The need of philosophy arises...when the aesthetic and religious life of the time can no longer sustain the sense of a living unity."[13] One could say that the rapturous enthusiasm with which four-hand playing was taken up in the nineteenth century emerged from the same "need," and that it was similarly understood to level of the same absolutized "oppositions."

In the nineteenth-century German-speaking world, four-hand playing was considered *Hausmusik* or *Salonmusik*; it was understood as linked to the private, domestic sphere. But Hegel had already suggested that the "substantial unity" of the family is necessarily and inevitably rent asunder by the alienating and divisive forces of civil society. "The family becomes fragmented and its members behave towards each other as self-sufficient individuals, for they are held together only by the bond of mutual need."[14] The four-handed monster was not a matter of the "animal kingdom of the spirit"[15] but, rather, of the "substantial unity" of the family. Its (literal) members must not be alienated from one another.

Unlike Nietzsche and Schopenhauer, Hegel was not understood as one of the great "music-making philosophers"[16] of the nineteenth century. But throughout his career he was interested in the ways in which music as such was "determined"— and that also meant "negated"—in particular performance practices. In a letter to his wife in 1824, Hegel praises the music of Rossini by noting that "music, having validity for itself, can also be performed on the violin, on the piano, etc., but Rossini's music has meaning only as sung."[17] Performing music meant making music finite. And Hegel was interested in how what we hear in a piano melody is, in fact, a mediated assemblage of individual strings: in a horn, different sounds are all organically produced within the same object. In a piano, each string can only produce one sound.[18] What the piano presented as an organic whole was a "second immediacy,"

---

[13] G. W. F. Hegel, *The Difference Between Fichte's and Schelling's System of Philosophy*, ed. H.S. Harris and Walter Cerf (Albany: SUNY Press, 1977), 20.

[14] G. W. F. Hegel, *Elements of the Philosophy of Right*, ed. Allen Wood (Cambridge: Cambridge University Press, 1991), 64.

[15] G. W. F. Hegel, *The Phenomenology of Spirit*, ed. J.N. Findlay (Oxford: Oxford University Press, 1977), 237f.

[16] Rudolf Louis, *Der Widerspruch in der Musik* (Leipzig: Breitkopf & Härtel, 1893), vi.

[17] Cited in John Sallis, *Transfigurements: On the True Sense of Art* (Chicago: University of Chicago Press, 2008), 107.

[18] G. W. F. Hegel, *Philosophy of Nature (Part Two of the Encyclopedia of the Philosophical Sciences)*, ed. J. N. Finlay (Oxford: Oxford University Press, 2004), 203.

composed in fact of an immense set of mediations—the same way Hegel characterized civil society.

The nineteenth century often seemed to treat the four-handed monster itself as a kind of substantial whole. In this, the treatment of four-hand playing contrasts in telling ways with the way the nineteenth century thought about other kinds of ensembles. Unlike the orchestra, four-hand players are not ready-made models for society at large—too focused, too private in their interactions; too undialogical, too instinctive in their ways of communicating. Theirs is a community of feeling, lacking any kind of mediating point of authority, such as a conductor. Of course, other chamber music groups similarly get by without a conductor, but their musical communities are differently constituted: when compared to the conclave of different instruments in, say, a quartet or a quintet, or even in a piano duet on two instruments, there is a "plus x" to four-hand playing—not least because the duettists share their means of production. The members of the quartet are exactly that—members, Hegel's "self-sufficient individuals." When they seem to come together, it is as an afterthought; it is external and secondary. As Hermann Wetzel-Stettin puts it, in watching a quartet the observer "follows with joy the threads that spin the four string instruments together into a quartet."[19] Even on a purely visual level there are no such threads in four-hand playing; whatever connects the players, it is much more mysterious and difficult to spot. What makes them tick, what makes them work, is as mysterious as the success of a successful marriage.

Theodor W. Adorno suggested that the members of the quartet are in a way ciphers for the subjects of classical liberalism.[20] They come together under a social contract, submit to one another only up to a point, make decisions through communication rather than command, and pool their different resources for the greater good of the whole. Four-hand players are illiberal, and even profoundly undemocratic. But Adorno also points to what they share with the players in a quartet: "to unify, in however limited a space, object and audience."[21] The orchestra presupposes an audience, to which it offers its music as a commodity. A quartet does not require such an audience, even though it may well have one. Just as the members of a quartet often sit quietly, listening to the others and reading along in the score until it is their turn to join back in, so four-hand playing tends to unite reader, audience, and performer.

But four-hand playing unites more than just the audience and its object. Producer and consumer, orchestra and concertgoer become one. Even the different means of cognition were thought to transcend their boundaries toward something

---

[19] Hermann Wetzel-Stettin, "Schuberts Werke für Klavier zu vier Händen," *Die Musik* 6, No. 7 (1906): 36.

[20] Theodor W. Adorno, *Dissonanzen: Einleitung in die Musiksoziologie (GS 14)* (Frankfurt: Suhrkamp, 2003), 272.

[21] Adorno, *Dissonanzen*, 272.

that encompassed them all equally (again, a concern Hegel's *Differenzschrift* prefigured). Modern social alienation was predicated on the alienation of the senses from one another. The four-hand player hears and feels the communal playing; he or she has to imagine the other's part, and remembers, at least in the case of a transcription, the faint echoes of the orchestral version. Four-hand playing creates, or at least demands, something like a holistic unity of different faculties of cognition—a unity that, as Schopenhauer remarked in his essay "On Noise," had become increasingly impossible under the onslaught of modern noise. The great intellect, Schopenhauer writes, depends on the fact that it concentrates the strength of its various faculties "on one point and object, just as a concave mirror concentrates all the rays of light thrown upon it." All the faculties should thus converge on one object of perception, and all their various perceptions should converge into one unifying point, but "noisy interruption prevents this concentration."[22]

Four-hand playing unites producer and consumer. The players constitute a tiny world economy—a completely autonomous structure of exchange, a musical Robinsonade. But as Karl Marx remarked in *Das Kapital*, the Robinsonade is the paradigmatic phantasm of capitalist society—the idea that a single person, a self-made man, could make an economy all by himself.[23] And indeed, while a musical sociologist like Adorno can describe the utopian content of chamber music in some detail, Robinson and his man Friday in splendid isolation on their keyboard are a much harder configuration to read sociologically. Adorno gives us a sense of the reason for this when he contrasts chamber music and orchestra: both ensembles depict a form of communal life—the quartet is the utopian vision of an unalienated community; the orchestra is the reality of a socialized *polis*. But it is much more questionable whether four-hand piano playing constitutes a community at all. Are the two players already an embryonic community, or are they perhaps only one four-handed monster after all, one that has nothing to tell us about being and working together?

This is why Gavarni turns to four-hand playing in order to depict the entirely unorthodox and explicitly anti-bourgeois way in which the brothers Goncourt produce their work. Four-hand playing has a more fraught and unsettled relationship to civil society than does simple duettism—and it can depict phenomena that likewise don't entirely fit into the organizing dichotomies of the bourgeois cosmos. That is because the nineteenth century was never entirely certain how four-hand playing fit into the basic constants of its understanding of politics and society: the individual, the community, and society as a whole.

We have already discussed the way in which the four-handed monster did not fit easily with bourgeois conceptions of individuality. Four-hand playing was often

---

[22] Arthur Schopenhauer, "On Noise," *Essays of Schopenhauer* (London: Scott, 1897), 28.
[23] Karl Marx, *Capital: A Critique of Political Economy* (Chicago: Kerr, 1915), 1:88.

understood as analogous to friendship, marriage, siblinghood, or love affair—that is to say, other relationships that bourgeois liberalism had a hard time getting a handle on. And the fraught question of whether such binary relationships could be extended into larger groups in any way that had first emerged among the Romantics had never really gone away in the decades after. Four-hand players were understood as an "ensemble fated by nature towards unification,"[24] and thus could embody the fantasy of a perfectly unified community. But their unification pointed to a problem rather than to its solution.

The Metaphors of Four-Hand Piano Playing

The nineteenth century found four-hand players hard to place. How did their relationship relate to other forms of sociability? How did it relate to the individual, to civil society, to the family? This made four-hand playing particularly powerful at a time when the orchestra was becoming a popular way of talking about society. As John Spitzer has shown, in the nineteenth century the orchestra underwent an important shift—but so did the way its contemporaries used it to talk about things other than music. In the eighteenth century, the orchestra had been largely the *target* of metaphors (the orchestra is like some other thing); around the turn of the nineteenth century, it increasingly became a *source* of metaphors (something else is like an orchestra).[25] The orchestra had become sufficiently stable in terms of its social and cultural shape and position that contemporaries could refer back to it as a stable reservoir of stable meanings.

The most important of these meanings represents a complete reversal of eighteenth-century usage, namely the relationship between orchestra and civil society. Schematically speaking, the eighteenth century saw civil society (or constitutional monarchy) as an instructive analog to the orchestra, believing that the ways in which a state or a society is run have something to teach us about the way an orchestra should be organized. By the end of the century, state and society were in tatters, subject to vigorous questioning even in countries where revolution had not upended them. At the same time, the ascendancy of the bourgeoisie led to the emergence of a much more stable, professional, and secure set of practices relating to the orchestra. By the nineteenth century, the orchestra suddenly emerged as an index of how a state should or might be organized, how a society could or should function.

During the same era, however, the relationship between four-hand playing and the orchestra was, of course, anything but settled. Four-hand playing allowed the domestic sphere to play at being an orchestra. Sometimes it was suspected of trying

---

[24] Wetzel-Stettin, "Schuberts Werke für Klavier zu vier Händen," 37.

[25] John Spitzer, "Metaphors of the Orchestra—The Orchestra as Metaphor," *Musical Quarterly* 80, no. 2 (1996): 234–64.

to usurp the role of the orchestra; others, like Saint-Saëns, presented it as finger exercises that had deluded themselves into thinking they were a concert piece. But even without this fraught relationship, the metaphors attending four-hand playing were never as clear as those that attached themselves to other musical actors: while the soloist onstage or in the parlor was a ready symbol for the individual, the harmonizing voices of the orchestra made it ideal for talking about society. The bundle of four hands on the keyboard was both too large and too small for any such straightforward analogies.

The nineteenth century liked to refer—at times semi-ironically—to quartets, quintets, and the like *Hausorchester*, or "orchestra of the home." Four-hand playing was never referred to in this way unless the piano was ringed by a gathering of other instruments. For instance, Percy Fitzgerald's novel *Diana Gay* refers to "the select 'orchestra' of the house, led by Mr. Jennings, consisting of the piano (*á quatre mains*), flute (Master Halliday), cornet, and violin (Gill), [which] struck up the well-known march from *Norma*."[26] In Germany, Johann Wolfgang von Goethe convened a "home orchestra," which actually had both an audience and a reading public. In *Goethe's Correspondence with a Child* (*Goethes Briefwechsel mit einem Kinde*, 1835), Bettina von Arnim writes to Goethe in Weimar: "The next postal carriage will bring you a pack of music, almost all of it arranged for four voices, and thus perfect for your house orchestra."[27] The *Letters* were thoroughly edited and fictionalized by Bettina von Arnim, but we know that the shape of the actual *Hausorchester* accorded with Bettina's description. And Goethe himself turned to metaphors to describe this domestic orchestra—even though it is not the state, but the body that functions as the source of the metaphor. In a letter, Goethe speaks of his house orchestra as "a borrowed-together body, with this limb then that limb falling off."[28] Goethe's cobbled-together orchestra can lose individual limbs and still go on. The corporeal schema of four-hand players is comparatively unstable.

Whatever political valences attach to four-hand playing, they are necessarily in tension with the actual *polis*. Some writers turned to four-hand playing for that exact reason. E. T. A. Hoffman, for instance, presents a story in *Prinzessin Brambilla* (1820) that brings together four-hand piano playing, questions of bodies and their boundaries, and questions concerning political order. But the story, which a charlatan relates in order to show "the strange foolishness, in which the I divides against itself," describes a decidedly counterfactual—and downright surreal—political situation. A princess gives birth to "dear princes, who, although twins, should really have been called 'ones,' seeing as they had grown together at their rear ends."[29] As

---

[26] Percy H. Fitzgerald, *Diana Gay: The History of a Young Lady* (London: Moxon, 1877), 23.

[27] Bettina von Arnim, *Goethe's Briefwechsel mit einem Kinde* (Berlin: Hertz, 1881), 107.

[28] Johann Wolfgang von Goethe, *Goethes Werke (Weimarer Ausgabe) Abt. IV, Vol. 24 (Briefe 1814)* (Weimar: Böhlau, 1887–1919), 221.

[29] E. T. A. Hoffmann, *Poetische Werke in sechs Bänden* (Berlin: Aufbau, 1963), 5:734.

explored in the fourth chapter, the emerging problem is that this twin/one occupies a position supposedly reserved for a single, autonomous ruler. The king is supposed to be a solo player. The ministers calm down the prince, "who was slightly worried by the double blessing," by pointing out that "four hands would be much firmer in their grasp of scepter and sword than two."

But this well-meaning support, of course, raises more questions than it settles: how many scepters and swords would this four-handed rat-king wield? Four hands would seem to require two scepters, but the two princes are supposed to rule the state as *one* sovereign. The reassuring metaphor that "the governmental sonata would sound even fuller and more powerful *à quatre mains*" points not to the fact that four-hand piano playing can easily depict what government is like, and much rather to the fact that it can only do so with some contortions. For Hoffmann, four-handedness thus means the impossibility of sovereignty.

The king decides to convene "a commission composed of philosophers and tailors," who will create a "double set of pantaloons" for the princes, although the more pressing question is "what the appropriate shape of the throne should be." Hoffmann's story personalizes sovereignty—it belongs to an individual person, not to a principle that could disperse into a system of checks and balances.[30] The sovereign thus cannot be two people, even if they are grown together at their rear ends. If one thinks it through, according to Hoffmann, the "governmental sonata" and "*à quatre mains*" turn out to be contradictory terms.

Hoffmann's charlatan tells this story in order to demonstrate the impossibility of the categories of person and personality, and whatever political points the story makes sneak in unbidden. But there is, of course, a connection between the vision of a person or subject who is split against him- or herself, who isn't the lone master of his or her own self, on the one hand; and of a state in which two princes rule back-to-back, with two scepters and two swords and four-legged pantaloons. This is what happens when nineteenth-century writers turn to four-hand playing as a metaphor: orchestra, soloist, quartet—all of these stabilize whatever they are adduced to metaphorize, be this the state, the person, or the body. Four-hand playing is always a sign of instability; it can depict only the monstrous aspects of the political, the schizophrenic, and nonidentity in categories of subjectivity.

But if four-hand playing was an uneasy fit for metaphors dealing with individuals and states, what about its semiotic relationship to its own native soil, the family? After all, the one thing Hoffmann's fairy tale *can* liken to the princes' sonata *à quatre mains* without too much friction is brotherhood. Four-hand playing could gather, structure, bound the family—but how well did it represent the family as a metaphor? Here, too, it turns out that four-hand piano was less than ideal in transporting straightforward points about an entity. For in musicalizing the family, the

---

[30] Warren Breckman, *Marx, the Young Hegelians, and the Origins of Social Theory* (Cambridge: Cambridge University Press, 2001), 9–14.

nineteenth century preferred to turn to the orchestra. Consider, for instance, a text that appeared in January of 1830 in the *Allgemeine musikalische Zeitung* in Berlin, which can count as symptomatic. In applying musical logic to family life, it avoids talking about chamber music or four-hand piano; instead, it orchestrates the family.

The way this orchestration proceeds gives us some clues as to the status of four-hand music as metaphor. The text is written under the pseudonym "Techo di Teczoni" and endeavors to describe "the concert of domestic life," "an opportunity for mutual instruction between heads of household and musicians."[31] The author is particularly interested in "how to distribute the voices in the orchestra of domestic life, such as to produce an effective harmony and pleasing melody."[32]

The "effective harmony" the author calls for in both the bourgeois household and the orchestra raises a number of questions: Who safeguards this harmony in each case? How are the individual members of the family or of the orchestra supposed to conceive of their relationships to one another? And finally, who gets to decide and enjoy the "effective harmony" and the "pleasing melody"? The answers to these questions show why "Di Teczoni" could not have used four-hand piano in his little text. The harmony in the orchestra of domestic life is intended for a listener who comes from the outside and is not part of the family or the orchestra. The harmony thus has nothing to do with the family/orchestra members themselves. The family described here is not self-sufficient, autonomous, or intimate; rather, it is a radically heteronomous small business, the job of which is to produce goods that please the outside world.

Moreover, "Di Teczoni" sometimes thinks that the individual orchestra *player* is somehow like a family member; at other times, he talks as though the *instrument itself* were representative of a family member. The first violin is the "mother of the house," who has to be "equipped with pure, not false strings." "One should," the reader is told, "check and inspect carefully" such an instrument before "procuring" one. The bass meanwhile plays the role of the paterfamilias, whose job it is to counteract the easily seduced violin: "The notes can flitter their beautiful plumage, the figures can be colorful and seductive"; the father and husband has to continue "providing the calm, powerful root of the chord which provides orientation for the other instruments, and to maintain the rhythm for the entire orchestra."[33] In this task he is supported by the lady-in-waiting (second violin), the secretary (cello), and the cook (viola). Around this inner circle, we have the children (clarinets, flutes, and oboes), the master of ceremonies (bassoon), the servants (horns), and riding guard and coachman (tympani and trumpets), "which only appear on the scene when the full household rides out in pomp and circumstance."[34]

---

[31] *Allgemeine musikalische Zeitung* (hereafter *AmZ*) (January 9, 1830): 1–15.
[32] *AmZ* (1830): 13.
[33] *AmZ* (1830): 13.
[34] *AmZ* (1830): 14.

As much as this text smacks of the unreflected prejudices of its era, there are a few truly telling aspects to the analogies "Di Teczoni" draws between orchestra and family. Among them is the fact that the writer assigns to the bass the role of the man of the house, rather than crowning him the conductor of the entire ensemble, as one might expect. This probably has to do with the fact that the conductor has a very different kind of authority (and that he does not lend a voice to the "concert of domestic life"), a kind of authority that has more in common with state authority than that of the paterfamilias. In the eighteenth century, the metaphor of the conductor as the sovereign of the orchestra was quite common. Charles Dufresny (1648–1724) described the conductor as "sovereign of the orchestra, a Prince so perfectly absolute that in raising or lowering his baton he regulates all the movements of his capricious little people."[35] Even though the role that the article assigns the bass-husband could well be performed by a conductor (in particular, the job to keep the violin's hysteria in check), the writer chose to leave the conductor out of his orchestra altogether. His kind of authority has no right to the domestic sphere in the nineteenth century.

It is unclear what status the individual family members have in this orchestra. Are they supposed to correspond to the instruments themselves or, rather, to the players who play them? In particular when it comes to the wife, the article never distinguishes between the two. It remarks that one should not depend "on a brilliant exterior" in "choosing such an instrument." At the same time, the writer speaks of the *Besetzung* of this part, meaning the players assigned to it. In the concert of domestic life, the wife thus seems to play the violin and at the same time is that violin.

While she is thus instrument and instrumentalist in one, the "lord of the household and husband" is explicitly said to strum the bass. The body of the bass does not come into view—we never find out if its exterior is brilliant, are never instructed to scrutinize it before allowing it into our orchestra. The instrument is not identical with the husband; it is the husband's instrument. Because the woman is player and instrument in one, she is particularly seducible. She "therefore all too easily abandons the correct rhythm, and then seduces the rest of the orchestra to follow her wanton example." This is why one has to check her strings and examine her body for "finesse and delicacy."

Another strange feature of the text has less to do with the gender stereotypes of the early nineteenth century and more with fairly profound assumptions its pseudonymous author makes: the article treats orchestra and concert as essentially the same thing. Especially if the author wants to suggest how the orchestra may teach his (apparently entirely male) readers about familial harmony, it is of course important to know what the author means by "effective harmony" and "pleasing melody." "Di Teczoni" seems particularly worried that the orchestra could lose its unifying rhythm, which "is an annoyance to the listener." But who is this listener, and what

---

[35] Charles Dufresny, *Amusemens serieux et comiques* (Amsterdam: Desbordes, 1699), 64.

business of his is it if the family travels to the beats of different drummers? And why should his annoyance matter to the family?

Symphony and concert exist for a listener who consumes its music without being part of the production of music.[36] The orchestra is not supposed to luxuriate in its own music; rather, its "sounding together" is intended for something outside of itself. But it would seem that "familial harmony" is something that exists almost exclusively for the harmonic family. Harmony is an end in itself rather than a means for another's viewing pleasure. At the same time, the family that "Di Teczoni" describes is not a nuclear family but, rather, a fairly extended household. It is what the ancient Greeks would have called an *oikos*—family plus servants, a small economy all to itself. All of this—the economic aspect, the extended household, and, yes, even the family's children—fall away in the metaphors of four-hand piano playing. Four hands cannot possibly provide the kind of subservience, the kind of stratification, or the kind of economic energy that the orchestral metaphor provides "Di Teczoni."

The Metaphysics of the Keyboard

While the strange dualism of four-hand players is harder to connect to, let alone reduce to, other social formations, four-hand piano playing seems to push all the more forcefully into the realm of metaphysics. If four-hand playing seemed to have a strange affinity with Hegel's critique of atomism, since in both the point was to transcend opposition in favor of an all-encompassing third thing, the reason lies in the fact that both phenomena were imbued not just with a "Romanticism of alienation" but also with a metaphysics of unification. In other words, for the nineteenth century, the uncanny solidarity and unspoken bonds of the four hands on the keyboard didn't just contain suggestions of a transcendence of particular roles; they also pointed to an all-encompassing, perhaps cosmic unity with another.

On the face of it, it may seem absurd that what in the end boiled down to a unique but not all that remarkable musical practice should attract such recondite speculation. The reason for this elective affinity had to do with the fact that music was frequently understood as somehow metaphysical in the nineteenth century, especially in the German-speaking world. Arthur Schopenhauer had proposed that, while the other arts dealt with the world of representations (quite literally in the sense that they based themselves on objects in the real world), music had its referent in the will that stood behind all reality. Music thus transcended the world of individual objects, moving in the direction of the substrate that lay behind the everyday world and the things that appear in it.

---

[36] Hanns-Werner Heister, *Das Konzert: Theorie einer Kulturform* (Wilhelmshaven: Heinrichshofen, 1983), 36.

While Schopenhauer's forbidding tome *The World as Will and Representation* probably found its way into only a select number of households in the nineteenth century, his ideas circulated much more widely. Richard Wagner did his part to popularize Schopenhauer's basic premise, as did his admirer-cum-critic Friedrich Nietzsche. At the time, the idea that music transcended the *principium individuationis*, the world of discreet and bounded objects, in favor of something more encompassing and harder to grasp was widespread. Given that contemporaries thought they observed something similar playing out on the four-hand keyboard, it is not entirely surprising that they understood four-hand playing in decidedly metaphysical terms. And it is likewise not entirely surprising that their English and French contemporaries had some trouble following them in this respect.

Hoffmann's Siamese princes stressed the inherent *duality* of four-hand playing, but other texts were far more interested in the *unity* behind the four hands. In literary depictions, in philosophical reflections, and in journalistic accounts, contemporaries marveled at both togetherness and unity. But in *The Man Without Qualities*, Robert Musil proposed a new interpretation of the unity of the four-handed monster, one that probably formed key cultural perceptions of four-hand piano playing much earlier. Musil understands the eroticism of four-hand playing, not in terms of closeness and touch (of hands and bodies), but in terms of a wholesale unification of a couple during play. Musil seems to have drawn the idea from his reading of the eclectic Romantic philosopher Franz von Baader (1765–1841), but it originated in Plato's dialogues. *The Man Without Qualities* seems to have been the first text to point to the siblinghood between the four-handed monster and the circular beings of which Aristophanes speaks in Plato's *Symposium*. In his speech on the origin of love at the titular banquet, Aristophanes postulates the existence of a prehistoric species of humans who were "rounded whole, with back and sides forming a circle," who not only each possessed the sexual organs of both sexes but also two faces, four legs—and four hands.[37]

In his speech, Aristophanes suggests that the point of erotic desire is to reunite the two split halves of these erstwhile circular beings. Hermann Wetzel-Stettin similarly speaks of an "ensemble driven by nature towards unification."[38] Hans Moldenhauer suggests that all four-hand playing strives for "an ideal of organic integration."[39] Playing four-hand piano means two things: becoming *one* (like the Platonic "rounded wholes," or Hegel's family) and dividing labor (like the orchestra described by "Techo di Teczoni"). In Musil's novel, Walter and Clarisse, two childhood friends of the protagonist's who have since married, play *à quatre mains* almost obsessively. Musil's narrator describes their playing as the "great unification" on the

---

[37] Plato, *The Symposium* (New York: Penguin, 1999), 22. (189e).
[38] Wetzel-Stettin, "Schuberts Werke für Klavier zu vier Händen," 37.
[39] Hans Moldenhauer, *Duo Pianism* (Chicago: Chicago Musical College Press, 1950), 189.

piano, as "twinned gestures of desperation and rapture,"[40] as a "balloon, wavering in outlines as it filled up with hot emotions,"[41] and as that "mysterious space in which self and world, perception and feeling, inside and outside, plunge into one another in the most indefinable way."[42] Whenever four hands touch a keyboard in Musil's novel, things swell, melt, plunge—borders break down and things become one.

But at this point, the translation obscures what Musil is actually saying about Walter's and Clarisse's four-hand playing. The narrator doesn't use the word "twinned" to describe their unification; instead, he uses the word *zwillingshaft*, "twinlike." Four-hand piano playing never actually manages to create the absolute identity that it is after. Only toward the end of the completed part of the novel is there such a unity, and when it arrives it isn't merely twinlike; it is the erotic unification of two actual twins. Instead of the avid four-hand pianists Walter and Clarisse achieving twinship, the man without qualities and his twin sister, Agathe, actually manage to attain the much sought-after goal of becoming truly one. When Musil's narrator strains to describe the fullness of their unification, he turns to a familiar metaphor: four-hand piano playing, with a distinctly Platonic hue.

> From some undetermined boundary on, they felt as one being: the way that two people playing piano four-handedly, or reading with two voices a scripture important for their salvation, a single being arises.... As in a dream, what hovered before them was a melting into one form—just as incomprehensibly, convincingly and passionately beautiful as it happens that two people exist alongside each other and are secretly the same.[43]

In this single image of twinned (rather than twinlike) unification, Musil's narrator manages to combine the four-handed monster at the piano and the shared voice of the instrument when it is played four hands. He compares the siblings' sexual unification to four-hand piano playing, and he compares it to two voices reading an identical text. The complexity of Musil's comparison suggests that he was uncommonly aware of the metaphysical niceties of four-hand playing.

But the relationship between unification and four-hand playing in Musil is a good deal more complex than the rapturous passage just quoted would suggest. For although in his climactic description Musil seems to connect the coming together of the twins with the twinlike attempts at unification at the piano, his actual descriptions of four-hand playing always imply that there is a good deal of distance between the two. There is a lot of room between the twinlike groping toward unification and the rapturous "melting" the siblings actually accomplish. Especially the scenes

---

[40] Musil, *The Man Without Qualities*, 152.
[41] Musil, *The Man Without Qualities*, 45.
[42] Musil, *The Man Without Qualities*, 151.
[43] Musil, *The Man Without Qualities*, 148–49.

involving Walter and Clarisse suggest that their twinlike gestures can never actually reach the kind of unification they strive for.

In the course of the novel, Walter also plays the piano by himself. When alone, he seems to prefer Wagner, while the two partners together seem to play mostly Beethoven. While Wagner runs self-sufficiently through the hands of the solo player, Beethoven's music arrives with an appeal to a communal effort, although it is a communal effort that rather spectacularly fails to come to fruition. This is because the two players are unable to fully invest in their playing—or, rather, almost compulsively invest it with extraneous concerns. They are afforded the opportunity to make music together as one person—an opportunity no cellist, no trumpeter, no guitarist will ever be afforded. And yet the two obsessively regard this opportunity as a sign for something else—in particular, the child that they might or could have together. They engage almost in a game of poker over this spectral child they will never have.

> His feelings were splashing like big raindrops on the keys. She instantly guessed what he was thnking of: the child. She knew that he wanted to bind her to himself with a child. They argued about it day in, day out. And the music did not for a second. The music knew no denial. Like a net whose entangling meshes she had not noticed, it was pulling shut with lightning speed. Clarisse leapt up in mid-chord and banged the piano shut; Walter barely managed to save his fingers.[44]

As mentioned earlier, Musil's narrator is not exactly subtle in drawing links between Walter's solo playing and masturbation. He depicts Wagner, whom Walter plays when he is alone at the piano, as somehow inherently autoerotic, but he presents Beethoven, and above all Beethoven played *à quatre mains*, as the epitome of allosexuality. It is no accident, then, that his wife forces her Wagner-loving husband to join her in playing Beethoven's "Ode to Joy." Where he would prefer to putter in his own musical man cave, she forces him to rehearse a piece that is all about unification with another. Friedrich Schiller's poem, after all, celebrates joy as that which brings together "that which fashion has divided." In the scene just quoted, then, we witness the four-hand version of the "Ode to Joy" as a kind of musical *coitus interruptus*. Walter tries to coax his wife musically, and she can escape only by closing the piano.

Even before he stages the mystical union of the twins Ulrich and Agnes as a kind of cosmic four-hand play, Musil presents four-hand playing in insistently metaphysical language. Wherever Walter and Clarisse meet to play piano, the circular humans of Plato's *Symposium* are never far behind; he speaks of the "great unification" or, rather, of the way four-hand playing always manages to fall short of it. He follows

---

[44] Musil, *The Man Without Qualities*, 155.

Aristophanes in postulating a great all-encompassing oneness, one that unites not just the two sexes in one being but even the senses. It is a oneness that undoes "a division of labor" between thought and emotion: "for in primeval times, our emotions as well as our sense sensations sprang from the same root, an attitude that involved the entire creature."[45] Aristophanes suggests that this kind of reunification is always already impossible, and Musil's loving descriptions of four-hand playing suggest that these twinlike attempts at reattaining a lost unity are similarly doomed to failure.

But what exactly is it that dooms it? When Clarisse forces Walter to try out pianistic sex with someone other than himself for a change, she seems to enjoy the act quite a bit. Still, she interrupts the musical coitus—but not because she is afraid of her own enjoyment, or of his. Instead, she realizes that he has ulterior motives, that he wants a child. Her reaction is strange: it would make sense if Clarisse were disgusted that her husband looks at the keyboard as an ersatz bedroom, but she has no problem with that. It's the fact that he connects their pianistic lovemaking with biological reproduction that arouses her disgust. Whatever mystical powers previous chapters (and nineteenth-century flights of fancy) may have imputed to four-hand playing, it is fairly clear that Walter's desire to musically impregnate his wife remains steadfastly metaphoric. Four-hand piano playing may be sublimated sex, in other words, but no one has yet gotten pregnant from playing four hands. Why, then, interrupt the metaphoric coitus?

The answer seems to be that not everything one creates in four-hand playing is created equal. In staging Clarisse's horror at her possible musical pregnancy, Musil thematizes the question of how the product of the strange, melding communion on the keyboard is to be understood. Clarisse reads Walter's feelings in the keys they share, and she realizes that whatever they produce in common, it won't be the kind of product he has in mind. She sees that he is making music with her, which has no substance or solidity and drifts out the open window never to be heard from again, but that he is interested in creating something far more permanent. Both Walter and Clarisse look to the keyboard, and to Beethoven's setting of Schiller's "Ode," to provide some kind of unification—but he perverts the kind of unification-in-the-moment she seeks by trying to turn that unification into a unified thing.

Musil's speculations on sexual unification and androgyny (in particular, the passages on the protagonist's relationship with his twin-wife Agathe) were heavily indebted to his somewhat eclectic reading of the equally eclectic Romantic Franz von Baader.[46] Baader, a friend and follower of Schelling, assigned the erotic an important function in his philosophy. He distinguished between a kind of erotic unification that created a child who exits his parents and becomes a thing of his

---

[45] Musil, *The Man Without Qualities*, 130–31.
[46] See Achim Aurnhammer, *Androgynie: Studien zu einem Motiv in der europäischen Literatur* (Vienna: Böhlau, 1986).

own, and another kind in which the child "doesn't live side-by-side with the parents, but rather inside them, and thus continues uniting the two inwardly and in solidarity."[47] Baader, whose theosophic speculations fused Platonism, German Idealism, and theology, understood the former kind of reproduction (the almost fecal expulsion of the unity from the united couple) as a debasement of an ideal communal pregnancy. Either the child is a "third thing," an alienated something, an external purpose; or (in "true love") the child exists as an unalienated, connecting substance that binds together the two lovers, and that "knows no wherefore."[48]

Musil adapts Baader's ideas in staging his scene of musical sex. He picks up on Baader's opposition: on the one hand, a communal producing that is never alienated into an external thing, and on the other, the far more straightforward (and somehow brute and shallow) alienation of love into a physical child. While Clarisse luxuriates in the infinite flow of their playing ("One would have to go on playing, till the very end," Clarisse muses, and at another point, "We should never have to stop playing"[49]), Walter seems terrified of that same infinity. Where she sees an eternally lingering moment, he sees only a rush to dissipation and early extinction: "In a wink, it would be over!"[50] What bothers him is what he perceives as the sterility of their playing (perhaps again as its masturbatory quality): the fact that nothing comes of what they do, that no something emerges from their activity.

Musil activates an old philosophical opposition—that between the world of being and the world of becoming—and uses it to have his characters articulate two opposing cultural attitudes toward art. Clarisse wishes for the complete submersion of life (in this instance, of erotic unification) in art, while Walter demands that art should be good for something after all, that it should produce something more tangible than a never-ending profusion of sound.

Walter's sacrilege against the Eleusinian mysteries of four-hand piano playing consists of nothing other than that he wants it to be good for something. He violates the aestheticist imperative that the community on the keyboard should "know no wherefore," or, as Gautier put it, "ne peut servir à rien." Musil places his duettists (a) in a kind of collaborative work relationship (albeit a work relationship that doesn't actually produce anything), and (b) in an erotic relationship (albeit one that never truly brings the lovers together). Musil's description doesn't allow us to assign it to one side or the other exclusively: it is either erotic labor or eroticism with a division of labor; either something that cannot but point beyond itself, or something that at least tries to come to rest in itself. Four-hand playing is a reversible image of the utopian imagination. The utopian idea of transcending all bounds of profession

---

[47] Franz von Baader, *Franz von Baader's sämmtliche Werke, Zehnter Band* (Leipzig: Hermann Bethmann, 1855), 344.
[48] Baader, *Franz von Baader's sämmtliche Werke*, 345.
[49] Musil, *The Man Without Qualities*, 153.
[50] Musil, *The Man Without Qualities*, 155.

and class turns on closer inspection into that of complete sexual unity with an other. The ideal turns suddenly into a matter of feeling, of presence, of nerves.

Many nineteenth-century commentators were befuddled by the way four-hand playing seemed to be located somewhere between unity and duality, or perhaps better, between being not quite one and not quite two. For those who looked to music as a source of stability for the wider world, or even to the wider world for ways to stabilize music, this had to be an irritant. But the same irritation contains the utopian force of four-hand playing: in it, the utopian yearning for overcoming modern atomism coincides with the kind of erotic longing described by Plato. The four-handed monster contains both—and its instability is both its semantic strength and its weakness. It proved useless—even dangerous—in describing the world as it actually existed; but it proved indispensable to those dreamers and crackpots interested precisely in describing a world that didn't exist yet.

The social utopia contained in the phenomenon of four-hand playing depended on the unification of spheres and moments that were otherwise polar opposites in nineteenth-century social life: four-hand playing was (1) work without product, an activity that can never be alienated from its producer or entered into general circulation; it was f (2) labor in the private sphere—that is to say, a sphere in which anything that had acknowledged work character was constitutively banished; and it was (3) family work, and that also meant work without division of labor. It was not just communal effort (as opposed to labor done and exchanged in the social world); it was work as sexual relationship, as marriage, as love. It was an activity that afforded recognition, not through the product but through the activity itself.

But as the texts considered in this chapter make clear, this utopian valence is never more than a glint in the players' eyes, a possibility that hovers over the scene and then withdraws. As noted, four-hand playing in its very appearance acknowledges this: the possibility of unity draws hands and bodies closer together, but only for moments. Then, as though by some divine command, the arms untangle, the hands rush off in embarrassment and busy themselves in distant corners of the keyboard. And the same players who only seconds ago appeared to be one four-handed monster, breathing in unison and moving in uncanny concord, suddenly sit like two laborers on a workbench, uncomfortable and inconvenienced by the other alien body on the stool, with their backs almost turned to each other.

Failing at Unification

Why would Musil choose Beethoven's "Ode to Joy'" as Walter and Clarisse's project *du jour*, and why would he choose to have his narrator dissect four-hand playing specifically on the basis of this piece? Significantly, Musil's narrator speaks only of the "Ode"—that is to say, the concluding movement of Beethoven's symphony;

Walter and Clarisse, he suggests, are cherry-picking their favorite parts of the musical canon. But the narrator is pointing to something else yet, since he makes direct reference to the millions who embrace in Schiller's poem, which Beethoven set to music. Walter and Clarisse aren't "just" playing a transcription of Beethoven's piece. By calling it an "Ode" and invoking a text the four-hand version doesn't have, Musil's narrator makes clear that Walter and Clarisse aren't just pulling an arbitrary score from their library, they are pulling out a whole lot of cultural baggage with it.

Schiller's "Ode," composed in 1785, represented a celebration of unification, oneness, and brotherhood so delirious that the poet (who wrote the work for friends) later disowned its philosophy. Joy's "beautiful, divine spark" will "heal what fashion has pulled apart." Under joy's influence "all men become brothers." And, perhaps most significantly, those who persist in animus and separateness "may forever steal away from our congregation [*Bund*]." Behind Schiller's celebration of joy's unifying power lies an ideology of unification in the Platonic mold. All men were once brothers, but "fashion" intervened and separated them from one another. Joy is able to (momentarily, ecstatically) bridge that separation, to restore what once was. Those who cannot bridge that separation, Schiller implies, those who cannot embrace joy's power to overcome wanton divisions, are somehow defective and unworthy of the congregation celebrated in the poem.

Musil's narrator thus places hapless Walter and Clarisse in dialogue with a poem whose dizzy raptures put the lie to the couple's own efforts at unification, either on the keyboard or off it, and which pronounces a rather severe sentence on people who fail at unification. But he raises the stakes considerably by explicitly invoking Clarisse's favorite philosopher, Friedrich Nietzsche. The remark Musil refers to in this passage constitutes one of the first explications of the Dionysian in Nietzsche's *The Birth of Tragedy*: "Transform Beethoven's song exulting Joy as a painting, do not hold back your imagination, when the millions sink shuddering into the dust; this way you approach the Dionysian." Nietzsche's conception, if anything, pushed Schiller's mania for unification, oneness, and plenitude to an extreme: "Under the spell of the Dionysian the bond [*Bund*] between man and man is finally restored, and alienated, hostile or subdued nature celebrates its feast of reconciliation with its prodigal son, man."[51] In Beethoven's rendition of Schiller's text, Clarisse's idol espies this rapturous reconciliation, the end of alienation, complete unification with the universe—the two players' experience itself, however, of course looks quite different.

Nietzsche never explicitly linked the Dionysian to four-hand playing, of course. But Musil, a careful reader of Nietzsche himself, would have been aware that the philosopher had placed a very similar demand for unity and reconciliation on four-hand playing as he had on Dionysian revelry. This was not by accident: after

---

[51] Friedrich Nietzsche, *Werke (Kritische Gesamtausgabe, III. 1)*, ed. Giorgio Colli and Mazzino Montinari (Berlin: de Gruyter, 1972): 25.

all, Nietzsche's *Birth of Tragedy* pinned its hopes for a Dionysian revival on Wagner, whose music Nietzsche had first encountered in a piano transcription (of the overture to *Tristan*). But Nietzsche was not just a passionate four-hand player; he also composed four-hand music. Louis Kelterborn, who by his own account played with Nietzsche "about ten times" in the early 1870s, reported that "what I got to hear and play here was exclusively Wagner and Nietzsche."[52] Nietzsche's own compositions for piano four-hands were not particularly imaginative, and Nietzsche abandoned his compositional efforts in the mid-1870s. Just looking over the titles makes it clear, however, that Nietzsche understood the togetherness of the two piano players as an allegory for other forms of social life. One piece was a "Hymn to Friendship," another subtitled "In Praise of Compassion; another traced the "Echoes of New Year's Eve."

The most potent of these forms of social life was marriage. In 1873, Nietzsche sent a piece, the *Monodie à deux*, to Gabriel Monod and Olga Herzen, daughter of the Russian-German writer Alexander Herzen, on the occasion of their wedding in Florence. Both the wedding gift's title and the fact that it was written for four hands were owed to the occasion. As the budding composer wrote to Carl von Gersdorff, the piece "may be taken as a divining rod [*prognostikon*] for a good marriage."[53] At the same time he wrote to his mother and sister about the piece: "If you understand what a monody is, then you understand what symbolic bearing it has on marriage."[54] This symbolic bearing turned out to resemble very much the *Bund* he had sensed in Beethoven's setting of Schiller—the *deux* of the title were to sound as one (*Monodie*). The togetherness on the keyboard was to become a symbol for togetherness in marriage; Nietzsche even specified that "the left part should be played by M. Monod, the right part by Madame Monod."[55]

The *Monodie à deux* was an adaptation of a portion of Nietzsche's much earlier attempt at a Christmas oratorio, but he added a new ending. These new final bars abandon the great majority of the keyboard, as both primo and secondo busy themselves in the same tiny range, getting so close that the editors of Nietzsche's piano works suggested that the primo take over for both parts. These bars, in *pianissimo*, are followed by a gradual *crescendo*, culminating in a *fortissimo* conclusion that once again utilizes the entirety of the keyboard and finds the couple playing in broad and representative formation. Only here, then, does Nietzsche's title make sense beyond the joke about M. and Mme. Monod: what the editors somewhat unromantically remove here is the challenge of having to operate with extreme delicacy in extreme proximity. The piece is a divining rod in the sense that it is a practice

---

[52] Friedrich Nietzsche, *Briefwechsel (Kritische Gesamtausgabe II, 7.1)* (Berlin: de Gruyter, 1998), 593.

[53] Nietzsche, *Werke*, 3: 1087.

[54] Friedrich Nietzsche, *Briefe: Mai 1872–Dezember 1874*, ed. Giorgio Colli, Mazzino Montinari (Munich: Deutscher Taschenbuch Verlag, 1986), 133.

[55] Nietzsche, *Briefe: Mai 1872–Dezember 1874*, 133.

course: demonstrate that you can interact in close quarters on the keyboard, and you will be able to do it in the household.

Walter and Clarisse, it turns out, of course can do neither. Musil's narrator chronicles their play with nearly sadistic exactitude and makes very clear that they are flunking the tests implicit in the source material, be that source material Schiller, Beethoven, or Nietzsche. In so doing, it seems, he manages to indict not just Walter and Clarisse and their pretensions; he also seems to echo the concern about whether four-hand piano can possibly live up to the expectations placed on it. Is it really Walter and Clarisse's fault that they fail the test jointly set up for them by Schiller, Beethoven, and Nietzsche? Or is the test perhaps rigged and deeply unfair? If Musil, more than any other writer, thematized the stratospheric metaphysical hopes attached to four-hand playing in the nineteenth century, he is also more brutal than most in showing how almost by necessity the practice fell far short of those hopes.

The utopian and erotic unification of the four-handed monster doesn't just succumb to the pressures of a familial prohibition; it is ultimately undone by its own social impossibility. The viewer's enjoyment depends on the change from moments of intimacy and moments of dispersal. So far, this book has treated this change primarily in terms of sexual intimacy and its censorship. But of course the same goes for the labor character of four-hand playing. Four-hand playing dramatized, albeit only in fleeting moments, the utopian vision of an unalienated community, a community that knows no division of labor. And then it dramatized its necessary undoing, its prohibition, its ephemeral character. When the two players strike their final chord, the two sets of hands are each in their corner like boxers. No touch, no single four-handed monster but, rather, two very distinct people, each with his own purview and job description, office drones of the piano keyboard.

Scenes like the ones Musil stages on the piano once again highlight just how overdetermined the scene of four-hand playing was in the nineteenth century. The fourth chapter of this book showed that contemporaries read four-hand playing both in terms of the fashionable determinism of their age and as a sign that such determinism could be transcended. Chapters 5 and 6 have shown that four-hand playing was caught in a complicated dialectic between labor and eroticism, changing from one to the other, pretending to be one and instead being the other, or even combining the two in ways not found elsewhere in the culture. The following chapter will continue the investigation of Musil's *Man Without Qualities* and its highly complex scenes of four-hand playing. It will show how a keen eye and philosophically savvy writer could use the very instability and overdetermination of four-hand semiotics to not only interrogate his own culture and his age but also to make it the first incision in a full-scale postmortem on the nineteenth century.

8

Kakanian Variations

Four Hands and the Passing of the Nineteenth Century

In the preceding chapters, four-hand playing on a single keyboard emerged as a fantastically charged scene; for the nineteenth century, it fulfilled wishes, unleashed fears, and set dreams into motion. The nineteenth-century bourgeoisie valued piano four-hands far more than related phenomena and ascribed greater meaning to it. The bourgeois salon liked to play quartets, too, but quartets did not merit discussion as much as the uncanny *pas-de-deux* of hands on the keyboard. To nineteenth-century eyes, the soloist also seemed deeply unsettling, even demonic, yet there were no comparable utopias or dreams of domestic bliss associated with this figure—quite the opposite.

It is no wonder, then, that four-hand piano became important "once again" or "one more time" (as Theodor Adorno titles his essay on the subject) at the point when the "dream world" of the nineteenth century turned into the twentieth—first, as an expression of this dream world, its vision for its own future; then, as a nightmare that had been latent in it all along. This chapter discusses two novels from the early twentieth century in this light. Both originate in a country that dragged itself across the finish line of the nineteenth century, only to collapse just a little distance into the twentieth: the Austro-Hungarian Empire. Or, as Robert Musil called it, in a scatological bowdlerization of the abbreviation "k.u.k." (*kaiserlich und königlich*, "imperial and royal") that attached to it so many of the country's dignitaries and institutions: "Kakania."

Both novels understand the parallel exertion of four hands and two players as a figure for the strange twin monarchy that had ruled the empire since 1867 (the "Imperial and Royal Monarchy"). Both are keenly attuned to four-hand piano's promise to create national unity out of components that did not easily or automatically fit together. They thought the unity effected by four-hand playing might provide a concrete image for the community and a shared identity that had a hard time springing up in Franz Joseph's far-flung and bric-a-brac empire. But not just this outsized promise makes itself felt in these novels; so does the profound absurdity of these ambitions—and the dangerous phantasms they harbored.

One of the novels takes place in 1913; the other was published that year. Robert Musil's *Man Without Qualities* (*Der Mann ohne Eigenschaften*) is probably better known today than when it first appeared, and is considered one of the towering achievements of the modernist novel. The second—*Grillparzer's Love-Story, The Sisters Fröhlich* (*Grillparzers Liebesroman, Die Schwestern Fröhlich*), by Joseph August Lux—is forgotten today. Perhaps this unabashedly kitschy novel of *Heimat* with its questionable politics and even more questionable taste deserves it. When it appeared, however, it was by no means a flop: throughout the German-speaking world, more than 40,000 copies were sold within a year of publication. Lux's novel lightly fictionalizes the life of the poet and dramatist Franz Grillparzer (1791–1872), and shows the writer interacting with a number of luminaries of early nineteenth-century Vienna, among them Franz Schubert.

These two novels are concerned with the "Imperial and Royal Monarchy," and they use piano four-hands to cast light on the Danube monarchy. By way of a physiognomy of Vienna in the 1820s, Lux's work seeks to distill an authentically Austrian essence—an essence that could never have existed the way Lux imagines it in the multinational Austro-Hungarian state. Musil's novel, on the other hand, performs an autopsy on the double-headed monarchy after its demise. Lux's subtitle indicates that *Grillparzer's Love-Story* is a "novel from Vienna's classical age." The work fictionalizes and idealizes the world of the 1820s: "We, the generation of today, look back upon that time and its great men with a kind of tender, familial pride; it stands close to out hearts; we wish to look into its dear face, read in its eyes, and embrace its soul and inner life."[1] Musil, by contrast, has some sympathy for this bygone state, most of it suffused with irony, and otherwise takes stock unsparingly of the land that Friedrich Engels had called "European China"[2]—a country that, in Musil's own words, "was somehow just playing along with itself."[3]

Compared to Musil, Lux treats the "Kakanian" inheritance much less critically; he was writing while the dual monarchy was still in existence. For all that, his backward-looking depiction of the "classical age" of Vienna evinces profound ambivalence, not just about the age he is supposedly celebrating but about his own age as well. First, Lux (1871–1947) was of two minds about the politics of what in German-speaking lands is known as the Biedermeier era—the years of political repression and social stasis following the Congress of Vienna. Second, his sense of history—although tending toward conservatism and nostalgia—was extremely

---

[1] Joseph August Lux, *Grillparzers Liebesroman—Die Schwestern Fröhlich* (Berlin: Bong, 1913), v.
[2] Quoted in Walter Kleindel, *Österreich: Daten zur Geschichte und Kultur* (Vienna: Ueberreuter Verlag, 1978), S:240.
[3] Robert Musil, *Der Mann ohne Eigenschaften* (Reinbek bei Hamburg: Rowohlt, 2002), 35.

self-reflective. Lux worked as a freelance author and critic in the orbit of the Wiener Werkstätte, an important institution of early modernist design.

He was friends with such secession luminaries as Joseph Maria Olbrich, with pioneers of modern design like Hermann Muthesius, and later even with the painter Wassily Kandinsky. In 1908, he broke with his associates because the Werkbund had become too anti-Catholic and modern for his tastes. But if Lux criticized modernism's rationalist tendencies in the following years, he also took a dim view of the historicist perspective that characterized the emphatically anti-modernist Heimatstil. As Mark Jarzombek observes, this meant that he "had no home among modernists or among conservatives."[4] After his career in design came to naught, Lux sought to make a name for himself as "a kind of Austrian cultural philosopher" through novels, aesthetic treatises, and critical writings. Although his works made the case for Austrian nationalism, from the beginning he maintained a critical distance from National Socialism and the annexation of Austria by Germany.[5]

Lux was interested in the efflorescence of especially domestic design during the Biedermeier era. Unlike many of his contemporaries, his fascination was not a matter of an anti-modern flight reflex, a rush to embrace the good old days, but stemmed, instead, from a thoroughly modern aesthetic program.[6] He understood Biedermeier designs, with their simplicity and their avoidance of either classical trappings or rococo frills as precursors to modernism. As a "conservative modernist," Lux was decidedly undecided about the "classical age" he depicted in his novel. When he turned back to the Vienna of the 1820s, he did not let his enthusiasm for Biedermeier aesthetics distort his view of the repressive social conditions under which they arose. During the Biedermeier years, when the burgher was no longer allowed to take to the streets to improve his lot, he took to his parlor and made it as pretty as could be. Lux, who authored a "collection of furnishings and interiors" (*Empire und Biedermeier*, 1930), as well as an influential book on *The Modern Apartment and its Furnishings* (*Die Moderne Wohnung und ihre Ausstattung*, 1905), celebrates this time, but is aware of its repressive undercurrents.[7] This posed a problem for Lux's novel: if the "classical age" to which he wanted to return his countrymen was purely an age of repression and stasis, how could its aesthetics hold any promise for a project concerned with modernity?

If his novel represents to some extent a vindication of Biedermeier aesthetics, Lux distinguished between an official Kakanian "majesty of court and state," and

---

[4] Mark Jarzombek, "Joseph August Lux: Werkbund, Promoter, Historian of a Lost Modernity," *Journal of the Society of Architectural Historians* 63, no. 2 (2004): 204.

[5] Jarzombek, "Joseph August Lux," 205.

[6] Jarzombek, "Joseph August Lux," 207–10.

[7] Joseph August Lux, *Empire und Biedermeier: Eine Sammlung von Möbeln und Innenräumen* (Stuttgart: Hoffmann, 1930); Joseph August Lux, *Die Moderne Wohnung und ihre Ausstattung* (Vienna: Wiener Verlag, 1905), 3–15.

its antipode, an explicitly domestic "true Austria." This is partly because the life of Grillparzer—unlike Goethe's life story, which Lux also treated in novelistic form[8]—is poorly suited to idealizing Vienna's "classical age." In the repressive atmosphere of the so-called Restoration Era, a time when the draconian Karlsbad Decrees regulated all kinds of artistic expression, Franz Grillparzer found himself thwarted at every turn by Viennese society and the Austrian state. Lux has Grillparzer judge himself a "failure! A failure in life!"[9] It is tempting to suspect that autobiographical reasons drew Lux to Grillparzer, as well: he saw in the rejection of his ideas by the Werkbund a parallel to Grillparzer's misfortunes.

But generally what Heinz Politzer has referred to as the "abyssal Biedermeier,"[10] the internal and external repressiveness that drove people into the domestic sphere, recedes far into the background in *Grillparzer's Love-Story*. Instead of external censors and frustration we get domestic togetherness and domestic design. Lux focuses on Grillparzer's early years of acquaintance with the sisters Fröhlich, who are, like all the novel's characters, drawn from history. Grillparzer lived with the sisters for years, and was engaged to Katharina Fröhlich, although they never married.[11]

Lux sidesteps any cognitive dissonance by simply positing the existence of two different Austrias: What turns Grillparzer's life into a "failure" is not his Austrian homeland as such, its people, its ambiance, its culture. It is the powers that be who run the Austro-Hungarian Empire (the "majesty of court and state"[12]), as opposed to just Austria. This peculiar brand of nationalism later made him both a defender of the Austrofascist state (because it came from within) and a critic of the so-called Anschluss with Nazi Germany (because it was imposed by another pan-European empire). Lux was enthusiastically Austrian and Catholic—a rarity for Austrian writers, even at the time. If he depicted the political world after the Congress of Vienna without too many illusions, he did not subject the Austrian nation to nearly as much scrutiny.[13] At the opening of the novel, he describes Grillparzer on a stroll through the city. An organic, folkish Vienna is set in opposition to the official, imperial capital. The city (and in later scenes, the whole of Austria) transforms into a private interior, a bourgeois apartment—as in the following two passages:

> The whole inner city resembled a single, capacious domicile, where there were many narrow and dark corridors, great, majestic halls and splendid chambers, but also secret corners and storage rooms, where human destiny can be experienced more strongly than in the vast, festive reception

---

[8] Joseph August Lux, *Goethe: Roman einer Dichterliebe* (Vienna: Speidel, 1937).
[9] Lux, *Grillparzers Liebesroman*, 2.
[10] Heinz Politzer, *Franz Grillparzer oder das Abgründige Biedermeier* (Vienna: Molden, 1972).
[11] Max Prels, *Grillparzers ewige Braut* (Berlin: Runge, 1922).
[12] Lux, *Grillparzers Liebesroman*, 15.
[13] Christian Otto, "Modern Environment and Historical Continuity: The Heimatschutz Discourse in Germany," *Art Journal* 43, no. 2 (1983): 148–57.

areas.... It is wonderful to know a city and feel at home, as if in one's own house.

He turns into the *Michaeler-Durchhaus*. It's as if one were walking in an apartment, through a series of doors and angular rooms that otherwise are never shown to visitors. He draws another breath at the *Josefsplatz*. Here, all is harmony. A great, measured beauty surrounds him. Ancient spirit, mixed with the ecstatic emotions of the Baroque—something that is dear to him, he doesn't know why. With love and awe, he gazes upon the beautiful monument by Zauner: Kaiser Josef on horseback as Roman imperator. Somehow, he feels at one with these things and experiences proud joy. Beloved Austria![14]

"Official Vienna" is a different matter entirely. On the way home, Grillparzer passes his workplace. "Now he experienced annoyance again, and it destroyed the harmony. Yes, back in the corner are the windows of the office stairs, where he had dragged his hopes every day, already for many years now, and always in vain."[15] Lux in these passages constructs a strange hybrid country that he then idealizes; borrowing Musil's terminology, we could say it is Austria without Kakania. Lux does not take aim at the Austrian state as a whole—the Kaiser, for example, cuts a handsome figure in Lux's narrative. Instead, his criticisms concern public life—or, more precisely, whatever happens in the public sphere: "the petty enmities in bureaucratic and court circles, the malicious attacks in critical pieces and newspaper announcements."[16] The opposition involves, on the one hand, the state apparatus and public life—which are different, yet in Lux's world belong together—and, on the other, the entirely private "apartment" of the poet's personal Austria.

It seems that domestic scenes from this "apartment" are what inspired Lux to write his novel in the first place. In a 1905 book on modern houses and interiors, Lux describes a music room with an image that clearly anticipates the scenes of piano four-hands in *Grillparzer's Love-Story*:

> Chance has placed in my hands a copy of a painting by Schwind. *An Evening of Schubert* is the title. An atmosphere radiates from the page, as delicate as the fragrance of dried roses; a breath of that legendary and dear Viennese sociability blows through the room. It is a burgher salon in the old Viennese style; heirlooms fill the space, hospitality and cheer, the spirit of the place beckons from every corner, a piano stands at the center of the room—one of those instruments like a spinet—graceful and slight, comfortingly different from the monstrous pianos we have these days. Schubert

---

[14] Lux, *Grillparzers Liebesroman*, 15–16.
[15] Lux, *Grillparzers Liebesroman*, 15.
[16] Lux, *Grillparzers Liebesroman*, 174.

is seated there, and a circle of art-lovers has assembled around him—the Fröhlich sisters and, of course, Grillparzer, too.[17]

The painting by Moritz von Schwind (fig. 8.1) that Lux mentions exemplifies his approach to the Biedermeier—and it underscores the importance of piano four-hands for making this approach. On the one hand, music plays a key role in structuring the interior; it is, so to speak, the *genius loci*. The piano must harmonize with the rest of the furnishings; indeed, home life and domestic culture decline in proportion to the growth of "monstrous" instruments, which grow bigger and more aggressive day by day. On the other hand, Lux takes Schwind's painting—which clearly depicts an idealized scene—as if it were a straightforward fact. Although it is certain that important aspects of the kind of sociability it depicts are historically accurate (the openness of the gathering, the mixed company of men and women, and so on), the painting is hardly a neutral document. Where music is concerned—and the same is true of his discussions of design—Lux is always most interested in how it relates to sociability. His glorification of the Biedermeier—its living rooms and piano evenings—registers a complaint about alienation in the twentieth century.

In the late nineteenth century, the sociologist Ferdinand Tönnies introduced the distinction between *Gemeinschaft* (community) and *Gesellschaft* (society) into the social sciences. The former term had the particular coloration of forms of intimacy that belonged to the Restoration period (that is, the Biedermeier years). Lux's novel draws on this model of life-in-community (or, more precisely, this *fantasy* of model life-in-community). In his construction of "Austria without Kakania," he employs all the clichés that remain associated with the Restoration period to this day; moreover, he amplifies them by giving them a generous coating of anachronistic nationalism. All the characters speak in heavy dialect (as also occurs, albeit with satirical intent, in the works of Karl Kraus); the descriptions are thoroughly archaic and the psychology of the characters is altogether conventional.

Among the many conventional elements of Lux's novel, the clichés of home life are easily the most cloying. Lux's characters are always meeting in drawing rooms and they spend their time chatting about domestic affairs. Schubert loses himself in romantic reveries, and the girls talk about their idyllic childhood in the countryside, yet we never leave the comforts of the parlor. Nature filters in through reminiscences, of conversation topics, and of course music; but the characters themselves circulate endlessly through a circumscribed set of domestic locales. The story takes place almost entirely in the inner sanctum of a feminized space—nature, the public sphere, the market place, all of them are relegated to the margins. It is abundantly clear that this domestic world is a kind of temple:

> How feminine and cozy the room was! The yellow-upholstered furniture with the dark, embroidered lines, the slow gait of the matronly clock,

---

[17] Lux, *Die Moderne Wohnung und ihre Ausstattung*, 112.

Figure 8.1 Schubert Evening (1868), by Moritz von Schwind (Bezirksmuseum Wien).

moving as faithfully as a mother's heart, the flowery coverings on the sofa and chairs, the soft, unnamable fragrance calling meadows and hay to mind, the delicately sweet scent of lavender sticking to the sisters' clothing, which the linen in the closet exhaled, the giant, carefully-arranged bouquets of fresh flowers in the vases....[18]

The scene is obtrusively feminized, and music in many respects is the pinnacle of that feminization. It comes from and sustains a world of excessively domesticated, politically neutralized, and reified femininity. "Now, besides the covenant of the heart, music also formed an all-embracing bond, and all three sisters were its votaries."[19] The sisters offer protection to Grillparzer against the vagaries of a profoundly debased public life: "This happened in that evil time, when Grillparzer was exposed to attack and no one stood by him.... And one day, when things raged most fiercely against him, the three encircled him and comforted him lovingly."[20] The "love story" promised in the title is actually not a love story at all. It is a story about the weaving of a cocoon—protecting a domestic stronghold against the wicked outside world.

To that end, Lux's novel frequently gathers Grillparzer, Schubert, Mayrhofer, and the three sisters Fröhlich of the title around the piano, where the "springtime of

[18] Lux, *Grillparzers Liebesroman*, 69.
[19] Lux, *Grillparzers Liebesroman*, 104.
[20] Lux, *Grillparzers Liebesroman*, 311–12.

love and poetry in these magical '20s"[21] is then performed. The novel's wholesome, love-mad, yet altogether chaste kitsch-universe is held together and structured by musical events. "In these '20s, which were full of song and melody...when music was the real stuff of life,"[22] the sounds from the "happy hearth" set the tone in the Fröhlich house. "Music and singing were to occur every day, for half an hour, at least."[23] The three sisters—all of whom contend (with proper modesty, of course) for the male characters' attentions—understand each other in a way that requires no words and comes out most naturally through musical activity. Sometimes one of the sisters plays while another sings; sometimes they look on reverently as little Pepi (Josephine) performs a solo piece. Never, however, do the sisters play four-hand piano when alone; that seems reserved for such time as when a man is present. Although it belongs to the private and domestic sphere, piano four-hands also points beyond the limited circle of the three sisters. Musically and otherwise, the three sisters are not self-sufficient. They yearn for a larger community, even though that larger community remains an altogether *private* one.

As previously mentioned, Lux seems to have considered music in the home an integral part of his aesthetic program—less for the sake of the music itself than for that of interior design. Not surprisingly, then, the scenes of music making in *Grillparzers Love-Story* represent nostalgia for a vanished form of sociability. For Lux, piano four-hands and similar phenomena can no longer blossom because the domestic culture that gave rise to them does not exist anymore. And if this domestic culture does not exist anymore, it is because the physical space of the bourgeois apartments has somehow degenerated:

> Traditional, home-made, honest home music is in decline. In truth, concert halls are not so much to blame as the decline of domestic life itself. The friendly spirits of comfort and hospitality, which were still to be found—even under much more modest circumstances—beneath every roof fifty years ago, have vanished from the cities, and especially the metropolises....It has grown cold and inhospitable around almost every hearth. Here, even the best compositions produce no harmony.[24]

This "harmony," which spreads from music to the people gathered to play it, is predicated on the most material factors of life: the sociability of musical togetherness mirrors the harmony of the way domestic space is arranged. Accordingly, Lux provided his novel with pictorial illustrations of the various interiors that the work describes. Just as the Austrian nation is reflected, above all, by the familiar, homey

---

[21] Lux, *Grillparzers Liebesroman*, vi.
[22] Lux, *Grillparzers Liebesroman*, 104.
[23] Lux, *Grillparzers Liebesroman*, 105.
[24] Lux, *Die Moderne Wohnung und ihre Ausstattung*, 113–14.

harmony of Viennese buildings and street design ("Here, all is harmony," "a great, measured beauty"[25]), agreeable coexistence is impossible in a dwelling that is not "in tune."

> In a household where noble colors and noble lines reign, as well as the good sense that derives beauty from everyday utility, one will, as a rule, encounter good music, too. A basic, artistic trait leads from visible harmony to the audible kind.[26]

Lux's primary interest is in furniture and design, but for him music making—and especially piano four-hands—was an important index of concord in the domestic utopia. As is the case in Schwind's painting, the piano provides the place of gathering for the group. The harmony and agreement between the players becomes that of those who observe them.

When the three girls take Grillparzer into their house, "it didn't last long before Franz, too, passionately devoted himself to playing the piano."[27] Courtship and love occur at the keyboard. While the novel does not feature explicit eroticism, the subliminal meanings of such scenes become very clear—as is so often the case in the texts examined in this study—once spectators are brought into the scene. The poet seems to play less with Kathi, the oldest of the three sisters and the main object of Grillparzer's desire; more often, sublime and artistic Nettl (Anne) is his partner. The way Lux stages the scenes at the piano emphasizes the trust and togetherness between Grillparzer and the sisters, but it also makes it clear that nothing more intimate can come of the relationship. That is because, at the piano as in real life, the poet is imprisoned within his own genius; he cannot stray beyond the confines of his own private universe, whether this world consists of his Austrian "apartment" or his part of the piano keyboard. "They start playing, but he can't keep time. First he plays too fast, then too slow. Just as it comes to him—the playing grows confused."[28] When the matter is brought to his attention, the poet grows angry and blames his playing partner. Grillparzer, we are given to understand, is a pianistic recluse—his inability to venture more decisively into the sisters' space on the keyboard signifies his inability to leave his own head.

Franz Schubert is entirely different. Kathi is deeply in love with the young composer and jealous of all the other young ladies with whom she must share him. Grillparzer and Kathi are clearly attracted to each other, too, but their feelings move back and forth, with the kind of mechanical regularity we might find in a soap opera, between disinterest and affection. Her devotion to Schubert is far

---

[25] Lux, *Grillparzers Liebesroman*, 15.
[26] Lux, *Die Moderne Wohnung und ihre Ausstattung*, 115.
[27] Lux, *Grillparzers Liebesroman*, 104.
[28] Lux, *Grillparzers Liebesroman*, 105.

more steady. While Nettl plays at the piano—a piece by Schubert, it so happens—Kathi sits there, enchanted: "Kathi was truly enraptured; as was her way, she held her little head slightly lowered and to the side, and seemed to breathe the notes in through her half-open mouth." Grillparzer immediately experiences the sting of jealousy: "Like a drinker at his cups, she's intoxicating herself with music."[29] Music, the "hashish of women," the source of male longing and envy: like a seismograph Lux's text picks up the aftershocks of the nineteenth century. But, as it turns out, he telescopes that century, collapsing phenomena from early in the age of four-hand playing with those at its tail end. In one scene, "poor little Schubert"—the "dear musician"[30]—plays a four-hand transcription of his *Trout* with Nettl at the piano. Their playing brings nature, the countryside, into their parlor—"like the cheeriest sunshine, it warmed their souls." But this moment of synaesthesia does more than just import the beauty of nature into the domestic sphere; it imports specifically Austrian nature. As the piece runs through the players' fingers, it suddenly unfurls a veritable map of the Austro-Hungarian Empire, traveling up and down Austria's rivers and streams: "The melody spread its sonorous waterfall, it contained the rush of the green Steyr and the blue Enns, two crystal-clear mountain streams that decorated, as they flowed together, a joyful city with their green and blue ribbons."[31] Then Lux's narrator sounds out a little creek called the Heiligenstädter Bach, "the holy rushing of the forests, the vivacious chatter of the brook and the mute song of the trout." Lux, who does not want to depict the past "by reconstruction, but by creating freely,"[32] reclaims Schubert as a national composer and *The Trout* as the quintessence of the Austro-Hungarian universe.

As we know, wide open spaces and piano four-hands were frequently linked in the nineteenth century, since scores for four hands often provided the only access to a modern repertory for people not residing in large cities (cf. chapter 2). One played new works by Brahms in arrangements for four hands because there was no opera, no concert hall, and no orchestra at home. It was one reason piano four-hands was often portrayed as somewhat provincial—for instance, in Schnitzler's "Frau Bertha Garlan," where Schubert marches played *à quatre mains* become a hated substitute for the rarified pleasures of the capital. Thus, in a letter from 1891, Martha Fontane wrote: "They went to the opera quite often and also made music at home: they play piano four hands! That's like something from Posemuckel."[33] Here, "Posemuckel" means "rustic," even if the geography

---

[29] Lux, *Grillparzers Liebesroman*, 68.
[30] Lux, *Grillparzers Liebesroman*, 72.
[31] Lux, *Grillparzers Liebesroman*, 60.
[32] Lux, *Grillparzers Liebesroman*, vi.
[33] January 1891, in Regina Dieterle (ed.), *Theodor Fontane und Martha Fontane: Ein Familienbriefnetz* (Berlin: De Gruyter, 2002), 389.

in question, like that of Kakania, was not of great duration: today, Posemuckel is called Podmokle, and is located in Poland.

For Frau Fontane, piano four-hands sounds the depths of the Germanic provinces, just as the four-hand arrangement of *The Trout* in Lux's novel evokes the breadth of Kakanian dominions. Four-hand piano playing was a way of making the metropolis with its galas, its concert halls, and its Wiener Musikverein present in places too far-flung for such pursuits; but it was also a way to make present the far reaches of the empire in a cramped living room in the medieval streets of Vienna. And for Lux, it was a way of integrating places on a map into an ideal whole—much more tightly than the disaggregated patchwork of provinces the Hapsburg monarchs had collected over the centuries.

Needless to say, Lux was not the only one connecting Schubert to this patchwork. The critic Hermann Bahr, himself far more critical of the Biedermeier era than Lux, employs the image of Schubert as an allegory for Austria in his writings on the Viennese Secession. He invokes Klimt's famous painting of Schubert at the piano to answer the question of what, exactly, an Austrian is. "I know only that I get angry when someone asks me if I'm German. No, I say, I am Austrian. 'That's not really a nation,' is the reply. 'It has become a nation,' I say.... That can be seen in Schubert, here."[34] In this likeness of Schubert, Bahr discerned something characteristic of Kakanian life and landscape. And, more to the point, in the image of Schubert that life and that landscape converge into a kind of unity they probably never possessed in reality.

Even if he viewed it critically, he seems possessed of a certain nostalgic longing for it—though Bahr wrote his text in 1900, and the state he laments is still very much with him! "This Schubert with the singing girls, who have something bourgeois yet almost holy about them, leaves me in an indescribable—I almost want to say 'happy'—melancholy. It is the same comforting sadness that the little mountains in the Bruhl region have."[35] No matter their stance toward the Austrian Empire, it seems, writers tended to regard Schubert as a kind of symbol for this vanished land—or use him to create this vanished land in the first place.

Lux's novel is not interesting for aesthetic reasons. Nor is the book particularly astute in capturing the 1820s particularly well. It is interesting for the way it illuminates the relationship that the early twentieth century entertained with the Biedermeier era. As previously mentioned, this relationship was of paramount importance to Lux. The novelist was also a critic of architecture and art. A desire to analyze the culture of the Biedermeier era is not the reason for the novel's obsession with domestic interiors. Rather, it stems from a certain *déformation professionelle* on the part of the writer. Lux was singularly fascinated by interior design, furniture, and

---

[34] Hermann Bahr, *Secession* (Vienna: Wiener Verlag, 1900), 123.
[35] Bahr, *Secession*, 124.

applied art. These objects of reflection are the focus of his theoretical writings about the relationship between the early twentieth century and the Biedermeier era.

In Lux's novel, piano four-hands is once again part of the furniture: it has the same function as the interior design of the bourgeois parlor. At the same time, the parlor is a metonymy for the entire Austrian cosmos. This is why Grillparzer can perceive Vienna as if it were a giant living room: "Somehow, he feels at one with these things and experiences proud joy."[36] Other scenes, which are elaborated in an analogous manner, include the whole of the Austrian landscape. The four hands playing *The Trout* have the same function as the Biedermeier furnishings: they fetch the cosmos into the home and privatize the public. The great, wide world becomes miniaturized, becomes manageable, becomes interior.

In fact—and as we saw in chapter 1—the bourgeois world in a parlor where music is played by four hands belongs, as a cultural phenomenon, to the mid- to late-nineteenth century. The form of sociability that Lux's novel takes as its model is the Schubertiade; only in terms of setting is it the same as salon music. To be sure, a great deal of four-hand piano playing occurred in Grillparzer's Vienna, and Lux used the poet's own autobiography when crafting his novel. But the assumptions he brings to bear on the world of the young Grillparzer and Schubert are those of the turn of the twentieth century. To be sure, Lux gets the basic outlines of four-hand playing around Grillparzer right: According to Marie von Ebner-Eschenbach's *My Recollections of Grillparzer* (*Meine Einnerungen an Grillparzer*, 1916), the poet did in fact play music with Anna and Josephine—four-hand arrangements of "symphonies by Haydn, Beethoven, and Mozart."[37] The two Fröhlich sisters were "respected piano and voice teachers," and they introduced Grillparzer to Schubert's compositions.

Yet the world that emerges from Ebner-Eschenbach's descriptions and those of other contemporaries has little in common with the idyllic community that Lux dreamt up. Lux presents his readers with an aestheticized vision of petit bourgeois life, which has withdrawn from the overpowering state apparatus into the (relative) security of the home. Ebner-Eschenbach concludes her anecdote by reporting how Grillparzer one day declined to play with his partners: "My fingers have grown stiff," the writer said, "It isn't working anymore." Grillparzer continues: "the spiritual conditions of my fatherland...poison my innermost soul";[38] from texts like Ebner-Eschenbach's and from Grillparzer's own correspondence emerges an image of a man adrift in the "classical age." Accordingly—and probably accurately— Ebner-Eschenbach understands piano four-hands not as a means of nostalgically

---

[36] Lux, *Grillparzers Liebesroman*, 15.

[37] Marie von Ebner-Eschenbach, "Meine Einnerungen an Grillparzer," in *Gesammelte Werke* (Munich: Nymphenburger, 1961), 8:229.

[38] Quoted in Hans Hoff and Ida Cernmak, *Grillparzer: Versuch einer Pathographie* (Vienna: Bergland, 1961), 65.

transforming and transfiguring an ideal community but as a symbol of the poet's resignation and withdrawal.

In another way, too, Lux's equation of home culture and the Schubertiade is anachronistic. The Schubertiade was not a homey, cozy affair. First, the groups that assembled at the house of Baron von Spaun were, as Alice M. Hanson has shown, much larger than the ones depicted by Lux.[39] Second, "Schubert evenings" were much more dynamic than a modest grouping of a select few persons around a piano in a bourgeois living room. Such evenings were more of an intellectual salon than the gathering of a substitute family. Whereas a cozy home with its grand piano was, so to speak, a reliable annex of the Austro-Hungarian state, the Schubertiade could represent protest and withdrawal or, as we would say today, an "alternative lifestyle." This aspect is apparent, not least of all in the fact that, immediately after the Carlsbad Decrees, Schubert and some of his friends were arrested for a short time.[40] The Schubertiade had far deeper and more dangerous political, erotic, and intellectual dimensions than what Lux shows. Schubert was less likely to be found "under a vine-covered pergola," lost in a "celestial concert"[41] that no one else could hear, than consorting with ladies of easy virtue, engaging in playful cross-dressing, or—if one accepts Maynard Solomon's controversial arguments—pursuing male prostitutes.[42] In general, the private sphere of the Restoration period was an asylum for forms of protest that the public sphere stifled. Lux takes all the fun out of the Biedermeier salon by forcing it to play piano four-hands.

The repertory of Lux's characters reveals that the novelist's version of the Biedermeier is, in fact, a retro-projection of late-nineteenth-century musical life onto the Biedermeier years. As previously mentioned, Franz Schubert and Netty Fröhlich are shown playing a version of *The Trout* for four hands, and Lux makes it clear that he is referring to the *Trout Quintet* (Piano Quintet in A major, op. 114) rather than the song on which it is based. Kathi requests this "number" as if she were at a small-town discotheque. Schubert obeys: "right away, he sat down again at the piano with Netty and played the piece, which, like the cheeriest sunshine, warmed their souls."[43] Lux permits himself more than a few liberties. Today, the *Trout Quintet* is one of the most famous pieces by Schubert, but it was never published in Schubert's lifetime, and no performance is known to have occurred while the composer was still alive.

---

[39] Alice Hanson, *Musical Life in Biedermeier Vienna* (New York: Cambridge University Press, 1985), 120.

[40] Dallas A. Weekly and Nancy Arganbrith, *Schubert's Music for Piano Four-Hands* (London: Kahn & Averill, 1990), 33.

[41] Lux, *Grillparzers Liebesroman*, 59.

[42] Maynard Solomon, "Franz Schubert and the Peacocks of Benevenuto Cellini," *19th Century Music* 12, no. 3 (1989): 193–206.

[43] Lux, *Grillparzers Liebesroman*, 73.

Hanson affirms that there is no reason to believe "that Schubert performed his more serious chamber or symphonic works"[44] at a Schubertiade, since songs and piano pieces of a more modest order were normally played in such a setting.[45] Moreover, an arrangement for four hands of *The Trout* was probably produced only after Schubert's death: Joseph Czerny (no relation to Carl) created it on the basis of a manuscript he acquired from Schubert's estate, and he published it together with the first edition of the original score. The first private performances of the piece seem to have taken place in the context of these publications. By the late nineteenth century, it seems that when someone said they played the *Trout Quintet* four hands, it was usually in a transcription by Hugo Ulrich from the 1870s. Lux, in contrast, uses the piece as a universally recognized shibboleth, a symbol of the familiar, communal spirit of the Biedermeier world. Everyone knows the piece, which represents a Kakanian Eden. In this fantasy world, *The Trout* is knowledge that creates agreement and concord; it is, so to speak, the seed of Kakania itself.

Lux's omission is extremely telling. The way Lux turns *The Trout* into a kind of musical evergreen represses the fact that the world in which *The Trout* is such an evergreen differs in fundamental ways from the "classical age" Lux apotheosizes. The community that Schubert's compositions represent does not share a musical culture and education with the score collector of later in the century. In fact, the Schubertiade excludes precisely the kind of music that one collects and points to as a universal sign of refinement. Lux's fantasy version of *The Trout*, known to all, playable by heart, requestable on a whim, is therefore the primal scene of piano four-hands: the fantasy that a posthumous musical score could call forth a living form of sociability; that the relatively uninspired performance of a score in a domestic setting could have anything to do with an actual evening with Schubert; that the reified, commercialized, and desexualized world of parlor music is comparable to the bohemian gatherings opposed to political oppression.

Lux's "springtime of love and poetry" serves the yearning of the late Habsburg Empire for an authentic Austrian identity that would not—as was the case with the real *Trout*—be a matter of reification and falsified tradition. In other words, Lux adheres to the fantasy that Schubert's circle and the citizens of Kakania felt the same feelings, and that these feelings—like the music that produced them—expressed a stable Austrian identity. This kind of nostalgia, which approaches the past by means of music pieces that are supposed to guarantee collective experience and shared knowledge, no longer has anything remarkable about it in the age of the CD. For this very reason, however, the anachronism is especially evident to us: in Lux's fantasy Vienna, Schubert's composition is treated as if it were a record from the 1970s—a hit the village DJ might play to get an elderly audience into the mood

---

[44] Hanson, *Musical Life in Biedermeier Vienna*, 121.
[45] Margaret Notley, "Schubert's Social Music—The 'Forgotten Genres,'" in Christopher H. Gibbs (ed.), *The Cambridge Companion to Schubert* (Cambridge: Cambridge University Press, 1997), 138.

and off their chairs. Of course, Lux did not attend parties of this kind, but the fact that we today witness the technological "realization" of this phantasm shows clearly how strangely discontinuous the phenomenon is. On the one hand, it anticipates a musical and social formation that only became possible some hundred years later; on the other hand, the fantasy's point of origin lies in a kind of sociability that even the nineteenth century, as it drew to a close, understood to be a thing of the past.

Parallel Actions, Twinned Gestures

An ideological critique of four hands at the piano must, therefore, begin with the promises that the instrument makes to the senses. It must reveal that what appears as immediate and communal—the result of unalienated and pure expression—is actually nothing more than the disciplining of self and surroundings. It must reveal that the very model of production against which the bourgeois fantasy of playing *à quatre mains* is directed creeps back in, undercover. Instead of domesticating and privatizing the exterior world, as occurs in Lux's novel, one must attempt to show the conflict within a unified-seeming gesture: the private realm is, in fact, only a repetition of what it believes it can exclude—namely the public sphere, masses, work, and power.

Critique of this sort occurs, in essayistic form, in Robert Musil's novel, *The Man Without Qualities*. Musil lays hold of the nineteenth-century fashion of piano four-hands at the moment it falls apart. Like many parts of his portrait of "Kakania," it is portrayed as a relic—a matter of pure habit that has, in fact, long been emptied of meaning by the progress of technology and science. Musil famously opens his *magnum opus* with a lengthy discussion of barometric pressure, air temperature fluctuations, and the phases of the moon, only to conclude, "In a word that characterizes the facts fairly accurately, even if it is a bit old-fashioned: It was a fine day in August 1913."[46] It is a world in which the categories of the past are being ground up by technological progress and the modernization of society.

Ulrich, the "man without qualities," tries to become "a great man" in a world in which racehorses are said to have "genius," in which mid-nineteenth-century concepts such as person, character and, well, quality have lost all meaning. Musil's narrator applies this same spirit of corrosion, of demystification, to the scene at the piano. The intimate scene in a private salon transforms into its opposite: labor, quantification, and piecework. In Lux's novel, "conventional, home-made, honest music"[47] stands in for an entire nation and its forms of sociability. Musil also uses piano four-hands to construct a country and an Austrian past; his view, of course, is much more critical. From Musil's diaries we know that he was aware of Lux's work,

---

[46] Robert Musil, *The Man Without Qualities* (New York: Knopf, 1995), 3.
[47] Lux, *Die Moderne Wohnung und ihre Ausstattung*, 113–14.

although it is doubtful he would have spent much time with the older man's novelistic output.[48]

One should not be surprised that *Man Without Qualities* chooses piano four-hands as a symbol. After all, "Kakania" itself, as simultaneously "imperial and royal," is not unlike the four-handed pair of (Siamese) rulers in E. T. A. Hoffmann's *Princess Brambrilla*. Moreover, the central irony of the novel's plot is based on the "Parallel Action" that the cast of characters plan for the year 1918—the seventy-fifth anniversary of the coronation of Emperor Franz Josef (that is, the man who embodied "Kakania" like no other) and the thirtieth anniversary of the German Kaiser's rule. The plan derives its bitter irony from the fact that both the German and the "Kakanian" monarchies lasted only as long as the projected year of celebration; unconsciously, the "Parallel Action" points to its own failure. Whatever stable parallels the characters believe they can rely on, the novel knows that behind them lurks chaos and destruction.

For all these reasons, it seems, Musil has his characters play four-hand piano. Just as the sounds of political decline are audible in the laying of plans for the "Parallel Action" itself, the "parallel action" at the piano signifies the built-in breakdown of its underlying idea. In either case, there stands behind the action an ideal of coordination, unification, and wholeness. In the play of four hands—as the narrator makes abundantly clear—that ideal is realized, but that realization turns out to be a perversion as well. Four-hand playing is not just about performing in tandem; it's also about individuals melting into one. In Musil's descriptions, the fact shines through that parallel actions never really lead to actual unity. If anything, parallel action comes to signify a forced synchronization, the way modern bureaucracies can brutalize the individual, the way industrial production can render the worker fungible.

We encountered Musil's piano players in the last chapter. One of them is Walter, a friend of Ulrich's (the "man without qualities") from university days, and the other is Clarisse, Walter's young wife—a slightly megalomaniacal disciple of Nietzsche. We first meet them—how else?—in the parlor, playing piano "so violently that the spindly reproduction furniture rattled and the Dante Gabriel Rossetti prints on the walls trembled."[49] Here, then, the piano does not represent a "harmonious" interior; instead, it seems to take possession of the interior by force. "In the days when Schubert sat at the piano," Lux had remarked, "this instrument had a shape that agreed with the other furniture." In contrast, the piano belonging to Walter and Clarisse terrifies the room and stands in an openly hostile relationship with its surroundings. There can be no question of things being in tune. The kind of gathering that occurs at and around the piano also has little in common with Lux's idylls or Moritz von Schwind's *Schubert Evening*. This is no Schubertiade—their guest waits forlorn until their "private commotion" is over.

---

[48] Robert Musil, *Tagebücher* (Reinbek bei Hamburg: Rowohlt, 1976), 1:397, 2:248.
[49] Musil, *The Man Without Qualities*, 150.

Whenever he got there, they were playing the piano together. It was understood that they would take no notice of him until they had finished the piece; this time it was Beethoven's jubilant 'Ode to Joy.' The millions sank, as Nietzsche describes it, in the dust; hostile boundaries shattered, the gospel of world harmony reconciled and unified the sundered. They had unlearned walking and talking and were about to fly off, dancing into the air.[50]

Later, the reader learns that Clarisse refuses to have sex with her husband; their sex is displaced onto the keyboard, though in keeping with the demystificatory thrust of the novel's narration, it is uniquely unerotic.[51] Whoever might expect an Aristophanic symposium at the piano is disappointed. The unification of people through music—the falling away of borders and barriers—remains the premise of the scene, but the execution belies it. Musil weaves numerous four-hand performances into the novel, but this is the only time he explicitly mentions which piece is being played. It is the "Ode to Joy" from Beethoven's Ninth Symphony.

Not just the four-hand form but also the piece itself takes becoming-one as its theme. The joint performance at the keyboard is supposed to create community, yet it only produces isolation. Schiller's "all men become brothers" now sounds like mockery. At very least, the commandment is one that the musicians can't seem to obey. Naturally, as was suggested in chapter 7, behind this commandment stand both the anti-capitalist metaphysics of unity professed by the Romantics and metaphysics of the Schopenhauerian variety, which sees in music the antidote to the false consciousness of the *principium individuationis*. Piano four-hands, like the joy that Schiller hymns, is supposed to bind together "what custom has strictly divided" (in the earlier version of the text, Schiller even speaks of custom's "sword"). All the worse, then, that such a piece should find the two musicians sit side by side at the keyboard more separate than ever.

Musil seems to have Schopenhauer's aesthetics in mind when he lets Walter indulge in his fantasy of a primordial, pre-individualized Will, almost gelatinous in its indistinction: "Like most musical people, he considered these billowing surges and emotional stirrings, all this cloudy, churned up, somatic sediment of the soul, to be the simple language of the eternal that binds all mankind together. It delighted him to press Clarisse to himself with the powerful arm of primal emotion."[52] Yet "primal sensation" is not just a matter of metaphysical unity with fellow man. Walter also means—and in a pretty concrete way, at that—to have his wife finally yield to him: "He wanted to bring Clarisse back, but not by force; the realization would

---

[50] Musil, *The Man Without Qualities*, 45.
[51] Stefan Howald, *Ästhetizismus und ästhetische Ideologiekritik—Untersuchungen zum Romanwerk Robert Musils* (Munich: Fink, 1984), 217–48.
[52] Musil, *The Man Without Qualities*, 151.

have to rise up from her innermost self and incline her gently to him."[53] Here, the connection between sex and music played by four hands—which the nineteenth century had always feared—becomes explicit. Unfortunately, Walter falls prey to a tragic error: four-hand piano playing is a displacement of sexuality, a substitution. Poor Walter believes that he can conjure up actual sexual intercourse just by the power of his hands.

Walter's fantasies of higher unity are exposed as simple sexual frustration. The book makes it more than clear that the physical coordination of bodies in no way leads to metaphysical or physical closeness. At the same time, the narrator observes, "Clarisse's thoughts had diverged as far from Walter's as is possible for two people who are storming along side by side with twinned gestures of desperation and rapture."[54] From time to time, Clarisse fantasizes either about Ulrich or Moosbrugger, an insane murderer of prostitutes. Here, as Jacques Lacan famously posited, "there is no sexual relationship": everyone is busy with his or her projection of the other.

> They sat stiffly in a trance on their little stools, angry, in love, or sad, at nothing, with nothing, about nothing, or each of them, at with, about something else, thinking and meaning different things of their own; the dictate of music united them in highest passion, yet at the same time it left them with something absent, as in the compulsive sleep of hypnosis.[55]

Nineteenth-century literature tended, as we have seen, to associate four-hand piano playing with love games and subliminal eroticism. There are a few voices to the contrary, such as Marie von Bunsen (1860–1941), who in one scene of her epistolary novel *Udo in England* (1895) describes how piano four-hands can destroy a romance. Udo wishes to court Agneta, whom he idolizes, but the noisy and aggressive playing of other parties makes this impossible:

> As long as the reverend's dutiful daughters were playing together, I could seize the moment; I stood next to Agneta in a dark corner and noticed how her hands were shaking; but the girls played too aggressively—so poorly you wanted to pull your hair out—and they made me lose my composure completely.[56]

Here, then, piano four-hands and erotic relations are not connected so much as they stand in direct opposition to one another. Musil goes a step further than von Bunsen. For him, four-hand playing not only disturbs eros it also projects a kind

---

[53] Musil, *The Man Without Qualities*, 151.
[54] Musil, *The Man Without Qualities*, 152.
[55] Musil, *The Man Without Qualities*, 151.
[56] Marie von Bunsen, *Udo in England: Eine Briefsammlung, Deutsche Rundschau* 83 (April 1895): 294.

of eroticism and then makes it impossible. Although Musil describes four-hand playing in Platonic terms as the "great becoming-one," his minute postmortems on this "becoming-one" suggest that what that occurs when Walter and Clarisse play together is really a kind of self-hypnosis—an artificially forged togetherness, manufactured by the pure speed of playing maniacally alongside one another. Instead of a community of feeling, Musil presents a self-induced adjustment to one another, a corporate merger of sensations. The illusion of shared feelings arises only in the "headwind" of the frenzied performance, and it does not derive from an abrogation of the division of labor (see chapter 7); rather, it stems from a division of labor that has become absolute Both players sit at the musical assembly line, "rigid and distant" in their terror, and the pure rage with which the motifs and manual operations seize them suggests unity that is purely mechanical:

> The next instant, Clarisse and Walter were off like two locomotives racing side by side. The piece they were playing came rushing at their eyes like flashing rails, vanished under the thundering engine, and spread out behind them as a ringing, resonant, marvelously present landscape. In the course of this ride these two people's separate feelings were compressed into a single entity; hearing, blood, muscles, were swept along irresistibly by the same experience; shimmering, bending, curving walls of sound forced their bodies onto the same track, bent them as one, and expanded and contracted their chests in the same breath.[57]

Here, it becomes obvious how far alienation has crept into the family unit. The narrator makes clear that family dynamics are no longer opposed but, rather, analogous to the dynamics of mass society. Musil reverses Lux's privatization of the cosmos: instead of four-hand piano playing harmoniously arranging the Enns and Steyr Rivers as parts of the domestic décor, it unmasks the family as a miniature version of the public sphere and of the modern city. The emotional release that the two players experience alongside each other is actually just affective piecework. Just as the audience in a cinema laughs in unison, and just as a crowd runs through the gamut of emotions as something that belongs to all and therefore to none, Walter and Clarisse feel what they feel simultaneously yet without any individual ownership. Therefore, the unity produced is emotional only on a secondary level: togetherness is generated *physically* ("compressed into a single entity"); only then, when breath and muscles are in alignment, do the two players have the "same experience."

In the preceding chapters, we have pointed out, again and again, that becoming-one at the piano—the "same experience"—most likely existed usually only in the eyes of the beholder. The supposed erotics of four-hand playing is rarely

---

[57] Musil, *The Man Without Qualities*, 150.

described from the perspective of the partners themselves; instead, a third party (usually male) brings erotic categories to bear on the phenomenon. Only rarely do we learn what it feels like to play four-hand piano from those whose fingers actually work the keys. When the players do get a word in, it is normally only one of them who shares his or her concerns, emotions, and perspective (as is the case, for example, with de Bernard's Gerfaut, Heyse's Aunt Leopoldine, or Schnitzler's young Else). The "twin" at the other end of the keyboard (the father, mother, teacher, lover) remains a mystery—and the nature of their "twinship" therefore always is a matter of guesswork. Musil's book is different: it brings both Clarisse and Walter into stereoscopic focus and finally portrays the "four-handed monster" in its entirety. However, at the very moment when literature grasps the phenomenon as a whole, that phenomenon is unmasked as deception and empty appearance. The bringing together of two perspectives (Clarisse's and Walter's) in the text puts the lie to the idea of an overarching unity. As soon as it achieves realization in the text—and in stereo, no less—the "same experience" is branded as something deeply unreal.

Musil's text makes it clear that this "experience" is only simulation. Walter and Clarisse's playing involves no real emotions—only the physiological symptoms of feeling. "The anger, love, joy, gaiety and sadness that Clarisse and Walter felt in their flight were not full emotions but little more than physical shells of feeling that had been worked up into a frenzy."[58] Speed, hypnotic suggestion, and simulation reinforce and condition each other. Instead of thoughtfulness and authentic feeling, it is a matter of an emotional speed-rush: "In a fraction of a second, gaiety, sadness, anger, and fear, love, and hatred, desire and satiety, passed through Walter and Clarise."[59] The four-hand playing at the piano is not the *expression* of an inner state (as Lux's novel would have it); instead, the inner state is produced by the pressure generated by that playing. What one hundred years of playing and observing four-hand piano took to be immediate and authentic, Musil's narrator reveals as always already mediated: the two players emote their way down a predetermined track, their feeling is literally labor.

Nothing is original or true in the Kakania of the year 1913; everything is repetition. The compulsion to repeat, which forces Clarisse and Walter to return to the keyboard time and again, has a historical cognate: what Musil's narrator forces them through is the emotional *parcours* of the Biedermeier era. Four-hand piano has not moved on since the days idealized by Lux: the view of the subject has changed, the world of work and the technology of the new age have nothing in common with those of a century prior, but four-hand playing, and its ideology, has not adapted. Walter and Clarisse sit down at the piano as though it were 1833, as though Schubert and Grillparzer and the sisters Fröhlich still sauntered through Vienna's "classical

---

[58] Musil, *The Man Without Qualities*, 151.
[59] Musil, *The Man Without Qualities*, 150–51.

age," unaware or unconcerned that the ground beneath their feet has shifted and is shifting still. When they sit down at the piano, nothing new can happen; they replay the rituals and regurgitate the ideas of the Biedermeier era—only this time as farce.

In the *Arcades Project*, Walter Benjamin drew attention to the fact that the ideological critique made by the great caricaturist J. J. Grandville had a Marxist insight at its core: the uncanniness of human beings and commodities having switched roles.[60] Musil's four-hand scenes do something similar. At the piano, Walter and Clarisse become parts of the instrument's hammer mechanism: "Faces flushed, bodies hunched, their heads jerked up and down while splayed claws banged away at the mass of sound rearing up under them."[61] Only the mass of notes does any bucking and rearing. The people who chop at it "in fits" are nowhere near as lively; they instead appear to be part of the machinery that should, in principle, be at their whim. But Musil has more in mind here than just the internal mechanics of the "sonic hearth." The picture that Musil invokes comes from the world of industry; it is the assembly line introduced by Henry Ford. The "mass of notes" glides down the keyboard, kneaded and chopped by robotic limbs. Whether these limbs are human or mechanical, it seems, is beside the point.

Musil's description suggests how elements of assembly-line production crept into the project of four-hand collaboration. He thereby anticipates Siegfried Kracauer's remark that the legs of the Tiller Girls were the counterparts of workers' hands in a factory.[62] What at first seems to be a counterbalance to the thoroughly rationalized production process reveals itself as a part of just that process. Now the libido only runs its course as piecework. In Musil's novel the erotic has not vanished but, instead of displaying itself in dialogue—intimate exchanges in speech, it occurs as the coordinated galloping of worked-up and overworked bodies. The partners "broaden and narrow" their "chests in the same breath." Tellingly, the absence of dialogue is accompanied by another omission: we learn nothing of the hands' movements—the "railroad tracks" moving by in a rush are all we see. A product replaces production. Musil writes of bodies, lungs, and the eyes, yet the moment of production itself—the creation of music—has dropped out of view.

It is entirely possible that Musil has the actual score in mind. Beethoven's "Ode to Joy" is a pointedly ironic choice for representing the epic nonmelting of two married people. A look at the most common arrangement of the Ninth Symphony in the nineteenth century, by Hugo Ulrich, suggests that Musil's musical selection was also based on empirical observation. Ulrich's arrangement endeavors to save as many notes as possible on the keyboard. Thereby, the magic of the symphony's concluding ode goes almost entirely missing. Moreover, it is striking how the first and second parts operate almost autonomously. Cross-playing and contact

---

[60] Walter Benjamin, *The Arcades Project* (Cambridge, MA: Belknap Press, 1999), 195f.
[61] Musil, *The Man Without Qualities*, 45.
[62] Siegfried Kracauer, *The Mass Ornament* (Cambridge, MA: Harvard University Press, 1995), 78.

are extremely rare. Significantly, only in the solo passages (for example, at the line, "Whoever has had the great fortune") do the hands of the two players cross. At the grand gesture of universal inclusion ("Be embraced, millions!"), the two parts call for complete separation—two parallel "railroad tracks," indeed.

The strange feature of this arrangement, therefore, is that the pairs of hands can complete the grand gesture and be "friends with an enemy" reasonably well, yet fail lamentably in "embracing" the "millions." And given Musil's descriptions of his characters on the keys, we almost have to look at the score. Their performance is observed *from the outside*, and the panic—the "wind" that hits them in the face—is an empirically verifiable phenomenon even with experienced performers. Hugo Ulrich's arrangement creates no all-encompassing unity; instead, it forces the two players to rush forward side by side, but lost.

It is also no coincidence that panic is written on the players' *faces*. Musil's observer does not look at what their hands are doing, but at their eyes. This perspective undermines the seeming immediacy of the creative community. If the narrator were to look at the players' hands, he might not recognize at all that agreement on the keys is only a function of the pressure to coordinate (which is exercised by the score). The eyes, however, reveal both the isolation of the players and just how forced their fleeting unity is. Almost fearfully, the performers' eyes turn to what is coming: "The piece ... came rushing at their eyes like flashing rails." The lack of communication in, and constrained nature of, these looks structures both the linearity in and parallelism of Musil's metaphors. When "their line of vision stands like four sticks poking out of their heads," industry has taken over in the domestic sphere.

The most haunting aspect of this scene is how much both the players accept what comes barreling toward them, how willingly their bodies yield to being bent into shape—*Bildung* occurs in a painfully literal sense. Musil's language calls forth gymnastics and athletic discipline: "It was the moment when the players stopped their pulse, in order to start again in the same rhythm." With discipline of this kind, it seems he means to say, one can also wage wars. Indeed, the truth that the 1913 parallel action foreshadows in the fictional world became visible with the eruption of the Great War in the real one.

Coda

Susan Buck-Morss has pointed out the connection, in the nineteenth century, between phantasmagoric mechanisms that shielded people from the industrial means of production ("anesthetics" is her term[63]) and the relations of production that,

---

[63] Susan Buck-Morss, "Aesthetics and Anaesthetics: Walter Benjamin's Artwork Essay Reconsidered," *October* 62 (1992): 3–41.

in their effects, almost resembled a state of war. While factories produced work injuries and amputations, physiognomists celebrated the human countenance and hand. While a hellish din filled the factories, the salons of the bourgeoisie grew better and better insulated from outside noise. While children were sent to work in mines, the bourgeoisie discovered childhood as an idyll free of labor. This division collapsed when actual war erupted in 1914: amputations, noise, and work invaded the parlors of the middle classes, and genteel piano playing—which was predicated on a division that had become inoperative—could not remain the same.

The destruction of the idyll was accompanied by the unsettling of the bourgeois world—and the "new music," which, according to Adorno, was not just "distressing" but "itself distressingly confused."[64] With Maurice Ravel, a fifth hand crept onto the keyboard; the fourth hand disappeared among English composers. At the request of Paul Wittgenstein, who was disabled in combat, Ravel, Paul Hindemith, Richard Strauss, and Franz Schmidt composed pieces for a single hand.[65] Just as the nineteenth-century cult of the human face lost its naïveté when the wounded soldiery returned from the First World War, the hand became problematic when amputation was a phenomenon not just in the factory but also in the drawing room. Almost all one-hand or three-hand pieces are consciously directed toward a *wounded* audience. Eighty percent of the former are written for the left hand, since most people are right-handed and injury is more likely on the dominant side.[66] There is a piano piece (in A major) by Carl Philipp Emanuel Bach for one hand, but the greatest number of compositions come from the late-nineteenth and early-twentieth centuries, including a number of transcriptions by Brahms, Wittgenstein, and others.[67] One-hand or three-hand piano concerts (at one or two instruments) were especially widespread in England. Benjamin Britten (who also composed for Wittgenstein), Arnold Bax, Arthur Bliss, and Malcolm Arnold all contributed to the genre.[68]

Apart from these special pieces—Hofmeister's *Handbuch der musikalischen Literatur* records, between 1870 and 1930, the more or less constant figure of ten new compositions a year—Ravel set the tone. Like Rachmaninov's works for piano four-hands, his pieces, with increasing frequency, are written for *four* hands at *two* pianos. Each set of hands needs its own sphere of action; it is impossible for them to share. Although, in France, extremely important four-hand music was still composed for players at a single piano (by, among others, Florent Schmitt, Gabriel Fauré, and Claude Debussy), four-hand playing at two pianos became the norm in

---

[64] Theodor W. Adorno, "The Ageing of New Music," in *Essays on Music*, ed. Richard Leppert (Los Angeles: University of California Press, 2002), 181.

[65] Donald L. Patterson, *One Handed: A Guide to Piano Music for One Hand* (Westport, CT: Greenwood Press, 1998).

[66] Patterson, *One Handed*, 10.

[67] Theodore Edel, *Piano Music for One Hand* (South Bend: Indiana University Press, 1994).

[68] Patterson, *One Handed*, 212.

"serious" compositions.⁶⁹ This also corresponds, of course, to the changing nature of symphonic music. The genres shifted in music for two pianos, too. There were fewer arrangements, fewer dances, fewer occasional pieces, and less music composed for the home. In exchange, suites and *bravura* pieces written specifically and originally for two pianos proliferated.

Throughout the nineteenth century, duets at two pianos existed alongside compositions for four hands at a single instrument. In principle, the practice is older: in an aristocratic salon, it was easier to set up two keyboards than to play four-hands at a harpsichord. Brahms arranged for piano both for four hands at a single keyboard and for four hands at two keyboards. Still, the greater part of new compositions and arrangements (to say nothing of potpourris, etudes, and variations) were still conceived for *one* keyboard. Helmut Loos collected data from the *Handbuch der musikalischen Literatur*. He found that only 0.2 percent of the piano scores recorded for 1817 are for two pianofortes. And while the percentage of four-hand works at a single piano increased regularly in the following decades (3% in 1817, 5.1% in 1828, and 7% in 1844), compositions for two piano remained at the same, minimal level.⁷⁰

Hofmeister's *Handbuch*—the "general, systematically-arranged register of musical works appearing in Germany and neighboring lands"—contains the following information. From 1844 until 1851, it lists literature for two pianos under the default heading, "For 2, 3, and 4 Pianofortes, and Pianoforte for 3 and 6 hands."⁷¹ Of these compositions, approximately 20 were written for four hands at two pianos; about as many were composed for eight hands. The same edition of the *Handbuch* records more than 2,000 new works for four hands on one piano! At the turn of the century, the picture changes, however. For 1890, Hofmeister's *Handbuch* records a total of 287 new works for four-hand piano. In 1900, the number is 163; in 1913, it is still a respectable 134; in 1925, only 27; and in 1960, the figure has sunk to 26.

In 1875, more than 300 new works appeared for piano four-hands, and there were about 20 works for four hands at two pianos. Piano four-hands dominated, then, by a factor of 15. By 1915, the gap between the figures had narrowed, though. Now, the 30 new works for two pianos came closer to matching the 80 compositions for a single piano. In 1925, the numbers stood neck-and-neck, and in 1935 the compositions for two pianos predominated. In total, volume 18 of the *Handbuch* registers, for the years between 1929 and 1933, 85 musical pieces for piano four-hands, and 125 for two pianos. And whereas the late-nineteenth-century list of musical works for two pianos consists almost entirely of arrangements, the twentieth-century repertory is much more interesting. The list for two-piano works contains many more famous names than the one for four-hand works on one instrument. Many of the two-piano

---

⁶⁹ Ernest Lubin, *The Piano Duet* (New York: Grossman, 1970), 158f.
⁷⁰ Helmut Loos, *Zur Klavierübertragung von Werken für und mit Orchester des 19 Und 20 Jahrhunderts* (Munich: Katzbichler, 1983), 8.
⁷¹ Friedrich Hofmeister, *Handbuch der Musikalischen Literatur* (Leipzig: Hofmeister, 1900), 11: 58.

pieces are still quite well known today, while the list of works for piano four-hands boasts such dubious offerings as John Philip Sousa's "Stars and Stripes Forever" and a piece entitled "Uncle Bumba Will Only Dance the Rumba." The previous volume (1924–1928)—in which pieces for four hands at a single piano are still a bit larger in number—lists 15 of about 150 publications under "Christmas Music."[72]

All the same, it is necessary to bear in mind that the rise of compositions for players at different pianos cannot be perfectly documented. The *Handbuch* lists only new publications and re-editions, and Hofmeister does not say how many copies of works were printed. The book's subtitle indicates that it is a "register of...works printed," but in many cases, it is doubtful whether the pieces for two pianos had any commercial distribution. Simply put, the shift, among new works, from one-piano music to compositions for two pianos also signified the end of the four-hand arrangement as an item for use or collecting. Even if one never actually plays it, it is nice to have, say, an arrangement of Beethoven for four hands lying open on the piano; the same cannot be said of a score that requires another grand piano.

After the First World War, then, published music for two pianos was intended largely for professionals and semi-professionals—people who needed the notes for public performances, musical festivals, or exams. Insofar as they were not suited for being played on one instrument, these publications are extremely similar to the piano scores of the nineteenth century—a form of notation that provides a reduced, abstract version of the orchestral score; the piano score was not actually conceived for any instrument at all, but for a trained reader.[73] These scores were tools of the trade, not fetish objects. No market existed for them, and they were not advertised or announced. Suppliers no longer found a demand; unlike at the end of Germany's Second Empire and of its neighbor "Kakania," there seemed to be no market.

The image that has guided us through this study—two persons, lost in reverie and intrigue, bent over a keyboard—must now give way to a new kind of picture: for example, that of Béla Bartók and Ditta Pásztory at their twin pianos. Arranged side by side, in parallel formation, they really do look like the "two locomotives racing side by side" that Musil described in his novel.[74] It almost seems that the two instruments could fly off the stage like silver arrows (fig. 8.2). The image of piano four-hands that Musil presented in *Man Without Qualities* is even more accurate for play at two separate pianos. And since, as a rule, music that is composed for two pianos is a good bit more complex than pieces for four hands at a single instrument, the panic that Musil connected with Walter and Clarisse expresses itself even more strongly on the players' faces.

Like horses, the two players gallop parallel—"hearing, blood, muscles, were swept along irresistibly by the same experience." It is easier to take stock of the

[72] Hofmeister, *Handbuch*, 17:109.
[73] Loos, *Zur Klavierübertragung von Werken für und mit Orchester*, 17.
[74] Musil, *The Man Without Qualities*, 151.

Figure 8.2 Béla Bartók and Ditta Pásztory playing a concert on two pianos (1939); photograph by Gyula Schäffer. (Collection Ferenc Bónis)

players' orientation in profile: as in *Man Without Qualities*, "walls of sound" force "their bodies onto the same track, bent them as one, and expanded and contracted their chests in the same breath."[75] The satirical thrust of Musil's observations reveals that four-hand piano play (which Lux transformed into sentimental kitsch) is, in reality, much more like playing at two different pianos than the dominant ideology would have it. Walter and Clarisse *are* Bartók and Pásztory—they just don't know it yet.

Even with two pianos, the example of Bartók and Pásztory shows that it is impossible to exclude romance entirely. The composer first had an affair with his student, then the couple married. At the same time, romance between two pianos is fundamentally different from the one that occurs when two pairs of hands are at the same keyboard. It is no longer physical contact that counts but, rather, the exchange of gazes. Normally, the two pianos in a concert hall are *not* placed parallel. Instead, they face each other, and the body of sound is organized and coordinated *visually*. "Solitariness and secretive craft,"[76] as Adorno describes it: only in a geometrical sense do the two grand pianos facing each other call to mind the unity they are supposed to produce. They fit together like yin and yang, but just from a bird's-eye view; such a perspective can only exist in the concert hall, not in a parlor. The unity of the playing becomes aerial photography—a view down upon the infernal machine.

[75] Musil, *The Man Without Qualities*, 151.
[76] Theodor W. Adorno, "Four Hands, Once Again," *Cultural Critique* 60 (Spring 2005): 1.

Musil's diagnosis is accurate on this point, too: if *Man Without Qualities* speaks of "eyes blazing out of their heads in four parallel axes"[77] like stalks, the novel indicates an orientation that becomes entirely dominant when playing occurs at two pianos. Body language—intimacy and eroticism—has disappeared from the picture, and the visual has taken the place of the tactile. The medium of immediacy is the studied reading of physiognomic expressions—not instinctive, subliminal collaboration. There is no higher unity, only mirroring. The narcissism that englobed the pair as it played at a single keyboard has transformed into narcissism that oscillates between two marked poles.

The pianists Greg Anderson and Elizabeth Roe (whose comparison of four-hand playing at a single keyboard to dancing a tango was discussed in chapter 4) have remarked on the altogether different nature of playing at two separate pianos. "It's as if the two players shared a whole orchestra and were conducting from different sides." The image of two conductors has something absurd about it. After all, the conductor personifies, in a sense, the unity of the orchestra. He is the "sovereign"— or, as Adorno put it somewhat derisively, a mixture of "whip-wielding stable master and head waiter."[78] Moreover, as Adorno makes clear, the conductor is also a stand-in for the public. In Anderson and Roe's image, we encounter two such figures, and the listener can side and identify with either one. The picture, then, no longer presents an impenetrable knot that seems impossible for the onlooker to unravel. Instead, the sides are clear, and one can alternately align oneself with the one or the other.

In chapter 1, we remarked that a feature of observing piano four-hands is the way it objectifies a relationship that, in essence, resists all objectification. The outsider's eyes may fall on the keyboard, but the eyes of the players are *basée[s] sur les touches*. The distinguishing characteristic of piano four-hands is that it takes place through touching and intuition—wordlessly and without exchanging glances. In both literature and fine art—whether it is a matter of describing or looking—one necessarily seeks to grasp a form of communication that relies upon neither words nor looks.

Such a picture contrasts with the scene of two pianos on stage. The wordlessness of the communication between the two players remains, but what breathing, little nudges, and hand movements had signaled when there was a single keyboard can now only be afforded by intentional gestures. The two players facing each other have become mutually legible; they are subjects in their own right, as well as objects for each other. Their exchanges do not occur by means of instinct and unconscious movement; rather, communication is a matter of what they consciously want to communicate. The exchange has a code: a certain way of breathing means "faster!" and tensing one's muscles in a specific way means "now!" The eyes and the hands signify in a systematic fashion; they perform denotative functions that belong to a

---

[77] Musil, *The Man Without Qualities*, 150.

[78] Theodor W. Adorno, *Dissonanzen. Einleitung in die Musiksoziologie (GS 14)* (Frankfurt: Suhrkamp, 2003), 294.

larger pattern of understanding. In the concert hall, the bodily and semantic immanence of piano four-hands is transformed by being distributed between two pianos. The order is legible, and it is supposed to be legible. The phenomenon is no longer private (that is, shared only with a partner), but now public—accessible, in principle, to anyone with eyes to see. And for that reason no different from any other group of chamber musicians. The special relationship between the players, and the special relationship with the audience their relationship enabled, have all vanished.

For the view from outside has changed as well. The experience of two-piano concerts is televisual. It is no longer a matter of indistinct nudges and hints, but of performance that is mediated by vision. The distinguishing characteristic of gazing upon the "four-handed monster," that Aristophanic super-being, was the visual encounter with something that was not itself visual, but tactile. Such a gaze was ashamed, and it represented, so to speak, a form of capitulation before something it could not grasp. No such capitulation occurs when gazing upon a performance at two pianos: one does not seek to unravel the secrets of the touch; rather, one looks at looking. The visual apprehension of something tactile was what lent piano four-hands its mystery and made watching it a kind of voyeurism. Now, the two players and the observer find themselves on the same playing field; the spectator can follow and project his thoughts onto each of the players, identify with him or her, and change position at will.

At first glance, this arrangement may seem more democratic. All the parties involved are at the same level, on the same playing field. Yet something has gone missing. It was precisely the alterity within a tactile relationship without words—which a gaze could not penetrate—that lent the phenomenon of piano four-hands its power of suggestion and "deeper meaning." Because the outside gaze could not solve—even with the utmost exertion of effort—the riddle of intertwining hands and two bodies pressed up against each other, four-handed play was monstrous. At the same time four-hand playing could suggest the seemingly impossible, the wondrous, and the utopian. Where the gaze from outside could not lay hold of—that is, comprehend—what was happening, there lay explosive power. Two pianos represent the victory of the external view. All alterity is absorbed and incorporated. The spectator sits like an umpire above what is taking place and can oversee the precision and coordination of events, much like the two players. Here ends not just our history but also the very possibility of telling the history of playing with four hands. Of course, piano four-hands continued to be practiced into the twentieth century. (Adorno himself, for example, indulged in the practice fairly regularly.) However, the twinned gestures are no longer put into words. The moment at which observing them might trigger nightmares, scandals, and utopias is over.

INDEX

adaptation. *See under* piano four-hands music.
addiction, 72, 80, 82–83
Adorno, Theodor W., 20–21, 35, 55, 67, 70, 75–76, 80–81, 88–89, 113, 129, 131–32, 165, 195–96, 212, 234, 237–39
ambiguity, 24
Anders, Fritz, 16
Anderson, Greg, 129–30, 238
André (publishing house), 58, 60
Andretzi, Gisela, 39
androgyny, 156
arrangement. *See under* piano four-hands music.
Auszüge. *See under* piano four-hands music.
authority, 201
authorship, 189–93
autoeroticism, 42, 44. *See also* eroticism, masturbation.
autonomy, 187–88

Baader, Franz von, 203, 206–7
Bach, Carl Philipp Emanuel, 2, 234
Bach, Johann Christian, 3
Bach, Johann Sebastian, 2, 142
Bakhtin, Mikhail, 86
Barthes, Roland, 88, 129, 150–51
Bax, Arnold, 91, 234
Baxandall, Michael, 25
Beethoven, Ludwig van, 94–96, 138; and Carl Czerny, 115, 135–36, 141, 143–44; transcriptions of music by, 21, 36, 59, 60, 63, 65, 67, 68, 73, 77, 92, 96, 113–16, 121, 126, 131, 137, 156, 205–6, 208–11, 223, 228, 232, 236
Benjamin, Walter, 29, 55, 75, 88, 142, 193, 212, 232
Berlioz, Hector, 5, 86, 114
Bertini, Henri, 35, 69, 112
bibliophily, 67

Bie, Oscar, 170, 172
Biedermeier era, 213–19, 223–25, 232
Bizet, Georges, 3, 154
Böcklin, Arnold, 70–71
Bodenstedt, Friedrich, 52–53
bodies, 14, 122–23, 168; excessive or lacking, 106; female, 13, 84, 140–41; interlocking, 9, 19, 108; metaphorical, 79; movement, 149–51; signifying, 124; still, 169. *See also* posture, touch.
Bolloch, Joëlle, 144–45
Bourdieu, Pierre, 168
bourgeoisie, 2, 5, 10, 22, 26, 38, 67, 70, 73, 83, 85, 88, 94–97, 101, 132, 165–66, 196–98, 223–27, 234–35. *See also* class.
Brahms, Johannes, 55, 75; transcriptions of music by, 18–19, 57n8; arranging for odd numbers of hands, 234; arranging others' work, 59–60, 112–15, 235; arranging own work for piano four hands, 18, 65–68, 113, 118–19; compositions of, 3, 66–68, 80–81; in literature, 13; in performance, 102, 221
Breitkopf & Härtel (publishers), 60, 64, 113–15, 128
Brett, Philip, 7–8, 91
Bruckner, Anton, 5, 37, 58, 61–62, 78–79
Burney, Charles, 2–4, 90
Burton, Tim, 110–11
Busch, Wilhelm, 106–8

calisthenics, 170–71, 178, 181–83
canon, process of definition, 64, 67; national, 66
Carus, Carl Gustav, 152–55
censorship, 84–85, 131–32
chamber music, analogy for social life, 200; arranged for 4HP, 20, 38, 56, 62, 65, 67, 69, 74; contrasted with 4HP, 34, 50, 65, 188, 195–95, 239; in private homes, 27, 34

241

chirognomy, 152–55, 160–62
chiroplast, 150, 177–79
Chopin, Frédéric, 4, 123, 138, 150
Christensen, Thomas, 1–2, 8, 28–29, 60, 64
Christmas, 20, 55, 126, 157, 210, 236
citizenship. *See* nationalism; philosophy, political.
class, social and economic, 5, 32, 94–96, 101, 143, 153, 155–57, 165–66, 234. *See also* bourgeoisie, labor.
Clementi, Muzio, 3, 150, 166, 182–83
Clésinger, Jean-Baptiste August, 138, 142
collaboration, 190–98
collecting, 138
collectivity, 118
commercialism, 75
commofidification, 70, 86
communication between musicians, 15, 131, 238–39
community, 7, 34, 50, 89, 120–21, 188–21
concert music, 235–37
concert programs, 61
Cone, Edward T., 15, 53, 89, 106, 122, 124, 126, 156
Constable, John, 44–48
consumerism, 70
consumption, 55–56, 72–73, 83
Coppée, François, 13–16, 39–40, 179
Couperain, François, 2, 38, 143
Couperin, Armand-Louis, 2, 150
criticism, musical, 4–5, 57, 60, 68–69, 76, 82, 114–16, 126
Czerny, Carl, as arranger, 58, 60, 64n31, 69, 115–16, 166; as composer, 60, 69, 166; as pedagogue, 69, 87, 139–41, 146, 149, 166–74, 176, 178–182, 186; as performer, 5, 135; memoirs of, 112, 135–36, 143; relationship with Beethoven, 135, 143–44

d'Arpentigny, Casimir Stanislas, 149, 152, 155–56
dance, 17, 26–27, 123, 130; folk, 66; humiliating, 16
danger, 101–2
de Bernard, Charles, 6, 17, 50, 119, 121, 231
degeneration. *See* heredity, Max Nordau.
democratization, 68, 77. *See also* bourgeoisie.
Desbarolles, Adolphe, 153–55
design, 214–17, 219–24
desire, 62, 94–97
determinism, 157–62
Dickens, Charles, 6, 92–97, 100, 102, 104
discipline, 150, 164–66, 170–84, 233–34. *See also under* gaze.
domesticity, 12, 27, 29, 35, 70–71, 83, 94–97, 120, 217–24, 226–27. See also bourgeoisie, family, private sphere.
Donizetti, Gaetano, 59

dreams, 98–100
duo-pianism, 53, 189
Dvorak, Antonin, 63, 66

education, 33, 51, 61–62, 98, 100–2, 166–84. *See also* pedagogy.
eroticism, 15–17, 31, 33, 44, 48, 50–51, 89–90, 99–100, 103, 120–21, 130, 139, 150, 155–56, 159–61, 179–83, 204–11, 237. See also autoeroticism, flirtation, homoeroticism, seduction.
essayism, 8
etudes, 166–69, 180–84. *See also* practice.

family, 2, 26, 29, 36, 44–46, 51, 63, 86, 89–90, 95–97, 101–2, 194–97, 199–202, 227–32; reading, 94
fantasy, 49
fathers, 92–93, 100, 106, 157–62; absent, 85
femininity, 14, 29, 39, 90, 102–3, 119–20, 163, 217–18
fetishism, 72, 79–80, 138
film, 110–11, 142
Fink, G.W., 5, 60
Flaubert, Gustave, 102, 189–90
flirtation, 16, 41, 119. *See also* eroticism, seduction.
Flothuis, Marius, 62–63
Fontane, Martha, 221–22
Fontane, Theodor, 6, 52
Fordism, 23, 175, 180, 183, 232. *See also* discipline, labor.
Foucault, Michel, 8, 67, 89–90, 168
Freud, Sigmund, 36, 70, 180, 182–83, 186
Freudian interpretation, 21, 36, 72, 79–80. *See also* psychoanalysis.
Friedlaender, Georg, 52
friendship, 52, 135
Frisch, Walter, 118

Gahy, Josef von, 91, 109
Gautier, Théophile, 192, 207
Gavarni, Paul, 190–93, 196
Gay, Peter, 101–2
gaze, 11, 15–16, 20, 26, 38–42, 50, 89, 91, 103, 237–39; comparative, 151–57; disciplinary, 92–94, 102, 137, 139, 16062; female, ; learned, 139; male, 14, 31, 84, 140–41, 219–24, 231–34; of artist, 8; photographic, 151; scientific, 144, 149
gender, 14, 31, 38–39, 119–22, 140–41, 153, 156–58, 163–64
Geothe, Johann Wolfgang von, 37, 55, 151, 198, 215
girls, 168
Gläser, Franz, 57–58

Gluck, Christoph Willibald, 2
Goldschmidt, Nocholas, 61–62
Goncourt, Edmond de, 6, 41, 44, 99, 123, 181–82; collaborating with his brother, 154, 188–94, 196; depicted, 190–93
Goncourt, Jules de, 6, 44; collaborating with his brother, 154, 188–94, 196; depicted, 190–93
Grenville Murray, Eustace Clare, 39–41
Grieg, Edvard, 16n28, 66, 89
Grillparzer, Franz, autobiography of, 36–37; in Lux's telling, 6, 23, 213–226, 231
guide-mains. *See* chiroplast.
guilt, 158
gymnastics. *See* calisthenics.

Habermas, Jürgen, 34, 71
habitus, 168
Hahn-Hahn, Ida, Countess, 92, 94, 97, 104
hands, 22, 47, 103, 135; contact, 121–22, 124; crossing, 108, 115–16, 233; disciplined, 177; disembodied, 110–11; evidentiary, 143; expressive, 142; guilty, 159–62; moving, 169; murderous, 142; observed, 136; photographed, 145–53; physiognomy, 22, 149, 152–57; sculpted or cast, 138, 143, 145; single, at piano, 234; spousal, 144
Hanslick, Eduard, 26, 29–33, 51, 56, 61, 64–65, 72, 90–91, 165, 169, 172–73, 177, 187
harpsichord, 37, 150, 169, 235
harpsichord, compared to piano, 169
Hauptmann, Gerhart, 6, 91–92, 137, 139, 157–61
Hausmusik, 10–11, 27, 34, 57n5, 70, 75, 154, 186, 194. *See also* bourgeoisie, domesticity, space.
Haydn, Franz Joseph, 3, 36, 55, 63; transcriptions of music by, 1, 58, 60–61, 63, 65, 223
Hegel, Georg Wilhelm Friedrich, 77, 152, 194–96, 202–3
Heidegger, Martin, 50
Helleu, Paul, 44–45, 47
Herder, Johann Gottfried, 77
heredity, 137, 154–62, 165–66
Heyse, Paul, 155–56, 231
Hobsbawm, Eric, 27–28
Hoffmann, E.T.A., 22, 77, 107, 125–28, 198–99, 203, 227
Hoffmann, Richard, 121–22
Hoffmeister, Adolph, 58–59, 62, 166, 234–36
homoeroticism, 31, 33, 42, 91

Idealism, German, 207
improvisation, 8, 172, 181–84, 187–94
individuality, 51–52, 108, 196–99. *See also* subjectivity.
infidelity, 91
interpretation of music, 8, 74
intimacy, 51, 89–90, 93, 98, 101–2

Jews, 96
Jones, Ernest, 98–99, 104, 180

Kalkbrenner, Frédéric, 112, 174, 177–78
Kammermusik. See chamber music, *Hausmusik*.
Keller, Robert, 60
Kinkel, Johanna, 33, 172–73
Kirchner, Aloisia (Ossip Schubin), 31, 121
Kracauer, Siegfried, 26, 232
Kraus, Karl, 10, 30, 217

L'Arrange, Adolph, 35, 124, 161
labor, 10, 23, 26, 50, 60, 83, 86–89, 103, 143, 156, 172–74, 183–84, 186–97, 226–34; shared, 199–211; unalienated, 188–89, 194–97. *See also* practice.
Lauterbach & Kuhn (publishers), 113
leadership, 121
Leppert, Richard, 7, 20, 28, 31, 38, 67, 170, 190
liberalism, 195–96
Liszt, Franz, 3; arranging others' music for 4HP, 5, 68, 113–14; depicted, 138, 146–47, 170–71; performance of music by, 29, 87; performing, 87, 123, 150; style, 170–71; writing, 113–14
Logier, Johann Bernhard, 23, 150–51, 168, 174–80, 183–84, 186, 190
Lombroso, Cesare, 22, 137, 142, 146, 149, 151, 153, 157
Löwe, Ferdinand, 61, 78
Lux, Joseph August, 6, 23, 28, 213–27, 230–31, 237

Mahler, Gustav, arranging others' music, 3, compositions arranged for four hands, 63, 73–75
Mann, Thomas, 6, 16, 41–43, 101, 180
Marlitt, Eugenie, 94–97, 104
marriage, 51, 52, 91, 144, 203–11, 215, 227–32
Marx, Adolf Bernhard, 26, 51, 57, 64 74, 116, 177
Marx, Karl, 72, 188, 196
Marxism, 21, 232
masculinity, 39, 119, 122
masturbation, 41–42, 99–100, 179–83
memoir, 13, 16
Mendelssohn, Felix, 136, 146–47, 153, 184, 186–87; transcriptions of music by, 5, 59, 61, 64, 117; compositions by, 163, 183–84
Merrick, Joseph, 106, 108
Meyerbeer, Giacomo, 58, 59, 66
mockery, 75, 83, 87, 170–71, 173–74
Mockwitz, Friedrich, 58, 112
Moldenhauer, Hans, 53, 203
money, 86
monogamy, 90–91
monsters, 22, 53, 126
monstrosity, 124, 129

Moscheles, Felix, 136, 139, 184
Moscheles, Ignaz, 136, 163, 167–68, 178, 182–84, 186–88
mothers, 55, 73, 83, 85–86, 98–102, 106, 157–60
Mozart, Wolfgang Amadeus, 3, 36, 63, 76; transcriptions of music by, 4, 58–60, 63, 65, 135, 223; as point of comparison, 166, 173; in literature, 12–13,
Müller, Max, 5
Musil, Robert, 2, 6, 14, 23, 29, 34, 108, 180, 186, 203–9, 211–13, 216, 226–33, 236–38

nation, 7
nationalism, 66, 96, 182, 212–17, 221–25
naturalism, 137, 156–57, 159–61
nature, 12, 217–18, 221–22, 226
Nietzsche, Friedrich, 5, 55, 194, 203, 209–11, 227, 228; as composer, 52–53, 210
night, 30
Nordau, Max, 142–43, 156–57

objectification, 4; of women, 84
Offenbach, Jacques, 86
opera, and nationalism, 5, 66; and urbanity, 26, 61, 221; in visual culture, 137–38; transcribed for piano four hands, 5, 56, 58–63, 66–67, 75
Orchardson, Sir William Quiller, 24–25
orchestra, as metaphor for society, 197–99; as metaphor for family, 200–2
orchestral music, 79, 173; accompanying 4HP, 86; arranged for 4HP, 4, 64, 69, 80, 114–18, 131, 135, 196; arranged for organ, 98; arranged for two pianos, 236; difficulty of arranging for 4HP, 38, 73–75; familiar through 4HP, 61; on radio, 76; performed by insufficient orchestras, 78
Orff, Carl, 103
organ, compared to 4HP, 97–100; contrasted with piano, 27; four–hand playing, 2; music transcribed for 4HP, 63–64; predecessor of piano, 2, 33
original (of artwork), 81

pedagogy, 22–23, 38, 139–40, 149, 163–69, 173–84. *See also* education.
pedaling, 124–25, 130
perception, modes of, 25
Peters (publishing house), 60, 117
philosophy, 52, 77; political, 53, 88–89, 170–71, 177, 195–96, 199, 212–17, 219, 221–28; of music, 119, 165, 194–98, 202–11
photography, 22, 76, 79, 138, 144–45
physiognomy, 146–47
piano, as bourgeois furniture, 21, 27–28, 38, 94–96, 108, 216–19; as hearth, 29–30, 34, 71, 83, 95–96; audibility of, 33–34, 43–44, 163; history of, 4, 28, 37

piano duets, 234–37
piano four-hands music, as status symbol, 10; as substitute for orchestra, 78–79; catalogs of, 58–59; collecting, 10, 21, 64, 65; commodification, 10; compared to chamber music, 34, 50, 65, 102, 188, 195–95, 212, 239 (*See also* chamber music.); compared to organ music, 98; compared to solo piano, 69, 114; desire for, 55; difficulty of, 19, 37, 60, 68, 114; excitement at new, 56, 62; fetish objects, 21, 62; fidelity of transcriptions to urtexts, 57; market for, 4, 22, 57–60, 63–65, 75–76, 235–36; mocked, 75–76, 86; narratives in, 19–20; other art forms "arranged" for, 70, 128; playability, 114–15; played by one person, 105–6; playing vs. reading, 113, 115; possession of, 9, 64; relationship of primo and secondo, 115, 117–22, 125, 128, 130–31, 167–69, 175; transcription for compared to composition for, 3, 59, 68–69; transcription, process of, 74, 76, 112–13; transcriptions as source of knowledge, 5, 9, 20–21, 61–64, 221–24; transcriptions compared to original instrumentation, 77, 232; transcriptions, impossible, 73–74, 78–79, 82; transcriptions, practicalities of, 10, 11; ubiquity, 5, 67
piano four-hands playing, and infidelity, 43 (*See also* seduction.); as diagnostic tool, 92–93, 97, 153–56, 181–82; as semi-public phenomenon, 9–10, 21, 26–27, 31–35, 37, 53, 71–72, 119, 193, 219–24, 226; as social event, 1; as status symbol, 32; as uncertain metaphor, 198–201; compared to solo piano, 70, 74, 89, 96; dangerous, 22, 71, 96–98; enjoyment of, 13; in concerts, 3, 87, 235–37; in drama, 16; in literature, 1–2, 5, 11–17, 23, 31–33, 39, 78, 83, 85, 105–6, 121, 123, 125–28, 136–37, 155–62, 164, 198 (*See also* Lux, Joseph August; Musil, Robert.); in painting, 24–25, 31–32, 38–39, 44–47; in private, 4, 9, 26, 83, 85; loudness of, 163; metaphor for collaboration, 190–98, 227; phenomenology of, 7–8, 22; relationship of partners, 90–91, 151; spectacle of, 9, 11–12, 20, 50, 71–72, 83, 94, 102–3, 108, 137, 151, 195–96, 237–39 (*See also* gaze.); tending to unity, 15, 5, 89, 108, 119, 195–99, 203–11; ubiquity of, 25, 30, 69–70
"piano plague," 41
Piazzola, Astor, 130
Pigault-Lebrun, Charles, 5–6
Platonism, 203–5, 207, 230
playfulness, musical, 118, 128, 130
pleasure, 80, 103, 165
poetry, and its creative process, 190; and painting contrasted, 39, 49; and piano four hands, 6, 11–13,

naturalist, 156. See also Franz Grillparzer, Friedrich Schiller.
posture, 170–72
Potter, Frank Huddlestone, 44–45, 47
practice, 22, 26–27, 69, 86–88, 134, 164–66, 172; as music, 75–76
Prinet, René-Xavier, 31–32
print culture, 3, 77, 94, 113, 169, 190, 213. See also publishing, reading.
private sphere, 70–71, 73, 79, 85, 88–90, 101–4, 119, 201, 226–27
Proust, Marcel, 78, 138
psychoanalysis, 36, 97–102. See also Freudian interpretation.
publicity, 63
publishing, 3–4, 21, 56–60, 63, 112–13, 190, 213; style in, 88. See also piano four-hands music, market for; print culture; reading.

Rachmaninov, Sergei, 70–71, 138, 151, 234
reading, 3, 113. See also print culture, publishing.
Reger, Max, 3n8, 63–64, 66, 70, 113
Reich, Steve, 132–34
Reich, Wilhelm, 49
Reinhart, C.S., 39–41, 48
religion, 98, 215
repetition, 231–2
reproduction, 204–7
Reventlow, Franziska (Fanny) Countess zu, 43–44, 49, 105
reviews. See criticism.
Rheinberger, Joseph Gabriel, 63–64
rhythm, 177
Riemann, Hugo, 141, 149, 174–75, 178–80
Rieter (publisher), 113
Robinsonade, 196
Rodi, Frithjof, 63–64
Roe, Elizabeth Joy, 129–30, 238
Rossini, Gioacchino, 59, 194
Rousseau, Jean-Jacques, 2, 120, 173, 180

Saint-Saëns, Camille, 3n8, 75–76, 86–87, 103, 173–74, 178, 180, 187, 198
Salonmusik. See *Hausmusik.*
salons, private, 11–12, 24, 31, 33, 102, 186, 216, 226, 234, 235; public, 84, 87; social events, 27, 34, 66, 76, 84, 212, 223–24
Schalk, Joseph, 61, 78
Schiller, Friedrich, 205–6, 209–11, 228
Schnitzler, Arthur, 6, 16, 61, 73, 83–86, 90–91, 96–97, 100–1, 165, 221, 231
Schoenberg, Arnold, 121–22
Schopenhauer, Arthur, 67, 119–20, 194, 196, 202–3, 228
Schott (publishing house), 21, 88, 114
Schubert, Franz, 3, 60, 119–20; transcriptions of music by, 55, 61–63, 75; composing for four hands piano, 69, 109, 117; in literature, 23, 61, 213, 216–24, 231; in amateur performance, 27, 34, 123, 223–25, 227; music and sexuality of, 8, 91, 121, 126; publication of music of, 56
Schubertiades ("Schubert evenings"), 27, 123, 216, 218, 223–25, 227
Schubin, Ossip (Aloisia Kirchner), 31, 121
Schulz-Beuthen, Heinrich, 70
Schumann, Clara, 113, hands of, 146, 148
Schumann, Robert, transcriptions of music by, 73, 75, 113; compositions of, 3; music reviews by, 5; writing of, 16, 174
Schwind, Moritz von, 216–20, 227
seduction, 17–18, 95–97, 201; by piano teacher, 31–32, 35; failed, 228–29; of teacher by student, 48
self-sufficiency, 50, 107
Sickert, Walter, 38, 44
Simrock publishing house, 57, 60, 66, 88
Simrock, Fritz, 67, 68, 113
Simrock, P.J., 65
space in which piano is played, 26–27, 97, 123, 219–22, 227
Spaun family home, 27, 123, 224
Spohr, Louis, 174–75, 180
sport, 170–71. See also calisthenics.
Stifter, Adalbert, 30, 139
Strauss, Richard, 234
Strindberg, August, 6, 13–14, 136–37, 144, 156
subjectivity, 7, 52, 118–20, 229–34, 238–39; surrendered, 108
surveillance, 97, 102. See also gaze.

Thackeray, William Makepeace, 6, 15
Thalberg, Sigismund, 27, 127, 138, 170, 178
Tolstoy, Leo, 6, 31–32, 91, 193
tone color, 75
tone density, 114–15
Tönnies, Ferdinand, 120, 217
touch, 15, 18, 90, 124, 209–11; foregone, 238–39; prevented, 179. See also hands, bodies.
transcription. See *under* piano four-hands music.
translation, 77; analogous to transcription, 75
twins, 203–4

Ulrich, Hugo, 60, 77, 112, 225, 232–33
uncanniness, 105–11, 208. See also monstrosity.
unification, 156–57, 202–17, 219–20; asexual, 228; failed, 229–34
unison, 132–33
unity, 15, 49
utopianism, 186–99, 207–11, 225–28

Vienna, "classical era" of, 23, 213–16, 222–25, 231–32; amateur music in, 26, 30; professional music in, 70

Vienna, golden age of, 213–26. See also Joseph August Lux.
violence, 150, 229–30, 234
visuality, 11–12, 14, 138
Vogl, Johann Michael, 119, 121, 126
voice, 34, 56n5, 76, 120–21, 129; of 4HP, 22, 75, 79, 109, 118–19, 125–27, 130–34, 175, 204; radio, 129
Voigt, Rudolf, 146–53, 157–58

Wagner, Cosima, 1–2, 5, 13, 136
Wagner, Richard, 1–5, 13, 27, 156, 203, 205, 210; transcriptions of music of, 58, 59, 61–63, 68–69, 75, 136, 180, 205; hands of, 146, 148, 153; metaphorical, 163–64, 167, 169, 176, 183–84
Weber, Carl Maria von, 163, 183–84
Weber, Max, 26–27, 78, 97, 172
Wedekind, Frank, 6, 48
Wehmeyer, Grete, 149, 166, 168–73, 181
Wetzel-Stettin, Hermann, 51, 69, 195, 203
Wilde, Oscar, 6, 105–6, 125–27
Wolf, Hugo, 5, 78–79
women, 38, 103. *See also* femininity, mothers.
Wöss, Josef Venantius von, 61, 74–75

Žižek, Slavoj, 102, 142